Play Production

Scene-sketches (See page 47)

Top and center, by Victor Jacoby; bottom, by Charles Allen

Play Production

FOR LITTLE THEATERS, SCHOOLS AND COLLEGES

BY

MILTON SMITH

Associate Professor of Dramatic Arts
and Director of Brander Matthews Theater
Columbia University

ILLUSTRATED BY WILLIAM STEINEL

APPLETON-CENTURY-CROFTS, INC.

NEW YORK

PREFACE

This book is a revision and an expansion of a similar one written many years ago. It is based on the same principle, that the first and most important approach to the art of the theater should be one which tries to discover its unity, and that theater practice involves the combining of many elements to make an exciting experience for an audience. None of these elements should be neglected by the practitioner who wishes to understand the art.

In the following pages, therefore, I have tried to describe these elements and to explain their relationship. While I hope that it will be possible for inquiring students to find sensible answers to many practical questions in the following pages, varying from those involving general process such as how to conduct rehearsals and how to manage a performance to specific details such as how to cover or paint a flat, my primary aim has been to rationalize and relate these processes. This approach is based on the belief that mere practice of an art does not necessarily, in and of itself, bring about improvement—except, perhaps, in the rare case of genius—and that true progress is likely to take place only when an intellectual basis for the criticism of that practice can be established.

However, in the course of more than thirty years of teaching theater, I have arrived at the melancholy conclusion that it is probably impossible to make generalizations that are philosophically unassailable, or to formulate principles of practice that are universally applicable. I am certain, therefore, that every experienced and thoughtful practitioner of the art of the theater will disagree with some of my conclusions and precepts. I hereby reserve the right to disagree with them myself; for in the

v

attempt to be brief, clear, and logical, many of them came out dogmatic and oversimplified.

Finally, I wish to express my appreciation and to extend my thanks to my colleagues and students, not only to those who will recognize their contributions to the following pages, but also to the many others who have helped to develop and process my thinking in this field during the past thirty years. I am grateful for their earnest and intelligent coöperation, and for what they have taught me, in many happy hours of labor in the process of making innumerable plays.

M. S.

Contents

Part I

THE THEATER AND THE SCRIPT

CHAPTER I

POINT OF VIEW AND DEFINITIONS

CHAPTER II

CHOOSING A SCRIPT

CHAPTER III

ANALYZING THE SCRIPT

Part II
DIRECTING AND ACTING

CHAPTER IX

THE FOURTH PHASE OF REHEARSAL: FINISH

CHAPTER X

THE THEORY OF ACTING

CHAPTER XI

THE TOOLS OF THE ACTOR

CHAPTER XII

STUDYING A RÔLE

CHAPTER XIII

THE PERFORMANCE

Part III
STAGECRAFT AND DESIGN

CHAPTER XIX

TYPES OF SCENERY

CHAPTER XX

DESIGNING SCENERY

CHAPTER XXI

HANDLING SCENERY

CHAPTER XXII

PROPERTIES

CHAPTER XXIII

COSTUMING

CHAPTER XXIV

MAKE-UP

PART I

The Theater and the Script

CHAPTER I

Point of View and Definitions

THE THEATER

One of the most universal of human traits is a love of stories. The theater is the institution invented by man for the acting out of stories. It springs, then, from the same human instinct that makes us read novels and listen to gossip. Theater historians are fond of pointing out that no human race has ever been found, no matter how primitive, in which there was not some form of theater. It may be only a primitive dance describing a victory over a neighboring tribe, or telling the details of a successful hunt, but to the degree that it involves the acting out of a story it is theater. Our modern theater is a more elaborate institution, involving special buildings, trained performers, and literate playwrights, but it springs from the same deepseated emotion—the desire to be entertained by enacted stories. We call these stories *plays*, so that the theater is often described as an institution for the giving of plays.

THE MODERN CONCEPTION OF A PLAY

Plays have been defined in many ways; as "the stage presentation of a drama," [1] or "a story in dialogue shown in action before an audience," [2] or "an imitation of an action." [3] None

[1] Webster's *Dictionary*.
[2] Brander Matthews, *A Study of the Drama* (Boston, Houghton Mifflin Co., 1910), p. 92.
[3] Aristotle, *The Poetics*, translated by Ingram Bywater (New York, The Macmillan Company, 1930), p. 15.

3

of these definitions sufficiently emphasize the fact that from the viewpoint of the theater, the drama or the story written down in a manuscript or printed in a book, the lines to be spoken and the stage directions to be carried out, are not in the truest sense a play at all. They are rather the directions from which a play can be made. They become a play by being played, in the same way that a song comes into existence only as the printed words and notes are sung. This idea is the basis of the ancient maxim that "No play is a play until it is acted."

But, according to the modern conception, acting alone does not create a play; for a play is not merely an intellectual understanding of an incident gathered from the actions and the words of the actors. It is a far bigger thing. It is an impression made on the spectators by ideas, sounds, colors, movements, lines, and all the other elements that move one in the theater. It is an emotional reaction to these elements and to many others that are too subtle to be analyzed out of the total situation. In brief, a play is an effect made upon an audience.

THE PLAY VS. THE SCRIPT

We would, therefore, clarify our thinking about the theater if we made a distinction between the play, which exists only in actual production in the theater, and the written set of directions which was its beginning. The correct and technical name for the latter is the *script*. The script is the written form of the play, just as the score is the written form of music. Music comes into being only when the score is played, for music is sound vibrations which exist in time and space, and not on paper. The theater, too, is a time-space art. The play is made by embodying the script in the terms of the theater, which are actors, their voices and movements, the colors and lines of the sets, lights, costumes, sounds, and all the other elements that we see and hear in the actual theater. The script, like the musical score, exists as long as there is a copy of it extant; but the play exists only while it is being played, or between the rise and fall of the curtain. In other words, between performances, plays exist only as scripts. Most professional theater people use these terms correctly, just as most musicians make the correct differentiation between music and the score. It is too much to hope that we can overcome the popular misconception, and the loose use of language, which calls the script a play. Nevertheless, it is a useful distinction in studying play production; for *the problem of play production is how to make a play out of a script.*

From this point of view, it is impossible to read a play. What one reads is a script. Sometimes, in the case of great playwrights, the script has such literary quality that it is delightful and exciting reading. Some playwrights—Barrie and Shaw, for instance—make reading versions of their scripts, by adding charming, elaborate, descriptive stage directions. Such a script we may read much as we would read a novel. It may even create such vivid impressions that we see the characters and hear them talk. But still we are not making a play, because it remains in our imagination. A skilful musician may take pleasure in reading a score and imagining he is hearing it, but he knows he is not making music until he completes the translation into actual sound. So we shall have a clearer and more helpful understanding of theater practice if we agree that a play is not merely a written composition, but a story actually played in the theater.

DEFINITION OF A PLAY

For these reasons, I propose that we define a play as *a story presented by actors on a stage before an audience.* Some critics object to the word *presented.* They prefer to say that a play is a story "devised to be presented," [4] and they point out the existence of many unproduced plays. But this word is the important feature of the definition: an unproduced play is not a *play*—it is only a *script.* Whether or not this definition can be

[4] Clayton Hamilton, *The Theory of the Theater* (New York, Henry Holt and Co., 1939), p. 3.

sustained philosophically is unimportant.[5] To those of us who work in the theater, a play is something that exists only in the theater. A play is a story *in the very act of being presented.* It exists only during the space of time that the curtain is up. This is the point of departure for all who engage in the exciting art of play production.

1. *The Story.* If we analyze this definition as a basis for our study of play production, we shall notice that its first element is a story. Because we are going to have to use this term so often, we shall find it necessary to be certain that we understand it. The first critic of whom we have a record who discussed this problem was Aristotle. In discussing the nature of tragedy—to Aristotle all serious play writing resulted in a "tragedy"—he states that "the proper construction of the fable or plot . . . is at once the first and the most important thing." [6] Then follows his often-quoted paragraph:

We have laid it down that a tragedy is an imitation of an action that is complete in itself, as a whole of some magnitude. Now a whole is that which has a beginning, middle, and end. A beginning is that which is not itself necessarily after anything else, and which has naturally something else after it; an end is that which is naturally after something itself, either as its necessary or usual consequence, and with nothing else after it; and a middle, that which is by nature after one thing and has also another after it.

This charming paragraph deserves reading and rereading, for it is the original statement of the idea that a fable, or story, should consist of a beginning, middle, and end. Some more recent drama critics think that the idea is clearer if restated thus: a beginning is that which comes first and which must be followed by something; an end is that which by its nature fol-

---

[5] "There is an advantage in insisting upon resolute definitions. Even if scientific precision is not to be hoped for, every writer gains by the sturdy struggle to make sure that at least he knows exactly what he himself intends by the words he employs." Matthews, *op. cit.,* p. 110.

[6] Aristotle, *op. cit.,* p. 15.

lows something, but which need not be followed by anything; a middle is that which must be preceded by something and followed by something! This leads to a definition most useful in the theater: a story is "a series of incidents with a beginning, a middle, and an end."

The problem of the playwright is to construct a series of incidents, and this is his plot or his story; and the problem of the theater artists—the director, the actors, the designers, and so on—is to embody this series of incidents in the physical objects which are the elements of theater practice. However, we must be cautious about two points:

a. By *beginning, middle, and end* we must not mean chronological order. The problem of the playwright is to determine the artistic beginning of his story—that is, the most effective place to start his telling of it. Sometimes the best beginning is actually the first incident, in which case he may arrange the incidents in chronological order and tell them as they occurred in time. Often, however, this would lessen our interest, and some incident near the chronological end of the story may be its artistic and logical beginning. For instance, the story of *Ghosts*, by Ibsen, covers many years, but Ibsen's artistic beginning is a dialogue between Regina and Engstrand that takes place only a few hours before the end of the play. The same is true of most of the great Greek plays: the playwright shows us only the concluding action of a long series of incidents. His beginning is very close to the chronological end. In other words, the beginning and the end are the result of an artistic decision, a choice on the part of the author, and are not merely a matter of time. An author has the duty of arranging his chronological incidents in the order that he thinks will make the most *effective* beginning, middle, and end.

b. The actual series of incidents need not be complicated or, indeed, exciting in and of themselves. In a melodrama or a mystery play, where we continually want to know what happens next, our interest may be held primarily by the series of incidents being presented. But in many plays, the story is simple and obvious, and we are more concerned with the unfolding of an idea or a philosophy, or the development of a character or a group of characters, or the portrayal of an interesting way of life that is new and unusual. Nevertheless, these things can exist only in terms of the development of some specific series of incidents which is always present as the basis of the action.

Therefore, we may conclude that the basis of every play is *a series of incidents with* (at least, in the opinion of the author!) *a beginning, a middle, and an end.*

2. *The Actors.* The first element in a play being the *story,* the second is the *actors.* Obviously, there must be characters involved in the series of incidents, and the actors are the persons who portray these characters. It is conceivable, perhaps, that by actors we need not always mean human beings. We may mean puppets, or animals. If we are going to try to expand our definition to include modern theater forms, like the motion picture and radio, we may have to devise some form of definition that will include actors represented by their pictures and their voices. But even in these cases, it is our impressions of the characters that interest us. So we may truly say that the actors are the *persons embodying the characters involved in the series of incidents.*

3. *The Stage.* The third element is the stage, which we must understand in a wide sense. In most modern theaters the stage is a shelf at the end of a room. But the stage may be a circular space surrounded by spectators, as it was among the Greeks; or an unadorned platform at the end of an enclosed tennis court, which was the stage of Molière; or a simple platform in the open air surrounded by balconies, similar to the courtyard of a medieval inn, which was the stage of Shakespeare. In a school, the stage may be the floor at the end of a classroom, or the center of a gymnasium. In presenting a play, there must be some space for the actors to play in. The stage will, therefore, be this *playing space.*

4. *The Audience.* The fourth element is the audience; and whether or not this element is necessary for the definition is a time-worn dispute. Suppose we have actors who have learned their lines and moves and who are in costumes and under light on a stage, are they not making a play, whether there is an audience in front of them or not? This question is somewhat similar to the apparently simple one often asked when one begins to study sound: if a tree falls in an uninhabited forest, does it make a sound? Ultimately the answer must be found in our idea of sound. If we define it physically, as vibratory disturbances or sound waves, of course the tree does make a sound. But on the other hand, if we define sound physiologically, as an effect on an ear, or psychologically, as an effect on a mind, then we must conclude that the tree makes no sound. In the same way, we may have a philosophical basis for the support of either side of the question of the necessity of an audience.

Practically though, everyone who works in the theater knows that his purpose in putting on a play, whatever his philosophy, is to make an effect on an audience. He wants this effect to be so pleasing that every spectator will urge his friends to attend, thus building up future audiences! The philosophical background for this practical attitude can be found among that group of critics who maintain that, "All art is a form of communication." Art is the attempt to communicate an idea or emotion to another person; and if the other person is not present, that communication cannot exist. In the theater, the other person is the audience. So, whether or not we accept this philosophy, in practicing the art of the theater, our attempt will be *to make an effect upon an audience.*[7]

[7] The most famous discussion of this point, that "we cannot conceive of a play without an audience," is found in an essay by Francisque Sarcey, written in 1876, called *Essai d'une esthétique de théâtre.* Translated by Hatcher Hughes as *A Theory of the Theater,* it was first published in English in 1916 (New York, Publications of the Brander Matthews Dramatic Museum, Columbia University, 1916, Third Series, Volume 4). It is reprinted, with

We can then summarize our discussion of the elements involved in a play by an extended definition, thus: *A play is a story*, or a series of incidents with a beginning, middle, and end, in the very act of being *presented by actors*, or persons who embody the characters involved in the incidents, *on a stage*, or playing space, *before an audience* in order to create an effect upon the audience.

DEFINITION OF PLAY PRODUCTION

If we understand this definition, the subject of play production becomes clear. *Play production is the process of embodying a story in actors and on a stage for the purpose of making an effect upon an audience.* Play production is the process of building up an effect, and the process involves four elements: (1) the story, (2) the actors, (3) the stage, and (4) the audience.

It is my purpose in the following pages to examine these four elements. In the remaining chapters of Part I, I shall consider choosing and analyzing the script, thus dealing with the *story* as it exists in its original written form. Part II considers the problem of how to embody this story in *actors*, hence it deals with directing and acting. The problem of embodying the story in the *stage* is considered in Part III, which discusses scenery, costumes, lighting, etc. And Part IV considers organization and management, or the securing and handling of an *audience*. To the degree that we understand these four elements and can combine them consciously and intelligently, we shall be practicing the art of play production.

PLAY PRODUCTION IN EDUCATION

Play production, properly used, can be a valuable tool in education. The practice of the theater has great appeal for most

---

many comments by famous critics on this and other dramatic theories, in Barrett Clark's *European Theories of the Drama* (see bibliography on page 467).

children and for many adults, and it has no superior, and few equals, as a general introduction to art. It has the advantage that it can be practiced by a small group, or by a whole country-side. But it must always be a socialized activity: no individual can practice the art of the theater all by himself. It requires and coördinates a multitude of activities—activities as diversified as directing, managing, designing, acting, writing, carpentry, painting, lighting, costuming, sewing, singing, dancing and many others. It is as all-embracing as life itself, for it involves at times the practice of all the other arts and all the other crafts. And the theater automatically creates a situation in which these other arts and crafts meet an acid test. A painter who is a stage-designer is confronted with the practical situation in which his work is exposed at once to public criticism. The carpenters must build the scenery so that it will stand the wear and tear of the performance. The actor exposes himself to the opinions of his audience. The accounts of the business manager must strike a balance. In a word, the theater offers an opportunity to test all these practices by performance. And in the process of doing so, it builds up a socialized situation equalled by few of the other tools of education.

The fear that some educators have of this tool and of the other arts in education is based on the false premise that art is a sort of emotional frenzy. Such is not the case with any true artist. Emotion may be the basis of art, but the necessity for the practice of an art is to direct and guide and control the emotion, and by a process of rationalized and intelligent decisions bring it to a satisfying expression. This is the point of view from which the practice of the theater is approached in the following pages.

In educational situations, play production may be practiced from either of two points of view. We may think of it as the practice of the art of the theater, or we may think of it as a therapeutic process. That is to say, just as in any of the other arts, we may emphasize either the *product* or the *process*. In the first instance, we should bend every effort to make the best possible play; in the second we shall try to use the most valuable and the most educational process, without too much regard for the product. The professional practitioner is confronted with no such problem; his purpose is always to make the best possible product, without regard to the value of the process. Perhaps any complete scheme for using play production as a tool in education should find room for both possibilities. Some plays may be produced with the emphasis on the product because there is an advantage to be derived from encouraging students to do their best. This emphasis would create a situation where the skilful would become still more skilful, which is the aim in many of our other school activities such as athletic teams. But a good program of physical education goes further and provides games and exercises to aid the unskilful. In the same way, the complete dramatics program might provide some activities where the emphasis is entirely on the process for the benefit of the participants, and where there is little or no thought of the product. This sort of play production need not lead to a public performance. Perhaps in many educational situations there will be no conflict between the two points of view; we shall be trying to make the best possible *product* by the most valuable educational *process*.

In the following pages, I shall many times refer to methods of professional practice in play production. I am guided by the idea that in so far as the practice of play production is an art it must have unity, just as do the arts of painting, or singing, or writing. It is unfortunate, I feel, that the word "amateur" has become so closely associated with play production, for this seems to many people to imply that amateur play production is a distinct and separate thing from professional play production. To set out to learn, or to teach, the art of amateur play production is as absurd as to study how to play the amateur violin, or how to write amateur stories, or how to speak amateur French. Every sensible person tries to learn to play the violin, or to write, or to speak French, as well as he can. In the same way, there cannot be one dramatic art for the professional and one for the non-professional. The only real division is between good art and bad, between practice that is successful and practice that fails. Students interested in the theater, of whatever age, should study dramatic art wherever they find it best practiced, and that is likely to be in the professional theater. In the schools the elements may be simpler, but they will not be fundamentally different. And we must not confuse simplicity with crudeness.

The action and reaction between the amateur and the professional practice of an art must always be a close and important relationship. Professionals, from the nature of the situation, usually develop a much more perfect technique than non-professionals. On the other hand, they often lose the spontaneity that gives pleasure in the work of the non-professional. Moreover, in the practice of dramatic art, non-professionals often have the advantage of being more independent of financial success; hence, they can be—or should be—much bolder in experimentations. Their aim may well be to keep their joyous spirit and their freedom, and to add the greatest possible measure of professional technique and excellence.

Of course, the aim of play production in education is not to make professional practitioners, any more than our aim in teaching composition is to make professional writers, or in speech to make professional orators. In the process of teaching these subjects, a few professional practitioners may emerge, but these will be the inevitable professionals. Writing and speaking and theater-going are common and important activities to persons living in modern society, whatever their professions. We are a nation of theater-goers—even those who rarely see a professional play. The moving-picture, radio, and television, bring the "theater" to every town and into every home. In such a situation, theater illiteracy may be just as bad—and just as dangerous—as any other kind of illiteracy. Perhaps our main purpose in educational play production should be to abolish theater illiteracy, for to many people, the theater is the gateway to art and literature and history.

Just putting on a play, in any old haphazard manner, is fun, and it may even have valuable educational results; but conscientiously practicing the art of the theater is more valuable and for most students it is much more fun!

CHAPTER II

Choosing a Script

THE DIFFICULTIES OF SELECTION

Every theater worker, professional or non-professional, who has any responsibility for play selection, is confronted with a problem. His problem arises from the difficulty of being forced to select from among available *scripts* that one that can be made into the *best play*.

How difficult such a selection can be is demonstrated daily during the theatrical season by the fortunes (and misfortunes!) of plays on Broadway. There, no producer has a record of uniform successes. The uninitiated—which may include some of the dramatic critics—do not understand how this can be. How could such a well-known producer, says the critic, be deceived by such a terrible play! The answer is, he wasn't! The producer was deceived by *the script*, and it didn't seem so terrible. In fact, even in the worst play, the script probably had elements of merit—such as an intriguing background, some unusual characters, or a complication that seemed amusing. By the time it becomes a play, its faults may be obvious; the producer himself may not like it! But he might be wrong! In any case, by bringing it into town he may cut his financial losses, even though he believes by now that it doesn't stand much chance of success. In fact, if he thinks it too bad, often the producer closes the play out of town, without a formal Broadway opening—thus, technically he hasn't produced it at all!

This suggests another difficulty that confronts the play producer. The theater is a difficult art to practice in secret! If a writer doesn't like the story he creates, he can confide it only to his waste basket; a painter can privately destroy his unsuccessful painting, or a sculptor his statue. No one even needs to know that he has been working on one. But by its very nature, play production is a different sort of an art. The act of gathering a group of actors and other theater artists for the purpose of turning a script into a play, makes secrecy difficult. Even if this were possible, ultimately the play-producer has to come right out in the open and practice his art in public, in the immediacy of a performance with an audience! His product cannot wait. The writer can leave his story for the judgment of posterity, and the painter may hide his painting until time is ripe for it—which may be long after his death. But a production in the theater must appeal to the contemporary audience, for only in them does it exist. No one can practice the art of play production secretly and in private. The play producer is then confronted with the necessity of deciding *in advance* whether or not *he can make a play out of the script he selects.*

THE PURPOSE OF SCRIPT SELECTION

The purpose of script selection is to choose a *script* out of which *a play can be made.* This is true, of course, only if the purpose *is* to make a play. If the intent is only to amuse or improve the persons participating in the production, the problem is different. In schools (see p. 11) the purpose may sometimes be purely therapeutic; hence choice will depend on the benefits to be derived by actors and other workers. But when the purpose is to make a play that will entertain an audience, as will often be the case with Little Theater, school, and college groups, the problem must be the same as in a professional production, how to choose a script that will make a good play.

Even a good script, however, does not always make a good play. The production may fail to do it justice, just as a good musical score may be so badly played as to be dull and uninteresting. On the other hand, the play may be better than the script seems to warrant; an unusually proficient bit of characterization, or a cleverly designed set, or unusually skilful direction may hide the deficiencies of the author. But in general, good plays are a combination of a good script and an efficient and imaginative production; there is a better chance of producing a good play if we start with a good script. The script tells the story, or the series of incidents, that is to be embodied by actors and stage technicians. The possibilities, then, of the play are inherent in the script.

ELEMENTS IN THE SPECIAL SITUATION

Sometimes these possibilities will depend on elements in the situation under which it is to be produced, such as (1) the financial nature of the production, (2) the timeliness of the story, (3) the amount of time available for working on the production, and (4) the ability of the director. All these are worth keeping in mind in the process of choice.

1. *The Financial Nature of the Production.* If one of the purposes is to make money, the question of royalty is one to be considered early. Royalty is the amount paid to an author for the right to produce his script. If a royalty is required, it must be paid to the publisher in advance of the performance. Some publishers have a sliding royalty, depending on the nature of the performance, whether or not admission is charged, the size of the auditorium, and so on. Occasionally, there is a situation in which the publisher feels that he can reduce the royalty. Early correspondence with the publisher is highly recommended before a definite selection is made. The author's rights in his play expire—after fifty-six years!—so many old plays have no royalty. There are many good plays, both old and new, for which no royalty is required.

Another and obvious way to make money is to keep expenses low. Therefore, in selecting a script, it is well to think of the elaborateness of production demands—the number of sets, the possibility of avoiding costume rental, the number and nature of properties and sound effects, and whether or not expensive lighting is involved.

2. *The Timeliness of the Story.* Many scripts depend for appeal on some current interest. War plays are often very popular in times of war, and a few years later they may have lost all their appeal. While the public is talking about some great discovery or some era-making invention, a play dealing with such an event may be more effective than it will be a few years, or even months, afterwards. Timeliness, then, is an element to be kept in mind. Plays that deal with ever present human problems, as do most of the great plays, rarely become dated, and in many situations are safer. However, local interest, the season of the year, the nearness to a holiday, or some special feature in the situation may guide the choice.

3. *The Amount of Time Available.* The time available is another obvious element in selecting a play. It should be sufficient to allow the workers to make a good production. Some scripts demand a long period of rehearsal, and if this is not possible, a simpler script is more sensible.

4. *The Ability of the Director.* This is probably a more delicate consideration, but it is one that cannot be ignored, even when the director is himself selecting the script. The success of the play may depend to a great degree on his skill and experience. It is his task to bring the story that the author has told in the script to life in the theater. A story that he does not understand, or one that he does not like, will probably not come to life very successfully. Directors without much experience will find that their best aid as a clear and simple story, which is, in and of itself, exciting.

ELEMENTS IN THE NATURE OF A PLAY

In addition to the elements mentioned above, which are inherent in the special situation under which the production is to be made, there are also certain elements, perhaps more important, that grow out of the nature of the theater. These appear in the definition of a play, previously discussed, and are the story, the actors, the stage, and the audience.

1. *The Story*. The main problem of the professional producer, who has at hand unlimited production possibilities, is the story. His financial purpose is always clear: to make a production, at any expense, which will be profitable because it is so good that audiences will flock to be entertained by it. He can take whatever amount of time is necessary. He can hire a director of great skill and experience, and can select suitable professional actors, designers, and technicians. If he fails in this purpose—and he often does—it is because he is wrong in his judgment. He finds out in the process of production that he is unable to make the *script* into a good *play*. The reason for his failure may lie in the quality of the script itself, and this problem has been the concern of thoughtful students of the theater for three thousand years. The stories of some scripts are of such a nature that they are exciting and interesting in almost any kind of a production. The characters, even if not well played, come to life and hence the incidents are thrilling and exciting. This quality of coming to life in the theater, possessed by some scripts but apparently lacking in others, we may call *theatrical effectiveness*. This is the first and foremost quality that the wise producer looks for in the script.

a. Theatrical Effectiveness vs. Literary Value. The qualities of theatrical effectiveness should not be confused with literary value. Perhaps we might say that the former is what makes a script *play* well in the theater, and the latter is that which makes the script *read* well. The quality that makes a script play, seems not to depend—at least, not entirely—on its literary value.

"Literary value" is that quality present in a play when "the finer attributes of structure and style are added to essential theatrical effectiveness." [1] Literary value is difficult to define but easy to recognize in a script. We feel that it exists when there is an underlying truth and beauty of perception in the story, an understanding of life, a rightness in the character portrayal and the dialogue, and a certain finality of expression. Literary value, however, is not present or absent as a chemical element might be in a solution. It exists in degree; therefore we are able to say that a certain script has great literary value, and another script has little. The latter script may have a simple and obvious idea, unconvincing characterization, hackneyed situations, and unoriginal resolutions. Yet it may still be entertaining, for the story may be told with sufficient craftsmanship to be amusing in the theater, even though it lacks any of the final attributes of great playwriting. Its playwright may be a successful workman, even though he is not a theater poet.

Theater poets, who combine literary quality and theatrical effectiveness, are rare in theater history. Their plays, although they may have no more immediate success, are likely to have a longer life both in and outside the theater. They write the theater classics. Some authors, famous in other fields—Tennyson and Browning are often given as examples—fail as playwrights. Their plays have the same high literary value as their poems. But they have little else—they lack theatrical effectiveness, and even the greatest actors do not seem able to bring them to life in the theater. Therefore, we must not think of literary value as a substitute for theatrical effectiveness. It is an added quality, desirable in a script, especially in an educational situation. If students are going to give time to learning lines and studying characters, they might as well be satisfying lines and truthfully-drawn characters. Also, repetition, in rehearsal and in performance, does not then become boring. Repetition increases our understanding—although the

---

[1] Brander Matthews, *A Study of the Drama* (Boston, Houghton Mifflin Co., 1910), p. 8.

poet stays always ahead of us—and brings increasing interest and growing delight. But all this may not help in the theater if the script lacks the quality of starting to life because of its theatrical effectiveness. This is what we must look for first in choosing a script.

b. Qualities of Theatrical Effectiveness. Unfortunately, there seems to be no absolute measure by which we can judge theatrical effectiveness. If there were, no play would ever fail, for it would then be a simple matter to avoid scripts which do not have it. However, the subject has been discussed by critics, and some of them have made suggestions concerning the essential nature of the kind of story that tends to come alive in the theater—and hence has theatrical effectiveness.

(1) *The Need for Conflict.* One of the suggestions often made is that the basis of every good play, hence of every good script, must be an obvious *conflict*. This theory is often connected with the name of Ferdinand Brunetière, and called the Brunetière theory. He was a great French dramatic critic of the last half of the nineteenth century.

Brunetière states that the basis of a play must be "the struggle of a will conscious of a purpose." [2] The chief character must desire something, and the story of the play will be his attempt to get it. He may be thwarted by some powerful antagonist, or he may be betrayed by some internal weakness in his own character, or he may be hindered by some social convention, but a play differs from all other forms of literature in that it *must always* deal with some exertion of the human will. It must represent a conflict.

Some critics have objected to M. Brunetière's dictum. William Archer, a famous English critic, says that the theory

[2] Ferdinand Brunetière, *The Law of the Theater*, (New York, Publications of the Brander Matthews Dramatic Museum, Columbia University, First Series, Volume 3, 1914). This essay is also reprinted, under the title *The Law of the Drama*, in Barrett Clark's invaluable book *European Theories of the Drama*, which contains many discussions of the theory by other critics.

would rule out as great plays *Agamemnon, Œdipus, Othello, Ghosts,* and "hundreds" of others. In these plays the heroes are not active wills: they are merely characters "writhing under the blows of Destiny." Mr. Archer therefore proposes to substitute the word *crisis* as one that more truly describes the situations found in many successful scripts. He says:

> What then, is the essence of drama, if conflict be not it? What is the common quality of themes, scenes, and incidents, which we recognize as specifically dramatic? Perhaps we shall scarcely come nearer to a helpful definition than if we say that the essence of drama is *crisis.* A play is a more or less rapidly-developing crisis in destiny or circumstance, and a dramatic scene is a crisis within a crisis, clearly furthering the ultimate event. The drama may be called the art of crises, as fiction is the art of gradual developments.[3]

Other critics have found difficulty in accepting Mr. Archer's suggestion to substitute crisis for conflict. Thus Henry Arthur Jones, the great English playwright, says:

> He (Mr. Archer) then goes on to sort out his crises, dividing them into those which are undramatic, and those which are dramatic. He establishes without a doubt, that when a crisis is dramatic, it is drama. On the other hand when a crisis is undramatic it is not drama. And unfortunately it appears that the crises which are undramatic are just as numerous and just as intrinsically important as those which are dramatic. Crises ought not to behave in this inconsistent way, if they are to prove Mr. Archer's theory. He has rejected "conflict" as the essence of drama. Yet I think if he carefully considers those crises which he calls dramatic he will find there is always a sense of conflict, active or implied; and often a conflict of the human will.[4]

In short, it seems difficult to understand the word *crisis* except as we define it as a turning point in a conflict!

Perhaps we could avoid this difficulty if we thought of a play in terms of modern psychology as an attempt at adjust-

---

[3] William Archer, *Play-Making* (Boston, Small, Maynard and Co., 1912), p. 36.

[4] Henry Arthur Jones, *Introduction to Brunetière's Law of the Theater.* Quotation from Barrett Clark's *European Theories of the Drama*, p. 467.

ment. Perhaps every play has as its basis a case of maladjustment. The play, then, is the hero's attempt to adjust himself to his surroundings. This he may do in a romantic melodrama by winning the girl of his choice away from the villain, or, in the case of Hamlet, by killing his father's murderer. Students constantly ask: "Why don't they write plays about nice, contented people?" The answer is that it isn't possible because well-adjusted people have no problems; hence the playwright would have no subject! Perhaps this is the basis of the facetious remark that "all good plays are about bad people!" Of course, there may be plays in which "good" people are in conflict with a bad environment, but in such a case the characters will be maladjusted and hence discontented and unhappy. So perhaps it may be truly stated that the struggle for adjustment makes material suitable for a play.

In any case, it is probably true that a play will be exciting to the degree to which it embodies some clear and important conflict, or, if you prefer, some interesting maladjustment. Hence, in choosing a script, we might ask such questions as: Is there a clear conflict? Is it about something that will interest the audience? Is the conflict given sufficient importance? Does it lead to a satisfying solution?

(2) *Obligatory Scenes*. Another idea regarding the essential quality of a story that will be interesting in the theater is advanced by Francisque Sarcey, whose *A Theory of the Theater* has been previously mentioned. Unfortunately, there seems to be no extant source in his own writings for his theory of *scènes à faire*, which may be translated as "obligatory scenes" or "scenes you must do." The theory is widely discussed, however, by other critics. Brander Matthews states Sarcey's theory thus:

. . . in every story which is fit to be set on the stage, there are certain episodes or interviews which must be shown in action and which cannot be narrated by the characters. . . . If any one of these essential scenes is shirked by the playwright, if he describes it in his dialogue, instead of letting the spectators see it for themselves, then the audience will be disappointed and their interest will flag. The spectators may not be able to declare the reason for their dissatisfaction; but they will be vaguely aware that they have been deprived of something to which they were entitled. They feel that they have been defrauded of their just expectations, if they are not made eye-witness of a vital incident which the inexpert dramatist has chosen to bring about behind closed doors or during one of the intermissions between the acts.[5]

William Archer expresses the same idea in this way:

An obligatory scene is one which the audience (more or less clearly and consciously) foresees and desires, and the absence of which it may with reason resent.[6]

A story will have theatrical effectiveness to the degree to which these scenes can be effectively presented. For instance, an audience would not be satisfied merely to be told that Iago has poisoned the mind of Othello. They insist on seeing, and have a right to be shown, the series of steps which change Othello from a trusting lover to a jealous and dangerous husband. The theatrical effectiveness of a script depends on the author's choice of the scenes he chooses to show.

Thus, in choosing a script, we might consider such questions as: Has the author shown us the obligatory scenes? Are some of the scenes dull because they are not obligatory so that they would be better told than presented? Has he omitted scenes that the audience will want to see?

(3) *Theatrical Conventions.* There is a third suggestion, which may be useful, proposed by Brander Matthews. He says that a script is likely to have theatrical effectiveness to the degree that it can be made vivid *within the conventions* of the theater. "In every art there is an implied contract between the artist and the public, permitting him to vary from the facts of life, and authorizing him to translate these facts and to

---

[5] Matthews, *op. cit.*, p. 103.
[6] *Ibid.*, p. 227.

transpose them, as his special art may require." [7] Some of these conventions, demanded by the very situation which exists in the special art of the theater, are that actors conduct themselves so we can see what they do; that they speak so we can hear all they say; that they all speak the same language, the language of the audience; that the dialogue be condensed and strengthened so as to have direct and instant meaning; that the action of the plot be telescoped and condensed, and events follow one another more quickly than they would in real life. These conventions explain the difficulties so often experienced by the playwright who tries to make a play out of a novel. The better the novel, the greater may be the difficulties because the conventions of the two arts differ. Therefore, if the story of the novel is such that it cannot be told in the conventions of the theater, it is not likely to make a good script.

We might ask, then, in considering a script, such questions as: Is the story such that it can be told successfully in the conventions of the theater? Can we believe the condensed and pointed dialogue? Can we accept the condensed time? Is the series of incidents suitable for telling in theatrical conventions?

These are some of the ways in which scripts might be examined to determine if they possess that essential quality, theatrical effectiveness. It is unfortunate, perhaps, that the measures of theatrical effectiveness, as it exists in the script, do not seem capable of being more exactly formulated. This arises from the fact that the theater is an art and not a science. The element of subjective judgment is ever present and all-important. In spite of this, we need not be forever satisfied and restricted by our limitations to selecting scripts that we vaguely like. We can, at least, attempt to form sensible judgments on a rational basis. Then we shall be better able to select *scripts* which by virtue of their fundamental nature have a reasonable chance of being turned into successful *plays*.

[7] Brander Matthews, *The Development of the Drama* (New York, Charles Scribner's Sons, 1926), p. 26.

2. *The Actors.* The three remaining elements that arise out of the nature of the theater are much easier to judge, and they may be briefly considered. The actors available obviously govern the choice of a script to be produced. Choice must be somewhat controlled by their number, their age, their sex, their maturity, and their ability and experience. The age of the actors, and especially their maturity and degree of sophistication, may determine the suitability of the script judged from its emotional tone. It is probably a true statement that the intellectual understanding of the actors may be exceeded, but never their emotional grasp. The emotions of the characters of Shakespeare, with but few exceptions, can be understood by high-school students, but the more subtle character portrayals of Ibsen may be beyond them. Actors of experience and trained ability can, of course, play a much more difficult script than those who are without much experience. Finally, the presence among the available actors of one or two persons of exceptional ability or peculiar physique may make possible some script that would otherwise be out of the question. It would seem unwise, for instance, to choose Henry IV, with no one available who would make a suitable Falstaff. In all these ways, and perhaps in many others, the actors govern the choice of script.

3. *The Stage.* Just as the actors help determine the choice, so must the stage on which it is to be produced. Determining features will be its size, the facilities for handling scenery, the lighting equipment, etc. Included with these physical factors should be one that is often forgotten, namely, the available staff. The number of backstage workers, their training in designing and in making and handling scenery, their skill in costuming and in building properties, and their ability to manipulate lights must be considered. A simple production, well done, which gives the technical staff courage and experience to carry over into more complicated work, is better than

an elaborate play less successfully done. Sustained and planned effort is the best method by which to arrive at ambitious and elaborate performances.

4. *The Audience.* A final consideration inherent in the theater situation is the nature of the probable audience—their age and experience, their degree of sophistication, their previous theater-going opportunities, and their reason for coming to the performance. A script suitable for an audience of adults may lack qualities to interest an audience of children; an unsophisticated group may enjoy a light comedy that would bore a sophisticated one. If the audience is a group of parents whose main purpose in coming to the production is to see their children perform, the script should be one that gives them an opportunity. On the other hand, if there is to be a normal audience situation, in which people pay to come to the theater for entertainment and amusement, the script must have these qualities. In this case, the non-professional producer is confronted with the same problem as the professional, that of choosing a script that possesses to the highest possible degree the quality of theatrical effectiveness.

METHODS OF SELECTION

The probability of making successful choices of scripts is likely to be greater if some systematic method is evolved in order that choice need not depend on accidentally stumbling on a good script.

1. *Bibliographies and Catalogues.* Choice demands that there be a number of possibilities. A preliminary sifting of scripts that seem suitable may be made with the aid of the many available bibliographies.[8] These usually give an idea of the story, the sets, the number of characters, the royalty, and the suitability of plays for various educational situations. A set

[8] Bibliographies, especially those listing current plays, rapidly pass out of date, and hence out of print, as they are replaced by newer lists. Most of the

of catalogues from play publishers [9] is also useful in this process. Catalogues are usually sent on request. The use of these bibliographies and catalogues aids to narrow the search, reduces the number of scripts that it is necessary to read, and speeds up the entire process. Members of a Little Theater, or a school or college group, may be encouraged to study bibliographies and catalogues, and the actual scripts in which they are interested may then be procured for further investigation.

---

following bibliographies are still available in libraries, even though some of them may no longer be purchased from the publishers.

American Library Association, *Subject Index to Children's Plays* (American Library Association, Chicago, 1940).

Ina Ten Eyck Firkin, *Index to Plays* (New York, H. W. Wilson Co., 1935).

Hannah Lagosa and Winifred Ver Nooy, *An Index of One Act Plays* (Boston, F. W. Faxson Co. First supplement, 1924-1931; Second supplement, 1932-1940).

Kate Oglebay, *Plays for Children* (New York, H. W. Wilson Co., 1928).

John H. Ottemiller, *Index to Plays in Collections, 1900-1942* (New York, H. W. Wilson Co., 1943).

Marjorie Seligman and Louise N. Frankenstein, *Plays for Junior and Senior High Schools* (New York, H. W. Wilson Co., 1932).

Frank Shay, *Guide to Longer Plays* (New York, D. Appleton-Century Co., Inc., 1925).

Frank Shay, *One Thousand and One Plays for Little Theatres* (New York, D. Appleton-Century Co., Inc., 1923).

Milton Smith, *Guide to Play Selection* (New York, D. Appleton-Century Co., Inc., 1934).

Ruth Gibbons Thomson, *Index to Full Length Plays, 1926-1944* (Boston, F. W. Faxson Co., 1946).

S. Marion Tucker, *Plays for Amateurs* (New York, H. W. Wilson Co., 1926).

[9] Publishers who issue extensive play catalogues:

Walter H. Baker Co., 178 Tremont Street, Boston, Mass.

Dramatic Publishing Co., 59 East Van Buren St., Chicago, Ill.

Dramatists Play Service, Inc., 6 East 39th St., New York, N. Y.

Samuel French, Inc., 25 West 45th St., New York, N. Y.

Henry Holt & Co., Inc., 257 Fourth Avenue, New York, N. Y.

Longmans, Green & Co., 55 Fifth Avenue, New York, N. Y.

Rowe, Peterson & Co., 131 East 23rd St., New York, N. Y.

2. *Reading Committee.* This process will probably be more successful if there is a small committee in the group whose duty is primarily to recommend suitable scripts. The final decision may be left, if it seems desirable, to a vote of the members; for it is usually a mistake to attempt to force a script on a group. The whole-hearted desire of the members to produce it is the director's greatest aid. But even the most energetic committee cannot do without assistance. If all the members of a group are encouraged to be constantly searching for suitable scripts, to bring suggestions to the committee, to discuss the problems of script choice with one another, there are always likely to be some good ones on hand.

3. *Early Choice.* But no matter what the method, the process of selecting a script is usually a long one. It should, therefore, be started early and worked at continuously. A good organization ought always to have several scripts on its list that it plans to produce whenever occasion allows, so that there never need be a mad, eleventh-hour search for something to play! The best safeguard against errors—which are so easy to make in play selection—is to have a carefully-planned program, which makes a hurried, last-minute choice unnecessary.

POSSIBILITIES OF THE ONE-ACT PLAY

The bibliographies listed above and the catalogues of publishers list many one-act scripts. In many localities, however, the one-act play has still to make its way. Often, especially in educational situations, it has many advantages. A program of one-act plays usually provides a greater variety of interesting problems in acting and production than one long play. And, in general a short play is easier for the non-professional actor since the problem of successfully creating a character to be seen for a short time only, under stress of a few incidents, is less than that of showing the consistent character development usually required in a longer play. A program of one-act plays must be carefully chosen to appeal to varying tastes. It is wise to make the program consist of various types, for instance, a fantasy, a serious play, and then a comedy or a farce. Interesting programs, such as "Three Sea Plays," or "Plays of Rural Life," or "Plays from Foreign Lands," can sometimes be made by selecting scripts with a common subject. So many delightful one-act plays now exist that they should not be ignored in arranging programs.

THE NEED FOR VARIETY

The ultimate test for script selection in the program of any non-professional organization—aside from the fact that the scripts must be capable of being turned into plays!—is probably variety. After a successful long play, a program of one-act plays might well be attempted. A realistic play of modern life might be followed by a costume play. To produce plays of only one type, out of the wealth of material that exists, is to lose much of the interest inherent in the practice of play production; to produce nothing but Shakespeare is, in most situations, as bad as to produce nothing but Broadway successes. Little Theaters and college groups, especially, might be on the look-out for unproduced original scripts. And there is always the possibility of some of the less well-known classics. The successful producing group has a planned and varied program of worth-while productions both behind it and ahead.

CHAPTER III

Analyzing the Script

THE NECESSITY FOR ANALYZING THE SCRIPT

No matter how much care the play producer has exercised in choosing his script, and no matter how successful he has been in selecting a good one, in putting it into the process of production, he faces another hazard and another problem. The problem now is to embody it in a production that will bring all its virtues to light. The experienced producer does not, therefore, rush blindly into production. Having chosen what he hopes is the best *script*, he begins to worry about how to make the best *play*. He knows that the play has two elements. The first is the author's concept which is described on paper, and the second is the embodiment of that concept in actors and on a stage for the purpose of making an effect on an audience. This second element is the production, and the problem is how to make this production embody the virtues of the script. Only a good *script* plus a good *production* will make a good *play*.

From this point of view, every production of every script results in a new and different play. The uninitiated in theater practice thinks of a script as a sort of phonograph record which always comes out the same. He says he has seen *Twelfth Night*. The truth is, he has only seen *a Twelfth Night*. Every production of *Twelfth Night* comes out a different *play!* It may have the same title, and tell roughly the same incidents, and contain characters of the same names. But the total of the production, the *play* called *Twelfth Night*, will have a different effect. Sometimes the effect will be good; hence it will be a good play; sometimes, alas, it will be bad! The script, meanwhile, hasn't changed at all! It is only the play that is different.

Most musicians know that they cannot hear Beethoven's Fifth Symphony, let us say, when they go to the concert hall. All they can hear is *a* Fifth Symphony, the one performed by the artists—the director and the instrumentalists—involved in the performance. Music lovers like to hear different conductors and orchestras play the same score because each performance results in different *music*—a different Fifth Symphony. It all depends on the *interpretation* that is being played.

So, if we are fond of the theater, we may like to see the same *script* embodied by different artists—directors, actors, scene- and costume-designers, etc. Every group of theater artists, whether or not they are conscious of the fact, will always make a different *play* because like music, the play *exists only in performance*. The effectiveness of the performance will depend, to a large degree, on the soundness of the interpretation shared by the artists involved in the production.

THE PURPOSE OF ANALYZING THE SCRIPT

The purpose of analyzing the script, then, is to reach a sound idea as a basis for the production. The process of producing a play—embodying the script in actors and a stage—involves thousands of decisions. Perhaps the director must decide whether or not this actor is better than that one. The actor has to decide how to play his rôle and to choose the best readings and gestures from an infinite number of possibilities. The scene-designer must ultimately choose between two chairs, or two kinds of wall-paper design, or two screens. The necessity for decision is ever present. The result is likely to be confusion if each of these artists proceeds along individual lines and selects only what he likes. Good play production results in one great unified design; it is the work of a group of artists laboring understandingly together to produce a unity of effect. This will be impossible unless there is some *common basis for choice*. The purpose of analyzing the script, then, is to arrive at this common basis which will lead to a unified interpretation. This is just as necessary—perhaps even more necessary—if the elements are few and simple, as they might be in a production by school children of a fairy tale, rather than numerous and complicated, as in a huge Broadway production. Either performance is likely to be more effective, a better work of theater art, if the elements are wisely selected to form a unified whole. This unity can arise only out of a common point of view, and the purpose of the analysis is to arrive at one.

THE CENTRAL IDEA

The common point of view, essential to unity in a production, may be imposed by the director (see p. 71), or arrived at by general discussion of all the participating artists. In either case, it must start with a study of the script, involving probably much reading and rereading, to deduce a basis for an interpretation that will be exciting to an audience. This basis grows out of the attitude that the author has embodied in his script—the philosophy of life which he represents. It corresponds to the atmosphere, or the aesthetic tone or mood, that should be created by any work of art. It may sometimes be described and discussed in general language as "atmosphere" or "mood," just as in any other work of art. Often, however, it is helpful to express this central idea as a *theme*.

1. *The Central Idea as a Theme.* The theme of a script is the abstract statement of its philosophy, the fundamental observation of human nature on which it is based. Sometimes an author consciously starts with a theme, in which case the theme is probably easily discernible. Plays with an apparent theme, resulting in a message, are often called thesis plays. The author may be attempting to criticize a contemporary evil, or to bring about some social reform. Thus, Galsworthy, starting with the observation that in England there is one kind of justice for

the rich and another kind for the poor, embodies his idea in a plot and writes *The Silver Box*. Many of the plays of the modern theater—those of Ibsen, Shaw, O'Neill, Brieux, etc. —are thesis plays. But even if a theme is not consciously embodied by the playwright, one is always discernible. An author, knowingly, or not, embodies his observations of human nature and his philosophy of life. This is to say, no one can write except out of his experience. If his experience is shallow, his observation inexact, and his thinking puerile, his theme will not be very important—and perhaps neither will his script. The theme, too, is somewhat a matter of opinion; different readers may draw different themes out of the same script. And different authors may embody identical, or almost identical themes, in varying plots. The important thing is that there should be agreement on the *theme to be emphasized in the production*, which tends to bring about a satisfying artistic unity in that production.

In the attempt to discover the theme, several points must be remembered:

a. The theme must be a statement. A single word cannot be a theme; it is only a topic. Ambition is not the theme of *Macbeth*, although it is the topic treated. The theme may be: "A man, essentially brave and generous, may have a flaw in his character, a consuming and unrighteous ambition, that will bring him to ruin and death." Another person may not agree with this theme, but say: "An ambitious man may meet such overwhelming opportunities to gain what he wants by false means that he brings about his own ruin and death." The topic of each of these themes is ambition, but the statements represent different points of view, and each should result in a different kind of production, hence a different play.

b. The theme must be abstract. The plot is the specific series of incidents in which the characters are involved. The theme is a generalization, an abstract observation, stating the point of view from which the story is developed. The *plot* of Dunsany's

A Night at an Inn may be stated thus: "Some English sailors steal a ruby that is the eye of a Hindoo idol; they succeed in killing the priests who come to reclaim the ruby, but are ultimately slain one by one by the idol itself." The *theme* for this plot might be that justice will be done, or that retribution for evil is certain, or some such idea.

c. The theme is not the moral. A moral is a little preachment, a lesson that grows out of the story. Not every play contains a moral. If the author is pessimistic or anti-social, his theme may actually be immoral, or at least unmoral. In his own time, Ibsen was regarded by many people as an immoral writer because his plays embodied themes that seemed anti-social; they questioned the teachings of church and state. It is not even necessary that we believe the theme to be true—although it is probably easier to make a good production if we accept the theme. What is important is that we try to understand the point of view of the playwright, if our purpose is to create an interpretation of his script.

d. The theme is often obvious and unoriginal. Not every play contains a unique and unusual theme. The most common of all themes are: Virtue will triumph, or Love conquers all, or Those who are good will be happy, etc. These themes are embodied by playwrights in scripts year after year and generation after generation. If the story in which these commonplace themes are embodied has sufficient originality in its craftsmanship, the play may be highly successful, for the theater tells and retells successfully the old stories that audiences like to hear. The theme is likely to be original and important only to the degree that the author has a profound understanding of the problems of life. Even among authors, such understanding is rare.

2. *The Central Idea as a Graphic Image.* The theme is often so commonplace and unoriginal that it does not provide a valuable point of view from which to make a production.

Sometimes, therefore, it is more helpful to define the central idea as a "graphic image." A graphic image is a *visual impression*, a picture, that corresponds in mood to the atmosphere desired for the production. Gordon Craig, one of the pioneers in the new movement in the theater, presents his idea of *Macbeth* in a graphic image:

I see two things. I see a lofty and steep rock, and I see a moist cloud which envelops the head of this rock. That is to say, a place for fierce and warlike men to inhabit, a place for phantoms to nest in. Ultimately this moisture will destroy the rock; ultimately these spirits will destroy the men.[1]

On the basis of a graphic image such as this, a unified and interesting production of the script could be made. How to carry the image over into actual production is the subject of many of the following pages.

Sometimes it is helpful to express the central idea both as a theme and as a graphic image. But in any case, the production is likely to be unified and successful to the degree to which we can arrive at an original and intelligent expression of the *central idea* of the script.

THE COLOR OF A PLAY

As we read and reread the script in order to find and state the central idea, we gradually begin to see, in our mind's eye, the production we hope to make. Certain colors begin to associate themselves with the idea. Perhaps the colors will force themselves upon us, and we may be unable to give a rational explanation of the fact that these certain colors seem to signify the play. We think of one play as red and green, and of another as dark red, brown, and yellow. We are not thinking as yet of the color of the sets, or of the costumes, or of any specific elements, but simply of the *abstract colors* that seem

[1] Gordon Craig, *On the Art of the Theater* (New York, Dodd, Mead, 1925).

best to represent the mood of the script. Perhaps we shall be able to intellectualize our feeling about the color.

This is what Craig proceeds to do in his discussion of *Macbeth*:

You ask about color? What are the colors that Shakespeare has indicated for us? Do not first look at Nature, but look in the play of the poet. Two; one for the rock, the man; one for the mist, the spirit. Now, quickly, take and accept this statement from me. Touch not a single other color, but only these two colors through your whole process of designing your scene and your costume, yet forget not that each color contains many variations. . . .

I know you are not yet quite comfortable in your mind about this rock and this mist; I know you have got in the back of your head the recollection that a little later on in the play come several "interiors" as they are called. But, bless your heart, don't bother about that! Call to mind that the interior of a castle is made from the stuff which is taken from the quarries. Is it not precisely the same color to begin with? and do not the blows of the axes which hew out the great stones give a texture to each stone which resembles the texture given it by natural means, as rain, lightning, frost? So you will not have to change your mind or change your impression as you proceed. You will have but to give variations of the same theme, the rock—the brown, the mist—the gray; and by these means you will, wonder of wonders, actually have preserved unity. Your success will depend upon your capacity to make variations upon these two themes; but remember never to let go of the main theme of the play when searching for variations in the scene.[2]

It is obvious that Craig thinks of *Macbeth* as a brown and gray play. We need not agree with him, but we understand his idea.

The entire matter of color is so subjective and psychological that objective values can be definitely determined no more than they can be in music. But for most people, musical sounds of a certain kind produce a definite feeling of cheerfulness, or depression, or some other emotion. In general, the same sort of thing is true of color. We may feel that a broad medieval farce, like *Pierre Patelin*, would best be represented by

[2] *Ibid.*, p. 23.

a combination of dull red and earthy brown. This combination, however, probably would seem inappropriate for a flashy, sophisticated modern comedy, such as *The Royal Family*. We might think of this as a cerise and green play. But the cerise and green combination does not strike the right tone for a delicate little harlequinade, like *The Maker of Dreams*. Color combinations give an effect that audiences feel, even though they are completely ignorant of color theory.

It is possible, however, to rationalize, or intellectualize, our reactions to color and color combinations and to work them out from generalizations made by generations of artists. It is helpful if all workers in the theater understand the importance and the possibility of using color skilfully to help act the play. This is true not only for scenic artists, but for directors, actors, carpenters, scene-painters, and even business managers!

1. *Definition of Color*. Color is the peculiar and mysterious quality that matter has of reflecting certain light rays and absorbing others. These reflected rays stimulate our eyes and give us the sensation which we call color. Thus, one object might reflect rays of a high intensity and create the impression that we call red. Another object may absorb these intense red rays, while it reflects rays of a lower vibration, which we call blue. All of these rays are present in white light. If we take a single beam of white light and pass it through a glass prism, the rays will be deflected, or refracted, at various angles. When these refracted rays fall on a white surface, they make a band of color, which is called the *spectrum*. Most observers see in the spectrum a band of color starting with red and ranging through orange, yellow, green, and blue, to violet. We know, of course, that there are colors that we do not see. Below red are beams of light which make no noticeable impression on the eye, and which are called infra red. Beyond violet are beams called ultra violet. The colors that we see, then, are limited by our eyes; and sometimes this color band is called the visible spectrum. A rainbow is the visible spectrum made

by a beam of light refracted by drops of rain and reflected on a convenient cloud.

2. *Color Theories*. There are many color theories, which the student will find fascinating and useful, even if they are contradictory. Some of them are physical, in that they are based on the actual study of light, the measurement of wave lengths, and the recording of these variations on the spectrometer. Others are physiological or psychological, starting with the study of the eye and trying to describe and measure physiological reactions to color sensation. Any system that allows us to think about color intelligently is useful.[3] Much of our confusion in attempting to think about color arises from the difficulty of describing it in words. Mr. Munsell states the case:

> The incongruous and bizarre nature of our present color names must appear to any thoughtful person. Baby blue, peacock blue, Nile green, apple green, lemon yellow, straw yellow, rose pink, heliotrope, royal purple, Magenta, Solferino, plum, and automobile are popular terms, conveying different ideas to different persons and utterly failing to define colors. The terms used for a single hue, such as pea green, sea green, olive green, grass green, sage green, evergreen, invisible green, are not to be trusted in ordering a piece of cloth. They invite mistakes and disappointment. Not only are they inaccurate: they are inappropriate. Can we imagine musical tones called lark, canary, cocatoo, crow, cat, dog, or mouse, because they bear some distant resemblance to the cries of those animals?

Most theories try to bring order out of this confusion by reducing color to some rational system. So far, no system has won general acceptance.

[3] Useful books for the further study of color:
  Albert Henry Munsell, *Color Notation* (Boston, H. Ellis Co., 1916).
  Wilhelm Ostwold, *Color Science* (London, Windsor & Newton, 1931).
  Faber Birren, *Color Dimensions* (Chicago, The Crimson Press, 1934). This contains an excellent brief history of the theories that have been held in regard to color, pp. 4-9.
  Bustanoby, J. H., *Principles of Color and Color Mixing* (New York, McGraw-Hill Book Co., 1947).

3. *The Pigment Theory*. Because much of our color in the theater is secured by the use of pigment, that is paint and dye, the pigment theory is perhaps the most useful one, although less scientific than other more recent theories. In this theory, there are three primary colors—the painter's primaries —red, blue, and yellow. These are primaries, because with these three colors (and black and white), it is possible to create all other colors. Orange is a mixture of red and yellow; green is a mixture of yellow and blue; violet is a mixture of red and

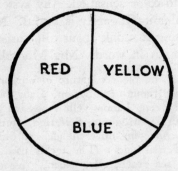

FIG. I. A COLOR WHEEL OF PIGMENT PRIMARIES

blue. These three colors, orange, green, and violet, are *secondary* colors. If we arrange the primary colors adjacent to one another, we shall make a *color wheel* of pigment primaries. By inserting the secondaries between the primaries in their proper places, we show the colors ordinarily recognized in the spectrum and make a color wheel which is *a graphic arrangement of all the colors showing their relationship*. Colors opposite one another are called *complementary* colors. Thus, red has green as its complement, orange has blue, and yellow has violet. The mixture of a color and its complement produces gray—although with most pigments, a very brownish gray is produced because of the impurity of the pigments. Colors next to one another are called *analogous* colors. Thus, the analogous colors of red are orange and violet.

Now, it must be understood that the space represented on the wheel by any one color—red, for example—is made up of all the possible variations of that color, and these variations are almost infinite in number. They are limited only by the ability of our eyes to perceive differences between them. These variations will depend on the amount of the other colors and the amount of black and white.

4. *Color Dimensions.* It is usually stated that color may vary in three possible ways, and each of these variations is a

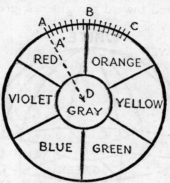

FIG. 2. A COLOR WHEEL SHOWING PRIMARIES AND SECONDARIES

change in dimension. We can describe a color completely only in terms of these dimensions. They are (*a*) hue, (*b*) intensity (or saturation),[4] and (*c*) value (or brilliance). In the complete color wheel, these may all be indicated graphically.

a. Hue. The variation in *hue* is that which is shown by movement around the circumference of the wheel. Thus, only in the very center of the space for red, at the spot marked A, will be found a true, pure red. This might be called the reddest red. As this point on the circumference moves toward B, we shall have an increasing amount of orange, until at B itself, we shall have a color half red and half orange, which for lack of a better name we may call red-orange. As this point con-

[4] Munsell calls this quality "chroma."

tinues to move towards C, the red will continue to grow less and less, and the orange more and more, until at C we shall have the point where there is a pure orange. As we continue to move this mythical point around the wheel, until we get back to red, we shall have passed through all the possible variations of hue.

b. Intensity. The second variation is determined by the nearness of the color to the center of the wheel. If we have a line from A toward the center of the wheel at D, this line will move from the reddest red toward the greenest green. As we move

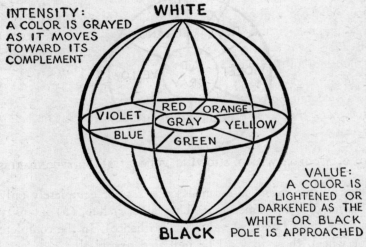

INTENSITY:
A COLOR IS GRAYED AS IT MOVES TOWARD ITS COMPLEMENT

WHITE

VIOLET   RED   ORANGE
GRAY
BLUE   YELLOW
GREEN

VALUE:
A COLOR IS LIGHTENED OR DARKENED AS THE WHITE OR BLACK POLE IS APPROACHED

BLACK

FIG. 3. A COLOR SPHERE

from A toward D, we shall decrease the *intensity* of the red. Thus, the red at A^1 will be slightly more gray than the red at A; the nearer we get to the center, the nearer we shall approach true neutral gray, which forms the center of the wheel. The variation in intensity is determined by the amount added of the complementary color.

c. Value. The third change is that of *value*, which is the brilliance of the color, determined by its blackness or whiteness. In order to represent it graphically, we shall have to transform the color wheel to a *color sphere* (See Fig. 3). If the top pole is white, and the bottom black, the value will change as the color moves up toward white, or down toward black. In popular language, the white values are often called tints, or pastel colors, and the black ones are called shades.

The main purpose of the sphere is to remind us that there is an infinite variety in every color. If we start with a pure red, we may change its (1) *hue* by moving it toward orange; we may change its (2) *intensity* by moving it toward green; we may change its (3) *value* by dropping it toward black. Each stopping place will be a different color, for color is a sum total of the three dimensions, and is capable of infinite variation.

Readers who recollect Craig's suggestion of brown and gray as the color of *Macbeth* may be worried by a lack of brown on the sphere. The color we call brown is only a variation of orange, containing a large amount of black; therefore, a dark value, or a shade, of orange. This illustrates the confusion of the names of colors. Many segments of the sphere are so common in nature or so widely used by man, that special words have been created for them, such as *brown,* and *pink,* and *purple.* But to an artist, brown is a dark value of orange, pink is a light value of red, and purple is a reddish hue of violet. Moreover, an artist does not think of a color as a single sensation, but as a *kind of sensation.* When Craig mentions gray as one of his colors, he thinks of the entire core of the sphere: perhaps a royal purple-gray for Duncan, a strong red-gray for Lady Macbeth, a robust blue-gray for Banquo, a slimy green-gray for the witches, etc. These are all united by the common quality of grayness and shown in opposition to the brown of Macbeth. And just like the gray, the brown has its infinite variety.

5. *Generalizations.* The arrangement of colors on a wheel or sphere leads to a few generalizations, made by artists, and useful in theater practice.

a. Complementary and Analogous Colors. Complementary colors, being opposite one another, are most unlike, and usually give a feeling of clash or opposition; while analogous colors, being close together or neighboring, express similarity and harmony.[5] Thus, a designer often decides to costume a group of characters in analogous colors to show that they are a harmonious group, and in complementary colors if he wishes to show the reverse. In the same way, we might expect that if the colors of the play are sharply complementary, the action will consist of a violent clash; if they are analogous, we expect milder action.

b. Warm and Cool Colors. Red, orange, and yellow are warm colors; whereas green, blue, and violet are cool. There is, however, overlapping; a green that contains much yellow, or a violet that contains much red, appears warm. The warm colors are those of highest physical vibration and are therefore most virile, lively, and exciting. We should not expect to find a feeble vacillating character dressed in red—in the theater. Perhaps another reason why the red-orange side of the wheel appears warm to us is that these colors are associated in nature with warm and forceful things, like fire, sun, and blood. On the other hand, the cool colors are not only lower in their rate of vibration, but are associated with the air, sky, foliage, sea, and other cool things in nature. In any case, we should not expect a blue-green play to have the forceful exciting quality of a red-orange play.

c. Primary and Secondary Colors. Primary colors have already been defined as the basic ones, out of which all the others can be made; and secondary colors are the made colors, orange, green, and violet. Some artists feel that the primary colors are cruder and more primitive, and the secondary colors

[5] These ideas are not to be confused with the theories that certain color combinations are pleasing and harmonious, whereas others are not. Any color combination is possible to a modern artist, even if disturbing, providing that this is the effect he wants.

more sophisticated. Thus, in choosing between two cool colors, like blue and green, they would say blue is a simple, more primitive, color, perhaps better for a calm heroine; while green, a derived color, is more sophisticated, better for a deep-dyed villainess. A primitive play might then be thought of in primary colors; and an artificial, complicated, worldly play in secondary colors.

However, the entire matter of color is subjective and psychological, and it is impossible to reduce it completely to objective values. The subtleness of the subject makes it impossible to lay down hard and fast rules. The beginner must not be worried. He should understand as much of the theory as he finds useful, but the only ultimate guide is his own reaction in the situation. As he learns to react carefully and truly, color will come to have more and more significance for him, and will become an increasingly useful tool in theater practice.

THE LINE OF A PLAY

Just as it is possible to think abstractly about the color that best expresses the mood of a script, so we may think about the line.

1. *Definition of Line*. The *line* is *the pattern* made by outlines, edges, and all the places where colors come together. If we place a piece of transparent paper over a painting and trace its outlines, we should have the *line pattern* of the picture. Ultimately, the production is going to make a line pattern. This will consist not only of the sets and furniture, but also of the actors, of the moves they make, of how they stand, and the positions they take. Therefore, line is the concern not only of the scenic designer, but of everybody participating in the production. The nature of the production, and hence its effect, will be somewhat determined by the appropriateness of its line. Therefore, this is one of the things that should be determined in the preliminary analysis, along with the central idea and the color. Like color, it is a generalization that grows

out of the central idea and helps to produce a unified artistic effect. We should not, at the beginning, think of the shape of the chairs or furniture, nor the pattern of the wall paper, nor of the lines the actors are to make with their bodies. We must think of the *abstract line pattern* that best represents the mood of the script.

Like color, line is a subjective element, and no definite rules can be laid down. But whether or not we know anything about the theory, line patterns will affect us. If we think of the mood of a script as noble and dignified, we shall probably think of long, straight vertical lines. This will not be very gay or comic, however, so we may think of the pattern for a broad comedy as in sharp curves and small circles. A fantasy, however, may suggest long delicate curves. Perhaps you will feel that there is a distinct difference in mood in the following line patterns:

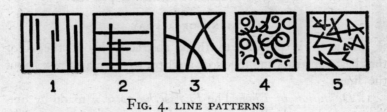

FIG. 4. LINE PATTERNS

It should be pointed out that these blocks do not represent any tangible objects; they are not pictures of anything. They are merely an attempt to suggest varying mood as abstract line patterns. Just as various combinations of color give an effect, so do various combinations of line.

2. *Useful Generalizations.* Most artists would probably agree to the following generalizations:

1. The most serious line is a long straight line, which is most noble, dignified and religious when it is vertical. (Line pattern 1.)
2. It is most earthy when it is horizontal. (Line pattern 2.)
3. Long slow curves are most sensual or fanciful. (Line pattern 3.)

OEDIPUS

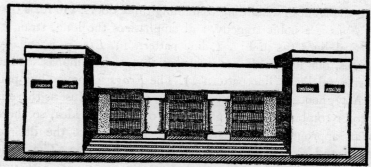

ELECTRA

FROGS

FIG. 5. SETS FOR THREE GREEK PLAYS, SHOWING VARIATION IN LINE PATTERN

47

4. Sharp curves and arcs of small circles are most comic. (Line
    pattern 4.)
5. Jagged lines and sharp angles are most exciting. (Line pattern 5.)

Thus, if the central idea suggests a noble and dignified play,
we shall not expect the line pattern to be predominantly short
curves and sharp angles, for this would deny the premise of
the central idea. In the same way, we should not expect a gay
farce to suggest long, serious, vertical lines. In the drawings in
Fig. 5, the artist has the same mechanical problem—to represent the front of a building containing three doors. He feels that
Oedipus is a noble tragedy, and emphasizes the long, straight,
vertical lines (as in Fig. 4, line pattern 1). *Electra* is equally
serious, but less noble and more earthy, so he emphasizes the
horizontal lines (line pattern 2). The *Frogs* is comic (line pattern 4), hence he introduces many sharp curves. Just as there is
a color combination that grows out of the basic idea, so there
is an appropriate line pattern that will suggest the desired
mood and thus help lead to a unified production. The three
scene-sketches (see frontispiece) illustrate this point. Although
the artist had in each case an identical mechanical problem, to
show a proscenium arch, a curtain, two proscenium doors, etc., he
had a different artistic problem. In the upper sketch, for *The
Beggar's Opera* the artist created a crude, strong, earthy quality,
by using a vigorous red and many sharp curves; in the middle
sketch, *The Way of the World*, the effect is intended to be
more elegant and decadent, and is secured by a cool and sophisticated blue-green, and flattened slow curves; in the bottom
sketch, for *The Knight of the Burning Pestle*, the lavenders
and greens, and the exaggerated and broken lines of the shingles
and windows, create what the artist hopes will be an exciting
burlesque. In a similar way, the plate facing page 296 shows a
completely unrealistic, gay, and exaggerated *Barber of Seville*,
consciously made so by the choice of color and line.

THE STEPS IN THE ANALYSIS

The steps in the sort of a preliminary analysis which should lead to a unified production are thus three in number:

1. Express the central idea in the most appropriate way, either as a theme or a graphic image.
2. Indicate the combination of colors most appropriate to the central idea.
3. Indicate the line pattern most appropriate to the central idea..

THE PROBLEM OF EMBODYING THE ANALYSIS

The problem now, throughout the entire process of production, is how best to embody the analysis, and this is a problem for all the artists involved. All decisions must be made in terms of the analysis, for the basis of the decisions should be the interpretation desired. The process of play production is the process of transforming ideas into physical things—actors, their voices and movement, costumes, sets, furniture, etc. In the theater, we are moved by these physical embodiments, and by them only. Through them, we perceive the ideas and the emotions that the artists are trying to communicate to us. If there are no ideas and emotions there, the physical things remain dead and meaningless; they do not combine to give us the emotional experience of a play.

Every one of these physical things must be selected, and the choice will be intelligent to the degree that it carries out the idea of the analysis. For instance, I have above suggested two possible themes for *Macbeth;* one, "A man, essentially brave and generous, may have a flaw in his character, a consuming and unrighteous ambition, that will bring him to ruin and death;" the other, "An ambitious man may meet such overwhelming opportunities to gain what he wants by false means that he brings about his own ruin and death." Each of these will make a different play, and these are only two of innumerable possibilities. If we wish to embody the first, however, we shall want an actor who can play a thoughtful, sensitive Macbeth—a Macbeth of internal weaknesses. We shall emphasize the poetry of the play, and our choice of all the other characters will be determined by this basic idea. The Lady Macbeth must be gracious and insinuating, rather than obviously forceful; and all of the characters must be so played as to allow the conflict of the play to be Macbeth's struggle with himself. A play based on the second theme would probably be more external and much more melodramatic. Our choice of an actor for Macbeth must be different, for now we want a less sensitive character. This Macbeth is not a poetic, brooding, Hamlet-like man; for we want him to be the victim of external circumstances, not of an internal struggle. These circumstances will be formed partly by the other characters; therefore they, too must be different. They must be more forceful and more varied, so as to be able to influence him more obviously. This should be no gentle and insinuating Lady Macbeth, but a domineering one who openly urges him on to murder. The Duncan must be a man born to be murdered! All the circumstances must combine to force Macbeth into his crimes.

Many other plays called *Macbeth* are possible. Some years ago Macbeth was portrayed on Broadway, by Lionel Barrymore, as a barbarian chief, brave, ferocious, and rather stupid. The castle scenes consisted merely of huge outlines of gothic arches set against a black cyclorama. As the play progressed these arches became more and more distorted. So did all the other elements in the scenery. This was an attempt to show the spectators a disintegrating world, as it might appear through the eyes of a criminal whose crimes lead him to insanity. This was a new and pathological *Macbeth*. Again, a group of negro actors once presented a jungle *Macbeth*. This was a red and green play, not the brown and gray one proposed by Craig. In this exciting production, the locale was changed to Haiti, although no lines were altered. Macbeth was a huge native chief, in a red coat, the witches were green voodoo women; and the whole tale became an exciting display of witchcraft. It was a new and savage *Macbeth;* and I am sure Shakespeare would have approved of the production, although he would never have thought of it! The nature of all great scripts is that they can be constantly interpreted and reinterpreted by new groups of artists for new generations.

But it is not only in the selection and directing of actors that a central idea is essential. It guides every decision. The heroine should see that a dress this color, however becoming, will not do; for it puts her in the wrong character group and destroys the color idea of the play. The designer cannot use this piece of furniture, no matter how handsome it may be, if it is curved and gentle and gay, whereas the idea of the situation demands that it be gloomy and threatening. A princess cannot sit on this chair, but only a gum-chewing stenographer. And so on, throughout all the physical elements that go to make up the play in the theater.

The embodiment of a new and exciting interpretation of a good script is a task for any group of artists. Just how it may best be done is the topic considered in the following chapters.

PART II

Directing and Acting

CHAPTER IV

Choosing Players

The first step in play production, after a script has been chosen and analyzed, is finding players. This process is called casting. In general, the problem is to find the best actor available to play each of the characters. But this presents the problem of determining who the best actor is. In the professional theater, there have been two distinct theories, each representing a different philosophy of casting.

1. *Casting by Ability.* The first theory maintains that casting should be based on ability; the *most capable actors should be chosen for the most difficult rôles.* This assumes that ability to act is more important than natural likeness to the character. Thus, the great eighteenth-century actor David Garrick, thought he could play any part in any play better than any other actor in his company; in *The Beaux Stratagem* sometimes he would play Archer, the hero, and at other times he would play Scrub, a comic servant. Even in the late nineteenth century, Booth and Barrett, on tour with Shakespeare's *Othello,* used to alternate between the rôles of Othello and Iago, exchanging rôles in alternating performances. Even sex might be no deterrent; skilful actresses might play men's parts and vice versa. Peg Woffington, in the late eighteenth century, won fame as Harry Wildair, a dashing, romantic lover. And Sarah Bernhardt, as the person of greatest ability in her company, often played the title rôle in *Hamlet.* The idea behind this kind of casting is

55

that the most capable and experienced actor should play the most important and difficult rôle.

2. *Type Casting*. In the modern theater, casting by ability has been replaced almost entirely by type casting. The director casts by type when he tries to find an actor who naturally resembles the character to be portrayed, in physical, vocal, and personality traits. It is the complaint of many old actors that type casting has ruined the art of acting. The modern actor, they say, doesn't have to be able to act; he never plays anything but himself! If he makes a success as a southern young man, he is doomed to play a southern young man as long as he is in the theater. And the dispute is on!

Whatever may be the philosophical truth, it is probably true that neither extreme exists, or ever has existed. Even in the old theater, while there may have been more variety in the kinds of rôles an actor played, he was quite likely to be most successful in one distinct type of part. This became what was called his line of business. Shakespeare, for instance, seems to have been an old man all his life; that is, even as a young man, he played dignified old men, like Adam in *As You Like It,* and the Ghost in *Hamlet.* Perhaps he did not have, and knew he did not have, those qualities as an actor that would allow him to play great emotional parts. And so, whatever the theory, there is probably always a limit of physical, vocal, or personality characteristics which prevents an actor from playing *any* part. On the other hand, even when the type theory of casting prevails, there are obvious limits to its use. No one probably ever thinks of getting a real idiot to play an idiot! The ideal of every director is, and probably always has been, to find an actor of just the right type who has the highest degree of ability.

3. *Anti-type Casting*. Sometimes, in school dramatics, a third theory seems to be advocated, and this we might call the anti-type theory. This is based on the feeling that persons of a reverse type should be chosen because of the educational value

that lies in the student's playing a part that takes him out of himself. Thus, a bashful boy might be chosen to play a braggart; or a forward girl, a timid country cousin. Whether or not this theory is true is perhaps open to question, for it assumes that an actor takes on in some way the characteristics of the rôle he plays. Otis Skinner once jokingly implied this about himself; after playing a long series of jovial rascals, he said he was now looking for a nice heroic rôle because he was getting to be afraid of staying alone with himself! In any case, whether or not there is a carry-over of acted characteristics into real life, there probably is educational value in playing parts to which the actor has little natural resemblance; and such activity may be valuable in the training of an actor. But this is not a good idea when the purpose is to make the best possible play.

It becomes quite clear, then, that our theory of casting must be somewhat determined by our *purpose*. If our aim is merely to give the actors experience, we may sometimes be guided by the *anti-type* theory. However, when the aim is to make the best possible performance, a large element of *type* casting seems the more logical method. Certainly, it simplifies tremendously the labor of the director and makes for a better production. And young people usually like best to play those rôles for which they are obviously best fitted, just as professional actors do. When we are fortunate enough to find a high degree of *ability*, in addition to rightness of type, we shall have made a long step towards a successful production.

METHODS OF CASTING

Whatever the theory back of our casting, we shall increase our success if we practice it through some intelligent method. In non-professional groups, where there is a permanent director, he will naturally do the casting, with more or less aid from other members of the group. If the organization is large, however, and does several productions a season under different directors, it may be wise to have a permanent officer in charge

of casting, even though in each individual production the director must have the final word. Most large professional producing offices have a casting secretary, who makes it his (or her)
business to know a great many actors. He is thus able to suggest
and advise, and help find the best possible cast.

The actual methods of procedure are only three in number,
and all of the many methods used really fall into one or the
other of these classifications:

1. *Tryouts*. Tryouts, which seem the most democratic method
at first glance, consist of competitive readings for parts in the
chosen play. This method implies that candidates have had a
chance to become familiar with the script and have made up
their own mind as to the rôles for which they are best suited.
If the script is unfamiliar, some way must be devised so that
they may have a chance to read and study it. Perhaps copies
may be left in some generally accessible place—the greenroom
of the Little Theater, or the library of the school. At definite
given times, candidates may appear before the director and his
assistants, and interpret the rôles they wish to play.

The advantages of tryouts are obvious. If they are properly
conducted, they furnish an opportunity in which new people
can demonstrate ability; and they may be so conducted as to
arouse enthusiasm and lead to the discovery of talent that might
otherwise remain unknown. The disadvantages, however, must
not be overlooked. They may consume a great amount of time,
and they are never reliable in result. There are persons who
read a part well, but who never get much better than they are
at the first reading. They do not work up in the rôle. On the
other hand, many a person who reads badly and who makes a
poor first impression may ultimately play a character better
than a person who reads well. Therefore, to cast entirely by
tryouts is, as a rule, not wise.

2. *Interviews*. Interviews, or informal conversations with the
candidates, are advocated by some directors. They feel that
competitive tryouts are poor tests because the candidates are

under such a strain. They prefer to judge candidates under more normal social conditions. Most professional directors interview actors whom they are considering for specific parts. Perhaps this is a method that might well be used in educational situations more than it is. Alert athletic directors in a school constantly urge good athletic material to try out for teams. Perhaps, in the same way, we can encourage hesitating candidates for dramatics to try out, by some system of planned interviews.

3. *Experience.* The past experience of the actors, according to other directors, is the only test. Probably it is true that the only real way of knowing what an actor can do is to have worked with him in a play. In amateur groups the past experience of the actors is sometimes not given sufficient weight. In the professional theater, experience is a most important item; it is the complaint of all young actors that you can't get a job until you have professional experience, but you can't get professional experience until you have a job! This leads to a discouraging and endless circle. Still, all professional actors have started somewhere.

BEST METHOD

Probably the best method of casting is some combination of all those described. Old actors of the organization who have proved themselves may be cast in important parts for which they are obviously fitted; whereas some sort of tryout system for less important parts will give new-comers a chance to prove their abilities. The director learns much about the ability of an actor from having used him in a play, and it seems only reasonable to take this into consideration. Character, willingness to coöperate, reliability, etc., are important things, and they cannot be learned from tryouts or interviews. On the other hand, tryouts and interviews lead to the discovery of new actors and thus constantly feed new life into the organization.

THE CASTING SHEET

The director will probably find it useful, whatever his theory or his method, to study the play in advance and decide what sort of actors he needs. This study may result in a casting sheet,

CASTING SHEET

"AS YOU LIKE IT" with actors from a High School dramatic club

DUKE	Thick set, mature boy, with deep resonant voice. Placid and pleasant personality.
FREDERICK	Younger brother to banished Duke. More slightly built, but taller in height. More energetic personality quality - a "go-getter".
ORLANDO	Hero of the play. Tall, masculine, and handsome. Must have charming, virile quality. Pleasing voice with variety — must be able to read well. Ability to wrestle desirable.
OLIVER	Orlando's eldest brother. Similar to Orlando in coloring and general quality, but should have a more sophisticated, perhaps even sinister, quality.
JACQUES	Another brother, older than Orlando, but younger than Oliver. Similar to them in physical and vocal traits, possibly with more romantic personality.
ADAM	Old servant. Tall, thin boy. Light voice. Orlando must be able to carry him.
CHARLES	Athletic boy, able to wrestle, big and strong, with heavy voice. Must have threatening and dangerous quality.
TOUCHSTONE	Slight boy, not too tall. Voice must be light and pleasing. Needs comic quality of some sort.
ROSALIND	Tall, athletic girl, but smaller than Orlando, with pleasing voice. Must read well. Must have exciting and interesting personality, and boyish quality.
CELIA	Different from Rosalind in coloring, and smaller in physique and lighter in voice. More gentle in personality.

FIG. 6. A CASTING SHEET

as in the illustration (Fig. 6). The casting sheet will be a description of the actors needed for the specific play. *It must be in terms of the actors and not the characters.*

Thus, the high-school director should not jot down that

he wants "a gentle old man, about seventy years of age, with a sense of humor." This describes the *character*, and not the *actor*. The problem is to decide what kind of an actor, among those available, will best embody the character presented by the author, or imagined by the director. There is not likely to be a gentle old man, about seventy years of age among the high-school students! In the terms of his material, the director must decide what kind of a high-school boy will be best. Thus, he may want a tall, thin boy, with a high voice, and a gaunt face; or he may want a stocky, thick-set boy, with a heavy voice. His problem is which one of these will make the most appropriate old man for the specific rôle.

The casting sheet, then, is useful only if it is carefully thought out in terms of the material. It will probably describe the physical, vocal, and personality traits desirable for each character; the special abilities demanded; and the necessary relationship to the other characters. A physical trait might be excessive height or size; a vocal trait might be a sweet and gentle voice; a personality trait might be the quality of appearing to be dangerous. An actor might have many good qualities for a murderer, but have such an innate gentleness that no audience will ever accept him as such. The special ability demanded might be to play the piano, or to be able to sing, or to act hysterical. And the necessary relationship to the other characters might demand that two actors look alike because they are twins, or that one be shorter than another, or that one appear stronger and more powerful physically than another. If, in a serious play, a character is to be arrested, and the officer is a thin, weak boy, the effect is likely to be unintentionally comic. To keep it serious and believable, the officer must appear to be able to dominate. Thus, casting a play is often not a matter of finding individual actors so much as a matter of finding the right combinations. This is why casting should be kept flexible until the best combination is found. The casting must not deny the fundamental facts that we want an audience to accept.

The casting sheet may be typed or mimeographed and sent to the members of the group. I have found this a most useful device in Little Theaters. In a school, the list may be posted on a bulletin board, or passed out to members of a group. If all members understand the basic problems involved, the process is greatly aided. A well-thought-out casting sheet helps to make these basic problems clear.

CASTING CARDS

Another helpful device is a casting card. There should be a casting card for each member of the group. It will contain his name, address, telephone number, appearance and coloring, height and weight, his dramatic experience, the record of his

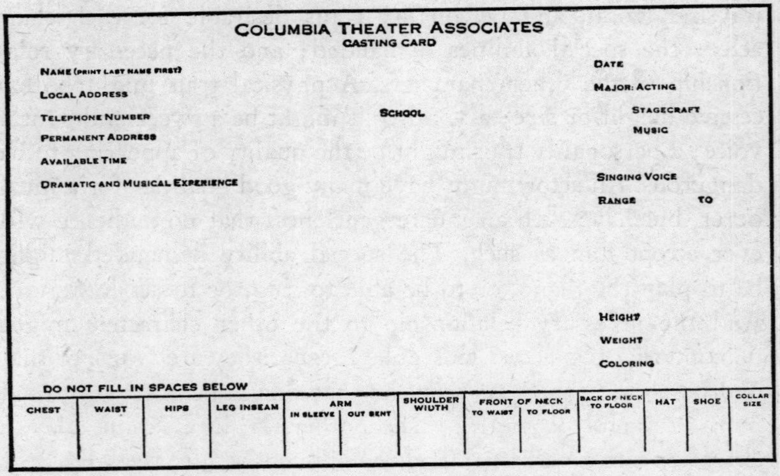

FIG. 7. A CASTING CARD

appearances with the group, and any other items the director thinks useful. If the director keeps an alphabetical file of these cards, he will be able in a moment to recall the important data for any actor. A study of his file will help solve his problem in casting a play. Most professional producers make such a file of the actors they interview. Many professional radio directors cast entirely from such a file.

UNDERSTUDIES

If there are to be understudies, they might be selected in this general process of casting. An understudy is an actor who studies another actor's part in order to be his substitute in an emergency. Sometimes directors in schools appoint an understudy for each character. Unless the understudy is faithful, really memorizes the lines, the movement, and the business, which involves attendance at all, or most, of the rehearsals, he is usually of very little use when the emergency arrives. The practice in most professional companies is to have two understudies, a man who is prepared to play any man in the play, and a woman who is able to play any of the women. There may be a special understudy for the star, or leading player. He (or she) rarely gets a chance to play, however, for if the star is incapacitated, the play is likely to close until he recovers.

A formal system of understudies does not always work well in a non-professional group. It is often better, if the emergency involves a leading player, to move a minor one into the part and to replace the minor one with a hastily recruited actor [1]— sometimes the stage-manager or one of his assistants. It is better still if no emergency occurs!

DOUBLE CASTS

Another educational device, rarely if ever used professionally, is double casts.[2] This involves the casting of two actors for each rôle—or, at least, for each important rôle. If there are two or more performances, the casts may play on alternate nights. But sometimes directors rehearse both casts and near the end

---

[1] In such an instance a good file of casting cards is useful!

[2] This may not be strictly true in musicals, which tax a singer's voice; so that in a difficult rôle, he may be able to appear only every other performance.

of the rehearsal period pick out those whom they believe to be the best players; the others automatically become understudies! This, too, is a device of doubtful usefulness if the object of the director is to make the best possible product. Among all these actors there must be some combination which is best, and this combination ought to be discernible early in the rehearsal process. If this combination can be selected and given the rehearsal time of both casts, the result will be far superior. However, a double cast has the advantage of using twice as many actors, and it eradicates worries about emergencies. There may be some educational situations in which it is a highly useful practice.

THE RESULT OF CASTING

Ignoring understudies and double casts, casting is the process of finding the best combination of actors, to "embody the characters involved in the series of incidents." This is always the aim of the professional director; and it should be the aim of the director of non-professionals—in schools, colleges, and Little Theaters—when he wishes to make the best possible play. The individual fitness of an actor to play a character is, then, only one of the considerations; another, and perhaps an even more important one, is his relationship to the other actors. Whatever the method used, the result can be successfully judged only in the early phases of rehearsal. Changes are often necessary at this time, not because an actor is *bad*, but because he is *wrong*. He is wrong because there is something about him that denies the fundamental premise of the story. Seen among the other actors, he is too large, or too small, or too forceful, or too weak. He just does not fit into the situation. Often a professional director regretfully finds that he must replace a really good actor with one not so good; some unchangeable characteristic of the first actor makes the story unbelievable.

For this reason, casting should be kept flexible during early rehearsals. An actor should never be allowed to feel that a part has been given to him, and now is his by rights. Shifts and changes are often necessary. The actor must know that if he doesn't work out properly, or if someone appears who can play "his" part better than he can, he will be dropped, just as would be the case if he were a candidate for the football team. In the professional theater, the first five days are a sort of tryout. This is by agreement between Equity, which is the actors' union, and the Association of Producers. A professional actor never tells his friends that he has a part until after these five days! If the director lets him come to rehearsal the sixth day, the part is his. The director cannot now let him go except by paying him two weeks' salary. On the other hand, and just to make the arrangement fair, an actor may leave a play during the first five days; but if he comes the sixth day, he cannot leave without paying the management two weeks' salary! This necessity for keeping the cast flexible, recognized by agreement among professionals, is equally important in non-professional productions. It is wise, therefore, to work out some fair scheme, just as the professionals have, to make it possible.

The kind of fundamental relationship between characters that must be tested during early rehearsals is probably obvious. Casting a family is an example. An audience cannot believe that this father and this mother are the parents of these three children if all five actors are different in race, coloring, culture, speech, etc. Casting a family is always difficult and full of hazards. There are usually similarities between parents and children that cannot be established by acting ability alone, however competent the actors are. Again, two persons who are going to appear together constantly, the hero and heroine for example, must not only have voices that are pleasing in themselves, but voices that are sufficiently different, and yet fit well together. In their case, height and size will be another important consideration. A hero who is much shorter and slighter than the heroine with whom he is supposed to be in love tends to be ludicrous; he may have to be discarded for a larger hero, even though the second may not act as well. In the same way, two persons of a similar type—for instance, two old men—are always difficult to cast and must be cast as a pair. Probably they must have dissimilar voices and unlike physiques—unless the point of the play is that they are alike, as might be the case if they are brothers. Many considerations of this sort complicate the process of casting, but at the same time make it interesting.

Sometimes critics say that a play is miscast. What they mean by this—if they know what they are talking about—is that the basic relationship of the characters, which must be accepted by the audience if it is to believe the story, is denied by the choice of actors. These four people cannot be a family, or these two persons are not believable as lovers, or these three men could not have been college classmates. The result of casting must be to avoid these impossibilities and to find the *group of actors* that reasonably embody the fundamental relationships necessary for the specific play.

CHAPTER V

The Process of Rehearsal

THE REHEARSAL AS A LEARNING PROCESS

Nothing is more important for success in play production, both amateur and professional, than the conduct of rehearsals; and unfortunately this is one of the most difficult parts of the process. One can learn from a book how to organize for a performance, or how to make scenery, or the important facts about lighting. But rehearsing, like the teaching process, is a very subtle thing, depending almost entirely on the influence of one personality on another. A good director, like a good teacher of any other art or craft, must be the product of experience.

Nevertheless, there are certain suggestions that may be given; and the most important of these is the fact that the rehearsing of a play is a learning process for the actor—and for the director, too—and that, therefore, like all learning processes, it consists of a series of distinct and recognizable steps. This is true if the actors are experienced professionals, or if they are young novices. The director will be tremendously aided if he will observe these steps and aid each in its turn. Like the wise teacher, he must know that he cannot teach everything at once. If his process is logical and follows the general method of learning, and if he is patient and tactful, many faults will correct themselves. He may guide and hasten the process, but he cannot twist it out of its normal course.

It is helpful, too, if he aids the actors to understand the process. They should know what is being attempted during each phase of the rehearsals—what is important, and what is, for the time being, unessential. Otherwise, they may be worried by the fact that they are not being aided to read their lines correctly when the director is wisely concentrating his attention on movement, or that the tempo seems too slow during the phase when the director is neglecting the tempo and bending every effort to work out each detail of characterization. In other words, in the process of learning how to act a play, there is a natural order of events; and the process is easier, sounder, quicker, and more pleasant if this natural order is the basis of the process.

THE PHASES IN THE PROCESS

There are, in my opinion, four distinct phases, or steps, which are discernible in any series of rehearsals, whether or not they are recognized by the persons involved. The sensible thing is to follow these steps consciously, and to make each one as sound as possible. They are:

1. *Preliminary study,* during which the actors should become familiar with the idea of the play.
2. *Blocking out the movement,* or deciding and learning the entrances, exits, and changes of position.
3. *Working out the details of characterization,* or learning the rôles and how to act them most effectively.
4. *Working for finish,* or pulling the whole play together to give unity and effectiveness of performance.

This series of steps grows out of the logic of the situation. It is not only unwise, but it is impossible to begin rehearsals by working for finish, for there is nothing to finish. In the same way, an actor cannot be expected to create a character while he is still trying to remember where he comes in, and when he crosses and where he should be standing during this or that speech. The logical process demands that actors get a general understanding of the play, go on to the details of movement and characterization, and then be brought back to a playing of the play as a whole.

These steps, however, are probably never all equal in duration of time. The third, working on the details, will probably require at least three quarters of all the time available for rehearsal. This step will be much shorter and more profitable if it has been preceded by the other two, a building up of a general understanding of the play and a skeleton of movement; and it needs always to be followed by a fourth, in which the play is rehearsed as a whole for general effectiveness. If some such definite plan is followed, all the persons involved will understand what is being done at any given rehearsal, and the entire process will be more rapid and more encouraging.

TIME ELEMENTS IN THE REHEARSAL PROCESS

It is difficult, if not impossible, to state just how much time is needed to prepare a play; for that will vary with the experience and ability of the actors and the director. In general, no competent director ever feels that he has enough time. Most professional companies rehearse eight hours a day for four weeks, with extra time during the final week, making a total of more than 200 hours. In fact, many professional companies probably spend 300 hours in rehearsal. Much of this time, however, may be spent in un-learning old scenes and learning new ones, as the director and the author rewrite the script! Also, during the first week or two, there are often so many changes in the cast, that it may be said that true rehearsals do not begin until the second or third week—and sometimes not then! Little Theaters and schools are rarely able to spend enough time on a play; and therefore it is especially essential, when time is short, to make the process as intelligent and as orderly as possible.

Probably a one-act play may be reasonably prepared in eight or ten rehearsals of two or three hours each. The first one may be used for preliminary study, the second and third to work out the movement, the next four or five for work on details, and the last one or two to pull the play together and for the dress rehearsal.

For a longer play, much more time is needed. I find that a convenient rough estimate is to allow *at least* five times as many rehearsals as there are acts; thus, a three-act play would need not less than fifteen rehearsals, each lasting at least three hours. This would make a total of only forty-five hours. This is a minimum, and it is possible only when rehearsals are efficiently conducted. Sixty to one hundred hours would be better, but the important thing is not to waste any of the rehearsal time.

During the first rehearsal, the entire play should be read and studied, and if possible, definite work on the first act should be started. Two or three rehearsals ought to be enough to work out the movement of the first act and to get well along in the work on details. By the fourth or fifth rehearsal, it is possible to work on both the first and second act, the first for further details, and the second for movement. Then the first act may be gone over only at every second rehearsal, and the third act started. Some scheme of this sort is essential. It is never wise to wait until the first act is perfected before going on to the others. They should all be moving along together, even though they are not all in the same phase. Toward the end of the rehearsals, it is often wise to work on the last act first, and then to review the earlier ones. Some definite scheme should be worked out for each rehearsal and announced to the actors. At the last two or three rehearsals—or more, if there is sufficient time—it ought to be possible to run through the entire play with the acts in their proper order. The important thing to keep in mind and to provide for in the scheme is that each individual act must go through all four phases. In the following chapters, each of these phases will be discussed in detail.

But first, it is necessary to point out that mere repetition is not true rehearsal. If the rehearsals are properly conducted, there should always be a sense of accomplishment. The movement of the play becomes more effective, or the readings grow clearer, or the characters are better understood and projected. Every actor improves at every rehearsal because he is being aided to see more clearly what he is trying to accomplish and the means he must use to accomplish it. Good rehearsals are guided learning, and not mere repetition.

CONFLICTING IDEAS OF DIRECTING

Just how the director will function in rehearsal will depend to a large extent on the theories he holds. There are at least two distinct points of view, each based on a different philosophy of theater practice:

1. *The Director as the Theater Artist.* The first point of view is that since the director is the artist in the theater, he should be an absolute dictator and shape the actors to carry out his ideas in every particular. Because this seems to be the underlying philosophy of Gordon Craig, who in his *On the Art of the Theater* preaches the necessity for complete unity in the theater, it is often called the Craig idea, or the Craig theory.[1] The basis of the theory seems to be that if the theater is to be an art, it must express the personality of *one* artist; for all art is nature or life seen through a personality. The director, therefore, must be this personality, who expresses himself by the aid of actors, scenery, lights, movement, sound, etc., in the same way that the sculptor expresses himself through stone, or the painter through paint on canvas. These theater media, therefore, should be as plastic and as unresistant as possible. The best actor is the one with the body and voice that is most completely at the service of the director. The less emotion the actor brings to his interpretation of his part the better. The director will supply the emotion. The actor need only be able to move and speak so as to express the director. Hence, the best actor would be the one with the fewest individual ideas or emotions to interfere with those of the director! Craig takes as his text a rather

[1] Gordon Craig, *On the Art of the Theater* (New York, Dodd, Mead, 1925).

ferocious statement attributed to the great actress Eleonora Duse: "To save the Theater, the Theater must be destroyed, the actors and actresses must all die of the plague. . . . They make art impossible."

2. *The Actor as the Theater Artist.* A second conception, quite different in theory, is that it is the actor who does the creating in the theater and that he is the theater artist. He is the personality through which the audience sees and feels the story, and the primary task of the director is to help the actor express himself by making him comfortable and by adding to his understanding of the story and the character. The director is merely a supervising artist who leaves the actor free to work out his individual conception. The fewer suggestions he is obliged to make the better. This may be called the laissez-faire idea.

THE PROPER IDEA OF DIRECTING

Both of these ideas have merit as theories, but it is doubtful if either extreme can exist in real life. A third, and probably more helpful theory, is that a director should be somewhere between these two extremes. He does not insist on imposing his own conception on the actors, nor does he hesitate to aid them when it seems desirable. This is certainly the most helpful idea when dramatics are conceived of as an educational process or when the actors are not being paid for their services, as in a Little Theater. In this situation, actors must be given a sense of accomplishment, they must enjoy the process; and this will occur only when they are encouraged to develop their own ideas about the characters they are playing. On the other hand, they must not be left to flounder, and the director should be experienced enough to know when his aid is needed. Even in professional situations, it is probable that some happy medium is likely to be most successful. The important thing, however, is that all decisions, regardless of whether they are made primarily by the director or primarily by the actors, be made in view of some basic point of view so that the play has unity.

The weakness of the Craig idea is that the superpuppet requires a superdirector. Directors who are not such are glad to have aid and suggestion from all possible sources. Even where the director has a very distinct impression of how the character ought to be played, the skilful actor may aid in clarifying this impression, or in changing it for the better, as rehearsals progress. The weakness of the laissez-faire idea is still more obvious, for the problem instantly arises as to what happens when two actors, both of whom are artists, conflict. Although producing a play is a democratic art, it *is* an art, and as such can exist only when there is a guiding and unifying force. This the director must probably be.

The true conception of rehearsals, then, is that they are *a process of continuous growth under the guidance of the director,* who both controls and is controlled by the actors and the situation. Only some such belief can justify dramatics as a worth-while cultural and educational process. And experience will teach that this concept will lead to better plays, more easily produced, in either a professional or non-professional situation. The director who makes it a point to encourage and use the enthusiasm of the actors is likely to be the most successful.

THE DIRECTOR'S STUDY OF THE SCRIPT

This concept of the director demands that he have all through the rehearsal process a complete and clear understanding of the script. He must know the events and the implications of the story, the relationships of the characters, the playing values of various scenes, and the probable reactions of the audience. The director should have this thorough understanding before the beginning of rehearsal. Therefore, he must prepare himself, by arduous and thoughtful study; and probably it is not too much to say that his success during rehearsals will depend to a considerable extent on the success of his work and study before the rehearsals start. A good director must do a large amount of homework. Not only does he study the script, but he informs himself on the subject and the period of the play. Thus, if the play deals with the American Revolution, as does Shaw's *Devil's Disciple*, he may read histories dealing with this period, biographies and autobiographies, letters and essays. If the director is doing *Julius Caesar*, or *Antony and Cleopatra*, or *Coriolanus*, he will want to brush up on his Roman history and will read biographies of the characters beginning—as Shakespeare did—with Plutarch. If the play deals with a department store, he will visit department stores with new vision in order to incorporate the right quality in his direction. If the play is mainly about China or India, he will study life in these countries. If it deals with banking, he learns all he can about the subject; if it treats the subject of illness and doctors, as do so many of Molière's plays, he studies medieval medicine. In every possible way, the good director tries to give himself a background of competency in the subject of the script. Then, and only then, is he ready to turn to a study of the script itself.

In his preliminary and pre-rehearsal study of the script, he will need to make many decisions, so that when he comes to help the actors in rehearsal, he can be clear and definite and quick. Some of these items might well be as follows:

1. A definite idea of the theme, color, line, and whole quality of the script which will give him a point of view from which to make a production. In other words, he will decide on an *interpretation* of the script. This is discussed in Chapter III.
2. The essential relationship of the characters, which will determine his choice of actors and what he is going to try to do with them after he has found them. This is discussed in Chapter IV.
3. The movement of the characters in the play, where they enter, leave, cross to and away from each other, where they stand or sit during various speeches, etc. This will be discussed in detail in Chapter VIII.

4. All the details of reading, gesture, business, etc., which create the character. These will be discussed in Chapters IX and XI.
5. The variations in tempo, emphasis, pauses, etc., which give finish to the performance. This will be discussed in Chapter X.

There are probably many other decisions that it will be helpful for him to make in advance, and these may well result in a series of little notes to himself, records of ideas he wants to remember. The wise director does not trust to his memory alone. He makes a record of this study in his script.

In order to do this, he will probably find it necessary to prepare his script by pasting it on pages of a large blank book so he will have plenty of margin on which to write. I find it useful, when using a script that has been printed, to cut a series of holes in a note-book, each hole slightly larger than the size of the type page. Then, if the pages of the script are pasted over the holes, it is possible to see both sides of each printed page (See Fig. 8). If the script is typed, perhaps the director inserts blank sheets between the pages of typing. The main point is that he needs plenty of room in which to record his preliminary study, and his notes need to be in such form that they will be instantly clear to him in rehearsal. Then actors need not stand around idly while the director cudgels his brain to invent a movement, nor while he tries to decide which is the most effective reading of a line. The wise director does much of this in advance, and he comes to each rehearsal with definite and clear ideas of just where he is and where he is trying to go.

THE IDEA OF SCENES

One of the most important theatrical ideas that might well concern the director during his preliminary study is that there is a fundamental difference between merely casual dialogue and playable dramatic dialogue. In ordinary conversation our ideas are not well organized; often we discuss a subject briefly, move on to something else, come back to the first subject,

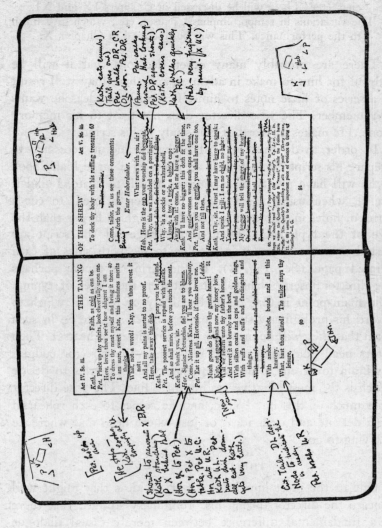

Fig. 8. Pages from a director's study of a script

interrupt it by a third idea, and so on. Casual conversation tends to be desultory and pointless. This can never be true of good dramatic dialogue. It can only *appear to be casual*. It falls into thought-groups; it develops an idea, and this idea leads on to another. For lack of a better word, let us call these thought-groups "scenes." Dramatic dialogue consists of a series of scenes, and it is the task of the director and his actors to indicate them. In a good play we have a sense of something happening, a sense of progress, because these scenes lead from one to another. We can follow clearly the thought processes and the emotional states of the characters. A good playwright groups his ideas, in the same way that a good essayist does, into progressive paragraphs. The material of a play is a series of actions or deeds, and the reactions of the characters to them. So we may find a series of scenes which begin with (1) the establishment of a fact, (2) the reaction of a character to this fact, (3) the reaction of another character to the emotion of the first character, etc. Each one of these ideas will be a little scene. Thus, the dialogue will have progression. This quality is perhaps one of the primary differences distinguishing a good playwright from a bad one, and it is certainly one of the primary differences between a good production and a bad one. Therefore, one of the primary tasks of the director, which he may well do in advance of rehearsal, is to break up the dialogue of the script into scenes.

The first obvious breaks will probably be at the entrance and exit of characters. In a well-written play, each character comes on for a purpose, which may be to bring in a fact, or to show his reaction, or to influence another character, etc. When he has accomplished this purpose, the author takes him off. Therefore, a scene almost always starts when a character enters, or when he leaves. These are sometimes called French scenes, because the classic French playwrights indicate new scenes at these points. Thus, in a play by Racine, an act will consist of twenty or thirty scenes, each one being a new combination of characters. These French scenes do not indicate a change of place, but merely a new combination of characters, hence presumably a new idea. The director will, therefore, help himself greatly by dividing the dialogue into French scenes, and by deciding the purpose of each one.

But each French scene, too, consists of a series of points, or smaller scenes. The French scenes are like the chapters in a book, and the scenes are like paragraphs. These scenes, like paragraphs, may vary greatly in length. Some will consist of only a line or two; some may be many lines in length. The division may not come at the end of a speech; often an actor, within a speech, ends one scene and starts another. There may even be scenes without lines; these would be complete bits of business or pantomime *making a distinct point*. Probably this breaking up of dialogue into scenes is often a matter of opinion. The actor may not always agree with the director as to where a scene begins or ends. The important thing is that there be a clear and interesting sequence.

The director will probably find it wise, then, to indicate the scenes in the dialogue during his preliminary study. I find it useful to do this with a short wavy line, as shown in the illustration (See Fig. 8). In the actual playing of the dialogue on the stage, the actors will indicate the scenes by pauses, by movements and gestures, by changing their readings in pitch and tempo, or by some definite sort of a transition. I shall discuss this further in the chapter on the final phase of the rehearsal, for it is a fundamental idea which need be ever-present in the process of preparing the play.

THE NECESSITY FOR FLEXIBILITY

It is probably both impossible and unwise for the director to feel that these decisions, made in advance, are unchangeable. This only makes for academic, dogmatic, and unpleasant directing. Many a fondly-thought-out bit of movement or business may prove in rehearsal to be impractical. Many a reading that the director has heard in his study cannot be done by the actor in the situation. Many a scene division turns out to have been in the wrong place. The wise director, therefore, will not cling to them foolishly and too long. He must adapt himself to the situation, and often he will find that what is worked out in rehearsal is really better than what he has thought out in his study. The point is that he comes to the rehearsals prepared, full of ideas and suggestions, and that in general he succeeds in staying far ahead of the actors in his understanding of the script—for he gives himself a head start! The purpose of his preliminary study is to arrive at this understanding; and to secure it he may study the script for days, or weeks, or months. Then, and only then, is he ready to put the script in rehearsal and to guide the process with ease and efficiency.

CHAPTER VI

The First Phase of Rehearsal: Preliminary Study

PURPOSE OF THE FIRST PHASE

The first phase of rehearsal is that during which the actors become familiar with the script. It should have a double purpose: (1) to arrive at an understanding of the plot or story of the script, the actual series of incidents that are to be the play and (2) to decide on a point of view, an interpretation, from which the story is to be played. The actors should master the plot, gain a clear conception of the characters they are to play, and study the interrelations of the characters on one another. But they should get beyond this merely factual understanding and by discussion and argument agree on a general method of approach. This would deal with the general nature of the production that they hope to make and might well be in terms of the most appropriate theme, graphic image, color and line, as discussed in Chapter III. Most of the decisions to be made during the process of rehearsal can be made intelligently only on the basis of some overall decision of what the main effect of the performance should be. Perhaps they decide that the most effective treatment will be as a gay, quick comedy with few or no overtones of seriousness; or perhaps effectiveness will demand the underscoring of a growing series of horrors. All decisions will depend on a common point of view, or else the play will lack fundamental unity. This is the kind of decision that the director and players in a symphony orchestra must make in approaching a piece of music—some of the players cannot play a rousing march, while others try to play a sentimental love song. A basic unity that will make all the rest of the process easier and more sound can be established during this first phase of rehearsal.

METHODS OF ACCOMPLISHING THE FIRST PHASE

Just how the first phase can be most economically accomplished is probably a matter of opinion, and directors differ greatly in their methods. There are, however, four common methods:

1. *The script read to the cast by an individual.* Sometimes the director, or the author, or some individual in the cast such as the star, reads the play to the actors. This reading, if it is well done, usually gives everyone a clear conception of the play, and of the various characters, which is the most desirable thing where time is short. It is supposed to have the disadvantage of imposing the reader's ideas, and sometimes even his mannerisms, on the actors. If important lines or scenes are read in a certain way, it is almost inevitable that many actors will imitate them. The better the reading, the more this is likely to be true.

2. *The story of the script told to the cast.* A variation of the above method is to have an individual, often the director, tell the story of the script and explain it. This has the advantage that the story can usually be made clear and interesting, and sometimes it is a way of selling the play to the actors. Young actors are often hazy or confused after the first reading of the script, and telling the story skilfully may overcome this difficulty. A director of my acquaintance invariably starts his rehearsals this way, but says that often actors come to him later, after they have read the script, and say reproachfully: "You lied to me! This part isn't half as good as you said." Probably a director who uses this method had better avoid overselling.

3. *The script read at home by actors.* Another common method is to have the actors study the play individually, before there is any general meeting. This process with young actors

may be wasteful since there is no way of correcting false impressions and of seeing that the actors agree on their general conceptions. They may bring ideas to rehearsals that have to be eradicated, and the most economical method demands that no false ideas be allowed to spring up. For this reason, some directors never allow actors to take their scripts or parts home during early rehearsals; they want all ideas to be developed in the group. Nevertheless, individual study before rehearsal enables the actor to use his ingenuity and imagination; and some actors work much better after a preliminary study of this sort.

4. *The script read by the actors in character*. The final method is a general reading as a group with each actor reading the lines of the character he is to play. The original impression thus comes from the actor. Such a reading frees the actors, but puts on the director the burden of seeing that the conceptions are correct. If a general reading is the method used, the actors should be seated in a group or around a table. They should not be allowed to walk through their parts until the play has been read once or twice without movement. Some directors like to have the play read in this way as many times as possible, perhaps five or six times, or even more. I know one director whose method is to make the cast read and reread the play until they grow nervous and restless, and then he says, "Oh, you want to act, do you? Well, come on!" By this time, the script is well understood and almost completely memorized. Other directors, after one complete reading, begin immediately on the second phase, and start to work out the movement.

Each director, and every group, must find out by experimentation which method is best. If a director has plenty of time and wishes to develop the initiative of the actors, probably he will find the last method best; if he reads well and has only a limited number of rehearsals, he may find the first or second a great time-saver. The third method is, perhaps, more adapted for groups of actors who are so inexperienced that they need the previous study to make the general reading have much value, or who are so experienced that they can do much for themselves.

In any case, no matter what method is used at the start, this will probably always need to be followed by the fourth, in which all the actors read their own rôles. This should lead to discussion of the values of the script, the point of view from which it is best played, and so on, for not until these things are determined are the actors ready to start on the movement.

SCRIPTS VS. SIDES

The actual method of starting rehearsals may depend to some extent on the physical condition in which the play is at this point. It may exist as a script, which means that it will be the entire thing as the author wrote it, with the descriptions of the sets, and the lines and business of all the actors. The ordinary printed copy of the play as it is obtained from a publisher is thus a script. But most professional companies work from sides, which consist of little typed booklets, each containing the business, cues, and lines of a single actor. There will be a set of sides for each character in the play. Usually these are half sheets of typing paper, with the directions in the second person. Thus, if you are playing The Thief in *Sham*, a one-act play by Frank G. Tompkins, your sides will probably start like this:

You are dressed in impeccable taste—evidently a man of culture. At curtain, you open the door and peer in cautiously. As soon as you see the room is unoccupied, you step inside, feel along the wall until you find the switch, which you light. From time to time, you bite appreciatively on a ham sandwich as you look about, apparently viewing the room for the first time. Nothing pleases you until a vase over the mantel catches your eyes. You pick it up, look at the bottom, and put it down hard. Then you speak, muttering, "Imitation."

As the illustration (Fig. 9) shows, it is customary to put in as a cue only the last four words of the preceding line. Thus, if an actor finds less than four words, he expects a short cue. His sides do not tell him who speaks the cue. He just waits for these four words; and when he hears them, he speaks his line. The number of pages in his sides give a rough idea of the length of the part, and actors commonly say they have five sides, or thirty sides, or sixty-two sides. The first will have a

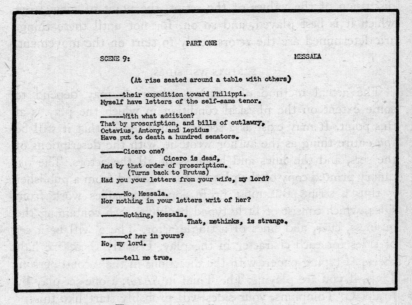

FIG. 9. A "SIDE" FOR MESSALA

short part (although parts of one side, or less, are not uncommon); and the latter will have a long part, probably containing several hundred speeches. The advantages claimed for sides is that they are easier for actors to handle in rehearsal, especially during the earlier ones when they are still reading the unmemorized lines. Moreover, after the actor has written in the movement and business given by the director, he has a complete record of what he must memorize. In a professional company, the leading players may have both scripts and sides,

SCENE 9

SCENE: Brutus' tent. Night. A table at
                         the center, around which are seated
                         BRUTUS, CASSIUS, MESSALA, TITINIUS,
                         LUCILIUS, and several other
                         OFFICERS.

                         The music fades, as BRUTUS speaks.

                Brutus
Countrymen, I have here received letters,
That young Octavius and Mark Antony
Come down upon us with a mighty power,
Bending their expedition toward Philippi.

                Messala
Myself have letters of the self-same tenor.

                Brutus
With what addition?

                Messala
That by proscription, and bills of outlawry,
Octavius, Antony, and Lepidus
Have put to death a hundred senators.

                Brutus
Therein our letters do not well agree;
Mine speak of seventy senators that died
By their proscriptions, Cicero being one.

                Cassius
Cicero one?

                Messala
                Cicero is dead,
And by that order of proscription.
                (He turns back to Brutus)
Had you your letters from your wife, my lord?

                Brutus
No, Messala.

                Messala
Nor nothing in your letters writ of her?

                Brutus
Nothing, Messala.

                Messala
                That, methinks, is strange.

FIG. 10. A PAGE OF MANUSCRIPT—FROM WHICH THE "SIDE" IN
FIG. 9 WAS MADE

but they are likely to do their studying from the sides. The disadvantage is that an actor with sides only can never read the complete story, and he has to depend on the rehearsals to develop his ideas. Some directors think this is an advantage.

In any case, it is probably a worthwhile experiment to see which method best fits any particular group and situation. If a group has worked from scripts, it is interesting to make a set of sides, and to see if they do not speed up the rehearsal process. Any clever typist can quickly learn to make sides. Some actors make their own, and this has the advantage of making memorization easier for them. Making sides is often cheaper and easier if but few copies of the script are available, which may be the case with a new play. And even when the script is in printed form, so that there are plenty of copies to go around, it may be advantageous for actors to make individual sides, for the ease that there is in working with them. If the actors work from scripts, it is important during this first phase of rehearsal for them to prepare their script for study by underlining their cues and checking their speeches.

DUTIES OF THE STAGE-MANAGER

One of the most useful methods of speeding work during this phase of rehearsal—and all phases—is to have a competent stage-manager. Even in a group of children there is usually an older child who will make an excellent one. His duties are to be in complete charge of the actors. He keeps discipline in the company, gives orders, checks up on absences, and in short, relieves the director of as much routine as possible. He should have the name, address, and telephone number of every actor. He keeps the actor informed about rehearsals—what is going to be done and who should be there. The director gives the stage-manager the orders, and he passes them on to the rest of the company. An experienced professional director does not come into the rehearsal and shout "All on stage for Act II!"

He says quietly to the stage-manager, "Call Act II," and it is the stage-manager's task to get the company ready for the rehearsal. If the time comes to break for lunch, the director gives the directions to the stage-manager, who tells the actors how long they have and when they must be back—and sees that they are back! The theory is that the director should be relieved of all this routine so that he can give his best efforts to artistic matters. He should be free to study the play, and an experienced director employs a competent stage-manager.

During this first phase of rehearsal, the stage-manager's task is to keep the reading going. He, of course, must have a complete script, in which he writes all the directions. Thus he is beginning his *prompt script*, which ultimately will be a complete record of the production. It will contain all the cuts and line changes, the directions for movement and business and reading. Usually the printed script of a play that has been performed on Broadway, and is later published, is basically the prompt script made by the stage-manager during the rehearsal period. If the actors are working from sides, as they always are on Broadway, the stage-manager, in these early rehearsals, reads the directions and describes the business, since otherwise the actors would not be able to understand the story. At the same time, he must see that the sides are correct. During all phases of the rehearsal, the stage-manager is a busy man!

THE DISCUSSION OF THE SCRIPT

Probably the wise director does not, during this first phase of rehearsal, confine his activities to a mere reading of the script. He takes the time, and finds it well spent, to lead a discussion of the problems involved in the production. The first one, as already indicated, will be the point of view from which the production may best be made—the theme or graphic image that he wants to bring out, the color, the line, the atmosphere, etc. There are, however, other lines of discussion that are sometimes profitable. One of these is the question of the dramatic hero.

In every play there is a character, or a group of characters, with whom the interest of the audience is mainly concerned. The interest of the audience in the play is likely to arise out of their concern for this character. His fate is involved in the story of the play. The audience feels and understands his emotions and his reactions. In a way, they see the story through his eyes. This character (or characters) is called the dramatic hero. "He" may be a woman, or a group of women. Conceivably he may be the embodiment of an idea in a large group of characters. Such would be the case in Hauptmann's famous play *The Weavers,* in which an entire group of exploited workers, none of them of great individual prominence, are the dramatic hero. He does not need to be the romantic hero, who is the chief personage in a love story, and he will be so only in those plays in which the love story is of primary interest and importance. The Greek name for this character was *protagonist,* which means the "first actor." If the first actor, or dramatic hero, cannot be made interesting to the audience, the play is liable to remain very dull. The audience need not sympathize with the desire of this chief actor; nobody can want Macbeth, for instance, to succeed in his crimes, or to "get away with it." But if Macbeth is not made an exciting and human figure, the play of which he is the dramatic hero will not come to life. This point is considered further on pages 151-158, but it may well be discussed by the actors during this early phase of the rehearsal, for it should lead to a more complete understanding of the play. The actors may well discuss such questions as to how the author makes the dramatic hero interesting, what incidents are especially important, how the other characters contribute to our understanding of him, and so on.

Another question that leads to understanding concerns the climax of the play. The *climax* is the turning point, or the point of highest complication in the plot—which we must remember is a series of incidents. At this point, we want to be sure that the incidents are clear, and they are likely to be clearer if we see what they lead to. The climax is usually the turning point in the fate of the dramatic hero. After this point his success is obvious, or his failure sure. If he succeeds, the play is a comedy; if he fails, it will be a tragedy. A good point to discuss, then, is the climax, so that each actor can be working for the same end—to make the climax as clear and as exciting as possible.

It is probably useful, too, at this point sometimes to discuss the shape of the play. (See illustration, Fig. 11.) According

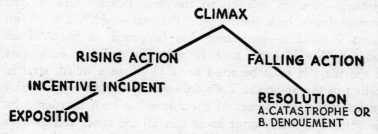

FIG. 11. SHAPE OF A PLAY

to this idea, the play will have definite parts: exposition, incentive incident, rising action, climax, falling action, and resolution. The exposition is the explanation necessary for the audience to understand the story. It describes the lives of the characters and the situation in which they are involved when the curtain rises. In old plays, these important facts were often gleaned by the audience from the conversation of a butler and a maid. In modern plays, we often gather them from a telephone call, in which a character explains them to another—who often already knows them! In any case, we can rarely understand a play without some preparation, and it is valuable to discuss this exposition with the actors. The more skilful the playwright, the less blatant and offensive is his exposition likely to be.

This exposition is usually followed by an incentive incident, which should be an actual occurrence that happens in front of us. Here is where the play actually starts, and we should be certain that we make it start. Sometimes a play begins with some incident which we may not altogether understand, and the exposition follows. This is called delayed exposition. For example, in a one-act play by Susan Glaspell, called *Trifles*, at the rise of the curtain we see three men and two women entering a disordered kitchen. The men hurry to the stove to warm themselves, but the women stand fearfully by the door. Then one of the men at the stove—he turns out to be the county attorney—says: "Come up to the fire, ladies." One of the women draws back and says: "I'm not—cold." This is an incentive incident—something has happened in front of an audience. But in order to have value, in order to be a start of the play, it must be acted so as to create a weird, strange feeling in the audience. Then follows the exposition, in which we learn that the owner of the house has been murdered by his wife. The actors must know this all the time, and give us a feeling of strangeness, otherwise they will not have started the play.

This incentive incident will be followed by a series of incidents which form the rising action. We shall expect that during these incidents the life of the dramatic hero will grow more and more complex until finally it reaches a climax. This climax will lead to a series of incidents called the falling action and will end in a resolution. This resolution may be a *catastrophe*, in which the hero usually comes to madness and death, or at any rate to a complete defeat; or it may come to a *dénoument*, which will be victory and success. In the first case we shall have a tragedy, and in the second, a comedy. This idea that a play has parts is often scoffed at by modern critics, but I find it exceedingly useful. Probably it is not wise to be academic about it, or to discuss it in too much detail with younger actors. But some literary discussion of the play which leads to an understanding of what it is all about, and how it is put together, will save hours of explanation in later phases of the rehearsal. And even young actors can profitably discuss such questions as: "What is the exposition? What is the incentive incident? Where is the climax? What is the resolution?" Thus they gain an understanding of the story that they are going to act.

This discussion may usually be done briefly. The wise director will not let it grow long and dull. It may even not always lead immediately to definite conclusions, for further work on the script in subsequent rehearsals will clarify ideas. The purpose of the discussion, and of first readings, is to get the actors started on a sound line of thought. The director should probably interrupt the reading as little as possible, perhaps only to correct gross errors or wrong pronunciations. He will not hope to get effective readings of the lines. That is the function of a later phase of rehearsal. He is trying to develop in the actors an accurate understanding of the story, and a point of view. This alone should be the purpose of the first phase; and having accomplished this, as briefly and as excitingly as possible, the director is ready to move on to the second phase.

CHAPTER VII

The Second Phase of Rehearsal: Movement

PURPOSE OF THE SECOND PHASE

The purpose of the second phase in rehearsal is to block out the movement of the play, to determine where actors are to come in and go out, and to decide their positions while they are on the stage. Incidentally, the general conceptions of the play, already agreed upon during the first rehearsals, will tend to be clarified during this process. But the primary purpose, on which every one should be concentrating, is the idea of movement. For a short play, one rehearsal, or even a part of one rehearsal, may be sufficient. For a longer play, this process must be gone through for each act, perhaps several times. These rehearsals should not be stopped for long discussions of the characters and their relationships; there should be no special attempt to read the lines with proper emphasis, although actors should read as well as possible and gross errors should probably be corrected. The fewer times the actors are interrupted for anything but movement the better, for the secret of good rehearsals is to concentrate on one problem at a time.

SOME DEFINITIONS

There are certain terms commonly used in the theater that we must understand at this point. The first is *movement*, which is *change of place or position*. It means coming in at a door, crossing to a chair, going to a window. It is actual change of position on the floor of the stage. When an actor waves his hand, that is not movement, but *gesture*. Gesture is the assumption of a body position to indicate an emotion or an idea. Another word often confused with movement is *business*. Business, in the theater, is characteristic activity, like limping, or smoking, or shelling peas, or paring potatoes, or knitting. When an actor limps, that is not movement. If he crosses to a window or a fireplace and limps while doing so, or smokes, or fans himself, that is a combination of movement and business. If he sits on a sofa and opens a letter, that is business only. There is a third word, often confused with movement, and the word is *action*. Technically action is a literary word, which should be applied only to the script. Action is the speed at which incidents are unfolded by the author. If the action of a play is fast, this means that the author has made incidents follow one another in quick succession; if it is slow, there is little incident. Theoretically, fast action would demand fast movement, but conceivably the actors might all be running around vigorously, which would be fast movement, and the play might still be dull and uninteresting because the action is slow. In this second phase of rehearsal, we are concerned primarily with *movement*. We want to create, as rapidly as possible, a pattern of movement, a pantomimic skeleton, on which we can hang the other elements of acting. Later we shall be concerned with gesture and business and many other matters.

Some directors make a differentiation between what they call *direct movement* and *indirect movement*, and perhaps this is a helpful distinction. Direct movement is the basic, essential movement that is necessary if the play is to happen. If the script demands it, an actor must be near enough to the heroine at a certain line so that he can embrace her; or he must be in such a position that the villain can strike him. As an actor, he has no choice about this matter. The director is concerned at first primarily with this basic, direct movement. However, within this basic pattern of movement, the actor has many possibilities. If the director tells him to cross to a chair, he may do it in many ways. He may make a curve above it and come down to it, or a curve below it and go up to it; or he may start the movement rapidly and slow down as he approaches it, or start slowly and continue at increasing tempo. The value of this concept is that actors need not be made to feel that they must, even in this phase of rehearsal, follow woodenly the directions given to them. Their task is to justify and embroider the basic pattern given by the director. This is the teacher's best answer to the school principal who says, "But Miss Jones, if you give all these directions, how can the children develop their originality!" Within the basic pattern of essential movement, there is room for all the variation that can be contributed by the most skilful and imaginative actor.

METHOD OF CONDUCTING BLOCKING-OUT REHEARSALS

In working out the movement of a play, the director is like an artist designing a picture. It is to be assumed that he has previously created a basic pattern of movement and recorded it in his script. This is part of his preliminary study, discussed in Chapter VI. In order to work out the movement, he must know the sets that are to be used, the position of the openings in the set, the arrangement of the furniture, the costumes that are to be worn, and all the other things that go to make up the picture. Scene-sketches, models, and costume plates (see Chapters XX and XXIII) will be of greatest value. Some directors work out the movement of the actors by using chessmen, or pins, as puppets to aid them in visualizing the movement. In any case, now his problem is to explain this basic movement to the actors as quickly and as accurately as possible. Usually he sits near the front edge of the stage, with the stage manager beside him, or perhaps in the front row of the auditorium. As he describes the movement, the actors should walk it, and if he is clear and accurate in his directions and the actors are properly trained, it should not be a long process.

One thing that will speed the process, is to have the set in lay-out on the floor. In the professional theater this is another job of the stage-manager. He is supposed to have secured from the designer the floor-plans (see Chapter XX) for the sets, and he reproduces these on the floor of the stage. Sometimes he makes the outlines of the walls on the floor with chalk, leaving clearly marked openings for doors and windows. Sometimes he lines up old furniture, or uses sticks or stage-braces, to indicate the outline of the set. With dilapidated tables and old chairs (every theater is well supplied with these), he indicates the furniture. Thus, three chairs side by side represent a sofa, or a bed, or a bench. An upturned box may be a fireplace, or a radio cabinet, or a sundial or fountain, or a kitchen sink. There should be something to indicate each item of furniture, and they should be put in their proper places as shown on the designer's floor-plan. Only by having the proper spaces can the rehearsal for movement have greatest value. Thus, it is impossible to rehearse for movement in a room smaller in size than the set.

With the set correctly indicated, the director can begin to give directions and the actors to move through the play. The directions should be given clearly and slowly enough so that the actors may write them down. Every actor should have a pencil and be able to write! He should write down in his script or sides the movement as it applies to himself.

At the same time, the stage-manager takes down *all* the movement and thus continues making his *prompt script*. This process takes a little more time at this point, but saves much time later. Now the actor has in his part not only the lines that the author has given him to say, but the moves that the director has given him to make. A good actor studies both. The movement may have to be changed as the rehearsals progress, but there need never be any question of what has been decided, for it has been recorded by each individual actor and by the stage-manager. The rehearsal need never, therefore, turn into a debate about what was done yesterday! This process of recording movement will be both easier and quicker if some system of notation is used by the entire company, and such a system has been developed by generations of actors.

SYSTEM OF NOTATION OF MOVEMENT

In the first place, the stage is commonly divided into certain areas, as shown in Fig. 12. The directions left and right are always from the point of view of an actor facing the audience. The part nearest the front of the stage is called down-

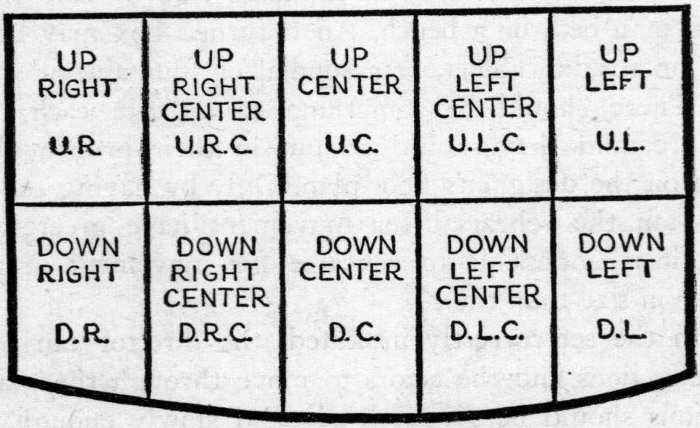

UP RIGHT U.R.	UP RIGHT CENTER U.R.C.	UP CENTER U.C.	UP LEFT CENTER U.L.C.	UP LEFT U.L.
DOWN RIGHT D.R.	DOWN RIGHT CENTER D.R.C.	DOWN CENTER D.C.	DOWN LEFT CENTER D.L.C.	DOWN LEFT D.L.

FIG. 12. PARTS OF A STAGE

stage, and the part above the center upstage—this grows out of the fact that old stages were usually higher in the back than the front, or slanted downstage, often as much as eight or ten inches; therefore when an actor went upstage he literally went up. By using this language, the director is able to give the actors specific moves. He does not need to point, or to tell the actor to come in there and stand here; he is able to say, "Enter at the door up left, and cross down to right center," or "Sit at the left end of the sofa," or "Look out the window down right."

Now the trained actor is able to write down these directions very briefly and in the same terms. He uses D for *down*, and

U for *up*, C for *center*, and so on. Probably he uses X for *cross*. Instead of writing "Enter at the door up left, and cross down to right center," all he need write is "Ent. UL, X DRC." The stage-manager is making the same brief and clear notation— and it is to be hoped that this is the note that the director has in his script as a result of his preliminary study. Thus, many directions can be given quickly and as quickly recorded.

Sometimes, perhaps, the stage-manager and the actor—as well as the director—will find it desirable to indicate the movements by little diagrams. I find that my preliminary studies of scripts get full of little thumb-nail sketches, thus:

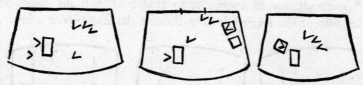

Fig. 13. Diagrammatic sketches of positions of actors

The set and furniture are shown by outlines with a few rough lines, and the actors are indicated by the little arrow-heads, or carets. The point of the caret shows the direction in which the actor is facing. If it is superimposed on a square or an oblong, this shows that the actor is sitting on a chair or sofa. Thus it is possible, with great speed, to indicate the positions of many actors at any given moment in the play. It is worth while taking the time to teach both the actors and stage-manager some simple system of notation of this sort. The important problem, however, still remains, and that is, how can the director create movement that will be effective in the theater.

PRINCIPLES OF GRAPHIC COMPOSITION

The movement in a play is likely to be good to the degree that it embodies the principles of good graphic composition. At this point in rehearsal, the director is like an artist designing a picture, and he must keep in mind the general principles of picture composition. The proscenium arch of his stage is the frame or the edge of his canvas, and within this space he is going to compose with actors, scenery, light, and the other graphic elements of the theater. He is going to try to make a *series of pictures, each in itself aesthetically pleasing and satisfying, and flowing naturally from one into another.* Thus, he is faced with a difficult task. Among the most useful ideas of graphic composition are (1) balance, (2) emphasis, and (3) variety.

1. *Balance.* Balance demands that we distribute the actors with some degree of evenness, so that they will not mass on either side of the stage.[1] It is as though the stage were a lever,

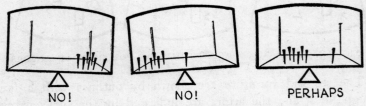

NO!　　　　　NO!　　　　　PERHAPS

FIG. 14. BALANCE IN STAGE COMPOSITION

with a fulcrum in the center. If we have one actor, he will naturally play near the center, and not be huddled over against one wall. Two actors will not, in general, both play, for any long period, on one half of the stage. If we have a group of half a dozen actors who are facing one, we shall try to distribute them (see Fig. 14) so that the stage remains in equilibrium. Of course, this may all be changed by some element in the stage set; two actors might play mainly down right if balanced

[1] Many of the illustrations in this book show clearly the points discussed in this and the following paragraphs. Note especially the *balance* in Plates I, IV B, V, VI A, VIII A, IX A & B, XII A & B, and XIII B; the clear *emphasis* on a single central figure in Plates IV B, VI A, VIII A, and IX B; and the *variety*, in the spacing and positions, in Plates V A & B, VI A, IX B, XII A & B, and XIII B.

by some large scenic structure down left, say a high crag, or a house, or a towering tree. The point to remember is that the scenery and actors are going to make a picture, and this picture will not be pleasing if all the weight is at one side of the stage. One of the old theater devices that may be helpful is the idea of fundamental positions. The fundamental position of one actor is the center of the stage; the position for two is facing each other, six feet apart, in the center; three actors make a triangle, with one in the center, and the others a little below him at each side; etc. The idea is that, in general, actors will be grouped in a semi-circle, facing front, as shown in the illustration (Fig. 15). This does not mean, of course, that

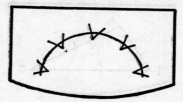

FIG. 15. FUNDAMENTAL POSITIONS

they will stand thus in a regular group like a glee club. Some will be sitting, they will face in various directions, etc. It only means that unless there is some good reason to the contrary, it is well to get actors accustomed to playing in the central area of the stage. A novice thinks he has made an entrance when he sneaks through a door; but when a director tells an old-time actor to enter, he comes to the center. This habit is probably a good one to inculcate in young actors, since it makes it much simpler to keep the stage in proper balance.

2. *Emphasis*. Emphasis is, perhaps, only another way of stating the principle that a well-grouped picture should have a center of interest, and one center only. The director must decide what the important action is, and emphasize that by his grouping. This will help the audience watch the important thing. In general, the upstage center will be the strongest

position. The old theater idea of a triangle is a helpful device.[2] If A is a character who is the center of interest, he should, as a rule, be made the apex of a triangle which has its base parallel to the front of the stage. B and C are other characters, less important for the moment. If B becomes the central figure, he and A may change places, and so on. Of course, there must be nothing mechanical about the movement; it must be made to seem as free and reasonable as possible. Perhaps there is a fireplace on the right wall in back of B, and at the given moment A moves to it to throw away his smoked cigar, or to place or remove something from the mantel, etc. In this case, B will naturally move to make place for him, and ultimately take

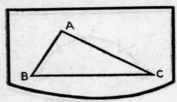

FIG. 16. TRIANGLE TO SHOW CENTER OF INTEREST

his position up center. One of the most interesting parts of the problem of directing is the inventing of natural movements to get the actors in the proper places to make satisfying pictures.

3. *Variety*. A third principle is that of *variety*. This is summed up by the old theater principle: "Avoid straight lines, and avoid even spaces." Experienced actors naturally avoid these pitfalls by slight adjustments of their positions. Thus in the illustrations (Fig. 17) the one at the left will result in a bad composition, even though it has a center of interest, in C. The grouping shown at the right is better. C is still the center of interest, but B has moved down towards A, D and E have

[2] Plate XII B is an example of a triangle of three actors, and Plate VI A shows a more complicated picture, which is still basically a triangle, even though it consists of a dozen actors arranged on several stage levels.

PLATE I. *Lorenzaccio*, by Alfred de Musset

A Hall in a Palace. A rich and elaborate effect created by one painted drop, hanging against black velour draperies, and a beautiful carved table and chair. (See p. 289.)

PLATE II (at left). A Baroque setting by Guiseppe Bibbiena, 1740

An interior for a dramatic festival at the wedding of Prince Elector of the Court of Bavaria, consisting of a drop, cut wings, and cut borders, all painted in elaborate perspective. (See pp. 264-265.) From the Cooper Union Museum Library.

PLATE III A (above). *Androcles and the Lion*, by G. Bernard Shaw

A scene in a forest. A famous non-realistic exterior by Covarrubias. (See p. 284.)

PLATE III B (below). *Iphigenia in Tauris*, by Euripides

Before a barbaric temple. A plaster sky-wall. Both sides are masked with high plastic rocks. The details on the front of the temple are also plastic. (See pp. 237-238.)

Columbia University: Columbia Theater Associates   *Gabrielse*

PLATE IV A (above). *Twist the Lion's Tail*, by Stanley Bortner

A sitting room in a mansion on the Eastern shore of Maryland, 1821. An interior showi
painted wall-paper and paneling. All the moulding, including that on the picture frame,
painted: only the fireplace is plastic. Designed by Margaret Anderson. (See p. 255 and p. 258

PLATE IV B (below). *The Inspector General*, by Nicholai Gogol

An interior created with black draperies, opened to show a sky drop. The design is made wi
white ropes, and the white spots are painted on a special proscenium frame.

Wesleyan University   *Booth*

drawn closer together, and F has fallen back slightly. Thus, they have broken up the objectionable features of the original composition. Straight lines and even spaces are especially to be avoided when the lines are either at right angles or parallel to the front edge of the stage—unless, of course, they are demanded by the situation, as might be the case with a file of soldiers, or a chain gang, or a quartet about to break into song.

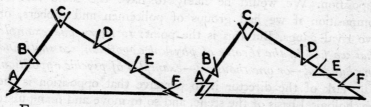

FIG. 17. TRIANGLE USED INCORRECTLY AND CORRECTLY

Another demand of variety is that pictures be not repeated— or at least, not too often. Even though there is a well-lighted sofa downstage at one side of the set, each set of characters indulging in a conversation must not sit side by side on this sofa. This is bad direction. Good direction requires that the director be able constantly to vary the composition.

PRINCIPLES OF SYMBOLIC MOVEMENT

But the task of the director is not over, even though he has created a series of pleasing and satisfying pictures. His problem now—and this is the fundamental problem of movement in the theater—is to give these pictures *dramatic meaning*. Sometimes this is called *symbolic movement*. The director is confronted with the problem of *translating the psychological, intellectual, or emotional idea of a scene into physical situations*. A play is a physical translation, the embodiment of an idea. Good movement on the stage must be more than pleasing; *it must have meaning*. Movement must help act the play by interpreting the fundamental ideas of the scenes. The director will find that the ideas embodied in dramatic scenes are fundamentally few in number.

1. *Opposition.* One of the most common dramatic ideas is opposition, which in the theater takes many forms. If we have two groups of soldiers, fighting with each other, we would naturally have one group at one side of the stage, and the other group facing them. This would be an embodiment of opposition. We would be likely to have the same sort of composition if we had groups of policemen and robbers, or two rival gangs. But this is the point: *to every one example that we find in the theater of physical opposition, we shall find one hundred—or one thousand—examples of psychic opposition.* The task of the director is to perceive that opposition is the psychological basis of the scene, and so to move and manipulate the characters that they embody this idea. Perhaps he has a group of men talking in a club, or a family discussion. If he sees that opposition is the basis of the scene, he divides and arranges his characters so as to express this idea. Then the movement will be symbolic, and the idea of the scene will be much clearer and more interesting. He will be translating a psychic idea into physical terms—and this is what the theater must do.

2. *Intervention.* Another very common theater idea is intervention. If the Duke, in *Romeo and Juliet,* comes upon the warring Capulets and Montagues and moves between them, that will be an obvious case of intervention. The theater is filled with characters who intervene between groups in conflict. A character intervenes when he pushes his way between two fighting men, or runs between a character and the window out of which he is about to jump. *To every example of obvious physical intervention, we shall find a hundred—or a thousand—examples of psychic intervention.* If a character walks into a club room where two groups of men are having a discussion, he does not intervene if he stands at one side of the stage. Some way must be found to get him between the groups. Two

ladies sit on a sofa having a most ladylike discussion, which nevertheless is a conflict; there must be some natural way to bring a third character between them if he is to intervene. In most scenes in the theater, the intervention will not be physical, but the scene will gain effectiveness from the movement to the degree to which we are able to make the translation into physical terms.

3. *Change of mind.* The theater is filled with examples of characters who change their minds. If two gangs of boys are arguing with each other and they have not yet come to blows, perhaps a member of one gang will change his mind and move over to the other, thus lining up against his former friends. This is a natural physical move, showing change of mind. This occurs constantly in intellectual and emotional situations. A man joins his wife against their children, or a mother sides with one child and against another. No physical violence is involved in these cases. Nevertheless, the movement will be symbolic, it will have meaning, only if the character makes an appropriate change in position which acts out the idea, and gives the scene meaning that it would not have otherwise.

4. *Enmeshing.* A fourth common idea is enmeshing or trapping. If some policemen come upon a robber busily engaged in opening a safe, they surround him. Two take up a position behind him, two go to his right, and the other three to his left. They enmesh him. The theater is full of psychic enmeshing, as when ladies gradually surround a tormented victim at a tea-party.

5. *Pounding.* Pounding involves the idea of hammer and anvil, as when in a physical struggle one character runs to another and delivers a blow and then dances back out of reach. Most argument is in the nature of pounding. Perhaps the victim sits in a chair, and an actor comes towards him to deliver an uncomplimentary opinion, draws back, and then comes forward again with a more scathing flow of words. If the victim rebels, he may rise and approach the other actor, and

thus become in his turn the pounder. The point is that an argument in the theater must not be a mere static scene, without movement; and the movement will have sense and meaning to the degree to which it can be made symbolic.

Perhaps there are other common dramatic ideas that might well be listed, but these five—with their opposites and combinations—suffice to solve almost all situations. If two or more ideas are evident in a scene, as is often the case, the director must decide which is the most important at the moment. And one idea may be quickly followed by another. For example, in the trial scene in *The Merchant of Venice,* we might embody the opposition with which the scene opens by having Shylock and his friends occupy one side of the stage, and the opposing force of Antonio, Bassanio, and their followers occupy the other. Intervention occurs almost immediately when Portia appears to help the Duke resolve the conflict. She intervenes by coming between the two groups and turning from one to another as the argument between them progresses. When she gives the decision, she shows her change of mind by approaching and standing with Antonio. And the idea of enmeshing may follow if, after the decree against Shylock is pronounced, Gratiano, Bassanio, and others of their group gradually surround him and separate him from his friends who fall away from him. Thus symbolic movement helps to show what is happening psychologically. In this way, by *translating the intellectual and emotional idea into physical terms,* the director is able to decide what pattern of movement is best. He is able to do things for a reason and to give meaning to the movement.

Movement that is real and lifelike will tend to be symbolic, whether or not the director and the actors are conscious of that term. When one actor separates two who are struggling by forcing himself between them, that is symbolic movement. When an actor shows that he has changed his mind by leaving one group and walking over and joining another, that also is symbolic. But many a less obvious situation and many a "talky" scene without much obvious movement may be quickly and easily solved if the director has this idea of symbolic movement consciously in mind.

THE RESULT OF REHEARSALS FOR MOVEMENT

These rehearsals should result in a definite pattern of movement, making a series of interesting, and varied, and well-composed pictures, each of which has meaning in terms of the scene. It has been said that the basis of every good play is an interesting pantomime. This pantomimic pattern should be the main concern of the director and the actors in this second phase of rehearsal. Often the pattern will have to be modified in later rehearsals because further study may show that it does not quite work. Often, too, it may need further elaboration. But the basic pattern—the direct movement—must be worked out and memorized by all the actors. Then, and only then, are they ready to start on the third phase.

CHAPTER VIII

The Third Phase of Rehearsal: Details

PURPOSE OF THE THIRD PHASE

The third phase is by far the most important, and it will usually take much more time than all the other phases together. Its purpose is the perfection of details, or, to use a more technical term, the building up of characterization. In other words, this is the point at which acting seriously enters the process. Up to now, the actors have concentrated on trying to understand the story and to memorize the movements. Now, in the pattern of movement that has been worked out, they should be concerned with building up their ability to play the parts. This is the process that actors call studying a rôle. It does not mean merely memorizing it—as young actors sometimes seem to think. *Studying a rôle* means developing a complete understanding of the character and making hundreds —perhaps thousands—of decisions, concerning how to walk, how to sit down, how to use face and hand, and how to read each line. It involves reacting to each other and bringing the characters to life. I shall discuss this process (from the point of view of the actor) in more detail in Chapters X, XI and XII. Here we are concerned with the problems of the director during this process.

Just how the director will work probably depends to some extent on his idea of directing, which is discussed on pages 71-73. Progress will be slow and halting, however, unless he has a definite plan. I find it desirable to have consciously in mind five kinds of details: (1) memorization, (2) vocalization, (3) reading, (4) gesture, and (5) business. These will be discussed, one by one, in the following pages. In the actual process of rehearsal, however, they will usually be intermingled. The director turns from the attempt to make one actor vocalize better, to a specific reading of a certain line; or while he works to improve the gestures of one actor, he tries to invent a bit of business for another.

METHOD DURING THE THIRD PHASE

The director's method of conducting the rehearsals during this third phase, whatever his theory, will probably involve constant interruption. This is the phase in which the play must be pulled apart. This bit of business must be tried over and over, and that line read again and again. Every individual detail must be tested. It may take hours to get through a single scene. The important thing is to arrive at definite decisions as to ways of doing things, and to drill them into the actors by repetition. The director will probably find it advantageous, too, to give the actors time to write down the decisions—and to insist, if necessary that they do so. The actors should under-line the words they are going to "plug," indicate pauses, jot down the business, etc., as described in Chapter X. During this phase of the rehearsals, the script or sides of the individual actor should become a complete record of the manner in which he hopes to play the rôle. This record, then, can become the subject of his study.

It is at this phase of the rehearsal that there is the greatest difference between directing professional actors and amateurs —or perhaps, good actors and bad ones. The director of professionals assumes that he will not have to concern himself very much with the *method* of acting. If he tells an actress to cry, or to laugh, he expects that she will be able to do so. But with novices, it may be necessary to teach crying and laughing. The director, then, may not only have to direct the play; he is likely, at the same time, to find himself obliged to teach acting.

This is one of the reasons why, in dealing with inexperienced actors, the third phase of the process assumes such importance.

DETAILS TO BE CONSIDERED

The director can best teach acting by helping the actors perfect the details of their characterizations.

1. *Memorization.* The first detail with which he will probably find it wise to concern himself will be the perfection of memorization. During the preliminary readings and the rehearsals for blocking out the movement, actors usually read the lines from their books, thus becoming more and more familiar with them. Then it is wise, at a definite place in the rehearsals, say after the fifth or sixth, when the lines are almost memorized by repetition, to announce that thereafter no more books are to be used. If the actors are not line perfect, let them be prompted by the stage-manager—this is another one of his many jobs—no matter how much prompting is needed. However, if every member of the cast needs constant prompting, perhaps the director has taken this step too early, and it may be wise to resume the use of books for one more rehearsal.

But it is to be supposed, at this point, that the actors are going to do some outside work for memory. Up to now, specific home work on memorization will be uneconomical, because the best sort of memory that an actor can have is a total one, of lines, moves, situations, business, etc. Therefore, most experienced directors do not wish actors to memorize lines before the movement has been blocked out. Another helpful idea that may be suggested to the actors is that it is better to learn long sections of their parts by repetition, and not to study for mere verbal memory, word by word. A better kind of memory is usually established by reading speeches over and over. Probably, too, it is wise at this point to insist on accurate memory, the speech as it is written. Some young actors—and some not so young—pride themselves on being able to give what they call the gist of the speech, but not the actual words of the author. This kind of memory is not enough! The actor's obligation to the author, the director, and the other actors, demands that memorization be accurate. The actor who prides himself on his bad memory can become a great nuisance if the director allows him to do so. I find it wise, once in a while, to excuse an actor—reluctantly, of course—who is "just unable to learn the lines." His memory usually improves miraculously. Memory is one of the tools that the actor must develop, and most good ones memorize easily, quickly, and accurately. Line rehearsals are sometimes a great help—in the old theater these were called prompter's rehearsals. During these the stage-manager works with the actors for their lines, and there is no attempt to do anything else. If actors meet in small groups and study their lines together, repeating them aloud and rapidly time after time in the proper order, with thought for little but the correctness of their readings, a group memory is established, which usually solves the problem. By some device or other, memorization must be assured early during this third phase, for further perfection of detail depends on it.

2. *Vocalization.* Another general detail—if there can be such a thing—that it is wise to work on early in this phase is vocalization. No good director suddenly discovers in dress rehearsals that the play cannot be heard in the auditorium. This is a detail that he works on early, so that correct vocalization becomes a habit with the actors. Correct vocalization has two elements, (1) audibility and (2) intelligibility; and the wise director thinks of both.

Audibility is the quality of being heard, and it depends directly on the amount of vocal sound that the actor produces. If he cannot be heard, he must make more sound, he must speak louder. There is no mysterious quality called projection which will make an audience understand a sound that they cannot hear! Of course, audibility will depend, to a large degree, on the acoustics of the auditorium, on its size, and on other noises that are occurring on the stage—or in the neighborhood. But the experienced actor thinks of all these things—he speaks more loudly if he has to speak upstage, or over music or in dark scenes when the audience cannot see his lips. Most directors believe that opening scenes—especially in a first act, when there is probably noise from late arrivals, and while the audience still hasn't settled down and become accustomed to the voices of the actors—should be louder than other parts of the play. As we become accustomed to voices, we hear and understand them better. The cure for inaudibility, then, is to insist on the actors making a greater volume. The danger in insisting on this is that sometimes actors are unable to increase the volume without some sort of physical strain that changes the quality of their voices. This, however, is one of the requirements for acting: that the actor be able to make himself heard, that he be able to increase the volume of his voice without strain and unpleasant quality. Probably all stage-speaking must be louder than ordinary conversation in a room. It must still, however, have the quality of ordinary conversation; even a stage whisper must be a whisper by virtue of its quality, and not by being low. Persons with weak and inflexible voices just cannot be successful actors—perhaps, they should imitate Sophocles, who, according to rumor, gave up acting because of his weak voice and became the greatest Greek playwright!

But audibility is only part of the problem. We can hear a voice and still not understand what is being said. The director must also work for intelligibility. This is the quality of being understood, or conveying meaning. It is perhaps primarily a matter of enunciation—what is sometimes called diction. Most actors secure this by a prolongation of vowels and an over-emphasis of consonants, especially final ones. Perhaps they have a slight exaggeration of enunciation—which leads to the accusation, offstage, that they have "actory" diction. This is, however, probably essential *in* the theater, for no actor—nor teacher, nor preacher, nor lecturer—can speak to one thousand persons as if he were speaking to one. Of course, exaggerated elocutionary speech should be avoided. But the advice to be natural is incorrect; the attempt of a good actor is not, and should not be, to *be natural*, but rather *to appear to be natural*. The good actor will have unnaturally clear, well-enunciated speech, which will appear natural on a stage.

3. *Reading of lines.* A third important detail, and probably one that will take more time than all the others, is the reading of the lines of the play. This is discussed in detail in Chapter XII. The director must weigh carefully the reading of every line and help the actor give it proper meaning. This meaning will naturally grow out of the character and the situation; that is to say, the kind of person the actor is portraying, and the incidents and situations in which the character is involved. Naturally the director will expect to help the actor (see pages 143-149) decide which words to emphasize, or "plug," and how to phrase the lines by insertion of pauses of the right length in the proper places. He will aid him with the important question of intonation or speech pattern, and advise him as to whether to read lines up or down. The actor, at this point, is trying to build up his individual performance, and it is the task of the director, while he is helping him to do this, to weld the scene into a whole. This will call for constant and careful analyses of the characters and of the effects that the actors are creating.

A useful device may be the inventing of silent lines, before or after audible ones, that the actor may think, or say, to himself. Actors call this *bridging*. Bridging is a device that helps an actor get from one place to another by the use of a thought sequence. Mitchell gives the following illustration: [1]

The line "Why, my lord!" is capable of being read in a score of ways. It may be outraged astonishment, *"Heavens, you're mad. Why, my lord! What do you mean?"* It may be frightened sur-

[1] Roy Mitchell, *Shakespeare for Community Players* (New York, E. P. Dutton & Co., 1919), p. 36.

prise, *"What has come over you?* Why, my lord! *You're ill."* It may be incredulity, *"I never heard of such a thing.* Why, my lord!"* . . . or in an effort to sooth, *"There's nothing to fear.* Why, my lord!"* . . . or reproach, *"Surely you were never guilty of that!* Why, my lord! *I'm ashamed of you."* In each case the italicized words are spoken under the breath and establish an emotional context which gives perfect accuracy to the short, awkward line.

It may be that the actors will need most help with the "short, awkward line," but it is probable that they will need help with all lines, to avoid the even, monotonous delivery that old-fashioned amateurs sometimes believed was demanded by acting. Varied and effective and natural readings demand constant attention and can be established only by much repetition.

4. *Gesture.* Another detail that will concern the director will be gesture. That term should mean to him not merely the waving of a hand, but the whole position assumed by the actor, with both body and limbs, for the purpose of expressing an idea or an emotion. Most young and inexperienced actors move too often. The director will probably find it constantly necessary to insist that there be no gesture without a meaning. Another bad habit of young actors is to make small, almost invisible, gestures. These express nothing. The gesture that *is* used should be broad and clear, probably slightly more exaggerated than it would be in real life. Trained actors usually gesture with the upstage hand; this is so as to keep the hands from cutting off the actor's body and face from the audience. Thus, if an actor sits facing left and must pick up a cup of tea from a table at his left, it is best to pick it up with the left hand, even if he is right handed, since otherwise his right hand has to move way across his body and back again, thus spoiling his open position. So the important thing for the director to watch, during this phase of rehearsal, is that actors do not gesture too often, that every gesture has a purpose, and that every gesture be broad, and clear, and

meaningful. The actor need not be afraid of keeping still; the longer he retains one position—providing it is a good one to start with!—the stronger is his position in the stage picture. When George Frederick Cooke, the celebrated actor, was questioned as to the most difficult and important part of acting, he replied, "Sir, it is to learn to stand still."

The idea of developing a master gesture for a character is sometimes helpful. A master gesture is one that is used repeatedly until it becomes part of the character. An old man may be fumbling with his beard, a young fire-eater fingers his sword or dagger, a nervous housewife rolls the corner of her apron, or a fat man keeps his hands folded on his stomach. Any repeated hand gesture, or any body position, which tends to characterize the rôle, is helpful to the inexperienced actor. Of course, the idea must not be abused, but the invention of master gestures is often helpful.

5. *Business*. Business is behavior, or activity, intended to interpret the character portrayed. Sometimes it is suggested by the author in his script. Sometimes, indeed, it is essential to the carrying-on of the play, for it is embodied in the lines. Often, however, it is invented by the director, and superimposed, for the purpose of giving lifelikeness to the characters. A good actress may sit quietly on a sofa and play a long scene; but a bad one may be aided by being instructed to knit, or smoke, or shell peas, etc. Of course, she should be the sort of character who would naturally do one of these things, but the invention of business which gives the inexperienced actor something reasonable to do is one of the profitable activities of the director during this third phase of rehearsal.

In short, the experienced director will, during this phase of the rehearsal, by considering all these details—and perhaps many others—help the actor so to use his body and voice as to create a character. He will leave nothing to "inspiration," for good acting is not an accident, but the result of building thousands of details by repetition into habit.

TRADITIONAL RULES OF ACTING

There is a body of material called *The Rules of Acting* which may be useful in these rehearsals for details. Of course, these are not rules in the sense that they are unbreakable regulations. They are merely the crystallized observations of experienced actors. They are a method of doing things that seem most effective on the stage. Sometimes they are ascribed to Talma, a great French actor of the early nineteenth century, and are called the rules of Talma. Some modern actors deny that any rules exist, or can exist. However, the traditional methods of doing things often help inexperienced actors. Here are the rules:

1. *Face the audience.* This does not mean that the actor should stand square-on, looking the audience in the eye. It does mean that, other things being equal, the face is more expressive than the back of the head, and it is easier to be audible facing front. Unless there is a good reason for the actor to turn his back on the audience, it's better if he faces obliquely downstage.

2. *Make turns towards the audience.* This is for the same reasons: in making upstage turns, the actor weakens his position.

3. *Stand with the downstage foot back.* The downstage foot is the one toward the audience; hence in facing left, the right foot is offstage of the left one, and vice versa. This again tends to let the actor easily and naturally face downstage rather than up.

4. *Makes moves with the nearest foot.* That is to say, if the actor is standing to the right of a chair, his left foot would be the nearest to the chair. Hence, if he were told to move to it, he would start with his left foot. In order to do this, he will need to have his weight on his right. If he starts with his right foot, his first step will be with his right foot across his left, which would tend to make him turn awkwardly upstage. Actors would say this makes him "walk around himself!"

5. *Enter with the upstage foot.* Again, this method has the purpose of bringing the actor on in a strong position, with his face downstage. In entering from the right, he crosses the threshold

with his left foot; in entering from the left, he crosses with his right.

6. *Exit with the upstage foot.* For identical reasons.

7. *Kneel on the downstage knee.* This again tends to make it easier to face downstage; and in addition, it is supposed to give a better costume line.

8. *The speaker enters last.* When two or more actors enter together, especially on an empty stage, the one who is to speak first enters last. This allows the speaker to throw his voice forward, towards the audience, and not back offstage, and makes the situation more natural.

9. *Eyes should be on the speaker.* In general, the audience watch what the actors watch. Therefore, actors help the one who is speaking by looking at him and thus appearing to listen—unless there is some better reason not to be looking at him!

10. *Never gesture on a pronoun.* The first—and only—gesture some inexperienced actors make is to point on "he," "you," and "I." On "I" they soundly thump their chests—or often their stomachs. This gesture is usually not necessary, and is better avoided—except in the case of a peculiar and vulgar character.

11. *Let gestures precede lines.* The ear is quicker in the theater than the eye. Many actors, therefore, when a gesture and a speech come at the same time, lead with the gesture. It is stronger to point dramatically and say "Go," than it is to say "Go!" and then point.

12. *Gesture with the upstage hand.* The upstage hand is more clearly visible when an actor is in a normal position, and it does not come between him and the audience, thus cutting off his face.

There are probably many other such rules; for every director and actor—if he believes in rules—will have his own favorites. Their advantage for the director who is working with inexperienced players is that they may help him avoid having to repeat corrections, and they aid the actors to do things in an easier way. It is not necessary to keep saying: "Use the other hand! Make the turn the other way! Start with the other foot! Kneel on the other knee!" If the director finds the rules useful, he may teach them to all the actors at once in a short time. Of course, he will not foolishly observe them when they should not be observed. Often there may be good reason for an actor's turning his back on the audience, or standing with this wrong foot forward, or gesturing with his downstage hand. Nevertheless, in general, actors are likely to find that the rules make playing easier and more effective.

SOME GENERAL SUGGESTIONS

Probably the most important suggestion to the director is to remember that he cannot correct every detail at once. Many defects will drop out naturally in a well-conducted series of rehearsals. The tendency of inexperienced actors is to drop out of character (that is, stop acting) when the speech is finished, and this is a fault that should be watched. A good actor holds his character. Some directors make it a point not to carry difficult scenes (love scenes, very tragic scenes, etc.) too far in general rehearsal. They may be rehearsed privately, so they will be effective when first performed before the other actors.

One of the most interesting tributes paid to acting in litera-ture appears in Fielding's *Tom Jones*. Tom and some other persons have taken Mr. Partridge, a country schoolmaster, to see David Garrick play Hamlet. After the play, they ask Mr. Partridge which of the players he liked best. He says that the King was the best actor. When they tell him that all critics have agreed that Hamlet was acted by the best player who ever was on the stage, he breaks out scornfully:

"He is the best player!" cries Partridge, with a contemptuous sneer, "why, I could act as well as he myself. I am sure, if I had seen a ghost, I should have looked in the same manner, and done just as he did. And then, to be sure, in that scene, as you called it, between him and his mother, where you told me he acted so fine, why, Lord help me, any man, that is, any good man, that had such a mother, would have done exactly the same. I know you are only joking with me; but indeed, madam, though I was never to a play in

London, yet I have seen acting before in the country; and the king for my money; he speaks all his words distinctly, half as loud again as the other. Anybody may see he is an actor."

It is in this important third phase of rehearsal that director and actors should be concentrating on the details that give the impression to the audience that in the situation and under the stress of emotion, "any man . . . would have done exactly the same."

CHAPTER IX

The Fourth Phase of Rehearsal: Finish

PURPOSE OF THE FOURTH PHASE

No matter how long the rehearsal period, the third phase of working on details is rarely long enough for the director to accomplish everything he wishes. There will always be readings he would like to improve, movement and business he would like to change, and characterizations that are not quite right. But the wise director at this point is very brave! He knows that now, in the remaining two or three rehearsals, the time for working on details is over. He and the actors must turn their attention again to the play as a whole. The idea now is to produce a smooth and confident performance.

This will be more easily accomplished if the director has in mind definite qualities, such as (1) clearness of story, (2) emphasis, (3) tempo, and (4) teamwork. Again, as in the preceding chapter, I shall discuss these one by one, although it is probable that in actual rehearsal the director can work for all of them at the same time.

METHOD DURING THE FOURTH PHASE

The important thing during these final rehearsals is to play the scenes or the acts through without pauses or breaks, so as to give the actors the experience of continuous playing. At whatever necessity for self-restraint, the wise director has a series of run-throughs. He is now like the conductor of an orchestra, and he turns his major attention to the ensemble playing. Faulty details if any still remain—and they always will—must be overlooked or covered by the proper perform-ance of the play as a whole. As the conductor of an orchestra cannot stop to teach an individual musician how to play a single note at this stage of the practice, so the director of a play must not stop to teach an actor some detail of characteriza-tion that has not yet been learned. Fortunately, the effect of the play on the audience will be the effect of a whole, and this whole is more important than any of its parts. Single faulty details are not likely to be fatal; a dull, faltering, ineffective whole will be.

There are two common methods of working during run-throughs. One is to take notes on parts that need changes or corrections, and after the completion of a scene or act, give these notes to the actors. Many professional directors work, at this time, with the aid of a stenographer, who rapidly takes down their muttered comments. Others take the notes themselves. The performance is likely to be better if the director does not trouble the actors at this time with too many unimportant notes. Inexperienced actors are not likely to be able to change the reading of a line just because they are told to change it, and they find it difficult to put in a new piece of business, or to modify a move merely from vocal directions. Therefore, if it is really important, it is worth while to take the necessary time to work on the reading with them and to give them time to rehearse the changed business or movement. If this is done at the end of each scene, the actors are likely to be able to incorporate them in the next run-through.

Another method is to attempt to produce the necessary changes in the run-through by directing it in a quiet voice, much as a conductor directs an orchestra. The director may say, "Faster, faster, that's it," or "Hold that pause, now," or "Don't change your positions yet," or "Now, emphasize this next speech," or "Look in this direction, all of you," and so on. Perhaps he may even move quietly, now and then, on to the stage, to give a direction to a specific actor, or to change a position of another. If he uses some such system, he will probably find it wise to have a specific noise, such as a whistle, with which to stop the rehearsal if necessary; and he will instruct actors to keep playing, not to stop at the sound of his voice, but only at the whistle. The main consideration is that actors must be allowed to build up the confidence that can come only from playing the play through.

QUALITIES TO BE CONSIDERED

Progress in the fourth phase is likely to be successful to the degree that the director has consciously in mind the qualities of a good performance.

1. *Clearness of Story.* One of the first of these qualities is clearness of story. He must be sure that audiences are going to understand the *plot*. There will be certain highly important lines stating a fact that the audience must get. Actors call these plot lines. They try to read such lines especially clearly and emphatically. The director might be noticing then, during run-throughs, how the actors are "making" the plot lines. There will also be some incidents of major importance, those that are necessary for the understanding of the other incidents in the story. These must be so played as to give them weight. Perhaps, he may feel that the audience will miss a point because a certain word is not given enough emphasis, or because a bit of business is too fast. In every possible way, the director will at this point try to forget that he *knows* the story, even though by now he may be nauseated with it. He will try to see if it will be clear to an audience seeing it for the first time.

2. *Emphasis.* A second point, perhaps growing immediately out of the first, will be emphasis. The director will try to get variety in emphasis. This will depend on the importance of the various parts of the play. A good performance changes constantly in volume and in tempo (which is so important that I shall discuss it separately below) and in the length of the pauses. In other words, the performance leads to a cli-

max, or to a series of climaxes. The director must at this point decide which are the more important scenes, and he may want to increase their volume; certain lines will need to be stressed, others will be better if—in the language of the theater—they are "thrown away." This means that they will be read without much emphasis. The director and the actors must remember that they can get emphasis only by making other parts less emphatic. If everything is emphasized, nothing is! because emphasis can exist only by contrast. Variety is the important key-word; there is only one really bad kind of emphasis, and that is the lack of emphasis which is the result of heavy, even playing.

3. *Tempo.* Just as there must be a variety in emphasis, so there must be a variety in tempo, or in the rate of speed at which the play is played. Some parts must be played slowly, and some rapidly. The director must decide on these variations and attempt to achieve them during this phase of rehearsal. It is a helpful general rule that the tempo of comedy is fast, and the tempo of tragedy is slow. This means that the general tempo in a light play will be more rapid than that of a serious play. But within this general tempo, there must be variety. Even in a light play, there will be more serious parts, perhaps even parts with tragic implications. These, then, might well be played more slowly. And even in a tragedy, there will be less serious scenes; and these should probably be speeded up. We should not expect the Porter in *Macbeth* to play with the slowness of Macbeth trying to decide whether or not to murder Duncan, or Lady Macbeth sleep-walking. Even in a heavy tragedy, there will be lighter, and hence more rapid, parts.

In the attempt to attain speed, inexperienced actors sometimes read so rapidly as to lose all intelligibility. This is not necessary. The best way to get speed is not by excessive rate of delivery of words, but by the rapid picking up of cues. Before one actor has quite finished, another one has started his speech. Speeches are thus overlapped. Of course, this is sometimes not quite natural; usually we need to hear a speech and decide what to answer. But in the theater an audience is not likely to be worried about this; and the best way to secure the effect of great speed is to pick up cues.

A well-directed play has a beat, almost like music. Some directors—the others call them "arty"—direct this phase of rehearsal with a baton and actually beat time on a music stand or a block of wood. The beat may be increased and decreased, and thus a variety of tempo be created. The important thing to remember is that there is only one hopelessly bad kind of tempo, and that is *even* tempo, especially slow even tempo, when the playing plods dully along, without change of pace. As in the case of emphasis, variety is of the utmost importance, and it is best if the variety is not accidental; it should grow sensibly out of the nature of the story.

4. *Teamwork.* Teamwork means playing together, and to secure this is another one of the functions of the final rehearsals. Actors must help each other secure the desired effects. They must learn how to listen to each other and how to reënforce the ideas they are trying to play. Here again, we come back to the general nature of the production (see Chapter III): the theme, the graphic image, the color and line of the production. Some must not be playing a heavy tragedy, while others are playing a frivolous comedy. They must all be playing the same play, and if possible, the same scene!

THE IMPORTANCE OF SCENES

Perhaps all the above discussion may be summed up by saying that during this phase of rehearsal the director must see to it that the play falls into scenes. This idea has already been discussed on page 75. It is to be hoped that the director has long ago broken the dialogue up into its component scenes and that he has had them continuously in mind during the entire process of rehearsal. Now, however, he should be certain that he has made scenes *in the performance,* as well as in his script. A good performance *is* a series of scenes. Each one is a little incident, the development of an idea; and like a play it has its beginning, and middle, and end. The actors must, in some way, indicate the break between the scenes. Commonly, they will do so by (1) a pause, (2) a movement, (3) a gesture, (4) a change in emphasis, (5) a change in tempo, or (6) a change in vocal pitch. More often, they are likely to indicate the change by a combination of two or more of these methods. Thus an actor may end a scene by reading a line emphatically down, to complete his idea. Then he may pause, turn slowly, look up, and raise the pitch of his voice as he introduces a new idea. Thus, he will begin a new scene. It is these constant changes that make something appear to be happening in the theater, and scenes are especially important in a play without much action. When a play is talky, the talk must be purposeful, or it will be dull. The purpose is usually to show or to create varying states of mind in characters. By breaking the talk up into scenes the actors are able to show these changing states of mind. The dialogue thus becomes dramatic, and does not remain merely static. These changes of mind are often called transitions by actors. An actor must be clear as to *where* his transitions are, and *what* they are. The director should be sure, during these final rehearsals, that actors understand their transitions, and these will normally come between scenes. A play without scenes will be dull and ineffective; this the director can help to avoid during this fourth phase.

DRESS REHEARSALS

The run-throughs will naturally lead into dress rehearsals, which are final rehearsals, as much like performances as possible, and complete in every detail—except perhaps for a lack of audience. Some directors like to have an invited audience in order to give the actors the feel of playing before people.

Almost all Broadway productions have several previews, or invited dress rehearsals; unless they play, as many do, several weeks out of town. No matter how skilful the director, he cannot take the place of an audience, and it is only by seeing actual reactions that director and actors can judge what is most effective. It is these weeks on the road that enable the director and actors to set the play; that is, to agree upon the final form in which it is to be played. Good actors are always playing to an audience, although they must not appear to be. To teach actors to ignore the audience is, then, doubtful wisdom. They must be taught *to appear to ignore the audience*.

The skilful director probably trains the actors—especially if they are inexperienced—how to play against the applause and laughter which he hopes they will get. The technique is this. As the laughter of an audience increases to the degree that renders it impossible to make the lines audible, the actors must stop and hold their positions and attitudes. As the noise dies down, so that they can again be heard, they should pick up the lines from where they stopped. It is as though a moving picture stopped for a few seconds while the audience laughed, and then continued. Perhaps the director will feel it wise to give his actors some experience in thus stopping and starting, and this he can do in final rehearsals if he indicates laughter by beating on a box, or some such object, with a stick. Of course, it is unnecessary to say that the actors should not look at the audience in delighted surprise when they laugh or applaud.

Another necessity during final and dress rehearsals, is to think of such things as movement and deportment *backstage*. Actors should rehearse getting into positions for entrances in time and without noise, and they should not be allowed to climb over the footlights to get ready to appear as they may have done earlier in rehearsal. They must get into entrance positions without creating confusion, or without conflicting with actors who are making exits. If an actor goes off on one side of the stage and enters on the other, he should rehearse this change of position. If he has to make a costume or make-up change, he needs to rehearse this, probably several times. Noises that do not seem noticeable in rehearsals, when the director is constantly interrupting, often seem very loud in the silence of an attentive audience. Therefore, if an actor needs to cross behind a drop or a wall, he must be sure that the audience will not hear his footsteps. In fact, the footsteps of all the actors are a thing that should be thought about; and their noise should be eliminated, both on stage and off, by proper shoes, or by a ground cloth, or by strips of carpet.

Another thing that should be rehearsed is curtain calls, if there are to be any. Some directors object to them, but personally I do not find them objectionable except when they are badly done. The audience knows that the actor is not dead and often feels frustrated if denied the opportunity to show appreciation. Curtain calls are bad when they are confused and accidental, when some actors stand stiff and fearful as though about to be shot, others move gaily about and bow to each other and the audience, and still others are caught pushing one another on and off the stage! In short, they are bad when they are unrehearsed. Each actor should have a definite position in the curtain call and should move to it quickly and quietly. They should all do the same thing, probably stand quietly and pleasantly at ease, smiling slightly, but not painfully. If any are to bow, all should bow together, but probably slightly. If there are to be changes, so that different actors appear in different calls, these changes should be listed, memorized by all, and rehearsed. The tradition in the old theater was as follows: (1) all actors who were on at the final curtain, (2) all actors in the last act, (3) the entire company, (4) the leading players—the minor players faded quietly away, and (5) the star or stars. If there were more than five curtain calls, the star often brought out an individual actor, or a pair or group of actors, or he might call out the entire company again. In the modern theater, the stage-manager usually posts a list of curtain calls, indicating the actors that are to be on for each. It is probably most satisfactory with non-professional companies to have all the actors remain on, in assigned and rehearsed positions, for all calls.

The bane of all companies, both professional and amateur, is the actor who is always changing his performance. He is inspired in the performance and suddenly makes a move or gives a reading that he hasn't tried in rehearsal. Perhaps he suddenly thinks his part is too small and invents some new lines or business. The ancient professional name for this vice is "gagging." It should be guarded against in the final rehearsals. The director should insist that the play be played as it was rehearsed. If the actor gets a sudden idea that really *is* better, he should save it until he has talked it over with the other actors and the director. Perhaps he can put it in tomorrow night! Good actors try to give accurate and identical performances, just as they were rehearsed. A good actor, in a long professional run, doesn't change even his tie, without showing it to all the actors who have scenes with him. This is to protect himself as well as the other actors; he is afraid that one of them will notice it, and during a scene say to himself: "Well! John must have a new tie! I never before noticed . . ." By this time the cue is past, the rhythm of the scene has slipped, and the actor with the new tie finds *himself* playing badly. A good production gets set, it develops a tempo, a definite method of playing, and anything unrehearsed is always harmful. The purpose of the wise director during the final rehearsals is to set the performance, and to instruct the actors to play it as set.

There is an old tradition that a bad dress rehearsal makes a good performance. This is a most false and dangerous doctrine. It is probably true that actors sometimes rise to the occasion, so that a performance will probably not always be as bad as a poor dress rehearsal. But nothing makes for a good performance like a skilfully conducted series of rehearsals leading to a complete and successful dress rehearsal.

CHAPTER X

The Theory of Acting

THE ACTOR IN REHEARSAL

In the preceding chapters, the process of rehearsal has been discussed at length, and much has been said about *acting*. However, the process of acting is so important in play production that it will probably be wise to discuss it in even more detail. There are those who think that acting *is* play production. I believe it was Dumas who said, "A play is some boards, two actors, and a passion!" In the modern theater, much more than acting is involved in play production—items like playwriting, scene building and scene-painting, costume-selection, lighting, business-management, etc. However, perhaps it is still true that acting is the one indispensable element, without which it is impossible to have a play. It is conceivable that actors could make up the story as they go along and so do without a playwright; they might play without special scenery or lighting effects; they might by chance gather some spectators; and so on. But without *characters* to be involved in a series of incidents —that is, without actors—we could have no play at all.

Acting is certainly one of the most interesting of the arts involved in play production—and one of the most difficult. The actor, like the artists who practice all the other arts, such as painting, or music, or writing, finds himself confronted with a double problem. The first part of the problem is the *purpose,* and the second is the *method.* In other words, first he must decide *what he is trying to do,* and then *how he is going to try to do it.* What effect does the actor wish to create by his acting, and how is he going to create this effect? The way the actor works in rehearsal and his entire method of study will be somewhat determined by his answers to these questions.

THE PURPOSE OF ACTING

Obviously the purpose of acting is to embody the characters described by the author in his script, and the purpose of the embodiment is to make an *effect on the spectators*. A child who plays he is an elephant or a locomotive is not acting; he is merely indulging in dramatic play. He is playing he is an elephant only for his own amusement. If, however, the child begins to try to convey to someone else that he is an elephant, acting has started. Acting begins when we have consciously in mind the creating of an effect upon another person, or group of persons. The complicated problem now arises of what kind of an effect we wish to create. As in the case of most of the other theoretical questions that we have discussed, we shall find that there are two opposing philosophies.

1. *The Theory of Illusion.* Most of the criticism of acting in the modern theater proceeds from the thesis that the main purpose of acting is to create an *illusion*. Many critics and many theater-goers feel that the highest compliment they can pay to acting is to forget that they are seeing acting. Acting, for them, is successful to the degree to which it imitates and reproduces life. They want an actor who plays a policeman, let us say, to deceive them into thinking that he is a policeman. The difficulty with this theory is that the spectator, to be so deceived, must bring a high degree of naïveté to the theater. Moreover, as its critics point out, this theory would make acting differ from all the other arts; for in no other art is illusion the end, or the purpose. In seeing a painting, we do not try to forget that it is a painting; when we listen to music, we remain conscious that it is music. "Nobody but the simplest creature," says Stark Young, "expects the sound to deceive us by making us think it is a storm, or pasture bells, a waterfall, or anything but

music." [1] However, perhaps it is possible that acting, being more directly an imitation of life, is different from the other arts.

2. *The Theory of Comment or Interpretation.* The exponents of the second theory do not believe this, however. The actor, they say, should not try to deceive us; his purpose is not to create illusion, but to show us the reality behind the surface likeness. They are fond of quoting Coleridge's remark that the purpose of the theater is "not belief, but the suspension of disbelief." The spectator, they say, can never be deceived. The purpose of the actor should be to *interpret* the character and *comment* on it. The actor, by showing us the character through his own emotions and understanding, enables us to see in it what we could never see by ourselves. His characterization thus becomes what Matthew Arnold says all art is: "a criticism of life." The greater the actor as an artist the more he contributes of criticism, or comment, and the greater his performance. Of course, the actor who tries to embody this purpose, is not going to be consciously unrealistic. Realism is the end in both theories. The question is whether the best realism is obtained by the actor who tries to imitate, or by the actor who tries to interpret.

If this sounds difficult and confusing, do not worry about it. The important thing for the young actor is to see as much acting as possible. He may well try to decide why it is good, or why it is bad. The attempt to understand the purpose of an art is valuable, even though it is impossible to arrive at definite conclusions. If the young actor is confused, he will be in good company. Critics have discussed this question of the purpose of acting in essays, books, articles, and reviews for three thousand years; and there still seems to be as much. disagreement as ever. If there are sound and irrefutable conclusions, they do not appear in the records.

[1] Stark Young, *Glamour*, (New York, Charles Scribner's Sons, 1925), p. 88.

CONFLICTING METHODS OF ACTING

The second problem of the actor, his *method,* is fortunately not so complicated or difficult. Not that there is agreement here, either, for the practitioners of acting are sharply divided on the question of *how it should be done.* The problem is charmingly stated in a delightful old book *The Autobiography of an Actress* by Anna Cora Mowatt, the authoress of "Fashion, or Life in New York," and other dramas of the middle nineteenth century:

There are two distinct schools of acting, and it is a disputed point which is the greater. The actor of one school totally loses his own individuality, and abandons himself to the absorbing emotions that belong to the character he interprets. His tears are real, his laughter real, as real to himself as to his audience. Frequently, they are *more* real to himself than to his listeners; for the capacity of feeling, and the faculty of expressing the sensation experienced, are widely different. The current upon which the actor is borne away may, or may not, be strong enough to bear the spectator upon its bosom. . . .

The actor of the opposite school, if he is a thorough artist, is more certain of producing startling effects. He stands unmoved amidst the boisterous seas, the whirlwinds of passion swelling around him. He exercises perfect command over the emotions of the audience; seems to hold their heart-strings in his hands, to play upon their sympathies as though upon an instrument; to electrify or subdue his hearers by an effort of volition; but not a pulse of his own frame beats more rapidly than its wont. His personations are cut out of marble; they are grand, sublime, but no heart throbs within the lifelike sculpture. Such was the school of the great Talma. This absolute power over others, combined with the perfect self-command, is pronounced by a certain class of critics the perfection of dramatic art.

Nearly every one who has dealt with the subject of acting falls into one or the other of these two schools. The members of the first feel that acting is primarily *emotional* and that the actor must live the part. Members of the second school think that acting is *intellectual* and that the actor merely suggests the character and does not live it. Most actors tell us that they belong to one or the other of these schools.

1. *The Emotional School, or Living the Part.* If we believe acting is primarily emotional, our chief problem as actors will be to try to feel the emotion of the character we wish to portray. We shall expect the director to help us, not by detailed directions as to gestures, readings, etc., but by describing the feelings we must have. We shall try to understand the past life of the character, and the psychology of the rôle will be our chief concern. We shall know, of course, that we shall not have had, in our own lives, all the emotions we are asked to portray in the theater. The advocates of this school overcome this difficulty by a device that they call the transfer of emotion.

The transfer of emotion implies that the actor be able to recall from his past experience some situation resembling that which he wishes to play. For instance, perhaps a young lady must enact the loss of her husband. In real life, she has not lost her husband—in fact, perhaps she never had one. She must think of something she has lost, say her purse, or handkerchief, or a valuable letter. She must recall the emotion she had on that occasion and try to raise it to the height necessary to portray this greater loss. Or perhaps a young man is called upon to kill a man in a play. He has never killed a man, but he has killed a mosquito, or a snake. He remembers his hate and loathing on that occasion and makes that memory the basis of his acting. The obvious fallacy in this theory is that he cannot be certain that his emotions, however sound, will be transferred to his audience. As Mrs. Mowatt says, ". . . the capacity of feeling, and the faculty of expressing the sensation experienced, are widely different." Moreover, there may be some uncertainty as to whether or not he can be sure of having his emotions at the right time, when they are demanded by the incident in the play. However, it is possible that there are some actors whose faces, bodies, and voices so instinctively reflect what they feel, that for them to have an emotion is to express it effectively. Perhaps they are the ones who belong to this school. Sarah Bernhardt, for instance, says that she was one of these. She implies that she always felt the emotion of the part she played. She says: [2]

If the actor retains his mode of living, of thinking and of behaving throughout the manifold characters that he successively impersonates, he cannot feel the passions of these characters; and, unless he can enter into the feelings of his heroes, however violent that may be, however cruel and vindictive they may seem, he will never be anything but a bad actor. . . . If he does not really feel the anguish of the betrayed lover or of the dishonored father, if he does not temporarily escape from the dullness of his existence in order to throw himself whole-heartedly into the most acute crisis, he will move nobody.

And again: [3]

You must weep real tears, suffer real anguish, laugh a real laugh which is contagious. . . . Diderot contended that the artist ought not to feel anything. This is an error and I declare Diderot to be wrong.

Thus she implies that when she played Jeanne d' Arc, she went through all the agony of being burnt alive every performance!

2. *The Intellectual School, or Suggesting the Part.* The advocates of the second, or intellectual, school point out that emotion is unreliable. The actor must think primarily of actual devices for securing effects, and he must be able to remember them and repeat them. If he must kill a man on the stage, it is not enough to remember how he felt when he killed the snake. He must know that in hatred and loathing our lips curl back, our eyes narrow, and we feel a tenseness in all our muscles. Our voice grows rough and hoarse, and we speak only with difficulty. Perhaps our hands tremble, and our body

[2] Sarah Bernhardt, *The Art of the Theater*, translated by H. J. Stenning (London, Geoffrey Bles, 1924), p. 103. (Published in New York, Dial Press, 1925.)

[3] *Ibid.*, p. 200.

PLATE V. *Lysistrata*, by Aristophanes

A famous constructivistic setting, which functions primarily as design rather than as place-indication. The elements of the set are moved into varying positions, so that the design is constantly changed. (See p. 312.)

PLATE VI A (above). *Catherine de Medici,* by Warren A. Silver

The Palace of the Louvre. Necessary scenic elements arranged on a space stage, with the acting areas used in different scenes pointed out by light. Designed by Lester Polakov. (See p. 312.)

PLATE VI B (below). *The Adding Machine,* by Elmer Rice

A Courtroom. A famous expressionistic setting by Lee Simonson. The set was designed to be flown. The rail, the judge's bench, and the judge—who is a dummy—were props, set and struck on the stage. (See p. 312.)

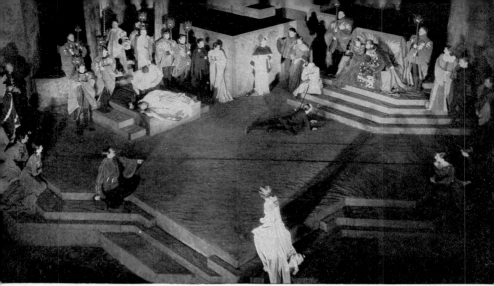

PLATE VII A (above). *Hamlet*, by William Shakespeare

The Players' Scene. An effective space stage to be used for all the scenes. Variation was secured by the use of properties and lighting. (See p. 312.)

PLATE VII B (below). The Same

The bare stage, showing the arrangement of platforms and steps.

New York Theatre Guild

Vandamm

PLATE VIII A (above). *The Three Sisters,* by Anton Chekov

A realistic exterior, designed by the Motleys, consisting of a painted drop, a plastic house, wood wings, and a plastic tree and fence. (See p. 278 and p. 423.)

PLATE VIII B (below). *Twist the Lion's Tail,* by Stanley Bortner

The rear terrace of a mansion in Maryland. The entire set, except for the tree, ground row, and sky-wall, is carried on a wagon. Designed by Margaret Anderson. (See p. 277.)

Columbia University: Columbia Theatre Associates

Gabrielson

leans forward. These, then, are the things that the actor must do in the theater to express hatred. It is not enough to feel hatred; the audience can tell what the actor feels only by what he does. An actor, then, must think of things to do that will explain how he feels. He should constantly observe how people act in real life. From these observations he is going to select details to use in portraying a character. He is going to expect from the director, not a description of emotions, but the suggestion of actual devices to secure effects. Constant Coquelin, the great French actor of the nineteenth century, a famous contemporary of Bernhardt, for whom Cyrano de Bergerac and many other famous parts were written, declared he was an actor of this school.[4] He says he never felt emotion in the theater. His motto, he says, is "Keep control of yourself."

There is evidence that the extremes described never exist in any practical actor. DeWolf Hopper, a famous American comedian, in a chapter entitled "How Not to Act," [5] says he was once backstage when Bernhardt was playing *Madame X*. Madame X returns after eighteen years to the husband she has betrayed and begs for the opportunity to see her son, whom she has not seen since he was a child. The husband brutally refuses, and in grief and despair, she walks to a door, sways, and supports herself with her hand on the door jamb. Finally she struggles through the door, leaving her hand still visible on its edge; the husband advances, wrenches her hand from the door, and flings it out. Bernhardt was famous for her playing of this moving scene. But Hopper says that while her right hand was still in view of the audience, she saw her stage-manager standing beside him. Waving her free hand, she said

[4] Coquelin, Constant, *Art and the Actor* (New York, Publications of the Brander Matthews Dramatic Museum, Columbia University, 1915, Second Series, Volume II) and *The Art of Acting* (the same, 1926, Fifth Series, Volume II). The latter is an interesting series of letters to one another by Coquelin, Henry Irving, and Dion Boucicault.

[5] DeWolf Hopper, *Once a Clown* (Boston, Little, Brown & Co., 1927), p. 100.

cheerily, "Hello, Eddie! Isn't it a wonderful house?" This little story he uses to illustrate the text that "Acting is an art, not a spasm." He says:

> The acrobat or the dancer may leave the stage exhausted, but an actress who knows her business no more swoons at the finish of her big scene than Whistler had to be revived with smelling salts on completing an etching. The poor actress puts her heart into the rôle, the trained actress puts her head into it.[6]

But on the other hand, there seems to be evidence that those who think they act entirely intellectually may not be altogether right either. Once I talked with an old actor who had played with Coquelin, and he said that he used to see him, in costume and makeup, strolling up and down backstage before making his entrance, gesticulating and muttering to himself, and giving every evidence of whipping up his emotion for the part.

THE TRUE METHOD OF ACTING

The true method, as usual, is probably some sort of a compromise between the two extremes; and we can best understand it, I believe, by remembering that acting is a *process*, and not an instantaneous deed. Those who advocate emotion are thinking of the steps they took in trying to understand a character; those who advocate intellect are describing the playing of a part in public. No doubt Bernhardt at some time in getting ready to play Jeanne d' Arc sympathized with her, felt her pain and agony, and hence suffered and wept. If she had not done so, she might not have been able to play her so well. It may be difficult, perhaps impossible, for an actor to play a part which he does not understand emotionally, with which, at some time or other, he has not attained some sort of emotional identity. This explains the often-repeated statement that "No actress is capable of playing Juliet until she is too

[6] *Ibid.*, p. 110.

old to play it!" The actor's emotion, however, is only the beginning, the jumping-off place, for a characterization.

In this respect, the actor is like all other artists. He starts with an emotion, but then, by every device that his intellect can suggest, he builds up an effect. Nobody ever wrote a love lyric in the throes of love! In the very process of trying to describe his feelings he becomes an artist, and is no longer the lover. He recalls his emotion and tries to put it into words. The same is true of the painter. He sees a scene—a sunset, or a romantic ruin, or a smoking factory, or a busy city street; he has an emotion of awe or wonder or pity. Now he turns to the problem of how to describe this emotion with paint on canvas, so that the scene will move other people as it has him. This may take him days or weeks. His emotion does not last all this time. In the process of painting, he has to make a hundred, or a thousand, purely intellectual decisions. Perhaps occasionally he can recall the emotion which overwhelmed him in the beginning and was his starting point. But it is always a recalled emotion, probably never as strong as when he first felt it. This is what is meant by the statement that *the substance of art is remembered emotion.*

The sensible actor works in this same manner. Obviously, emotion cannot completely guide him *at the moment of acting the rôle.* If it did, he might not do the things that the play demands. If he has to come on the stage and face his enemies, the time might come when his emotion would tell him to walk off, and not continue his struggle against these stupid people. Or if he is a villain, his emotion might cause him to fight so hard on some particular night that he would overcome the hero and give the play a new ending. In the theater, whatever an actor says, he can never really live the part, and be controlled entirely by his emotions. If he were, he might change the play at every performance. By the time he is ready to present his characterization in public, he has a carefully thought-out performance. The emotional school makes the error of concentrating on the first part of the process, and the intellectual school concentrates on the longer second part. Neither extreme is true, for the answer lies in what part of the process is under consideration.

ACTING TECHNIQUE

It is the actor's ability to repeat this thought-out performance that is acting technique. A bad actor may give occasionally a good performance, but he is never quite sure how he secured his effects, and he cannot repeat them. A good actor, with technique, can repeat his effects night after night. He has decided, with the help of the director, exactly what he is going to do at each moment in the performance, and he is able to do it. He has technique. Perhaps he never completely loses the emotion of his first understanding of the character. If he does, he may have technique *only*. His acting will be mechanical. All good acting is mechanical, but even a slight element of warmed-over emotion prevents it from being *only* mechanical. Most actors say they usually feel in any part this slight emotion. But the good actor controls it in performance—if he feels it at all.

There is an instructive little story about the great Italian actor, Thomas Salvini. Salvini was an actor of huge size and terrific energy, whose vitality and apparent emotion in performance was famous throughout the world. Once, just as he was about to make an entrance, he burst out in a rage over an incident that occurred backstage. Upon his entrance on the stage immediately afterwards, he showed no trace of the preceding real emotion. He seemed to be living entirely in the emotions of his rôle. Afterwards, when bystanders expressed surprise at his ability to do this, he said:

How can this surprise you? I learned to do that, you know. I have finished with my rôle. Therefore, I can play any scene at any moment, whatever you want and whenever you want it. If you should get me out of bed at night and tell me to recite the monologue before the murder of Desdemona, I should recite it exactly as I do in the evening on the stage, and should have the same emotion while doing it, namely, none. It is only that I have learned how to say it so as to make others believe in my sincere emotion. And once I did feel it, too . . . when I studied the rôle! Then I felt it, completely, even to the point of physical pain. But after I have mastered it, I no longer worry about anything. I have it at my fingers' ends. I play the emotion the way the pianist plays the piano, without looking at it. Acting is a physical exertion only, not in the least a mental or spiritual one.[7]

Thus, if we may believe Salvini, even an actor who has a reputation as an emotional player, depends on his ability to repeat, that is, on his technique. The truth probably is that "the artistic work of the actor is divided into several phases, *separated as to time.*"[8] The confusion exists between the schools because they do not agree as to whether they are discussing the first reading, or the period of private study, or the time of rehearsal, or the actual performance. Probably all good actors, whatever they profess, work much the same way. They start by developing an emotional understanding of the character; during rehearsal they decide on details that will give the effects they want and practice these effects until they become a vocal and physical habit. By the time a good actor is ready to play a part in public, his performance has become habitual, so that he is able to play the emotion of the rôle, as Salvini says, "without looking at it." In this way, and only in this way, is he sure of being able to repeat his performance on demand, whatever his state of personal emotion at the actual moment of performance. He has learned to act!

[7] Lorenz Kjerbuhl-Petersen, *Psychology of Acting* (Boston, The Expression Company, 1935), p. 200. This is, in my opinion, the best and most complete study that has yet been made of this difficult subject.

[8] *Ibid.*, p. 201.

CHAPTER XI

The Tools of the Actor

THE DIFFERENCE BETWEEN ACTING AND OTHER ARTS

The tools that the actor is to use in portraying his character are really only two, his own body and his own voice. Perhaps it would be truer to say that his tool is only one, *himself*. In this respect the actor differs from most, perhaps from all, other artists. The material of the writer is words, of the painter colors and canvas, of the sculptor stone and clay and wood. But the actor is his own material, for he must shape *himself* into the character that he is going to show to his public. This assumes that he be familiar with this material that he is going to shape. Obviously an actor must know every possibility of his own face and body in order to carry on his profession. A man may paint a picture, or a musician may write a song, without ever looking into a mirror; but an actor in the process of creating a character *out of himself* must risk the possibility of being misunderstood by spending many hours studying himself in the glass. "The *matter* of his art, that which he has to work upon and mould for the creation of his idea, is his own face, his own body, his own life," says Coquelin.[1] He goes on to explain how the actor is able to use himself as "the *matter* of his art."

Hence it follows that the actor must have a double personality. He has his first self, which is the player, and his second self, which is

[1] *The Art of Acting* (New York, Publications of the Brander Matthews Dramatic Museum, Columbia University, 1926, Fifth series, Vol. 11), p. 5.

the instrument. The first self conceives the person to be created, or rather—for the conception belongs to the author—he sees him such as he was formed by the author, whether he be Tartuffe, Hamlet, Arnolphe, or Romeo, and the being that he sees is represented by his second self. This dual personality is the characteristic of the actor . . . the first self works upon the second till it is transfigured, and thence an ideal personage is evolved—in short, until from himself he has made his work of art.

Most thoughtful actors would probably agree with this description. Mr. A. B. Walkley [2] says the same thing in these words: "No doubt, in the actor there is really a double consciousness. One side of him is acting, the other side is watching himself act, regulating and noting his effects, in short, controlling his art." If we accept some such theory of double personality, the problem arises as to what we are going to do with our second self. How can we make our second self an instrument that will best serve to express the ideas formed by our first self?

THE BODY AS A TOOL IN ACTING

One of the obvious steps is to develop skill in expressing ideas with our body. This is commonly called pantomime. Pantomime is a sum total and must include facial expression, body carriage, the use of the hands and arms, the manner of walking and sitting down, and all the other things that we must do in the theater. Obviously the greater our body flexibility and the more clearly we can express ideas physically, the greater will be our skill as actors. The actors of the old theater knew this and worked hard to attain trained and flexible bodies. They studied how to walk, how to sit down, how to fall; they studied fencing and dancing; they understood that a skilful actor must have complete control of this instrument. Many modern actors seem to have forgotten this necessity. They can play *a* part, but they cannot *act*. Perhaps some of the blame

[2] A. B. Walkley, "The Psychology of Acting," *Vanity Fair* (February, 1926).

for the prevalence of type casting must fall upon them. The good actor is not contented with being able to play a part, he wants to make himself capable of playing many parts. He knows, therefore, that he must have complete control over that part of his instrument that is his body.

Certain fundamental principles of the body in acting have already been discussed in Chapter VIII, but probably it will be useful to summarize them from the point of view of the actor.

1. *The Body as a Whole.* A first and fundamental step in creating a characterization is the ability to assume a general body position. The way the body as a whole is carried and used suggest the quality of a character. An angry man, full of hatred, will have a tight, tense body; and this will color all the moves he makes. An irritated, impatient person betrays his irritation by small aimless movements. A noble young man carries his body erect, and his actions are full of vitality and vigor. An ill old man is bent over and feeble, and he moves with a slow heaviness. For every character there is some appropriate use of the body as a whole to indicate the nature of the character, and the finding of it is the first step towards a characterization. An audience finds it difficult to believe the lines spoken by an actor if his body quality denies these lines. He can state and restate that he is an energetic and ambitious young man, but this is all in vain if his body indicates that he is ill and feeble.

2. *The Use of the Eye.* It is an old rule of pantomime that "the eye always leads." This may not always be true, but it is true that the eye is one of the most important features in acting. The actor makes another long step towards the creation of a character by deciding how he will look at objects and at people. We believe a character to be treacherous and insincere if his eye is shifty, if he never looks directly at persons with whom he talks, and if his glance is sly and restless. On the other hand, the honest man—in the theater, at least—looks everybody

straight in the eye. Humility, scorn, thoughtfulness, and an infinite number of other qualities, may each suggest some distinctive use of the eye that will help to suggest the character.

3. *Breathing.* In the same way, there is an appropriate form of breathing for every character, or even for each mood of every character. Some will breathe slowly and evenly, some rapidly and irregularly, some shallowly, some deeply. This will depend on whether the character is young or old, ill or well, in repose or in high emotion. But if the actor can decide on some basic quality most appropriate to the general impression he wishes to create, this will be another step towards his portrayal of a character.

4. *Gesture.* Gesture includes all of the moves an actor makes, like pointing, picking up objects, and so on. This has been previously discussed on page 112 but perhaps it is important to repeat again: do not gesture too much. A good actor is not afraid to stand still. He is not really standing still because his body, his breathing, his eye, are always carrying an idea. A good actor is acting while he is standing still! But many young actors feel that they are acting only while they are in motion, while they are doing something. This leads to gesticulation, and not gesture. Use gestures sparingly, only when they are needed, but then make them visible and clear. And make them *appropriate.* This means appropriate not only to the thing the actor must do at the moment, but appropriate to the character he is portraying. For instance, an actor playing a famous and successful surgeon may be directed to set a clock, or wind his watch, or pick up a cup of tea, or take up a knife and fork. He must match his gesture to his character by setting the clock accurately and quickly, by winding his watch precisely, by picking up the cup with great accuracy and economy of movement, by seizing the knife and fork as though they were surgical tools. If he is a banker, or a scholar, or a clergyman, he might do every one of these things differently. He should do them differently if he is a bungling surgeon. But if his idea of the

successful surgeon is quick, accurate moves, then his idea will color every gesture.

These are some of the ways—probably there are many more —that an actor uses in making his body an instrument to express the character conceived by his first self. But these are for the eyes of the audience only, these are only visual. The audience also has ears. The play is not only a pantomime, and so the careful actor thinks how his voice can be used to reënforce these visual impressions.

THE VOICE AS A TOOL IN ACTING

In order to use his voice as a tool of acting, the actor must be sure of two things, that he *can be heard* and that *he can be understood*. In more scientific language, his speech must have (1) *audibility* and (2) *intelligibility*. Here again many actors of the old theater are full of scorn for those of the new. DeWolf Hopper says, "Inaudibility is the curse of current acting. There is no more serious offense in the theater. Of what avail to be realistic if the unfortunate back of row F can not hear what you say?" [3]

1. *Audibility.* Audibility depends on the amount of sound that an actor makes, the actual volume of his voice. If the volume is not enough to carry to the last rows of a house, the only cure is for him to make a greater volume. In other words, he must *speak louder*. The good actor, therefore, trains his voice so as to be able to change the volume on demand. He knows how to produce more volume without shouting, or without so tightening his muscles that the quality of his voice changes. He must be able to increase or decrease the volume, just as we turn a radio up or down; and this is a matter for practice. The volume must always be enough so that the audience does not have to strain to hear, and never so much as to be over-loud and unpleasant. We cannot understand speech that

[3] DeWolf Hopper, *Once a Clown* (Boston, Little, Brown & Co., 1927), p. 116.

we cannot hear, however perfect it may be; therefore a good actor's first endeavor is to create a sufficient volume of sound.

2. *Intelligibility.* The next thing he must think about is *intelligibility,* for it is quite possible to hear speech and yet not understand it. Intelligibility depends on enunciation, or the clearness with which words are formed. The speech of most good actors is slightly more exact than the normal speech of ordinary conversation. The actor forms the vowels more exactly and gives them greater value. He exaggerates slightly the consonants in a word, especially the final consonants. Of course, he tries not to use over-exaggerated speech. But just as the size of the theater makes it necessary for him to use a greater volume than he would need in the living room of his home, so the size demands that his enunciation be more accurate. He will, of course, unless he is speaking verse, use the elisions and the weak forms of conversational speech. But he will use them with the slight exaggerations of volume and enunciation that makes for audibility and intelligibility, however realistic he wishes to appear. "The art of the actor," said Mr. George Arliss, "is to learn how not to be real on the stage without being found out by the audience."

3. *Reading for Meaning.* However, it is not enough merely to be *heard* and to be *understood.* The actor is now confronted with an even more difficult vocal problem: *how to read.* Reading in the theater is concerned with the interpretation of the lines that the character speaks. The actor's first concern is to *convey a meaning.* When we read a novel or a poem, we are able to go back and read again what we have not understood. But this procedure is impossible in the theater. The actor must make the meaning so clear that we understand it at first hearing. This involves much more than merely understanding the words he says. Therefore, the problem arises as to how in speech the actor can convey thought. The common answer is that the thought conveyed depends on three factors: (1) emphasis, (2) phrasing, and (3) intonation. These words are rarely used

by actors, for the theater has a language all its own, but the ideas are ever present.

a. Emphasis. Instead of emphasis, the actor talks about *plugged* words, and by that he means the words which he pronounces with extra force. The meaning of any sentence depends to a great extent upon what word, or words, are *plugged.* If no words in a sentence are plugged, the sentence is likely to convey little, if any, meaning. But the meaning will *change* with the plugging of different words. Therefore, in studying how to read a sentence, most actors begin by deciding which words to emphasize. Perhaps this will be clearer if we take an example of a simple sentence and see how many meanings we can give it. Suppose we are faced with the problem of reading the following line: "I didn't say he stole the dog." This sentence can be given at least six meanings.

1. *I* didn't say he stole the dog (but somebody else said so!)
2. I *didn't* say he stole the dog (but I am perfectly willing to say so!)
3. I didn't *say* he stole the dog (but that's what I thought!)
4. I didn't say *he* stole the dog (but somebody did!)
5. I didn't say he *stole* the dog (but he got it somehow!)
6. I didn't say he stole the *dog* (but he stole everything else!)

Thus we have many possibilities, even in a simple sentence, of changing its meaning by emphasizing different words. This is the constant concern of a good actor, and often he tries many readings before he arrives at one that satisfies him. Usually he underlines the word he decides to plug, for this is the standard way of indicating this decision. Sometimes several words need to be emphasized in a line, and sometimes only one. Never must all the words be emphasized equally because that would be equivalent to emphasizing none. Emphasized words exist only by contrast to unemphasized ones. Sometimes it is obvious at first glance which word should be plugged, but sometimes it demands much consideration. Correct plugging is the constant concern of the actors—and directors—in the professional theater and is a continuous and interesting problem for any alert actor.

b. Phrasing. Phrasing is the process of opening up a spoken sentence by inserting *pauses.* The professional actor rarely talks of phrasing, but he talks a lot about pauses. They supplement and reënforce plugging by making word-groups. In a way, pauses may be considered oral punctuation, corresponding to the punctuation marks in written sentences. Actors talk about putting in a comma, by which they mean making a slight pause; or they talk about framing a word, which means giving it importance by a short pause both before and after the word. Punctuation is not a safe guide to the proper breaking up of a sentence with pauses because most modern authors punctuate grammatically and not rhetorically, but punctuation is a rough guide that serves as a beginning. Many actors mark their lines to indicate the length of pause with a short vertical line, thus | . For a longer pause, they use two lines || , and for a very long one three ||| . Perhaps they are unconsciously influenced by a famous eighteenth century actor named Macklin, who used to say he had three pauses: a pause, a long pause, and a grand pause. One night, according to the story, while he was playing at the Drury Lane Theater, a new prompter held the book and constantly annoyed Macklin by prompting him. At length, the audience was astounded to see the star rush to the wings, seize the poor prompter, drag him out on the stage, and cuff him. Then turning to the audience, Macklin said, "The fellow interrupted my grand pause." A burst of cheering greeted the explanation, showing the concurrence of the audience with Macklin's estimate of the value of the grand pause. Any audience is grateful to an actor who knows the value of a pause, whether it is a pause, a long pause, or a grand pause. This device, intelligently used to group words properly so as to convey thought easily, is the constant concern of the actor. Often the pause is filled in with an unspoken thought, in which case it may be called a bridge, as explained on page 111.

c. Intonation. The final factor in reading for meaning is

intonation. This means the general sound pattern of the line, especially the pitch pattern. We might call it the modulation of the line, its inflection, or its melody. Intonation is a very subtle thing, but it is very important in conveying meaning. If we have difficulty in understanding the speech of an Englishman, one of the principle causes is likely to be that his intonation patterns differ from our own. Actors do not talk much about intonation but the melodic pattern is one of the things they argue in considering how to read a line. They commonly discuss whether to read a line up or down. If a line is read up, the pitch at the end is higher than the pitch of the preceding part; if the line is read down, the final few words are lower in pitch.

Actors have all sorts of rules about this phase of reading. One is that, on the stage, many more lines are read up than in ordinary speech. This serves the purpose of making the conversation more continuous and, hence, more interesting. Up readings are usually bright and gay, down readings final and tragic. Actors say, "Read comic lines *up*." It might be better to say, "*Read all lines up unless there is some overwhelming reason why the line should be read down.*" Such a reason would be that the line ends a scene (see p. 122), or is an exit line, or is a line expressing firm decision, like "I will not do it." A down line usually indicates some sort of finality. The actor reading it is ending a conversation. Another actor, speaking after him, is confronted with the problem of starting over again. But dialogue in the theater should not start and stop with each line; the convention of the theater demands it be kept going. One of the best ways of doing so is to read lines up wherever possible.

Perhaps another way to say this same thing is that, in the theater, we must predicate each sentence. A sentence consists always of two elements. The first is the subject, the thing we are talking about, and the second is the predicate, the idea we are connecting with the subject. In ordinary conversation we tend to state the subject clearly, but often we fade out before we have completed the predicate. The idea does not need to be expressed completely because the person to whom we are talking indicates that he understands and starts to reply. But even though the character understands, the audience may not. Usually, in the theater, we must express the meaning completely; we must be able to carry a thought to completion by carrying the force of our voice to the end of the sentence. In general, this is done by reading lines up.

But even to be able to do this, is not all. Most trained actors, by plugging the proper words, by pauses in the proper places, by reading the line with correct intonation, can read meaning into—or out of—almost any sentence at sight. That is the characteristic of a good reader: he conveys meaning. The actor still has another problem, and that problem is to decide on the meaning he wishes to convey. The good actor gives us the *right* meaning.

4. *Establishing the Right Meaning.* The right meaning of a line in the theater grows out of the situation, the total idea of the scene and the character, and the impression that we want to make on the audience. Therefore, we are often confronted with the problem of selecting from a number of possible meanings, the one that is *most* right. It will be most right because it is the most effective.

Even such a comparatively simple thing as plugging the right word must grow out of the situation and must be an answer to the preceding line. If an actor is quarreling with his sister and she says, "Let's leave it to *Father*," he must hear this line and answer it. The reply that the author has given him is, "All right! Let's leave it to Father." He might say "All right! *Let's* leave it to Father," or "All right! Let's *leave* it to Father." But if he says, "All right! Let's leave it to *Father*," this seems to be nonsense, because it does not contain the quality of a reply. In reading the line in this manner, he is introducing the idea of Father, but his sister has already introduced this idea. If, on the other hand, there has been an argument about whether to leave it to Father or Mother, then his reading, "leave-it-to-*Father*," even though it repeats her reading, might be the best one. The important idea is that the right meaning is the one that is the best answer. If one actor changes his reading, a second is likely to have to change his in order to make it answer, therefore a good actor always repeats, as exactly as he can, the reading that has been decided upon in the process of rehearsal. The characteristic of good reading in the theater is that it make the utmost sense in the situation.

Perhaps this is only another way of saying that in the theater every line grows out of an emotional background.[4] In this emotional background there are always two elements: (1) the situation, or what is actually happening in the scene, and (2) the character being portrayed, who is being affected by the situation. A good actor is constantly asking himself such questions as: "What is my emotion at this moment? How did that remark or that action affect me as a character? How can I show that I heard it? How can I read my line so as to reply to it?" In other words, an actor always works from the apparent emotion of the character he is acting, and he knows that *every line must be colored by this emotion*.

Emotion, in the sense that it is used here, does not mean merely anger, hatred, fear, delight, joy, and other such obvious reactions. Emotion on the stage must include every possible variation of *state of being*. To be dull, to be uninteresting, to be thoughtless, to be unmoved—all these, and thousands and thousands of other states of being, must be thought of as emotions. In this sense, having no emotion *is* an emotion. A character can never have no emotion, for that would mean that the actor would have nothing to act—he would have no reason to be making any impression on the audience. A good actor finds

---

[4] Of course, this means the emotional background of the character, not of the actor, and the discussion of emotion in acting, on pp. 130-137, should be kept constantly in mind.

a way to play every character from an appearance of vital emotion, and this gives color and life to every line he reads.

THE NECESSITY FOR BODY AND VOICE TRAINING

If the actor's body and voice are his tools, it follows that they should be as flexible and controlled as possible. He should be able to use them well. His body must be poised, his movements accurate. In other words, he must work to develop the most graceful and economical use of his body. In the same way, he must develop the most pleasing voice; and he must learn how to produce this with the least strain and effort. This does not mean, of course, that he will always, in every character, have a graceful body and a pleasing voice. But having learned to be graceful, he now knows how to make his body heavy and blundering, and his voice grating and nasal. And he will do these things when they are appropriate to the rôle, and when they make the playing of his character more effective. There is probably no awkwardness of body and no disagreeableness of voice that is not sometimes right in the theater; these qualities will be right when they reveal most clearly the character demanded. Acting skill demands the utmost flexibility and control of body and voice because these are the qualifications which enable an actor to assume many parts.

CHAPTER XII

Studying a Rôle

THE PURPOSE OF STUDYING A RÔLE

Studying a rôle is the process of getting ready to play it. It involves much more than merely learning the lines, and when to enter and exit, and how to move around in the set. These are only the elementary steps in the process, just as being able to play the right notes is the basic step in getting ready to perform a musical composition. A child, when he can do this, may think he is performing the piece; but a good musician knows better. He studies a composition that he is to perform by playing every note and every bar and every melody over and over again in the process of deciding just how it should be performed. His purpose is to create an *interpretation*, and only after he has done so does he feel competent to play it in a concert. In much the same way, the good actor knows that memorizing his lines and movement is only the beginning; he works to find the utmost value and meaning in every word he has to say and every action he has to perform.

Probably no two actors study a rôle in exactly the same manner. As in any other art, each artist develops his own method. Nevertheless, observation leads to the belief that most actors go through much the same process. In other words, there are certain definite steps in the process of studying a rôle, just as there are definite phases in the process of rehearsing a play. The two processes are closely related. However, in the rehearsal process, we are concerned with the manner in which the whole play is being shaped under the guidance of the director by all the actors together; in the process of studying a rôle, we are concerned with the thought processes of the individual actors.

In studying a rôle, the actor's process may be accidental and uncertain, or it may be carefully planned. His progress is likely to be greater to the degree that he develops a definite and intelligent process.

1. *The Function of the Character in the Play.* The actor's first step should be to decide the function of his character in the play. In the series of incidents that is the plot of the play, there will be certain characters whose fate is determined, or changed, by the events portrayed. The audience must want to know what happens to them and why it happens. These are the principal, or major, characters—*the characters whose story is being told in the play*. Therefore, an actor playing one of these major rôles—actors call them leads—is faced by the problem of making his character, his second self, as interesting as possible, so that what happens to him becomes important to the audience. (See the discussion of the "dramatic hero" on p. 88.) If Hamlet is a dull young man, we shall never be excited by what happens to him. If Romeo and Juliet are merely silly young lovers, we shall not be much interested in their fate. If Macbeth is only a stupid soldier, we shall be bored by the process by which he brings about his own ruin. Any play depends for its success primarily on the interest that can be established in the fate of the principal characters, and this depends upon how interesting and exciting the leading players can be. A lead, then, must study his character from all angles and from every possible point of view, in order to see how he can make his portrayal most exciting. Good leads in a production often make a poor script seem much better than it is because they bring, by virtue of their own stimulating personalities, interest and excitement where the author has supplied very little.

But the majority of the characters in most plays are *minor* characters, or what in the theater are called supporting players. Their purpose in the play is to affect, at some time and in some way, the fate of the major characters. Often these minor characters appear only briefly, and we do not know much about the complete story of their lives. We are interested in them only to the degree to which they affect the major characters. They are friends or acquaintances of the major characters—servants, messengers, soldiers, courtiers, and so on. They form the background against which the major characters live that part of their lives which is the plot of the play. But in any good play, these minor characters have a reason for being; and this reason lies in the way they influence the leading players.

The primary problem of a minor character, then, is to decide how he is to play his rôle so as to create the right kind of influence. For example, in *Hamlet*, we find three young courtiers, Horatio, Rosencrantz, and Guildenstern, who are friends of the major character, Hamlet. Any study of the script will make clear that Horatio is an upright and noble young man, a true friend. On the other hand, Rosencrantz and Guildenstern are false friends, ready to betray Hamlet at the slightest prospect of finding favor with Claudius, the treacherous king, Hamlet's enemy. Obviously, then, the actor playing Horatio must from the beginning make us like him; if he has any quality of slyness, any lack of open honesty, we are going to think that Hamlet is a fool to trust him as he does. But Rosencrantz and Guildenstern, who in the beginning of the play have friendly scenes with Hamlet, should even in these scenes make us distrust them. We must feel from the beginning that they are false friends, or else when Hamlet destroys them by a trick, as he does near the end of the play, we may dislike Hamlet for this deed. It is possible for the two actors playing Rosencrantz and Guildenstern, by playing frank and noble young men, to distort the plot and defeat the purpose of the author.

The same is true of almost any minor character in any play, and a skilled actor, studying a minor character from this point of view, never feels that his rôle is unimportant. His purpose is to give importance to his rôle by playing it so it will be most effective.[1] Often a good actor asks the director at the beginning of rehearsals, "What impression do you want me to make? Do you want the audience to like me?" A bad actor never asks such a question. The good actor is already beginning to think of the importance of the effect he hopes to create. He knows that somewhere in the play, perhaps many scenes later, he is going to give the heroine some advice; and he is already thinking that he can make the audience feel, by the kind of person he is, that the heroine should accept it or reject it. Most minor rôles have at least one important moment in a play, a big scene, a moment when they obviously influence a major character. The good actor knows how to play his entire part so that this moment has the greatest possible effectiveness.

But even if there is no such scene, the minor character has a reason for being—or the actor must give it one. If an actress plays a serving-maid with six lines to speak—even with one line, or none—her rôle is important. By being a certain kind of a maid she makes us like the heroine, but by being another kind she makes us dislike her. She helps create the atmosphere in which the heroine lives, and she can support her by helping create the proper atmosphere. She is efficient, kindly, intelligent, happily obedient to a sensible mistress; or she is slovenly, disgruntled, sly, and surly. In this way, because we judge the principal characters in the light of what the minor characters do and say, and *how* they do and say it, she gives her rôle its true value in the play.

Thus, by studying the script the actor decides what character he must create to best serve the play, and this character is the *idea* which is going to guide all the rest of his work. It

[1] P. S. He gets the jobs!

is the point of view from which he is going to make the many necessary decisions.

2. *The Physical Traits of the Character.* Having arrived at an *idea* for the character he is to portray, the actor must next turn to his tools—his body and his voice—and shape them so as to express the idea in the most effective manner. First, he shapes his body to represent the character he has in mind; he creates a basis for his pantomime.

Perhaps it ought to be said here that actors commonly say that there are two kinds of rôles, *straight* and *character*. A straight rôle is one much like the actor; it is a young man playing a young man, or a young woman playing a young woman. A character rôle is one in which the actor plays a part unlike himself; a young man plays an old man, or an American plays a Chinaman or an Eskimo. This is probably an unfortunate idea. A good actor rarely, if ever, plays straight, for that would mean that he is exactly right for the character, and this is rarely true. Even a young man playing a young man says to himself if he is a good actor, "How can I make the young man that I *am* into the young man that I *should be* to express the idea of this character?" He knows that he must change his walk, his manner of sitting down, his way of looking at objects and of picking them up, his bearing in meeting people, and so on.

In shaping himself to be the *right* young man, he is no longer straight; that is, he is no longer just himself. Perhaps he is naturally too vital and vigorous to be the tentative character demanded by the play; perhaps he must be much more alert and forthright. "What kind of a body," he says to himself, "must this young man have?" Suppose he is a coal-miner, or a farmer, or an automobile mechanic, or any character with a background of hard physical labor. Then, he may think, this character should have heavy slow-moving muscles; perhaps he is slightly stooped from long labor; perhaps his horny hands, from years of handling a pick, or a hoe, or a wrench, never completely close. In short, he is going to be different in many physical aspects from what he would be were the character an artist, or a lively student, or a society butterfly.

He may even wear his clothes differently, to make himself look taller or shorter, or stouter or slimmer. He may wear a loose, ill-fitting, unbuttoned coat with padded shoulders and big sleeves to give himself additional weight; he may add an inch or two to his height by wearing over-large shoes with many inner soles; he may make his head appear larger or smaller by the way in which he has his hair cut and combed. No natural feature is neglected in the process of making-over his second self.

If his character is young, he is going to decide what basic body action, such as erectness, springy vigor, directness of movement, will best portray this idea; if he is old, he is going to move more slowly because of general muscular weakness, and be slightly bent over, and transfer his weight more carefully from one foot to the other when he walks, and assume a weakness of shoulder muscle that allows the palms of his hands to turn slightly forward, and so on. By such a process of thought, the natural second self of the actor must be changed by the assumption of those physical traits which make the best basis for whatever character he has decided to portray.

3. *The Vocal Traits of the Character*. Next, the thoughtful actor thinks of the vocal traits most appropriate for the rôle he is to play. He is not as yet concerned with readings or meanings, or emotional backgrounds of lines, or shades of expression; he is concerned primarily with the *sort of voice* that best expresses his idea. Like Bottom, he can speak in a "monstrous little voice," or he can roar like a lion. The normal human voice has a wide range. The question to decide is what part of our range is most suitable for the character we are to portray. Probably most of us have many voices that we have never used.

I remember once hearing an actress who was playing Gina,

in Ibsen's *The Wild Duck,* to the acclaim of all critics, explain that for this part she had cut down her voice to four or five notes in her middle register. Gina is a hardworking drudge, the wife of a flashy and unreliable photographer; and for many years she has worked early and late to keep the household together. It goes without saying, of course, that the actress represented Gina with a slow and heavy body that portrayed her physical and mental exhaustion. But to this she added the narrow voice range of a woman dulled by years of discouraging toil. She did not allow her voice to become monotonous, for inside the limited range of voice that she had decided to use, she read with great variety. The point is that when she read a line up, she did not go to the top of her natural range, but to the top of Gina's range, and when she read a line down she stopped at Gina's bottom note, and not her own. Thus she created a variety in monotony—intelligent, dramatic, and exciting monotony, not mere dullness.

In the same way, for any character there is an appropriate range of voice. For some characters it may be high, and for some low. Sometimes the range is wide, and sometimes narrow. Inside of this pre-decided range there must be as much variety as possible. Of course, I am not advocating a "fake" voice, such as the falsetto used by so many bad actors in portraying old men, for instance. That implies a distortion of voice, and the actor's voice should never seem unnatural. Rather, within his own natural range he should, by study and experimentation, find that part that best suggests the character he plays. Perhaps, if you are playing a shrill-voiced southern belle, you decide to omit some of your lower tones, but you must not introduce a false shrillness; if you are playing a big-voiced business man, you use only the lower part of your natural speaking voice, but you do not produce a low indistinct rumble. The point is, perhaps, that the good actor, by developing the greatest possible variety in his natural range, is able to appear to have more than one natural voice. So he is able to adapt his voice, as well as his body, to a wide range of characters.

4. *The Details of Performance.* Having made these basic and preliminary decisions—the idea of the character, and the body and voice most appropriate for it—the actor is now ready to embroider his rôle with detail. This is going to be his concern during the greater part of the rehearsal periods. It is in his ability to vary these details that a good actor proves his skill, for he is able to give meaning to everything he does and says in the light of some thought-out idea. All of his decisions, such as how to make this gesture, or how to read this line, will be colored by his basic idea; therefore they will have a unity that will give distinctness to his rôle.

There are thousands of details to be considered in any rôle, even the shortest one, and many of them must be worked out by the actor playing the individual part. Even the most brilliant author finds it impossible to describe in detail every action he asks the actors to perform, or to annotate in detail the shades of meaning in the lines he wants the actors to read. If he tried to do so, his one-hundred page manuscript would expand to many volumes; and the very voluminousness of his script would defeat his purpose—nobody would be able to find the time to read it. In the same way, the director, no matter how skilful he is, cannot help each actor with every minute detail. If he did, the rehearsal of one short scene would be a process of months. The author describes his concept in general terms, and the director is concerned with the correctness and effectiveness of the interpretation as a whole; but the actor must create many of the details within this framework. The more the actor can contribute, the better the play is likely to be.

He asks himself many questions: "Where am I coming from on my entrance? Have I ever been in this place before? Do I like the people in the room, or do I hate them? What has happened to me since the audience saw me last? How has my relationship to the other characters in the play changed? How do my relationships change in this scene? What is the effect of that remark upon me? How can I show my mood at this moment?"—and so on. A good actor may ask himself hundreds of such questions in the process of studying a rôle; and his skill as an actor depends, to a large extent, upon his ability to find the right answers. Then he must be able, with his body and voice, to show the audience the answers he has found.

THE RESULT OF STUDYING A RÔLE

An intelligent actor who has this idea of studying his rôle finds rehearsing an exciting process. He must avoid the error of making decisions too early, and he must be willing to change his ideas when change is demanded. But he is able to bring comment and illumination to the parts he gets an opportunity to play. He knows that acting is not a series of accidental reactions. He agrees with Gordon Craig: "Accident is an enemy of the artist. Art arrives only by design." He sees the importance of his part, no matter how brief it is, in the total design that is the play. This vision makes him an actor-artist.

CHAPTER XIII

The Performance

THE ATMOSPHERE OF A PERFORMANCE

The process of rehearsing, which for days or weeks has consumed the energy of the director and the actors, must at length lead into a performance. This can be an eagerly-awaited event, or a dreaded one. Perhaps, in most cases, it will be an exciting combination of both. In any case, the performance is likely to be most pleasant if it is not complicated by a hysterical atmosphere backstage!

One of the devices used in the professional theater to avoid this, is to allow no backstage visitors. Friends and relatives must curb their excitement until after the performance. Perhaps, therefore, it's a good idea to post a large sign, saying:

POSITIVELY NO VISITORS
UNTIL AFTER FINAL CURTAIN!
THIS MEANS YOU!

A second device is to promote relaxation among the actors by having some definite place in which to await their entrances. They should not be allowed to stand around behind the scenes and with misguided zeal help the stage crew shift the scenery, or give a hand with properties. A smooth performance demands that every person backstage, both actors and crew, do his own job, and his own job *only*. Traditionally the place where actors wait for their appearances is called the greenroom —nobody knows why it is so called. Many modern theaters are built without a greenroom, and actors then wait in their dressing rooms. For non-professional groups the idea of a greenroom is a good one; it is even beginning to come back in the professional theater. If no room is available, some definite corner, or hall, or staircase, may be the station of the actors who are waiting for their cues.

Finally, it is wise to discourage "temperament!" There is no place for it backstage during a performance. It is unfortunate that in some schools, acting is considered an emotional orgy; and actors are rather encouraged to show temperament by fainting, either before or after a performance. In the real theater, everyone is too busy and too concentrated on his job to have time to faint. In performance, a good actor is calm and collected. If he forgets a line, or makes a mistake, he does not let it throw him. All phases of theater work demand self-control, especially the performance.

NUMBER OF PERFORMANCES

Each performance in a series should be smoother and better than the preceding one. Even in the professional theater, the first is likely to be different from the following ones—sometimes it is better and sometimes it is worse! This is caused by the excitement of discovering what kind of an impact the play is going to make on the audience. A quality of nervousness arises from this uncertainty. But in the professional theater, playing soon becomes routine; and the repetition of the play before an audience gives the actor steadiness and skill in playing his part. It is desirable, therefore, from the point of view of the non-professional actor that the play have as many performances as possible. Playing gets to be fun, and it should be the reward for many weeks of effort.

It is unfortunate that in many educational situations, weeks of rehearsal so often lead to but a single performance. The quality of the dramatic work in a school will improve more rapidly if there are several performances, for they allow the actor to develop skill. Even though the total audience is limited, it is a more educational experience to play for several small audiences than the single large one.

THE STATION OF THE DIRECTOR

In the professional theater, the duties of the director—and his pay!—stop with the rise of the curtain on opening night. He does not have to be backstage. The performance is controlled by the stage-manager. This is the ideal for the director in a school or non-professional group; and by a well-conducted series of dress rehearsals, he can usually attain it. Only by seeing the performance from the front can he form an intelligent opinion of audience reactions, and so help the actors to improve their playing on succeeding nights.

It is unfortunate that there are some directors, especially in educational situations, who never see the play they direct except through holes in the set. If the director is out front, he can take notes, just as he did in run-throughs, and work them into subsequent performances. Even if there are none, he learns much about his directing and the skill of the actors from seeing the play. So, he becomes a better director.

He need not be completely cut off from the performance. Perhaps he can sit in a definite place in the rear of the auditorium so that he can be reached in an emergency, should any arise. Probably he will come backstage in intermissions, to report on progress. He is the only one who should be allowed to do so—no other visitors!

If the actors are very young, or if there is a need for chaperonage, or if the principal insists on having one or more adults at hand, perhaps the director can persuade some colleague to be his substitute. In any case, the performance should be so organized that it does not depend on his presence. There should be no necessity for him to push the actors on and off, pull the curtains, handle the properties, shift the scenes, and prompt the lines. As suggested in the preceding chapters, a good director develops an efficient organization to run the performance.

THE STAGE-MANAGER IN PERFORMANCE

In the discussion of the rehearsal process, the stage-manager has been mentioned many times. Now, in the performance, he shows his true mettle. Smoothness of performance depends to a large degree on his skill and level-headedness. His duties are to check up on the actors, to supervise the stage crews, to give all the signals, and to prompt. In the professional theater he gets the blame for everything that goes wrong, and very little of the credit when everything goes right!

1. *Checking in the Actors.* His first task is to see that all the actors are present and ready for the curtain on time. This he does by checking a list as the actors appear and then by calling time. He may begin with the half-hour which means that he will tap on each dressing room door and call, "Half-hour, please!" Now all the actors know they have a half-hour to curtain. He may, if he is especially conscientious—or if he has a company of slow actors!—call quarter-hour and five minutes. In any case, a few minutes before he intends to take his curtain up, he calls "Places, please!" If the show is a musical, he may call "overture!" This means that actors who are on stage at the rise of the curtain, get there; those who make early entrances go to their positions; those who enter later may stay in their dressing rooms or go to the greenroom, but they should be ready. He must know where they are because as their entrances approach, he will need to send an assistant— in the old theater this would be a call-boy—to warn them. At this point, a careful stage-manager takes a hurried look at the actors to see that each one has his costume on right, that he hasn't made any improvements on it, that he hasn't forgotten that stick or handbag or fan, etc. It is his task to see that the actors follow the directions that have been given them, and he

is the one who is blamed if an actor enters the first act in his second-act costume!

2. *Supervising the Crew.* After the actors are in their places, the careful stage-manager takes a last quick look around the set. The chief carpenter is responsible for seeing that it's right, that all the furniture is in the correct place, that the doors work, etc., etc. But the stage-manager is responsible for seeing that the chief carpenter *is* responsible! If someone has forgotten to turn the button on the back of a door, so that the actor who walks up to it grandly for his exit has to bang it and shake it and then climb out a window, it's the stage-manager's fault! So he usually sees that everything that is supposed to be practical really works. If a window has to be opened, he tries it; if a lamp has to be turned on, he tests it; if a victrola has to play, he makes sure it will play! Now he is ready to start.

3. *Giving signals.* The actors and the stage both ready, the stage-manager rings up. First, he must signal the electrician, who arranges the lights for the opening and signals back that all is ready; and then he signals curtain. Throughout the rest of the play, he will probably have to give a succession of signals: for sounds and offstage effects, for light changes, for the fall and rise of the act curtains, etc. He must, therefore, have a clear method of giving signals. Signals can be clear only when they are in two parts, one for warning and one for go. These he has written in his script. In giving hand signals, which is possible only when he can see the other workers and they can see him, the warning should be a waving of his hand above shoulder level for a few seconds. The "go" will be indicated by swinging his hand sharply down, not just a few inches, but several feet. If he gives signals by pushing a button and thus lighting a small bulb, he should light it for the warning, and put it out for the go. Whatever kind of signals are to be used, they must be carefully worked out so as to be as clear as possible.

4. *Prompting.* In addition to all these duties, the stage-

manager now must prompt the play. Some non-professional groups pride themselves on having no prompter. If the actors forget lines or make a mistake, they must get themselves out of it. Their argument for this practice is that it leads to more conscientious memorization. Maybe so! In the professional theater, there is always a prompter; even after a year's run, there is always a possibility that something will happen. The skilful stage-manager, no matter how many other duties he has to perform, never takes his eyes off his prompt script. He reads the lines to himself while the actors read on stage. Then if he must prompt, he does not have to find his place. He follows his script conscientiously at every performance, although by this time he may have memorized the play better than any of the actors. It is always at the moment that he relaxes, or stops to talk to somebody, or concentrates on something else, that the prompt is needed. If he has to prompt, he prompts quickly and loudly enough to be heard by the actor. He gives the next few words, and this is usually enough. A quick-witted stage-manager, who knows his business and who knows the script, by a judicial skipping of a line or two, or by bringing the actors back to the text at the right place, may often save the play in case of slips—which should never occur, but sometimes do.

5. *The Time Sheet.* Even after the end of the performance, the stage-manager is not through. He is usually required to make a time sheet. This is an accurate record of the time at which the curtain rose, the playing time of each scene or act, and the length of the intermissions. Thus the producer is able to see whether or not the performance starts on time, if the playing time of scenes varies from night to night, if the intermissions are held to the right length, etc. Usually the variations are slight and can be easily accounted for. If, however, one scene begins to grow longer and longer, the producer knows that it is not being played as rehearsed; and he can do something about it.

The duties of the stage-manager are so many, so varied, and so important, that he may well have several assistants. One of them may act as prompter, and one give the signals, and one watch the time and do the calling, whereas the stage-manager himself oversees everything. The experienced stage-manager saves himself much labor by putting as many as possible of his communications in writing, thus avoiding the misunderstandings that arise when vocal orders are given. The traditional method is to post everything on the call-board, which all trained theater workers consult both on their way into the theater and on their way out of it. A call-board is a useful and time-saving device in a non-professional theater. If the stage-manager wishes to communicate with two or three actors, he heads his notice with their names. If he wishes to be sure one of his assistants gets certain instructions, he places the assistant's name at the top. If he wishes everybody to read it, he marks it "Company Notice"—to tell the truth, everybody usually reads all the notices!

One of the stage-manager's final duties, not previously mentioned, and especially important in the non-professional theater, is to supervise the cleaning up after the performances have run their course. He should see that scenery is replaced in the dock, that borrowed and rented properties are returned to their owners, that other properties are put back in storage, etc., etc. The duties of the stage-manager are not over until everything has been cleaned up and all is ready for the start of a new play—with perhaps, another stage-manager!

THE AFTERMATH OF PERFORMANCES

In educational dramatics, the wise director probably concerns himself with the post-performance effects on the participants. He tries to see that the students involved in it do not have the false idea that it was the most perfect performance possible, nor does he allow them to be unduly discouraged by believing that it was worse than it was. All performances might, then, be followed by a discussion with the actors and the crews. Those who did well should not be allowed to think that they were perfect; there was probably room for improvement even in the best elements of the performance. And the poorest performers had some good points which might well be indicated. The director should create a situation in which his actors and other workers will develop neither egotism nor frustration. And the result of the discussion ought to be to lead to a determination to do more and better plays!

PART III

Stagecraft and Design

CHAPTER XIV

The Physical Theater

In the modern world, *theater* is a word often applied to the total institution that has been built up for the giving of plays. This would include building, actors, authors, managers, technicians, designers, costumers, scene-painters—in short, the sum total of equipment and personnel necessary for the continuous production of plays. However, the word is also used in a more limited sense to mean a building designed for the presenting of plays. This was the original meaning of the word *theater*, for it is derived from an old Greek word meaning "to see" or "to view": hence, a place for the display of a spectacle.

The modern theater is a building having two main parts: (1) an auditorium [1] for the accommodation of an audience, and (2) a stage on which the play may be performed. Perhaps it is even true to say that a modern theater building is *two adjacent buildings,* one to hold an audience and one to hold a play, joined by an opening through which the audience can see and hear the play. This opening is called the proscenium opening, the wall separating the two buildings and containing the opening is the proscenium wall, and the arch surrounding the opening, the proscenium arch. The proscenium opening is filled

---

[1] As the Greeks apparently didn't have a word for it, we use the Latin word auditorium for that part of the theater assigned to the spectators. This is derived from a word meaning "to hear." Thus the spectators, who came to *see*, became the audience, who come to *hear*. Probably it's best when they can do both.

by a curtain which may be drawn up or pulled aside during the performances. The word, *proscenium*, is also Greek in origin, and means literally "in front of the tent," as the earliest Greek theaters were sloping hillsides, for the convenience of an audience, with a tent pitched at the bottom of the hill in which the actors could change their costumes and masks. The playing-space was then the proscenium, or space in front of the tent.

This fact suggests that early forms of the theater building were very different from modern ones. Even in its most highly developed form, the Greek theater was an open-air auditorium, roughly semi-circular in shape, with rising tiers of stone seats surrounding a circular playing-space called the orchestra, or dancing place. The tent became the façade of a narrow building, pierced with doors through which the main actors entered and left. Roman theaters were modifications of the Greek, but the Romans allowed prominent persons to sit in the orchestra, thus originating orchestra seats. The earliest English theater, probably built in 1576, consisted of three balconies surrounding a courtyard open to the sky, with a large platform projecting into the yard. Our modern theaters grow out of Renaissance Italian ballrooms, where a platform was often erected at one end of the room to serve as the playing-space. The important fact to be noted is that the kind of building that is thought of as a theater in the modern world is recent in origin, and it is entirely possible that it may undergo many further modifications. Great changes have already been made recently in moving-picture theaters to make them more suitable for their purpose. Nevertheless, most modern plays are written to be produced in a modern theater, which means a theater having a proscenium opening and a curtain, not being merely a platform. Therefore, it is desirable to understand the nature of a building of this sort.

The ideal theater would be one having the most adequate auditorium, for the accommodation of the audience, and the most practical stage, for the presentation of the play. This leads to the necessity of trying to determine what makes an auditorium adequate, and a stage practical.

TESTS FOR AN ADEQUATE AUDITORIUM

An auditorium will be successful to the degree to which it allows the audience to hear and see the play and to the degree that it is comfortable and pleasing. We may then judge any auditorium for these four particulars:

1. *Acoustical Properties.* A good auditorium is so constructed that sounds made upon the stage can easily be heard in all parts of the auditorium. This depends on the length of time the sound continues in the room, or upon what architects call the period of reverberation. It can be tested by making a sharp sound, like a pistol shot or a blow of a slapstick, and counting with a stop-watch the number of seconds the sound can be heard. Usually, people who talk about bad acoustics mean that the period of reverberation is too long. This is likely to be the case when there are large blank spaces on opposite walls, or where the ceiling and floor are completely parallel. These spaces reflect the sound waves and prolong them so that they overlap and cut into each other, thus creating continuous indistinct speech. However, bad acoustics may also result if the period of reverberation is too short, since in this case the sound has insufficient reflection and dies too quickly to be heard. In a good auditorium it is necessary to avoid either extreme. Most authorities agree that an ideal period of reverberation is 1¼ to 1½ seconds.

2. *Sight Lines.* The sight lines of an auditorium are the lines of vision, and they may be represented on the floor-plan of a theater by two lines from each seat, one drawn to each side of the proscenium opening. The worst sight lines are always those from the front corner seats, that is, those in the front row at the extreme right and left; so it is from these seats that we must make the test. A spectator nearer the center, or

farther back in the auditorium, will have better sight lines. In the perfect theater, the sight lines from each and every seat would cover the playing space. Every person in the audience should be able to see all of the action of the play, regardless of the part of the stage in which it is taking place.

3. *Hygienic Conditions.* In hygienic conditions, we may include all those elements which make for the physical well-being of the audience. Heating and ventilating is one important aspect of this problem. Often it may be necessary to have all

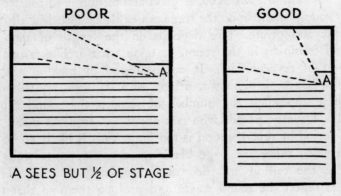

POOR   GOOD

A SEES BUT ½ OF STAGE

FIG. 18. SIGHT LINES

the windows closed—for, of course, it should be possible to darken a good auditorium for performances in the daytime— so that there is a greater need for successful ventilation here than in other rooms. An audience gives out a large amount of physical heat, and even though the auditorium is reasonably cool at the beginning of a play, unless it is properly ventilated, it is likely to be uncomfortably warm by the end of the evening. On the other hand, too much ventilation may dissipate the necessary heat and be very uneconomical. How to keep a proper balance between heat and fresh, cool air is a constant theater problem; for no audience can enjoy a play if it is freezing or being stifled—or both alternately. The nature of the theater seat is another problem. It should be as comfortable as possible, and yet it must not take up too much room. An audience which is in the process of being crippled and distorted by the theater seats will probably not really enjoy any play. A final problem is the arrangement of the lobby, lounges, toilets, and other rooms that must be provided for the use of the audience. Such rooms should be large enough to handle the audience comfortably, near enough to be easily accessible, and yet so arranged that noise in them will not be audible in the auditorium. This element of theater practice—the art of making an audience as comfortable as possible—comes within the province of the house manager and will be discussed further in Chapter XXVIII.

4. *Aesthetic Qualities*. Finally, it is desirable that an auditorium be a pleasing sort of room, the kind in which an audience will be in a frame of mind to enjoy a play. This will depend on its structural qualities and on how it is painted and decorated. As has been previously stated, old theaters often were modeled on Italian Renaissance ballrooms, and they were often —for modern taste—over-decorated and over-elaborate. Most modern theaters are built more simply and finished with subdued and harmonious colors. Modern theory is that the proscenium opening, through which the audience hears and sees the play, should be as inconspicuous as possible, instead of being ornate and gaudy and exciting. The proscenium curtain is part of the design and should be so considered. Of course, the lighting should be soft and pleasant, and yet sufficient so that it is possible to read programs without eyestrain. In short, the ideal for an auditorium is the same as that for any other charming room, for in the last analysis that is all an auditorium should be.

Thus it might be possible to test the quality of any auditorium by answering the following questions: (1) Are its acoustical properties such that actors can easily be heard in every part of the house? (2) Are its sight lines such that the audience can see all the action? (3) Are the hygienic conditions proper? (4) Does it make a pleasing aesthetic appeal?

TESTS FOR A PRACTICAL STAGE

A stage is practical to the degree that a play can be presented on it with ease and efficiency. The first problem is usually one of size. The stage is the space back of the proscenium wall, and it can hardly be too big. It is necessary, however, to make a distinction between what is commonly called onstage and offstage. Onstage is the space immediately behind the proscenium opening—that space in which the actors become visible. Offstage is all the rest of the space back of the proscenium wall which separates the stage from the auditorium. This is the space that should be as large as possible. The onstage space is defined by the width of the proscenium opening, and this is one of the most important dimensions in a theater building because the sight lines will depend on the relationship between the width of the proscenium opening and the width of the auditorium (See Fig. 18).

1. *The Size of the Proscenium Opening.* There is, in the theater, only one unchangeable dimension, and that is the size of the actor. The size of the proscenium opening, then, must be considered in light of the size of a human being. Probably the minimum practical opening is fifteen feet in width and eight feet in height. In a space narrower than fifteen feet, three or four persons side by side look cramped and crowded. In a height less than eight feet, the gestures of the actors go up out of sight. This minimum proscenium opening is practical only for plays containing a few characters. The maximum width is probably forty-five feet, and the maximum height twenty or twenty-five feet. In a bigger opening, actors look dwarfed. Professional stages rarely have openings larger than this. One authority [2] suggests that the professional minimum is twenty-four

[2] Irving Pichel, *Modern Theaters* (New York, Harcourt, Brace and Co. 1925), p. 30.

by twelve. I have found thirty by fifteen to be an excellent size, and unless the auditorium is exceptionally large, or unless the production of huge musicals and spectacles is planned, those dimensions will be found satisfactory.

2. *Necessity for Movable Teaser and Tormentor.* Whatever the size of the proscenium opening, but especially when it is unusually large, it should be possible to cut down its size with a teaser and tormentors. A teaser is a curtain hanging over the opening; and tormentors are upright pieces, usually frames covered with canvas or other material, one of which stands on each side of the opening, a few inches, or sometimes on a large stage several feet, in back of the proscenium wall (Fig. 19). The curtain, whether it pulls up out of sight or opens on a track, works in the space between the tormentors and the proscenium wall. The front teaser which, with the curtain fills the proscenium opening, is often called the "Grand Drape." The teaser should never be fastened in a permanent way to the top of the arch, but should be rigged, like any other drop (see p. 178) so that it can be raised and lowered, for often it is desirable to cut down the maximum height of the opening. When a small interior set is used, such as a cabin, a kitchen, or a room in a poor home, it is often effective to use an opening not more than nine or ten feet in height. In the same way, the tormentors may be moved in to decrease the width of the opening. One of the first and most important of all principles in regard to stage equipment is that everything should be as flexible as possible. The dimension of the proscenium opening in any given stage is a maximum, that of the built arch; and in the professional theater this maximum is rarely used.

3. *Backstage Space.* As there can hardly be too much room backstage, the problem is largely one of determining the minimum limits. Every theater man wants as much room backstage as possible—unless he happens to be paying for it! The depth of the stage depends on the width of the opening. The stage should have the proportions of a generously-large room, and

eighteen or twenty feet is a normal depth for a twenty-five to thirty-foot opening. A good rule is that the minimum depth should be at least two-thirds of the width of the proscenium opening. On each side of the arch there should be space for the storage of properties and scenery. Six feet is probably a minimum, and this is what has been shown in Figure 19. It has been argued that the spaces to the right and left of the proscenium arch should at least equal the center space within

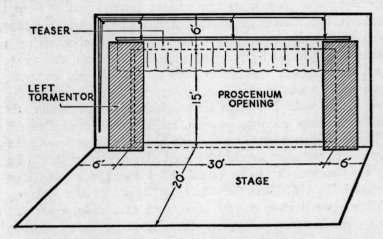

FIG. 19. A STAGE WITH MINIMUM OFF-STAGE SPACE

the arch, but perhaps this is the counsel of perfection. For practical purposes, twelve or fifteen feet is sufficient, and that is all there is in many professional theaters. This space should, of course, be cleared space, and not cut into rooms by unnecessary partitions. This backstage space need not be symmetrical. If it is more convenient, the greater part of it may be on one side. This side with the largest space is called the *working side,* and here may be stored the extra scenery, properties, etc. However, the wall on the short side should be at least six feet from the edge of the proscenium arch, and ten or twelve feet would be better.

4. *Overhead Space.* The one dimension that remains to be considered is the height of the stage from floor to ceiling. In the modern theater, much scenery is flied, that is, hauled up into the space over the stage above the line of vision of the spectators. This implies that there be as much space above the top of the proscenium arch as there is below, plus whatever space is needed so that scenery hung in the flies will really be above the line of vision (Fig. 20). Most recent theaters have twice as much space above the top of the arch as there is

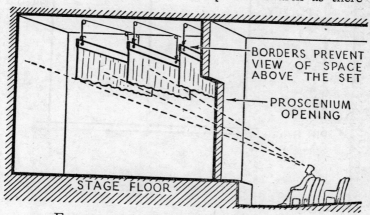

BORDERS PREVENT VIEW OF SPACE ABOVE THE SET

PROSCENIUM OPENING

STAGE FLOOR

FIG. 20. SIGHT LINES FOR OVERHEAD SPACE

below it, which means that the distance from the floor to the roof is three times the height of the proscenium opening. This is perhaps desirable, but it is not absolutely necessary. However, some overhead space is essential. Perhaps six feet is the absolute minimum, and ten or twelve feet will be much better. If there be as much space above the top of the arch as there is below, or even a little more, the theater will be a nearer approach to the ideal.

5. *Rigging.* The purpose of this overhead space is to provide room for the rigging—the arrangement of pulleys and ropes that allows scenery to be flied. Most modern theaters are equipped with a *gridiron,* which is a strong steel grating

fastened six feet or so from the ceiling at the top of the over-head space. Men may walk around on top of the gridiron, and blocks and pulleys may be fastened to any part of it. Three (or more) pulleys fastened to the grid at equal distance from each other, and in a line parallel to the proscenium wall, make

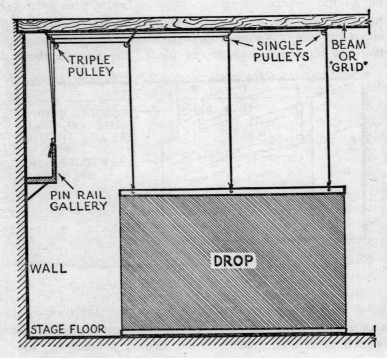

FIG. 21. A DROP ON A SET OF LINES

This diagram shows under-slung pulleys, but in normal professional practice the pulleys would be on top of the gridiron.

it possible to support a drop of any length. The ropes that go from the top of the drop—or whatever scenery is being moved —should all be turned in the same direction, run through a multiple pulley, and down toward the floor to some place where they can be tied-off (see Fig. 21). A set of pulleys and ropes so arranged that they hold a drop is called a *set of lines*. The ropes are stout manila, never less than one-half inch, and larger if the grid is high or the load unusually heavy. It may even be desirable to use wire cable. If the pulleys rest on the top of the grid, it is impossible for them to tear loose. Some theaters have more than three lines to a set, the extra lines being for the purpose of helping to distribute the weight and making it easier to keep the drop level. In a three-line set, the lines, for obvious reasons, are often called "short," "center," and "long." The more sets of lines the theater has, the easier it is to handle drops, lights, and other units of scenery that are to be suspended. A good professional theater may have from forty to seventy-five sets of lines. The lines are handled from a *pinrail*, a stout railing containing *belaying pins* around which the ropes may be tied off. The entire system is similar to that by which sails are handled on a ship, and from which, indeed, it is been developed. In some theaters the pinrail is on a raised gallery, built out from one of the side walls of the stage (Fig. 21). This has the advantage of keeping the stage floor clear of ropes and leaving the side walls free for the stacking of scenery under the gallery. In smaller theaters, the pinrail is usually built against one wall (Fig. 22). The illustration (Fig. 22) shows the lines tied-off, with a half-hitch, directly on top of the pin. However, in order to make the tie-off safe, and so that the lines can be snubbed under the pin when the load is lowered, it is necessary to put the lines under and over the pin once before tying the half-hitch. The newest theaters have elaborate counterweight systems, or even motors to move the lines, so that one man can move and control the heaviest pieces. Where the older manual system is used, it is always possible to counterweight heavy units by tying sandbags to a set of lines, so that the sheer lift need never be excessive. One of the tests of the practicality of the stage will be, then, the amount and quality of the overhead rigging.

6. *Stage Walls and Floor*. Another test will be the construc-

tion of the walls and floor. As the walls of the theater will always be masked from the sight of the audience during the play, it is not necessary that they be finished with elaborate paneling, wainscoting, and architectural details. They are more useful if left plain and workmanlike, for scenery and all sorts of properties must be piled against them. So that they will have the utmost usefulness for this purpose, they should be pierced by as few openings as possible. The doors should be placed so that they leave the maximum of stacking-space. Windows are unnecessary if there is any other means of ventilation, and they are likely to be a nuisance in that they let in light and noise. The one wall that is useful if finished in the right way is the back wall. If this back wall is free of openings and can be roughly plastered and properly painted, it makes a beautiful and useful sky (see p. 278). It is convenient to have one large door giving access to the street, so that scenery, properties, lumber, and all the other necessary material can be moved into the theater with a minimum of effort. The nearer trucks can drive to this door the shorter is the necessary carry.

Like the walls, the floor is part of the machine; and in a professional theater it is always built of soft wood. A hardwood floor is a tremendous nuisance, since stage pegs and nails cannot be driven into it easily. In most modern professional theaters much of the stage is *trapped,* that is, it really consists of a series of sections each resting on a frame of heavy beams. Thus, it is possible at almost any place in the stage floor to make an opening into the cellar. These openings are not only useful in that they allow stairs from the cellar to provide for the entrance of actors, and make the scene an upper story in a house, but also they allow scenery and properties to be dropped into the cellar for storage. A basement, or a cellar under the stage, serves many useful purposes.

As the floor of a stage often becomes rough and uneven, it is common during performances to cover it with a floor cloth, or ground cloth. Usually this is made of heavy brown duck, as cotton wears better than linen. It should extend off-stage a few feet at each side, and be finished at the edges with webbing through which it can be tacked down with carpet tacks. It can easily be pulled up and the tacks removed from the webbing, so that it can be folded and stored until wanted again. Duck is sometimes made with one brown side and one dark green side, and a reversible floor cloth made of this material is useful for both interiors and exteriors.

If the stage in a school is used as a chapel, for assembly programs, debates or concerts, the unsightly floor and walls, which make the stage suitable for play production, may be covered by a floor cloth and rugs, a cyclorama of handsome draperies (see Chapter XVII), or even by an appropriate stage setting made especially for these purposes.

7. *Accessory Rooms.* Aside from the stage itself, the number and size of the adjacent rooms is one of the tests of its usefulness. Some provision is necessary for dressing-rooms to be used by the actors. In modern theater buildings, the attempt is made to isolate these rooms and not to have them open directly on the stage floor or on galleries above the stage, as was once the common practice. The rooms should be so arranged that the slamming of doors, the sound of voices, and the chance of the inopportune opening of a dressing-room door letting a beam of light onto the stage, is reduced to a minimum. A dressing-room will be most useful if it has a long shelf or narrow table along one wall about thirty inches from the floor. It is convenient to have a drawer under the shelf to contain make-up, and there should be a closet or wardrobe in which costumes may be hung. Above the shelf there should be a good mirror with lights placed at each side, so that they will illuminate the face of the actor as he makes up. A *greenroom,* or a lounging room for actors awaiting calls or entrances, is another useful accessory (see p. 159). Finally, there should be as many workrooms as possible. The ideal number of workrooms in a theater is probably two for each department, one

a combination shop and office, and the other a storage room. As there are at least four separate departments—scenery, properties, electrical, and costume—there would be eight required rooms. Some of these would need to be much larger than the others; for instance, scenery requires much more storage space than lighting equipment, or properties. Many of the older theaters, especially those presenting repertory, had a *scene dock*—that is, a storeroom for scenery, just offstage. Probably few theaters will be supplied with all these desirable rooms, but one of the tests of the stage will be the number, size, and location of these working spaces.

TESTS FOR A THEATER

In view of the above discussion, it is possible to examine any theater and to determine its probable usefulness for the giving of plays. Any group having a theater at its disposal might well find it a profitable undertaking to make a survey of it. This survey may be conducted in terms of the following questions:

A. Auditorium.
1. Are the acoustics satisfactory? What is the period of reverberation?
2. Are the sight lines correct? From what proportion of the seats are they perfect? Are there seats from which the sight lines are hopelessly bad?
3. Are the hygienic conditions satisfactory in regard to ventilation? heating? toilet facilities? Is the auditorium accessible from the street? Can it be darkened for afternoon performances?
4. Does the room make a pleasing aesthetic appeal?

B. Stage.
1. Is the proscenium opening at least fifteen feet wide and eight feet high, yet not so large as to dwarf actors?
2. Is there a movable teaser and tormentor, so that the opening can be decreased in size?
3. Is the backstage space at least six feet wider at each side than the proscenium opening? Is the depth at least two-

thirds of the width of the arch? Is the backstage space as large as possible, or can it be increased by removing unnecessary partitions?

4. How much overhead space is there?

5. Is there some sort of grid, with pulleys and lines so that scenery can be handled from overhead? Is the rigging scheme as flexible as possible?

6. Are there spaces against the walls, and are the walls properly unfinished, so that materials can be stacked against them? Are the doors and openings arranged to give maximum space? Is the back wall a plaster sky? Is the floor of soft wood? Is it trapped?

7. Are there dressing-rooms so located that they will not be inconvenient in regard to noise, letting out light, etc.? Are they equipped with make-up tables? mirrors? lights? closets or wardrobes? running water? Is there any space that can be used as a *green room*? Are there any back-stage rooms that can be used for workshops and storage rooms?

Probably few groups will have a theater satisfactory in every particular, but to the degree that it meets these specifications, it is likely to prove completely satisfactory.

IMPROVING A THEATER

It is an interesting and valuable project for a school, or college, or Little Theater group, to improve the facilities of the theater in which it works. This may be a long-term project, preceded by a survey and followed by a plan. Probably the most obvious defects should be corrected first, and others can wait until money is available and the time is ripe.

1. *Improving the Auditorium*. The acoustical properties of an auditorium can often be improved by simple devices. Where expert advice cannot be secured, experimentation may be resorted to. If the period of reverberation is too long, curtains may be hung on the blank walls that cause the echo, or the ceiling may be covered with some material that will deaden the reflection. There are many suitable materials on the mar-

ket, such as special plasters and wall boards. Hair felt is excellent for this purpose, and it may be covered with some suitable cloth. People are one of the most absorbent of materials, which explains why some halls in which there is a very bad echo when they are empty, have comparatively good acoustics when they are crowded. This is likely to be especially true if the floor is a hard surface, like wood or concrete. So perhaps the best way to improve the acoustics is to pack the hall with an audience! Covering the floor with a carpet often brings about a noticeable improvement also. In theaters where the acoustics are bad, the actors must pay greater attention to their enunciation and to the manner in which they use their voices to make this defect less serious.

Bad sight lines can sometimes be improved by widening the proscenium opening and by rearranging the seating. Sometimes it may be necessary to take out a few of the worst ones, those in the front corners—or at least, not to sell them in performances. Careful direction of the play may also help to overcome the defect of bad sight lines. The action can usually be brought forward and to the center of the stage, so that it will be visible from all parts of the house. A clever designer can help by making scenery that will aid in bringing the action into general vision. The aesthetic appeal can often be improved by repainting and redecorating. Carpeting, wall hangings, new light fixtures, and many other such changes may be desirable. Care and foresight will do much to improve the hygienic conditions. Perhaps there are rooms available, which although not originally intended to be lounges and comfort rooms, can be rebuilt for such use. A small and inconvenient lobby may be improved by changing the location of the box office and by the proper handling, on the part of the house-manager and ushers, of audience traffic. No progressive group should be satisfied until they have done everything in their power to make their auditorium as comfortable as possible.

2. *Improving the Stage.* The stage may be a more difficult problem, but real improvements can often be made very easily. Perhaps the size of the proscenium arch can be changed to make it more suitable. The curtain can often be re-rigged so that it will work more easily and more quietly. A teaser and tormentors can be provided. Sometimes the backstage space can be made more useful by taking down unnecessary partitions. Unnecessary doors and windows may be filled in, so as to give more clear wall space. The switchboard can be re-located, and perhaps a platform, or perch, built for it to get it off the floor. Openings in the back wall can be filled in, so that it can be plastered and painted; and perhaps traps can be built into the floor. Convenient rooms can be rearranged to make them more useful as dressing rooms, as a greenroom, or as work and storage rooms. Above all, the rigging can often be improved.

Few non-professional groups will probably have a complete grid and the elaborate rigging that is found in most modern theaters. But even the smallest theater should have something that serves for a grid, though it be only a heavy beam or two solidly fastened to the ceiling. This will allow stage ceilings, overhead lights, drops and borders, and many other essential scenic elements to be suspended. If necessary a framework of wood or piping can be supported from the floor of the stage. Even though there is not sufficient overhead room so that drops can be hauled up out of sight, the overhead rigging will be useful. Drops can be tripped (see p. 321), or they can be lowered and rolled, and then pulled up against the ceiling. Often a rudimentary and useful grid can be made by leaving the beams in the actual stage roof exposed, or, if they are not in themselves suitable, by fastening small I-beams at right angles to the proscenium arch, as shown in Fig. 22. Three or four sets of lines and pulleys so arranged will often be sufficient in a small theater. The pulleys may be moved forward and backward on the I-beams, and fastened at different times at whatever spot they will be most useful.[3] Thus, they will serve the purpose of many fixed sets of lines. In rigging, as in all other elements, flexibility will allow units to be used again and again in different places and in different ways. Underslung pulleys of this sort must be carefully fastened; and the lips, bolts, and nuts by which they are attached to the beam should be of the best tested steel. But if they are good quality, carefully used, there is little danger of their failing to hold

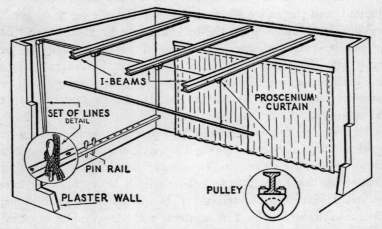

FIG. 22. I-BEAMS SET IN THE STAGE CEILING TO SUPPORT PULLEYS

any weight to which they are likely to be subjected in the course of ordinary play production. All overhead rigging, including ropes, must be frequently inspected to see that no weaknesses develop from wear.

ADVANTAGE OF IMPROVING THE THEATER

True play production demands the best equipment that can be devised, just as a good violin is most desirable in attempting to play violin music. It is true that a good violinist may be able

[3] Such pulleys may be secured from J. R. Clancy, Inc., Syracuse, N. Y. Catalogue sent on request.

to produce recognizable sounds with a string strung on a cigar box. However, this is the practice of ingenuity, and hardly the practice of the art of music. Sometimes non-professional play-production groups seem quite proud of their insignificant equipment and glory in telling what they have done with meager means. Much more praiseworthy would be an attempt to build up a better equipment. There is little danger of true ingenuity being stifled by adequate equipment. Quite the reverse is true; adequate equipment frees ingenuity to study the plays presented so that they may be given in the best possible way and with the utmost beauty and effectiveness—and this is the only true end of dramatic art.

CHAPTER XV

Building a Theater

If a non-professional group has no available theater of the sort described in the previous chapter, often it is possible to find, in the school or in the community, some large room in which a theater can be built. Building a theater can become a valuable and exciting project. The theater does not even need to be a permanent one; with proper planning, the proscenium wall, the curtain, and even the stage itself, can be made removable, so that the room can quickly and easily be made from the theater back into a gymnasium, or library, or lunchroom. If the original room has a platform of proper size for the stage, the process is much easier; but if the platform is too small, it can be extended, or an entire platform can be built if necessary. To try to turn a room into a theater by building merely a proscenium arch and curtain, without any device to raise the action from the floor, is usually unsatisfactory. If there is no platform, and if one cannot be built, it is wiser to use central staging, or some similar device, as suggested in Chapter XVI.

SIZE OF ROOM

The first and most important consideration is the size and height of the room. A stage that is smaller than fifteen by twenty feet is too small for much use, and a larger one is better. The stage itself should not take up more than one-third of the room, or else there will be no space for the audience.

Therefore, probably it will be unwise to attempt to turn any room less than twenty feet by fifty feet in size into a theater. Some ingenious things have been done by organizations with smaller rooms, but to do much is difficult. A larger room is more desirable. Height is another important consideration. A stage should be raised at least thirty inches from the floor if the floor of the auditorium is level, or else the actors cannot be seen sufficiently well from any but the first two or three rows. If the auditorium is large, three feet, or even three feet six inches, is a better elevation for the stage. The proscenium opening should be at least eight feet in height; otherwise the actors look cramped and out of proportion. Twelve feet, or more, is a still better height for the proscenium arch. There should be a space of at least four or five feet above the proscenium arch. In a really well-proportioned theater, there is as much room above the top of the arch as there is below; that is, the top of the proscenium arch should be half-way between the floor of the stage and the ceiling. Probably few rooms are high enough to allow this to be done, and it is not absolutely essential, since the scenery can be handled in some other way. But allowing three feet for the height of the stage, eight for the proscenium arch, and five for the space above the opening, it may be seen that the room to be turned into a theater should be at least sixteen feet in height. If this height is not available, the space above the opening, rather than any other dimension, had better be reduced. The minimum size of the room that can be successfully turned into a theater should be, then, about twenty feet by fifty, by sixteen or more in height.

PERMANENT STAGE AND PROSCENIUM

If the room can be turned into a permanent theater, the problem of building a platform and proscenium arch is not difficult. The undertaking then assumes the form of building a wall to cut the room into two parts, the smaller of which will contain the stage, and the larger the auditorium. In this wall will be left the large opening called the proscenium opening. The stage must be solidly built and should be floored with soft wood, so that stage braces may be screwed to the floor with stage screws. The proscenium wall may be built of beams and covered with beaver board or some similar substance. It is still better to have it plastered, or finished in the same way as the auditorium itself. The color should be subdued and harmonious, and if it is desired to outline the proscenium arch in some way, a plain dull black, or a dark finish of some sort, is much more suitable and artistic than the gilt, ornate effect so often found in old public theaters. Persons wishing to turn a large room into a permanent theater will find a wealth of suggestion and aid in Irving Pichel's admirable volume, *Modern Theaters*.[1]

MOVABLE STAGE

More often, perhaps, especially in schools and colleges, the problem is to turn a room into a theater only temporarily. Here, the stage and the proscenium wall must be movable. It must be possible by a few hours of work to transform the room into a theater. Of late, several theatrical dealers have begun to make Little Theater equipment which can be thus set up and taken down, but there is no reason why an energetic dramatic organization cannot make its own.

The stage is the most difficult thing to build, for it must be made solid. No general plan can be suggested that will be universally satisfactory. A series of strongly-built sections, each of which has permanent legs like a table, which can be fastened together, is perhaps the easiest sort of stage to manufacture. It requires considerable storage room, however, so that it will usually be necessary to make a stage that can be stored in less space. The illustration (Fig. 23) and the explanation of it should suggest a possibility. A good grade of lumber should be used, if possible, otherwise the warping of the stage makes

[1] Irving Pichel, *Modern Theaters* (New York, Harcourt, Brace and Co., 1925).

it difficult to put up and take down easily. The short cross-beams supporting the planks of the floor of the stage should be near enough together to hold them absolutely rigid—fourteen or eighteen inches apart, at the very most. The cross braces may be fastened to the short upright beams that hold the sections with bolts and winged nuts, and the sections may

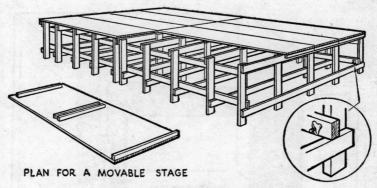

PLAN FOR A MOVABLE STAGE

FIG. 23. A MOVABLE STAGE

Sections of flooring are nailed together on cleats and supported by a framework of two-by-four beams. The section of the framework shown at the right, consisting of five uprights and two long beams parallel to the floor, may be nailed or screwed permanently. The long beams running the other way should be fastened to the uprights with bolts and winged nuts (as shown in the detail). The uprights may be braced further with diagonal ties in the same manner if necessary. Uprights should not be more than eighteen inches apart. As many sections can be made and fastened together as necessary to make a stage of the desired size.

be fastened to the frame and to each other in the same manner. A stage that is built in this way will hold almost any weight, and it may be put up and taken down without the use of a tool. If a movable stage is to be built, it pays to put as much money and labor into it as is necessary to make it absolutely rigid; for good play production is difficult on a shaky, unsatisfactory platform.

MOVABLE PROSCENIUM WALL

For the proscenium wall there are two possibilities. The wall may be made of covered frames or of draperies.

1. *A Temporary Proscenium of Frames*. A temporary wall of frames should cut off the stage end of the room, by extending from wall to wall, and from floor to ceiling. In its simplest

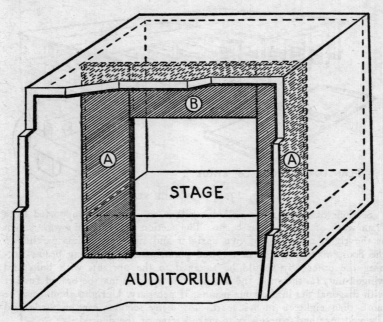

FIG. 24. PROSCENIUM WALL

form it should consist of three pieces, two tall frames (A) standing on the floor, and a crosspiece (B) reaching from the inner edges of these frames, and placed up against the ceiling. An arrangement of this sort, however, needs to be supported by the side walls of the room, or by the platform, or in some other way. Often it is not permissible to attach things to the walls or the ceiling. In that case, it is possible to devise a

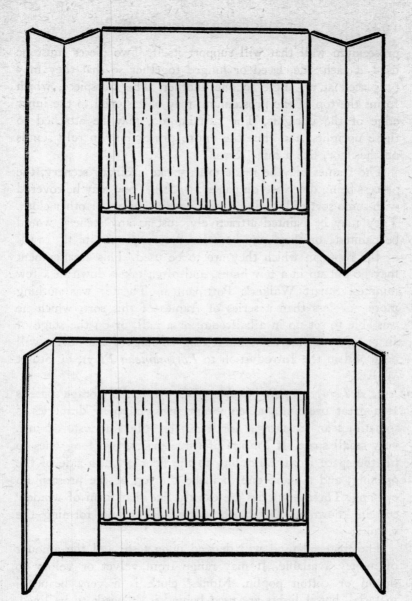

FIG. 25. PROSCENIUM OF FRAMES

proscenium wall that will support itself. Two pieces must be used at each side, laced or hinged together so that they may be placed at an angle to one another. The crosspiece, which forms the top of the proscenium, may be fastened to the inner edge of the uprights. The curtain, too, may be attached to these uprights, and thus the entire proscenium merely stands on the floor, like a huge screen.

The frames may be made exactly like ordinary scenery, the process being described on pages 219-228. They may be covered with some sort of building board, or with canvas or other cloth. They may be painted attractively, just as any scenery would be painted; or they may be colored to approximate the walls of the room in which they are to be used. This arrangement may be put up in a few hours, and often taken down in a few minutes. Stuart Walker's Portmanteau Theater was nothing more nor less than a series of frames of this sort, which he was able to set up in a ballroom, or a hall, or on the stage of an ordinary theater. An interesting account of his device will be found in the Introduction to *Portmanteau Plays*, by Stuart Walker.[2]

2. *A Temporary Proscenium of Draperies.* If storage space is at a great premium, a temporary proscenium of draperies is sometimes an advantage, for it can be rolled and stored in a very small space. It consists of three pieces, two long ones to fill the space from the ceiling to the floor on each side of the opening, and a short one to make the top of the proscenium opening. These draperies are exactly like that form of window curtain known as Dutch, the short top curtain forming the valance.

The material used will depend upon taste and the amount of money available. It may range from velvet or velour to denim or cotton poplin. Monks' cloth is a very beautiful material, but if lights are used behind it, it needs to be lined.

[2] Stuart Walker, *Portmanteau Plays* (New York, D. Appleton & Co., 1917).

FRONT VIEW

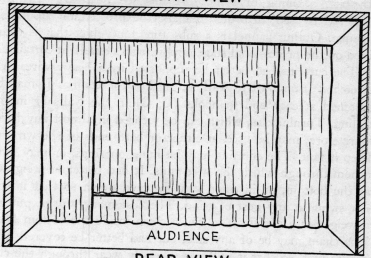

AUDIENCE

REAR VIEW

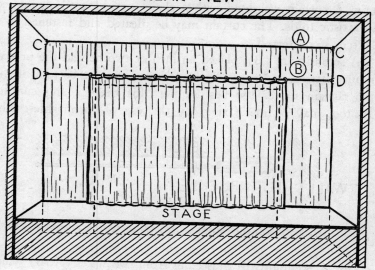

STAGE

FIG. 26. PROSCENIUM OF DRAPERIES

In fact, a lining of some sort may be necessary whatever material is used, in order to make the proscenium absolutely opaque. Outing flannel is a substitute for velvet that is often used on the professional stage, and it makes excellent curtains.

The curtains had better be supported by a heavy wire (A), stretched from wall to wall, up against the ceiling. It may be fastened at each end to hooks (C, C) in the walls or in the ceiling. Turnbuckles, which can be secured in almost any hardware store, may be used at either or both ends of the wire, to keep it taut. The curtains may be hung on rings, or may have a hem through which the wire runs. It had better be weighted at the bottom, or in some way fastened down so that it will not swing at any gust of wind. The customary way of putting a weight in a curtain is to run a chain inside the bottom hem. The chain may be of any size, but had better be covered with canvas first, so that it will not so easily wear through the curtain. A curtain weighted with a chain may be easily arranged in artistic folds. The curtain may be pleated and fastened to a batten, if preferred.

A second wire (B), placed an inch or two behind the proscenium curtains, and six or seven inches above the bottom of the top curtain makes the best support for the opening curtain. It, too, may be made rigid by the use of turnbuckles. The

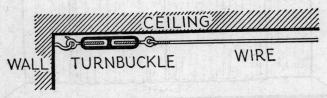

FIG. 27. METHOD OF TIGHTENING WIRE WITH TURNBUCKLE

entire proscenium will thus hang from two wires (A, B) which depend on four firmly fastened hooks (C, C, D, D). The hooks may be made inconspicuous and can usually be left permanently in position, so that to put up the proscenium it is necessary only to slip the ends of the wires over the hooks, tighten them by the turnbuckles, and shake out the curtains.

THE CURTAIN

Whichever form of temporary proscenium is used, the making and hanging of the opening curtain will be an identical process. In fact, the operation will be the same for a permanent proscenium, in many cases. A double curtain opening in the center is probably most satisfactory; for a drop, or guillotine, curtain is difficult to arrange unless the overhead space is sufficient so that it may be hauled straight up. If there is sufficient overhead room, a drop curtain may be arranged to run by pulleys and ropes, just as any drop is (see Fig. 21). Sliding curtains may be run on a track-and-pulley system, which will be supplied by any dealer in theatrical materials. For any but a very heavy curtain, however, it is possible to rig up a satisfactory arrangement in the following manner:

Run a heavy wire from wall to wall, or from support to support, in the manner described above, for the proscenium

FIG. 28. METHOD OF HANGING THE CURTAIN

curtains. It may be tightened with turnbuckles; and if it has a tendency to sag, it may be supported by a wire hanging from the ceiling in the exact center. The curtain may be run on this wire on sliding rings or small pulleys. On one small stage, the deed was done with little wooden spools. The rings or pulleys should be placed on the curtains so that they come about six or eight inches apart; therefore, the number required depends entirely on the width of the opening. The rings had better be put in place by sewing or with curtain pins, so that it falls into the desired folds or pleats. Now it is necessary to tie the rings together at the proper distance, with a light, but strong, cord. This cord (M) goes from ring to ring (Fig. 29), and its purpose is to prevent the rings from moving apart when the curtain is pulled by one corner, which would otherwise straighten out the folds. When the rings in the corners of the curtain (A and B) are pulled forward or back, the curtains will follow, and they will remain in folds, as arranged.

It is necessary to devise a rope for opening and closing the curtains. To do this, a single pulley is necessary at one side, say

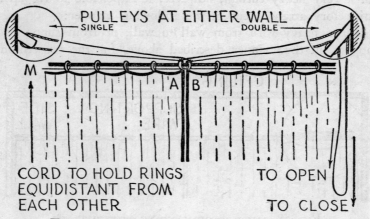

FIG. 29. METHOD OF PULLING THE CURTAIN

the left, and a double pulley at the right. The curtains will be worked from the side where the double pulley is placed. The curtains must be tightly closed, just as they should be when in position, and a light, strong rope tied to the corner of one (A), run through the single pulley, and brought back and fastened to the corner of the other (B). It is very important that this rope be tight and that it be just twice as long as the distance from where the curtains meet to the pulley. Then a rope must be run through one sheave of the double pulley and fastened at the corner of a curtain (A), and the other end of the rope run through the other sheave and fastened at the other corner (B). When the rope fastened to the near curtain (B) is pulled, the curtains will open evenly and equally; and when the rope fastened to the other corner (A) is pulled, they will both close. The principle of this operation is exactly the same as that used when two portières are made to open and close by the pulling of a single cord, and probably any upholsterer or decorator will explain it to any one who finds it difficult to follow the printed directions. Nevertheless, whether or not the principle is understood, the curtains will work if the directions are carefully followed.

The one difficulty with curtains so rigged is that they sometimes leave a small gap where they meet in the center. To

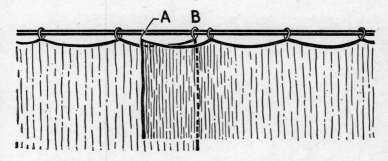

FIG. 30. METHOD OF OVERLAPPING CURTAINS

overcome this difficulty, two devices are possible. Two parallel wires may be run, one for each curtain, so that they can slide by one another. Simpler yet, the first ring on one curtain may be set back six or eight inches, so that this curtain overlaps the other by that amount. In that case, the ropes for working the curtains must be tied to the corner (A), and not to the first ring. The other ends should be tied to the first ring on the other curtain (B), just as usual. In this case, in order to keep the draw-line taut, it must be tied off to a cleat except while being used to move the curtain, or its slackness will allow the loose edge of the curtain (A) to fall. Better yet, a pulley may be fastened to the floor below the double curtain pulley, and the line passed through it when the curtain is being rigged. This will hold the draw-line taut at all times.

CHAPTER XVI

Producing Without a Theater

PLAYS WITHOUT A THEATER

Play production by no means depends upon the existence of a modern theater, such as has been described in the preceding chapters. In fact, this theater, with its proscenium opening and curtain, is a late development in the world of drama. It was universally used in Europe only after 1650 or so. Most plays antedating this were written for a stage without a proscenium arch. They are well adapted to be played without a theater in the modern sense. The plays of the Greeks and Romans, and those of the Elizabethans, are in this classification; so perhaps the greatest drama that has yet been created was written before the modern theater developed. It may be surmised then that producing without a theater is a fascinating process, in which there is room for all possible inventiveness.

USING A PLATFORM WITHOUT A CURTAIN

Where a platform is available, even though there is no proscenium arch and no curtain, the problem is not altogether unlike that of performing in the usual theater. The fact that it is impossible to hide the platform from the vision of the audience makes it necessary to find some other device for the changing of scenery, or for the disclosing and the hiding of characters who might normally be found on the stage as the curtains are opened or as they are closed. There are a number of possibilities.

1. *Using a Single Scene.* In the first place, it is possible to

choose a play that can be played without a change of scene of any sort. The platform can be prepared for the play before the audience enters, and no attempt need be made to hide the scene at any time. The method used by Reinhardt in *The Miracle* as produced at the Century Theater, New York City, is an example. In that noteworthy performance, the entire theater was transformed into a cathedral. As one entered, he saw its Gothic arches and pillars, and its altar surrounded by a huge grille. Occasionally monks, or church attendants, crossed in front of the altar. Finally an old verger tottered out and lighted the candles. The music of the organ commenced. The characters began to enter and the play started. The time that the audience had waited in the auditorium had enabled them to orient themselves in the proper atmosphere much better than would have been possible had the medieval cathedral suddenly been disclosed by the opening of the curtain.

A play of this sort must be directed so that the characters move off the stage naturally at the end of scenes, which can never be cut off by the curtain. The stopping of the action in an exciting situation by the curtain is, at its best, an unnatural theatrical convention, anyway; so perhaps the inability to do this is not a very great handicap. The Elizabethan dramatists were not able to do so; therefore, their plays are especially suitable for a curtainless platform. The platform can be arranged to approximate an Elizabethan stage. Chinese plays may be made very interesting played in this manner. In fact, almost any play, even a modern realistic one, may be played successfully on a curtainless platform if it is directed with that sort of performance in mind and if sufficient ingenuity is spent in adapting the platform.

2. *Curtain Substitutes.* It is possible, indeed, to perform plays that demand curtain situations. Darkness may be used instead of a curtain. When the play is ready to begin, a bell or some signal may be sounded, the lights may be turned off for a few seconds during which the characters enter and take their posi-

tions on the stage. The lights may then be turned up, and the play begins with the characters on the stage. The same device may be used at the end. With the curtain line, the lights may be turned out, the characters disappear; and when the lights come on again, the empty stage announces intermission or the end of the play. There is no need to do even this, however. It is surprising how soon an audience accepts any convention. At the end of a scene, however dramatic the ending, the actors may hold the position for a moment and then very frankly and obviously drop out of character and walk off. Of course, these devices are more adapted to student performances before fellow students, than to public performances, for which it may be better to adapt a play to the curtainless situation by using a suitable one-scene piece, as suggested above.

3. *Dramatic Scene-shifting.* Sometimes, however, even for public performances, it is amusing to change the scenes openly, somewhat as may have been done in the Elizabethan theater. This may be called dramatic scene-shifting. That is, the scene-shifters are in character, too, as well as the actors of the play. In a Shakespearean play, Elizabethan pages may do the work; in a Molière play, seventeenth-century French servants. Sometimes lines may be invented for a head scene-shifter of some sort. An example will illustrate this possibility. In a performance of MacKaye's *A Thousand Years Ago*, done without a front curtain, the scenes were set by a force of half a dozen Chinese coolies, under the direction of a Chinese property man. All the scene-shifters were in costume and make-up. The performance was given in front of a beautiful gray cyclorama, and the scenes were changed by moving several small platforms, by displaying brilliant Chinese screens and vases, by using necessary furniture, and above all, by changing the lights. The audience, on coming into the auditorium, saw at one end only the great gray cyclorama, or curtain, which hung straight down with a hidden slit in the center. When the

play was about to start, a gong was sounded, the lights went out, and a spotlight played on the center of the curtain. The property man bounded through, and with arms outspread called for silence. Then he spoke:

Sh-h-h! Silence, lords and ladies, if you please,
That you may hear our play with greater ease.
And, friends, I beg you, do not take it ill
I called you "lords and ladies"; if you will
You may be clowns, or peasants, or—let's say—
You're palace walls! only you're *in our play!*
For you must aid by every subtle means
Imagination knows to change the scenes.
With *my* assistance, if you truly try,
You'll find your parts are easy. Who am I?
See, lady, below the other names, there! see!
The Master of the Properties, that's me.
And though I'm at the bottom of the page,
My part's important, for I set the stage.
And then—I guess I might as well confess—
That I'm the Prologue—that is, more or less.
I come to take you with me far away
From all this modern world to old Cathay
For that's the place we're going to have our play.
   (*Takes scroll from belt, unrolls it, and looks for directions.*)
"Outside of Pekin Gate, the city wall . . ."
   (*Looks around for something to serve as wall.*)
This curtain here will do, but strong and tall
You must imagine it, as with a frown
Its crenelled towers watch o'er the sleeping town;
For here there dwells in power, and pomp, and state,
The Emperor of China. (*Consults scroll.*) Now, "a gate."
   (*With aid of other property men, he loops up curtains, making an opening for the gate.*)
There, that will do, I think. Lastly, "a row
Of severed heads!"
   (*Property men raise "severed heads" above the top of curtain.*)
(*Shuddering pleasantly*) Like evil plants they grow!
But, friends, I pray you, do not yield to fear,

Our play's a pleasant one, and full of cheer.
    (*Consults scroll again.*)
"Sunrise." A little light, a little light.
    (*Claps hands, and lights come up.*)
The city now awakens from the night.
    (*Looks through gate, and whispers confidentially to au-
    dience.*)
And all is stir and bustle there within;
I think our play is ready to begin.
Far down this road people I see appear.
Silence, now, not a noise! just hark and hear!
    (*Takes seat with other property men in front of audience.*)

Act I was then played before the created city walls, and at
the end of the action, after all the characters of the play had
disappeared, the property man bounded up from where he
had been sitting and consulted his scroll of directions again.

"A Harem." Here's where Turandot does dwell,
Like all true Princesses, as you know well!
    (*Music while the Property Man and his assistants set the
    scene for the Harem. When all is ready, he claps his
    hands, the music stops, the lights change, and he looks
    around to see that everything is in place.*)
All's ready now. Here's everything we need.
Quiet, sh-h-h! quiet! Let the play proceed.

There was a similar process before each scene; and the parts
of the scene-shifters were concluded, after the final scene had
been set, by the following lines:

Again we need the thrones, "the Hall of State,"
Where rules our Capocomico, the Great.
    (*Property men set the scene as before.*)
There! Now our task is done! And, by the way,
This is the last you'll see of us to-day;
So, if you like the way we've done our task,
You—well (*with mock hesitation*), you know, it's hardly
    correct to ask,
But (*shows empty pockets*), it's a struggle, and if you'll—do
    —so (*indicating applause*)

The Manager might (*pantomime of paying money*)—well,
you know, you know!
(*Bows, and exits, followed by the other property men.*)

A device of this sort may be interesting and amusing and
can easily be adapted for almost any sort of a romantic play.
One point to be noted is that it must not be allowed to become so long or elaborate that it steals interest away from
the play itself. The use of the chronicler in Drinkwater's
Abraham Lincoln, and the ballad man in MacKaye's *Washing-
ton*, and the stage-manager in Wilder's *Our Town*, is essentially
nothing more nor less than dramatic scene-shifting.

CENTRAL STAGING

Another possibility for producing plays without a theater
lies in the use of central staging. This, too, is a tried and true
device of great antiquity. The playing of little scenes in the
medieval church with the congregation on every hand; the
Elizabethan stage which was surrounded on three, and even
sometimes on four, sides by the audience; the experiments of
Max Reinhardt in Das Grosse Schausspielhaus in Berlin—all
these are essentially examples of central staging. A large room
or a hall is the main requirement. Even dramatic organizations
having a fully equipped theater will find that central staging
offers great opportunities for unusual effects if a good-sized
hall can sometimes be used in place of the theater. Often it
will solve the problem of organizations which find themselves
temporarily theaterless.

1. *Method of Central Staging.* In central staging, the play
is performed in the middle of the hall, whereas the audience
is placed in a circle on all sides of the performers. Several rings
of chairs may be placed around the outside of the hall, leaving
the center clear as the playing space. If more than two or
three rows of spectators must be accommodated, it becomes
difficult to see the action unless it is raised; and in any case, a

small platform in the center to raise the important action is helpful, although it is not absolutely necessary. This platform, and the space around it, and all the aisles leading to the space may be used for playing, and so becomes the "stage." If this central space can be lighted by overhead lights, or by spots and floods from concealed sources, many interesting effects can be secured. It is necessary to be certain that lights of this sort do not shine into the eyes of the audience. The proximity of the actors to the audience gives a feeling quite different from the picture-frame stage and for some plays is unusually effective.

2. *Examples of Central Staging. Prunella,* by Laurence Housman, was done in this manner with success. A small raised platform in the center was made into a garden, with a sundial, a stone bench, and a bed of tulips. Entrances into the garden, which is the scene of the entire play, were always made either from a house, or through a gate which is supposed to lead to a passing road. A broad aisle through the spectators led to a house at one end of the hall, with a door through which characters entered, and a window. At the opposite end of the aisle, at the other side of the hall, was an iron gate, making a second entrance. Characters who are supposed to be in the house when the play starts enter the playing-space through the door of the house, and the others come through the gate. The story is of a band of strolling mummers led by Pierrot, who wanders into the garden. He falls in love with Prunella, who lives in the house with her three aunts, and he runs away with her. Of course, he and his followers enter from the road; Prunella and her aunts come from the house. When Prunella elopes with Pierrot, she climbs through the window in the house, and they run out by the gate. The entire action works out very clearly and well. The playing was on the small platform, in the space around it, and up and down the aisle. By having several aisles, with a set piece of scenery, or something to indicate a distinctive entrance at each end of every

aisle, it is possible to have as many entrances as any play demands.

Molière's amusing farce *The Doctor by Compulsion*, is another example of a play successfully done with central staging. This time the attempt was made to turn the entire hall into a seventeenth-century room. Canvases, brilliantly painted to represent tapestries, were hung around the walls. A huge chandelier of silver ribbons hung over the small platform in

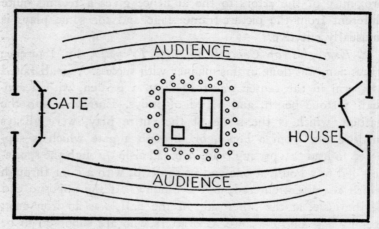

FIG. 31. "PRUNELLA" IN CENTRAL STAGING

the center of the hall. The platform was small, about six feet square and eighteen inches high, with a single step all around it, so that it could be easily mounted from any side. The only furniture on the platform was a small square box, covered with the same colored canvas as the platform itself. The audience sat at tables, placed in rows around the playing space, and refreshments were served during the two intermissions in the performance. The action in *The Doctor by Compulsion* takes place in several different places: a hut, a place in the forest, a boudoir, a drawing-room. No attempt was made to indicate these places. The play was written, as a matter of fact, to be played without any scenery in the modern sense; the place of the action is very unimportant, and the audience learns from the lines of the play where that place is, in practically every instance. After the audience had been quieted by the ringing of chimes, the turning out of the lights in the hall, and the lighting up of the central space by a number of concealed spotlights, the play opened with the entrance of Sganarelle, a woodcutter, and his wife Martine, from the audience at one

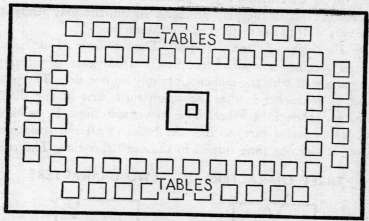

FIG. 32. "THE DOCTOR BY COMPULSION" IN CENTRAL STAGING

end of the hall. They are quarreling loudly. Still quarreling, they advance into the center and upon the platform, where Sganarelle seizes a slapstick and beats his wife. From the other end of the hall a neighbor, M. Roberts, rushes in and attempts to separate them. Both turn upon him fiercely, and he is driven out in discomfort. Sganarelle then attempts to pacify his wife, who pretends to be reconciled to him. Promising to cut a large supply of wood he goes out as he entered, through the audience. Two gentlemen are heard talking in another corner of the hall, and they move slowly into the lighted space discussing the trouble they are having in finding the famous physician for whom their master has sent them. Martine has been sitting on the platform meditating revenge. The gentlemen finally see her and approach. Seeing her opportunity, she tells them that Sganarelle is a marvelous physician, but that he is queer and doesn't like to admit his skill. The gentlemen can make him admit that he is a physician by beating him. Sganarelle is heard singing, and he staggers in with his bottle. Martine runs out in the opposite direction, and the two gentlemen wait for Sganarelle and try to persuade him that he is a noted physician. And so the play proceeds. Again, the play lends itself very well to the method of central staging.

3. *Technique of Central Staging.* The technique of successful central staging is somewhat different from that of playing against a wall with the audience entirely on one side. The play must be rehearsed so that the action turns first in one direction, and then in another. The movement must be worked out with unusual care, so that the backs of all the actors are never at any one time turned in the same direction. The rule

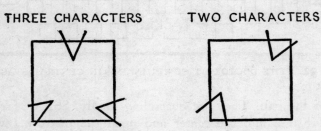

FIG. 33. DIAGRAM OF CORRECT FACING IN CENTRAL STAGING

should be that every spectator should be enabled to see the face of at least one actor at any time. Thus, if three persons are talking, they should stand in a triangle, each with his face to the center. Two persons must face in opposite directions, and never be left standing side by side, and facing the same wall. If the director, in directing a play for central staging, constantly changes his position, he will have little difficulty in working out positions that will be interesting from all angles. In central staging, since there is little scenery, a play that allows brilliant and interesting costuming is better than one for which costumes are dull. The costumes may be made to give the tone to the play. Make-up must be unusually correct and careful, owing to the fact that the actors come so near to the spectators. A good lighting system, that allows the lighting of the central playing space to be varied, aids greatly, too. And if large groups are used, they must be kept out of the central space as far as possible, or they obscure the action of the important characters. If, for example, a troop of soldiers were to be introduced in some play centrally staged, it would be wise to keep them back against the setting at the end of an aisle, while their officer, or one or two men only, advanced into the center to arrest an important character.

Groups desiring a novel form of play production, with great possibilities and opportunities for experimentation, need not be prevented from practicing play production by lack of a theater. Play production existed long before there was any modern theater. The practice of the theater does not depend on having a building; it is rather a state of mind—the desire to act out a story as effectively as possible so as to make an effect on an audience. Central staging is an ancient theater device, and it has many possibilities for the most up-to-date group.

CHAPTER XVII

Building Scenery

DEFINITION OF SCENERY

Scenery, in a strict sense, is the background before which the play is performed. Normally it consists of the hangings, or the painted cloths, that surround the playing-space. The non-professional designer will, however, be greatly aided if he will bear in mind a broader definition and conceive scenery to be the articles that create the place in which the action is occurring. The term will then include furniture, rugs, pictures, tapestries, and all the other possible elements that may aid in giving character to the place. A table and two chairs, carefully chosen, may do more to set the scene successfully, than all the painted cloths or hangings available. It is the delusion of some non-professionals that they are able to do plays without scenery. But, whatever the audience sees as a background for the playing is the scenery. It may be accidentally chosen scenery, or it may with luck be inconspicuous scenery, but a play without scenery is just an impossibility. If a play is performed on an empty stage, the walls of the theater are the scenery; if it is performed out-of-doors, on a hillside, the bushes and trees and skies of the background are the scenery. To choose this background so that it will be most effective in terms of the play is, therefore, the task of the designer. This task will be discussed at greater length in Chapter XIX. Our present problem is to become acquainted with the mechanical possibilities of scenery.

CLASSIFICATION OF SCENERY

Scenery may be roughly divided into two main classes: (1) *draperies* of unpainted materials, which are left their natural colors or dyed in solid colors; and (2) *painted scenery* of the more or less traditional type.

Many amateur organizations, especially in schools, use draperies almost exclusively, under the impression that painted scenery is impossible for them. This is a mistake. Audiences grow tired of seeing the same set of draperies play after play. Painted scenery, that may be remade and repainted for different performances, is much more satisfactory; and if properly planned and executed, it is by no means excessively expensive. Professionals use painted scenery, for the most part, because of its great superiority to any other device yet discovered, and non-professional groups may well follow this lead. There are times, of course, when draperies may be used, and occasionally they are capable of giving the effect desired. The well equipped theater might, therefore, possess one or two sets.

DRAPERIES

1. *Materials for Draperies.* Draperies may be made of velours, flannel, monks' cloth, hessian, denim, burlap, cotton velvet, poplin, or almost any material dictated by taste or price. With two sets of draperies, one a good light gray and the other a black, almost any play may be set. With proper lighting, excellent effects may be secured.

2. *Methods of Hanging Draperies.* Wires may be used on which to hang the curtains, and they may be stretched from wall to wall and tightened with turnbuckles as already described for proscenium curtains (p. 194). Sometimes wooden battens may be hung with hooks between two wires. They will keep the wires parallel, and curtains may be fastened to both battens and wire. This device works well only when distances between points of support are not great and when the curtains are light-

weight. Another method, traditional on the professional stage and more suitable when the scenery can be hung from overhead, is to build a frame in the desired shape, to which the curtains may be fastened (see Fig. 34). An even better method would be to hang the draperies from three tracks, one long track in

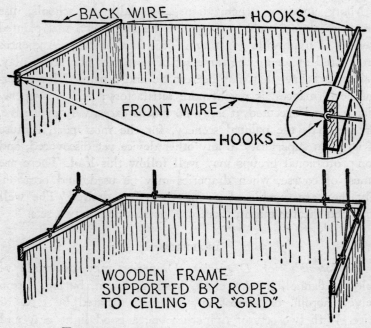

FIG. 34. METHODS OF HANGING DRAPERIES

back of the playing space, and two shorter ones on each side placed up- and downstage. This makes it possible to open and close all three of the curtains that make up the cyclorama.

3. *Making Draperies.* Professionally made curtains are usually gathered on a piece of webbing two or three inches wide, in which there are grommets, and short pieces of cord, by which the curtain may be tied to the frame (Fig. 35). They are weighted at the bottom by a chain run through the hem.

A narrow bag of shot or of sand may be used for the same purpose. But many times, the non-professional producer will find it to his advantage not to have his material made into curtains at all. It can merely be cut into strips long enough to reach from his supporting wire or frame to the floor. Each of these strips may be fastened to webbing, so that they may be tied to a support; or they may be cut long enough so that

WEBBING SEWN TO
TOP OF DRAPERIES

WEBBING PIERCED BY
GROMMETS AND TIES

FIG. 35. DRAPERIES WITH WEBBING, GROMMETS, AND TIES

they may be folded over the support at the top and pinned. They should overlap each other about six inches. Short strips, reaching to within six or seven feet of the floor, will make openings for doors. In fact, entrances may be made between the strips at any point. Curtains of this sort are much more flexible than an ordinary cyclorama enclosing the stage.

4. *The Use of Plastic Pieces with Draperies.* Whatever the system, it is helpful to vary the effects by the use of door frames and practical doors, windows, pictures, hangings, fireplaces, and whatever else may be made to function with curtains. Methods of making all these things will be described later in this chapter.

KINDS OF PAINTED SCENERY

Painted scenery may be divided according to its structure and use into three classifications: (1) flats, (2) drops, and (3) plastic pieces.

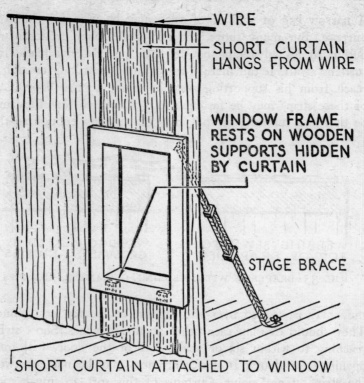

WIRE

SHORT CURTAIN
HANGS FROM WIRE

WINDOW FRAME
RESTS ON WOODEN
SUPPORTS HIDDEN
BY CURTAIN

STAGE BRACE

SHORT CURTAIN ATTACHED TO WINDOW

FIG. 36. METHOD OF SUPPORTING WINDOW FRAMES IN DRAPERIES

1. *Flats.* The most common variety of painted scenery is a flat, which is a framed piece covered with material, like the single panel of a screen. The walls of an interior setting usually consist of a number of such pieces, edge to edge. The height of the flat depends on the size of the room desired, the most common professional height being fourteen or sixteen feet. For a smaller theater, especially where there is no balcony, twelve feet is a useful height; but in many school theaters, it may be well to establish a standard height of nine or ten feet. The standard professional flat never exceeds five feet and nine inches in width, and the width of

covering materials and the difficulty of handling makes a flat that is much wider impractical. In a normal stage room there may be, however, many flats less than five feet nine inches in width; they are called *jogs*. A *jog* may be defined as a piece of standard height, but less than standard width. The question of size is discussed on page 294 in connection with the problems of the designer. A plain flat is one that contains no opening. A door flat has an opening for a door, and a window flat one for a window (see Fig. 37).

2. *Drops.* A drop is an unframed piece that must be suspended or hung from overhead, usually by sets of lines from a grid (see Fig. 21). Drops can be used only where there is a method of suspending them, hence the importance of some sort of overhead rigging, even on the smallest stage. A *full drop* is one large enough to cover the entire back of the playing space; that is, several feet wider and a few feet higher than the proscenium opening. Many smaller drops are, however, useful in the theater; and these have special names. Thus, a *border drop* (commonly called a border) is a short drop; several borders, suspended one behind the other over the playing space, are sometimes used to mask the ceiling of the stage (see Fig. 20). A border drop, which is not carried across the total distance of the playing space and which might be used to represent the foliage at the top of a tree, is often called a *tab*.[1] Drops are also named in other ways. Thus, a drop or a border that represents foliage is often called a foliage drop or a foliage border. Because such a drop might be cut along the edges to represent leaves, it is sometimes called a cut drop, or a cut border. It is possible that a full drop might not touch the floor at every point along its bottom edge, as would be the case were a hole cut in the center to represent a space in a forest, or an entrance to a cave. Such a drop would be a leg drop. The important thing that classifies a piece of scenery

[1] Technically, a *tab* is a narrow drop suspended on a single line, but the term is rarely used with complete accuracy.

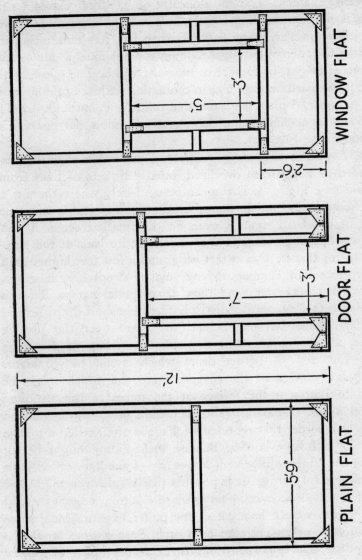

PLAIN FLAT

5'-9"

DOOR FLAT

12'

7'

3'

WINDOW FLAT

5'

3'

2'6"

Fig. 37. FRAMING OF PLAIN, DOOR, AND WINDOW FLAT

218

as a drop is that it cannot support itself from the floor; it must be suspended. From this point of view a cyclorama is a drop. A cyclorama is a large curtain that encloses the playing space, running roughly in a semi-circle from one side of the prosce- nium arch around to the other. Thus, the cyclorama of draperies, described on page 213, is technically a drop.

3. *Plastic Pieces.* Both drops and flats have one characteristic in common; their thickness is only the thickness of the material used. Often in the theater we wish to represent objects having a third dimension. Such pieces might be doors or windows, pillars, round trees, posts, fireplaces, stairways, platforms, etc. These are called plastic pieces.

Most sets are made up of a combination of all these kinds of scenery. We might represent the walls of a room by a series of flats edge to edge. If there are openings in the back wall, such as windows, and we wish to show a landscape through the windows, this might well be painted on a drop. If the room has a three-dimensional fireplace, or a stairway, or door and window frames, these will be plastic pieces.

BUILDING A FLAT

The ability to build a flat quickly and accurately is essential in the practice of stagecraft, for flats are basic units of scenery used in many ways. The process is similar whether it be a plain flat of standard dimensions, or a flat containing an open- ing, or a flat of irregular size or distorted shape. It consists of three steps: (1) building the frame, (2) reënforcing the frame, (3) covering the frame.

1. *Building the Frame.* The process of building the plain flat shown in Fig. 37 will illustrate the method of framing. It will require two long upright pieces, and three crosspieces. The long pieces in the frame of a flat are called stiles, and the crosspieces are called rails or stretchers. The middle stretcher is called the toggle-rail. Thus, to build the flat illustrated, we shall need two stiles and three rails.

The best material will be *Grade A white pine*. This should be selected lumber, straight and free from knots and blemishes. What is called tight-knot pine (usually Grade B) is possible, and in emergency fir or spruce may be used. These, however, split and warp so easily that when possible, pine should be used for framing. Flats built of Grade A white pine may be rebuilt and recovered, and will give satisfactory service for years. The size of lumber usually used for framing flats, except flats of great height, is one inch thick and three inches wide, or what is called one by three (and written thus: 1″x3″). The lumber should be finished (that is, planed at the mill) on all four sides. Sometimes this is called dressed lumber. The commercial dimension of lumber comes from the size in which it is cut from the tree, before it is planed; therefore, 1″x3″ will actually be one inch thick and three inches wide only as it is sawed. After planing it will be about three quarters of an inch thick and 2⅝ inches wide. This must be taken into account in cutting the stiles and rails.

The first problem will be joining the stiles and rails together at the corners of the flat. Most professionally made flats have mortise and tenon joints, but these are difficult to make without machinery, and necessary only for hard wear. The simplest kind of a joint for the beginner is a butt joint; that is, all cuts are right angles, and the end of one piece is merely butted up against the side of the other (Fig. 38). A decision must be made at this point as to how the corners are to be fitted together. Probably it is best to make the top and bottom rail the full width of the flat (5 feet, nine inches in this case). This requires that the stiles be the desired height *minus twice the width of the lumber*. The lumber is probably variable, so in each case its width should be measured. If it is two and five-eighths inches in width, the length to which the stiles must be cut would be twelve feet minus twice two and five-eighths inches, or eleven feet and six and three-quarters inches. The toggle-rail must fit between the stiles, so it should be cut the

width of the flat *minus twice the width of the lumber*, or
five feet, three and three-quarters inches. The cuts at the end
of the lumber should be as square and accurate as possible. The
five pieces—two stiles, a top rail, a bottom rail, and a toggle-rail
—are now ready for assembling.

The stiles and end rails can now be placed on the floor to
make the rectangular frame of the flat. We must be sure that
the stiles are *inside the rails*, otherwise the flat will come out

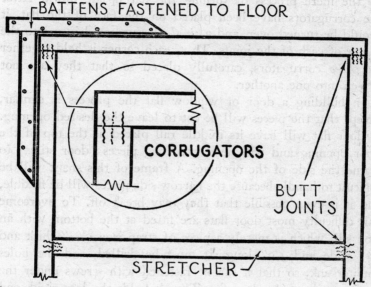

FIG. 38. ASSEMBLING A FLAT—BUTT JOINTS AND CORRUGATORS

with incorrect dimensions. The easiest way to hold the corner
together is with corrugated fasteners, which are commonly
called corrugators. The best kind of corrugator to use is a
saw-toothed ⅝"x5. They can usually be purchased in any
large hardware store. Two should be driven into each joint in
the position shown in the illustration. There is less probability of
the corrugators splitting the wood if they are placed at a slight
angle. It is desirable to hold the flat as square as possible

during this process. It may be squared with a carpenter's framing-square; or, if a number of flats are to be made, a right angle may be made on the floor with short pieces of wood (see Fig. 38), into which the corner of the flat may be held during the nailing process. In the same manner, the toggle-rail should be inserted. Usually, it is placed five feet from the floor; a better idea, however, is to place it *seven feet from the top;* then it will be possible to build in a seven-foot door by the mere process of turning the flat upside down. After the corrugators have been placed on the face of the flat, it should be turned over, and a *single* corrugator driven into the *center* of each of the joints. Thus, each corner is held together by *three* corrugators, carefully placed so that they are not driven into one another.

In building a door or window flat the process is similar, except that the pieces will be cut to leave the desired opening. A door flat will have its middle rail placed at the top of the door opening and will need two long pieces (door stiles) to frame the side of the opening. A frame of this shape will be difficult to handle because the narrow side pieces will be flexible, and it is even possible that they may break off. To overcome this difficulty most door flats are fitted at the bottom with an iron sill, which is merely a piece of strap iron, $\frac{3}{16}''$ thick and $\frac{3}{4}''$ wide and $5'9''$ long. It must be drilled, and the holes countersunk, so that it can be fastened with screws under the bottom rails of the door flat. Thus it holds the legs rigid, and keeps the bottom of the door hole its proper width. The stiles of a flat to be made in this manner must be $\frac{3}{16}''$ shorter than the finished height of the flat. Sometimes sill irons are made a foot or so shorter than the width of the flat: in this case part of the rails must be sawed or chiseled out, to make a rabbet into which the sill iron can be fitted.

To build a window flat it will be necessary to use two middle rails, one at the top and one at the bottom of the opening, and two window stiles to frame the sides. To make a flat rock, or flat tree, it is only necessary to lay out the material (see Fig. 50) to make the desired shape. In case of an irregular shape of this sort, the joints will rarely be right angles, but they can still be butt joints made by cutting the pieces at the required angles. Rails and reënforcing framing can be put in wherever necessary.

2. *Reënforcing the Frame.* Whatever the shape of the framed piece, the corrugators will not hold it together with sufficient strength to make it usable in the theater. Each joint needs now to be reënforced. It is customary to nail a corner-block on each corner joint, and a keystone on each T-joint. *Corners* and *keystones* are made out of ¼" plywood—thin

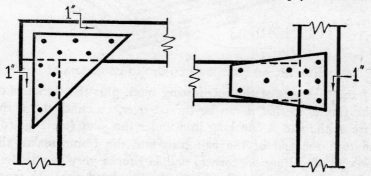

FIG. 39. REËNFORCING BLOCKS—CORNER AND KEYSTONE

sheets of wood (usually three in number) glued together under pressure. As the grains are crossed, plywood is very tough. Corners and keystones may be purchased from theatrical-supply stores or lumber yards, and come in various sizes. The size of a corner is determined by the length of the sides making the right angle; the size of keystones by the overall length. For ordinary use, ten-inch corners and eight-inch keystones are most satisfactory. Corners and keystones may also be homemade, especially if a mechanical saw is available. The plywood may be purchased in sheets, usually 4′ x 8′. It is often called in the theater, where is has many other uses (see p. 266 and p. 279), profile board.

Corners and keystones may be screwed onto the joints, with seven-eighths inch or one-inch screws, or they may be fastened on with nails. A special theatrical nail, which can usually be purchased only at theatrical supply houses, is made for this purpose. It is a square, soft-iron nail, with a large, flat head, called a clout nail. It comes in varying lengths. For normal building, the most useful size is the one and one-quarter inch clout nail. The nail should be a little longer than the total

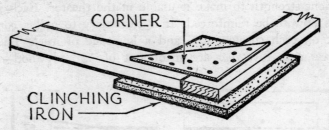

FIG. 40. METHOD OF CLINCHING CLOUT NAILS

of the thickness of the reënforcing block plus the thickness of the frame, so that it can be turned over, or clinched, on the face of the flat. A clinching iron under the joint (see Fig. 40) to turn the end of the nail back into the frame makes the process of nailing on corners and keystones very rapid. Both corners and keystones should *always* be placed one inch from the edges, so that completed flats can be set at right angles to each other and make a smooth corner. It is most important that frames be kept square during the process of fastening on the reënforcing block, since once reënforced, they are completely rigid. It is probably unnecessary to say that all the blocks should be on the *same side* of the frame, the back, leaving the other side, the face, clean for the covering.

3. *Covering the Frame.* The frames may be covered with any material on which it is possible to paint. Three materials are commonly used for this purpose: (1) theatrical canvas, (2) enameling duck, and (3) unbleached muslin. The theatrical canvas is the best material, but the most expensive. It is

a tight square weave of *linen*, commonly two yards in width, preshrunk and flameproofed. Just as lumber is named by the size to which it is sawed, cloth is named from the width it is loomed; thus, two-yard wide canvas loses two or three inches in the process of being shrunk. This material is often only sixty-nine inches wide—which is another reason for making flats not wider than five feet, nine inches. Canvas is very tough and gives a beautiful painting surface. Enameling duck is similar to canvas (and it is often called canvas), but it is made

FIG. 41. FLAT PLACED ON HORSES FOR COVERING

of *cotton*. It is usually half as expensive, normally between fifty and sixty cents a running yard—which, of course, is two square yards. Like canvas, theatrical duck is preshrunk and flameproofed. Unbleached muslin is also a cotton cloth, but its weave is not nearly so tight; therefore, it is not the equal of canvas or duck in either wearing or painting quality. Muslin comes in many weights, and the heavier it is the better for covering. It is usually not flameproofed and is rarely used in making professional scenery, except for big drops that will not receive heavy wear. It has the advantage of coming in varying widths, so sometimes wastage may be avoided. Also, it is made very wide—sometimes twelve or fifteen feet—hence a large drop can be made with few seams. It is, however, not very serviceable for covering flats, and duck is preferable.

Whatever the material, a piece should be cut roughly a little larger than the frame (an inch a side is sufficient allowance), laid over the frame, and tacked along the inner edges with ordinary carpet tacks. This process may be done with the frame face up on the floor, but it is less back-breaking if the frame is placed on benches or horses that will raise it to waist level. In professional studios, most of the framing and covering is done on a large waist-high bench, with clinching irons built in at the proper places. This is a useful aid, if the workshop is large enough to contain such a bench. In tacking, the center of the long sides should be the starting points from which the tacking should continue to the end of the frame. It is important to keep the weave of the material as square as possible and not to twist or warp it. It takes at least two workers to

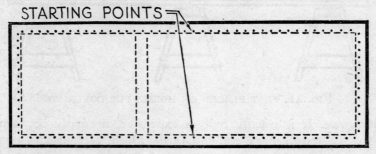

STARTING POINTS

FIG. 42. TACKS ARE PLACED ALONG THE INNER EDGE OF THE
BATTEN, BUT NOT DRIVEN WAY DOWN

cover a flat properly, one working on each side, tightening the material by pulling it away from the center and away from each other. Four persons, working in pairs, make the process very quick. After the material is tacked to the stiles, it should be tacked on the ends in a similar way, again starting in the middle of the end rails. The tacking is always along the inner edge of the face of the frame with the tacks six or eight inches apart. The tacks should not be driven way down, but left projecting a quarter of an inch. Painting is going to shrink the material, so it must not be too tightly stretched. On the other hand, if it is too loose, the canvas will remain flapping even after painting. Probably only experience will teach just how tightly it should be stretched, but it is safe to state that it should have no noticeable sag and should be smooth and unwrinkled.

Now the material must be glued to the frame. The cloth is

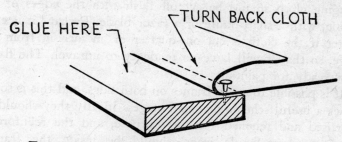

GLUE HERE — TURN BACK CLOTH

FIG. 43. METHOD OF GLUING CLOTH ON FRAME

turned back everywhere to the tacks, exposing the greater part of the wood (see Fig. 43). The wood is painted with glue thickly applied, the cloth pulled back over the glue and set into it by rubbing the surface out from the center with a cloth dampened with hot water. Use ground glue, which can be

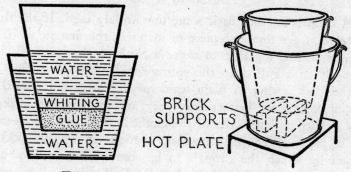

WATER
WHITING
GLUE
WATER

BRICK SUPPORTS

HOT PLATE

FIG. 44. METHOD OF PREPARING GLUE

secured from any hardware or paint store, melted in an ordinary iron glue pot, or in a double-boiler arrangement of buckets. Whiting should be added to the glue, making what is called white glue, so that the canvas will not be discolored along the edges by the glue. A common formula is one part of whiting, two parts of glue, and six parts of water (see pp. 240-241). After the glue is thoroughly dry, the tacks may be removed with a claw hammer or a pair of pliers. The overhanging cloth should be cut off flush with the edges of the frame, with a sharp knife or a razor blade. Perhaps it is even better if the cloth is cut one-quarter of an inch in from the edge, so that it will have no tendency to unravel. The flat is now ready for painting.

It is possible to cover frames on both sides, and this is sometimes a useful scheme on small stages. Ideally they should be mortised and tenoned for this purpose, and the reënforcing pieces—perhaps angle irons—should be inside the frames. However, it is not impossible to cover the back, right over the corners and keystones, which will not be too visible, especially if they are beveled. Double-covered flats may be hinged together in many ways, and an ingenious designer using this scheme can often make elaborate set changes with slight off-stage space.

BUILDING A DROP

A drop is another basic scene unit widely used. If the drop is to be larger than one piece of material, the first step will be to sew widths together to make a cloth of the required size. Usually in a full drop the seams run lengthwise as this demands less sewing. A plain seam may be used, but lapped or double seams are better, since they are stronger and make a flat surface on both sides of the cloth, thus allowing both sides to be painted. The next problem is to fasten on the sticks of wood by which the drop is to be suspended (see Fig. 21). This wood is usually called a batten.[2] Full drops will probably have a batten both at top and bottom. Short drops, such as borders, will have a batten only at the top.

---

[2] This is another example (see p. 179) of nautical language transferred into the theater, perhaps by early sailor-stagehands. To a sailor, any long thin stick is a batten. Thus, he "battens down" a hatch, by nailing thin strips of wood over the edges of the tarpaulin that covers it.

PLATE IX A (above). *The School for Husbands*, by Moliere

A charming exterior designed by Lee Simonson. A modern, decorative version of the perspective street scene of the 17th and 18th century theater. Sliding panels in the front houses allowed the audience to see their interiors. (See p. 310.)

PLATE IX B (below). *Henry VIII*, by William Shakespeare

An exterior, designed by David Ffolkes. A castle is suggested by a palace wall, built in false perspective, against a sky-drop. (See p. 312.)

A

B

C

PLATES X AND XI. *The Man with a Terrible Temper* and *Stratonice,* operettas by Mehul

Designed by Richard Bernstein

A. The False proscenium and roll curtain used for *The Man with a Terrible Temper.*

B, C and D. Steps in the process of folding and striking the proscenium. (See p. 270.)

(See p. 270.)

E. The exterior for *Stratonice,* set permanently behind the other settings. The colonnade is a flat cut-out, in one plane, with painted shadows.

F. Detail of the door, at left in E, which is also flat with painted thickness.

Gabrielson

Columbia University: The Morningside Players

Mulhollan

PLATE XII A (above). *If Booth Had Missed*, by Arthur Goodman

Lincoln's office in the White House. The set consists of five flats set inside a black cyclorama
Designed by Sherman Raveson. (See p. 311.)

PLATE XII B (below). *The Boor*, by Anton Chekov

A parlor. Another spot set, consisting of three flats, masked by a black cyclorama. Designe
by Arnold Hoskwith.

Columbia University: Columbia College Players

Mulholla

If the drop is light in weight, a single batten may be sufficient. In that case, the cloth may be placed on the face of the batten and glued and tacked just as on a flat. It is very important, if the drop is made in this manner, that the material be merely placed smoothly on the surface, and *not pulled*. The cloth of the drop will shrink with painting; therefore the edge must not be stretched. In order to avoid this possibility,

GLUE HERE

FIG. 45. SCARF JOINT

it is often better to paint the drop first and to mount it on the battens after painting.

Often it will be necessary to make the batten by joining two pieces of lumber end to end. For light weight drops, 1"x3" may be used. For heavier drops, it is customary to use 1"x4", or even 1¼"x4". In any case, the method of joining two sticks end to end is identical. A wedge is cut off each end of the two sticks, making a lap, which may be one and a half or two feet long. The two cut surfaces are then fastened together (see Fig. 45) with glue, screws, and small nails at the edges. This is called a scarf joint.

A double batten is made by placing one piece of wood on the top of another, with the cloth in between, and fastening them together with screws or nails. In this case, it will not be necessary to use many tacks to hold the cloth, since there should be sufficient pressure between the battens to hold it. It is better if both battens have been scarf-joined to a sufficient length, but this is not absolutely necessary. By using shorter pieces of wood, so placed that end to end joints on the one are covered by the solidness of the other, thus acting as cleats, it is possible to make a double batten of sufficient strength for many purposes. This is called a lap joint.

MAKING PLASTIC PIECES

The final basic scene unit is those elements having a third dimension and called plastic pieces. These will doubtlessly be of great variety. For some of this building, we shall need lumber wider than one by three inches. A useful assortment consists of 1"x4", 1"x6", 1"x8", and 1"x12".

1. *Doors and Window Frames.* Probably the most common plastic pieces that will be needed are door and window frames. They should be used with every set. Nothing looks more amateurish, in the worst sense, than scenery in which the doors are mere holes in the flats and which show that the wall has no thickness. The frames are made so that from the front they appear just like ordinary frames in a house. They may be wide or narrow, plain or ornate. The lighter they are, the easier they are to handle, and the less must they be braced. They should fit snugly into the hole, but they should slip in and out without pounding. A few screws through the batten of the hole and into the frame will hold it securely in place against the surface of the flat or it may be held in place by strap hinges on the door frame (see Fig. 46), which when opened will wedge it against the door stiles. If the door hole into which the frame is to be fitted has a sill iron, it will be necessary to cut a groove in the bottom of the sill to fit over the iron.

Professionally-made door frames usually have a clearance of two or three inches in each dimension. This allows the door frame to be reënforced with corner blocks, or wooden triangles, which are securely glued and nailed into the angle made by the facing and the jamb. However, this means that the door hole must be made extra-large, which is not always desirable in non-professional building, and door frames made as indicated in the illustration are satisfactory for all but the heaviest usage. In fact, often when there is no facing (see doors and windows in Plate XIV A), or when the facing is to be painted (see Plate IV A), the jamb, or thickness, may be nailed directly to the flat. It may consist of three, four, six, or eight inch wide pieces

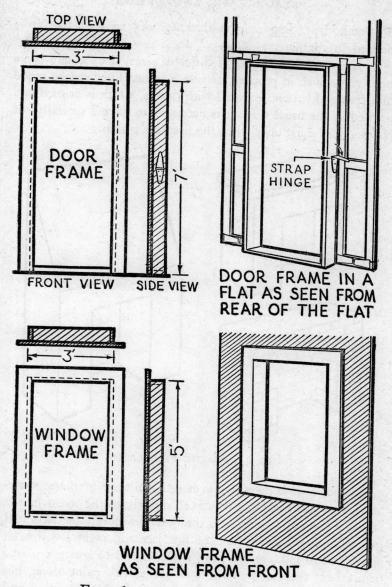

TOP VIEW

3'

DOOR FRAME

FRONT VIEW

SIDE VIEW

7'

STRAP HINGE

DOOR FRAME IN A FLAT AS SEEN FROM REAR OF THE FLAT

3'

WINDOW FRAME

5'

WINDOW FRAME AS SEEN FROM FRONT

FIG. 46. DOOR AND WINDOW FRAMES

of wood, depending on the thickness of the wall that it is desired to simulate.

2. *Fireplaces*. Fireplaces of different sizes, shapes, and colors help very much in properly setting a scene. They can be made of a frame of battens, covered with canvas, which is primed and painted in the usual way. It is necessary to have a specially cut opening in the flat only when the fireplace is thin.

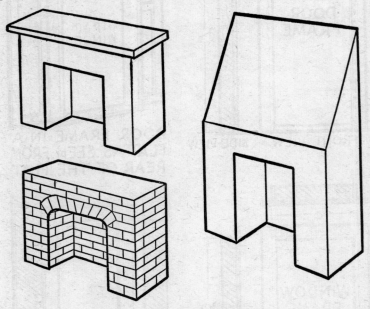

FIG. 47. PLASTIC FIREPLACES

It is not always necessary to have a built-out fireplace: sometimes a mantel shelf can be affixed directly to the flat over the fireplace hole, and sometimes the hole can merely be decorated (see Plate XIII A). Often the fireplace and mantel will need decoration to indicate the proper period and to create a plastic trim effect: this can sometimes be done with paint alone, but often it may be better if actually trimmed with moulding and papier-mâché (see Plate IV A). Whenever there is an opening in the flat for the fireplace, the opening will need to be masked with small pieces arranged to represent the back and sides of

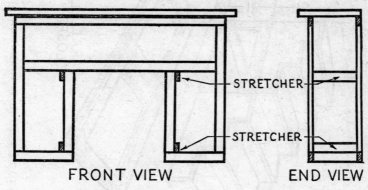

FRONT VIEW   END VIEW

FIG. 48. FRAMING OF A PLASTIC FIREPLACE

the firebox. The presence of a fireplace in a setting often is a great aid toward interesting lighting. A "fire" in the fireplace (see Fig. 98), sometimes reënforced by a hidden spot light, is often a valuable light source. If the fireplace is thick, so that there actually need be no fireplace hole in the flat, the cable to the lights can be run along the floor under the flat, so that no hole need be made in it.

3. *Posts.* A post, or a column, may be made in a similar way of a wooden frame covered with canvas. A number of wooden circles may be fastened together with long wooden slats. Square posts and beams can be made in the usual manner by nailing long boards together at right angles, leaving off those in back which will not show.

4. *Platforms and Steps.* Platforms and stairs are often very useful pieces. The illustration shows a common design for a platform, which has the advantage of folding flat, so that it can be stored in a small space. A platform made in this manner is called a parallel. Notice that there are hinges on each inner corner of the supporting frame. When the frame is opened out it

STAIR AND PLATFORM UNITS

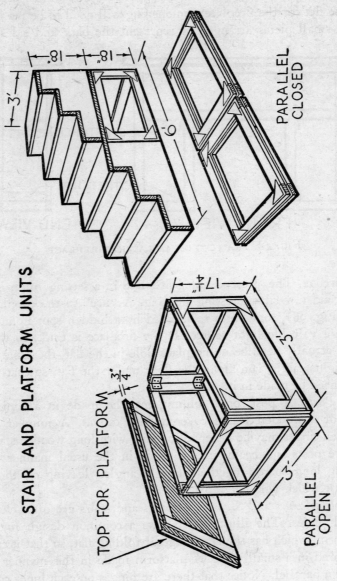

FIG. 49. DESIGN FOR STAIR AND PLATFORM UNITS TO BE USED IN COMBINATIONS

TOP FOR PLATFORM

PARALLEL OPEN

PARALLEL CLOSED

234

may be braced if necessary, although if the top is made carefully enough it ought to hold the frame rigid.

The parallel, shown in Fig. 49, is essentially the method used to build most platforms in the theater. Often the parallel frame is constructed with a bottom rail a few inches off the floor, so that only the uprights (the stiles) touch the floor. This helps to prevent rocking if the surface of the stage is uneven. Sometimes it is necessary to build cross-braces into the frames: they may run from corner to corner in narrow frames, and in wider ones from the middle of the top rail to the lower corners, where the stiles and bottom rails meet. Parallels may be built almost any size; but when a large platform is wanted, it is common practice to make the top the size of the required area, but to support it with several small parallels, which may stand two or three feet from each other. If the parallel is large, say three by six or eight feet, instead of the three by three feet shown in the illustration, it is often necessary to put in an extra center frame. This makes the unit consist of five frames, instead of four. In this case, the two side frames must be identical in size, and the two ends and the single center frame must be identical. The latter are all placed inside the side frames, and the hinges must now be placed on alternate surfaces of the end and center frames, so that the parallel will fold. A little experimenting with the placement of the hinges will make the necessary arrangement clear.

Stage stairs usually have a lower riser than ordinary ones, and a wider tread. This makes them easier for the actors to play on. The standard dimensions are for the riser six inches high, and for the tread one foot wide. If stairs and platforms are made to a similar dimension, interesting combinations may be made. Thus, in the illustration, where the standard size is three feet long, three feet wide, and one and one-half feet high, the platform placed at the end of the stairs raises the unit of stairs so that a continuous flight of steps is made. With a number of

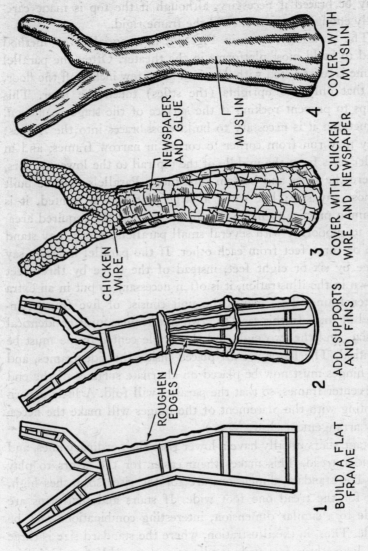

ROUGHEN EDGES

1
BUILD A FLAT FRAME

2
ADD SUPPORTS AND FINS

CHICKEN WIRE

NEWSPAPER AND GLUE

3
COVER WITH CHICKEN WIRE AND NEWSPAPER

MUSLIN

4
COVER WITH MUSLIN

FIG. 50. STEPS IN BUILDING A PLASTIC TREE

236

units of both stairs and platform all sorts of interesting combinations are possible.

5. *Trees and Rocks*. All the plastic pieces previously suggested are built much in the same way as they are by carpenters in a house. There is one type of plastic piece, widely used in theater practice only and based on *papier-mâché* (which literally means "chewed paper"). Papier-mâché is a paper pulp mixed with glue or paste which dries into a hard, tough substance. The usual method of building a tree, a rock, or a similar object is to make a framework of the required shape, to cover this frame with chicken wire, and to make a coat of papier-mâché on the wire. This process is not difficult, and there are many objects which can be successfully made in no other way. In making a tree, for example, the first step will be to build a flat tree (see Fig. 50) of the desired shape, leaving it uncovered. A plastic tree needs rarely to be more than half, or at the most three-quarters, round, as the back can be seen only by the actors. Therefore, it is necessary to build a thickness only on the front. This can be done by cutting a series of boards, each shaped to be the cross-section of the tree at the place where it is to be fastened. These cross-sections or fins, may be four or five feet apart; and the straight edge will be nailed to the flat from the back leaving the board projecting forward. The bottom cross-section forms the base of the tree. The cross-sections must now be reënforced by nailing three or four pieces of wood between them, the number depending on the size of the cross-section. If we wish the surface of the tree to be rough, or curved, we may roughen the outer edge of these supporting pieces with a knife or hatchet. The next step will be to cover the framed tree with chicken wire. Wire with a not-too-large mesh, say one and one-half or two inch, is preferable. It may be cut as necessary with tin shears and fastened to the frame with small staples. Now this wire may be covered with papier-mâché, which may be made by tearing newspaper into small pieces, boiling it until it becomes pulp, then adding white glue until we

have a sticky, clay-like substance. This can be molded on the wire. Another, and perhaps an easier method, is to cover the wire with a number of coats of newspaper dipped in glue. Wheaten paste, such as is used in paper hanging, may be used in place of glue and is much cheaper. Some builders make an adhesive of half paste and half glue. The final step in the process is to cover the paper coat with a cloth one. This may not be necessary if real papier-mâché is used. Muslin is useful for this purpose; and if a rough surface is desired, it should be left wrinkled to simulate the bark of a tree. Sometimes it is easier to make this cloth coat out of small square pieces, say eighteen inches square. Then each piece may be dipped in the paste, rung out, and applied. Of course, the squares must be slightly overlapped. After the tree has been allowed to dry, it is ready for painting. Pictures of plastic trees are shown in Plate VIII A and Plate VIII B. In the same manner, a rock can be built by making a flat of the proper shape; building thickness on it; covering it with chicken wire, and coats of paper and cloth. If the rock is to be practical (that is, such that actors can walk on it), it must be planned so that the top surface, even though it is roughened with papier-mâché, is a platform.[3] Sometimes it is simpler to build rocks out of boxes, covered with canvas, and stuffed so as to be irregular in shape. Of course, rocks—and trees—need not always be realistic. Plate XVI shows some interesting conventionalized rocks, which were used in changing combinations. In fact, the only limit to the possibility for plastic pieces is the ingenuity of the designer and the builder.

[3] Any stage article is said to be practical if it can function. Thus a practical rock is one on which the actors can walk, a practical window is one that can be opened, a practical lamp is one that is wired so that it can be turned on, etc.

CHAPTER XVIII

Painting Scenery

Like all other painters, the scene-painter uses pigment to make color. This pigment cannot be applied directly to the surface of an object we wish to color. It must be mixed in a medium, or vehicle. When it is mixed with oil or turpentine, as is usually the case in painting a house or in decorating a room, the result is oil paint. When it is mixed with water, the result is water-color. The scene-painter nearly always uses water-color.

The pigments used by the scene-painter commonly come in two forms: *dry colors,* which are powders, and *pulp colors,* which come in containers in paste form. Either may be used. The most brilliant and powerful colors are often obtainable only in pulp form because it is impossible to grind them dry. They sometimes are more expensive in cost per pound, but their brilliance and intensity may make them go much farther. However, much scene-painting can be done with dry colors only; and these will probably be the basis of the scene-painter's palette. Every painter will probably have his own favorite assortment of colors. For general use, the following colors are recommended:

American Vermilion. This is the cheapest common red. English Vermilion is better, but more expensive. American Vermilion is not a permanent color, but this doesn't matter to the scene-painter. Normally, sixty cents a pound.

239

Chrome Yellow Medium. A good cheap yellow, slightly golden. Twenty-five cents a pound.

French Ochre. A tan or buff-colored yellow; very useful as it mixes well with any other color. Twelve cents a pound.

Burnt Umber. A rich dark brown. Twelve cents a pound.

Burnt Sienna. A useful reddish brown. Fifteen cents a pound.

Chrome Green Medium. A useful grass green. Twenty-five cents a pound.

Ultramarine Blue. A warm medium blue, slightly purple. Thirty cents per pound.

Italian Blue. A powerful, turquoise blue. Sixty-five cents a pound.

Drop Black. A carbon, blue black. Ivory black or Bone black (which is a brown black) are probably better, and easier to use, although more expensive. Drop black is good enough for most purposes. Twenty cents a pound.

Whiting. Powdered calcium carbonate, used by the scene-painter in large quantities. The cheapest paint in the palette, but it pays to get a good quality of sifted, or bolted, whiting. Three or four cents a pound.

With the above colors at hand, the scene-painter will rarely find it impossible to make the color he needs. The amount of each that he will find it wise to keep on hand can be determined only by experience. I find it useful, however, in addition to twenty or thirty pounds each of the above colors, to have available a few pounds of each of these special colors: *Van Dyke Brown,* a rich, deep brown, very good for graining or painting wood; *French Orange Mineral,* a brilliant red-orange, difficult to make; *Hanover Green,* a bright, warm green, useful for foliage; *Royal Purple,* a cool purple, useful for shadows; and *Zinc White,* useful when Whiting is not sufficiently white.

The medium used in scene-painting is not water alone because if it were, as the water dried, the pigment would fall off the canvas. The water must contain glue to bind the pigment. We may say then that the ingredients of scene paint are (1) pigment, (2) water, and (3) glue. The glue should be heated in a double boiler (see Fig. 44), so a stove, or an electric plate, is indispensable. Glue is used continually, both in painting and building, so it is usually wise to prepare a bucket of saturated solution, by soaking three or four pounds of ground glue for several hours in just sufficient water to cover it. It should then be heated—but not boiled. This strong glue, which should be the consistency of heavy cream, can be diluted with water as it is to be used. When only a small amount of glue is necessary, or when there is no provision for heating it, cold furniture glue (which may be purchased in pint or quart cans) may be substituted. The combination of glue and water is often called size or sizing. An approximate formula for making size is one part strong glue to three parts of hot water. These proportions may vary greatly, however, since glue varies in strength, no matter how carefully it is prepared. To test the strength of the size, dip the fingers into it and press them together for a few seconds. If when one endeavors to separate them, they adhere slightly, the size is right. If the fingers adhere quickly and firmly, the size is too strong and needs thinning with more hot water. Size that is too strong will make the painting shine when dry and gives it a tendency to flake off. If the size is too weak, the paint will continue to fall off as powder. Fortunately the range of good size is fairly wide, and a little experience makes it possible to gauge the proper strength. For metallic paints, such as bronze and aluminum powders, which may be extensively used in painting properties and costumes, dextrine is a better medium than glue.

There are two common ways of mixing the size and the pigment. Sometimes the pigments are added to the size directly; thus the scene-painter stirs up wet in a bucket the color he is making. He must know, in this case, that *the wet paint will be several shades darker than it will appear when dry.* He can, therefore, judge the color accurately only by putting some on a piece of cloth and allowing it to dry. For this reason, some painters mix the dry color first. Colors mixed dry (they must be mixed very thoroughly) appear approximately the color of the dried coat. The size is added to the mixed color. In painting a surface which cannot be finished in one work period, this method has the advantage of allowing the size to be added as the paint is needed.

Paint to which the size has been added sours as it stands and becomes very disagreeable. This tendency can be prevented, or at least delayed, by adding a spoonful of disinfectant such as carbolic acid. Some of the dry colors, especially red and black, which are greasy, do not readily mix with water, and they will mix much more easily if a small amount of alcohol is added.

If paint is to be made by mixing several colors of dry pigment, it is often difficult to match. It is wise, therefore, to make a generous amount. Unfortunately, there is no accurate rule for the amount necessary to cover any given surface. In general, a two-gallon pail of paint will cover six standard flats—except for the first, or priming, coat (see below) which may take much more. If the paint does not cover the surface properly, it is too thin, and more pigment must be added; if it is hard to paint with, and drags the brush, it is too thick and should be thinned with more hot water.

In painting drops, or pieces of scenery that are to be rolled or folded, paint made in the above manner has a tendency, no matter how carefully it is prepared, to flake off. This can be prevented by using gelatin glue in place of ordinary ground glue. Gelatin glue can be prepared and used in the same manner, except that it needs to be soaked longer. It is more expensive and dries much more slowly, so it is not as useful for general scene-painting.

If the flats have previously been painted, and the old paint tends to bleed through, this can often be prevented by first painting on a thin solution of alum. Or, the flats may be washed. This is best done out-of-doors, where the flats can be stood against a building. They should be placed on blocks to hold them off the ground. A hose is almost essential, and it is better if the water can be hot. The paint should be well soaked with warm water, loosened by rubbing not too vigorously with ordinary scrubbing brushes, and then flushed off with the hose. If the tacks have previously been removed from the face of the flat, it had better be retacked before washing, as the process is likely to loosen the glue. If necessary, after washing, the canvas can be re-stretched and re-tacked. Ordinarily, however, unless dye paints are used, a flat may be painted a number of times before it needs to be washed. The signal for washing will be the flaking off of the numerous coats of paint as the flat is handled.

TOOLS OF THE PAINTER

As suggested above, the scene-painter needs some method of heating glue, and a well-built electric stove, of one or two plates, is sufficient in a small theater. The larger amounts of paint will probably be mixed in buckets, so he needs an assortment of two and three-gallon galvanized pails. Many small

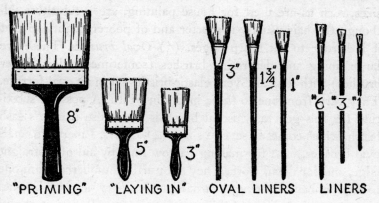

"PRIMING"   "LAYING IN"   OVAL LINERS   LINERS

FIG. 51. KINDS OF BRUSHES

cans will be useful for making small amounts of paint. His main tools, of course, will be brushes.

The brushes used by professional scenic artists are especially designed; they are made of extra long bristles which are extremely elastic, and they are well-balanced and easy to work with. They are more expensive than ordinary brushes and obtainable only at scenic-supply houses. If properly cared for, however, they last a long time and may in the end be cheaper than a succession of less expensive brushes. Proper care means that they should never be allowed to stand in paint, even for a short time, that they should not be used to stir paint, and that they should be thoroughly washed after each using in warm (*not hot*) water and hung up to dry. A school theater might well, then, have a growing collection of good scenic brushes. Four types of brushes will be useful:

(1) *Priming brushes*. Scenic priming brushes are long-haired, and seven or eight inches wide. They are used to paint large areas. A cheaper substitute would be ordinary calsomining brushes. (2) *Laying-in brushes*. These are similar to priming brushes, but not so large. The ordinary sizes used are three inches, four inches, and five inches. Ordinary brushes of these sizes, such as are used for house painting, are a substitute, although the hair usually is shorter and of poorer quality so that it is harder to cut sharp edges. (3) *Oval brushes*. These are large lining and decorating brushes (sometimes called Fisher brushes) with long and very elastic bristles set in an oval ferrule. They vary from one to three inches in width. A possible substitute for this generally-useful brush is the house painter's sash brush, which comes in several sizes. (4) *Liners*. Liners are small oval brushes, used for making narrow lines by aid of a straight edge, and for detail work. They are usually numbered from one to six, number one being the smallest. Ordinary one inch brushes are a possible substitute. The scene-painter will find it useful to have a varied collection of small brushes of all sorts.

In addition to brushes, the scene-painter applies paint with many other tools: sponges, pieces of cloth, rolls of paper, feather dusters, whips of rope and cloth, even his hands. Many of these methods, and other useful tools, will be discussed later in connection with specific processes.

PAINTING A FLAT COAT

One of the most difficult things to do in scene-painting is to paint a good even flat coat. The paint must be well-mixed and of the right consistency. It should be stirred occasionally with a stick to prevent the pigment from settling; and in making more than one bucket, the paint should be poured back and forth in the buckets to secure a constant color. The method is to use a large brush, a primer, and to make brush strokes promiscuously in all directions, so that the surface is thoroughly covered. This is called a weave.

The commonest use of flat painting is for the first, or priming, coat, which will give a smooth surface on which to paint the colors. This first coat fills the pores of the material, and applying it is often called sizing a flat. The material used is sizing water and whiting, and the method of preparing the paint has been previously described. This mixture of sizing water and whiting is also often called sizing. If a priming brush is too heavy for the painter, the priming may be done with a laying-in brush.

There are a number of things to be remembered in laying on a flat coat. The amount of paint on the brush should be only the amount that the brush will hold (the better the brush, the more it will hold), so that it should not drip all over the floor and the surface. The excess paint should be wiped off gently on the edge of the bucket. With inexperienced painters, it is often a good idea to fasten a wire across the diameter of the top of the bucket from the ends of the handle; this can be used for wiping off the excess paint, which will then drop into the bucket and not run down the outside to the floor. The correct stroke is the weaving stroke already described, and each stroke should be feathered off at each end. Start at one corner of the surface and cover as you go. The brush should be held almost at right angles to the surface, which should not be scrubbed with the side of the brush. The working part of the brush is the tip, and a good brush does not need much pressure. The surface should be completely covered as the painter works along, so that he does not have to come back and splash a little paint on some untouched area. The technique of painting a flat coat is worth acquiring, and careful thoughtfulness in the beginning will lead to the development of both skill and great speed.

In professional painting, the priming coat is usually white. This is partially because whiting is much cheaper than any of the colored pigments. Sometimes, especially when one or more of the methods of pointillage—to be described later—are to be applied, it is worth while to add a basic color to the priming coat. In a small set, the difference in expense is not great.

For this painting, and for all that is to follow, it is usual to hang the drops vertically and to paint from a ladder or a bridge. A bridge is an elevated platform, so placed that the drop may be raised or lowered so that each part of its surface can be reached. However, it is perfectly possible to spread drops out on the floor for painting. Flats may be placed either vertically or horizontally, but they should be nailed to a paint frame, a flat wall or a floor, so they will not warp. The painting shop should be supplied with an assortment of old canvas (paint cloths) which can be spread on the floor under the surfaces being painted. This makes the task of cleaning up less onerous.

THE VALUE OF BROKEN COLOR

Having described the process of painting a flat coat, it now becomes necessary to say that the modern scene-painter does it as seldom as possible. Instead, he gives the impression of a flat surface by the use of broken color. This means that the desired color is analyzed into basic color elements, and each of these elements is applied individually as a series of small spots. For instance, if he wishes to give the tone of a stone wall, he may apply spots of gray, and brown, and gray-green. If he wishes to produce a green surface, he may cover it with spots of yellow, blue, and green. The old scene-painter would have mixed all these colors together and painted a flat coat; the new scene-painter breaks up the desired color into its elements and applies each individually. Thus he creates a lively and vibrant surface, capable of great variation under light, and having much more the quality of solidity. The eye mixes the colors thus applied in spots, and sees them as a whole.

This method of painting is not unique with the modern scene-painter. It is used extensively by many modern artists, especially those who call themselves *Neo-impressionists*. They call this method of painting in small spots *pointillism*. In the theater it is more often called pointillage.

COMMON METHODS OF POINTILLAGE

There are many methods of applying pointillage, and non-professional scene-painters would do well to use them wherever possible. Broken color surfaces are much easier to do and much more interesting in result.

1. *Stippling*. Stippling is done by pressing the end of a medium full brush against the surface, so that the tip of the brush makes a pattern of small spots. The brush must not be twisted on the surface, but it must be constantly turned in the air so as to vary the pattern. Sometimes a feather duster can be used for this purpose. If necessary, the feathers can be cut short so as to make a better pattern.

2. *Spattering*. A brush, usually a primer, is dipped in paint, which is spattered on to the surface by shaking or snapping it so that the paint falls on the surface in small drops. Sometimes the brush is struck against the wrist or palm of the other hand. This is, perhaps, one of the commonest means of pointillage in professional studios. The surface to be spattered may be vertical or horizontal; but if it is vertical, it is necessary to have the paint sufficiently thick so that gravity will not cause the spots to run. Another method of spattering is to use a short-haired brush (a common scrubbing brush sawed in half is

excellent), and by holding the brush at right angles to the surface and drawing a knife over the ends of the hairs, snap the paint on to the surface. The paint must be medium thick, and the surface must be vertical. This gives a pattern of smaller

STIPPLING   SPATTERING

FIG. 52. METHODS OF STIPPLING AND SPATTERING

spots than stippling with a long-haired brush, and is excellent for shading, or changing the general tone of a surface, without dimming the details.

3. *Cloth-rolling*. A piece of cloth, twelve or fifteen inches square, is dipped into the paint, wrung partly dry, and then *while still twisted*, rolled across the surface to be painted. The twisted cloth must be rolled in varying directions, so as to avoid a distinctive pattern. This may be done with the surface in either position, but it is easier for the beginner if the surface is horizontal.

4. *Sponging*. A large sponge is trimmed so that it has a flat surface. The trimming should be done with the sponge completely dry. The sponge is dipped into the paint, wrung out, and the flat surface is patted on to the surface to be painted. The result is a pattern of spots made by the face of the sponge.

The sponge must be constantly turned to left and right during the pattern, so that the outline of the sponge will be lost in the larger pattern of spots. But it must not be turned *while it*

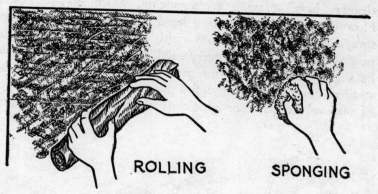

ROLLING   SPONGING

FIG. 53. METHOD OF CLOTH ROLLING AND SPONGING

is on the surface. The surface to be sponged may be either vertical or horizontal. This is a useful and rapid method.

5. *Puddling.* The surface to be covered is placed horizontally, and the paint is poured on, then pushed about and blended with a large brush. Several colors may be used, usually variations of the same color, such as two or three shades of green and a green-yellow. This process can be very rapid if one person is appointed to take a bucket of each color and simply pour on a small puddle as it is needed, while one or two others with brushes blend the edges of the puddles by running them together. Those using the brushes must be careful to leave the center of the puddles the original colors and merely to blend the edges. This is a quick way to create a varied background of browns or grays for a stone wall. Another method, which is somewhat similar in effect, and which may be done with the surface vertical, is to use a different brush for each color and continually change brushes, painting only a small area at a time and blending it, while still wet, with adjacent areas.

6. *Spraying*. Spraying is painting with an air-gun. The surface must be vertical. Motor-driven spray guns are available and are used in most professional studios. Sometimes vacuum cleaners have spraying arrangements, which may be used. However, a tank spray with a hand pump, such as is used for spraying poisons in gardens, is highly satisfactory and should be part of the equipment of every small theater. The paint should be slightly thinner than for most jobs and should always be strained into the tank through a piece of fine cloth since lumps of undissolved paint or glue will block up the nozzle. The

SPRAYING

FIG. 54. METHODS OF SPRAYING

size of the spots will be determined by the amount of air pumped into the tank, the greater the pressure, the finer the spray. The worker should always be opposite the surface to be sprayed, so he must spray the top of a flat from a ladder or platform. The nozzle should be four or five feet from the surface and should be kept in constant motion. The first and last burst from the gun, as it is turned on and off, will usually be blotchy, so it is necessary to start it pointed at the floor, away from the flat, and to turn it off only after it has been aimed away from the surface. In spite of care, much spray will fall on the floor, so it should be completely covered with paint cloths. This is the fastest method of making pointillage, and is very useful. Often this is the final step in any kind of painting, for a thin coat of spray smooths out irregularity, pulls the surface together, and gives it depth and solidity. Often—say over painted bricks, or wall paper, or woodwork—the final spray coat is purple or blue-black.

These methods of pointillage are often used in combination. For instance, to make a rough plaster wall, the painter may start with a light-tan priming coat. This may then be rolled or sponged with a darker brown, and smoothed out with a spray of purple-black. On the other hand, the surface of a blue-green room may be made by spattering on a coat of light blue, one of dark blue, one of yellow-green, and one of dark green. The order of the coats is not important, but it is easier to see the process if the lighter coats are put on first. Each coat must dry thoroughly before the next is applied.

Sometimes the walls of a room made by pointillage do not come together quite as the designer intended. This may be helped by a *glaze*. A glaze is a final watery coat of the basic color painted on as quickly as possible to help pull the spots together. It must be used with discretion, of course. Sometimes shellac thinned with alcohol is used as a glaze to give a glossy finish—especially on painted wood or marble. However, shellac tends to darken the painting.

SPECIAL SCENE-PAINTING TECHNIQUES

Not all scene-painting is done with pointillage, of course, for there are many effects for which it is not appropriate. Some of the other most commonly used methods are the following:

1. *Using Brush Strokes.* This is especially useful in painting foliage rapidly. The inexperienced scene-painter tries sometimes to paint individual leaves. The experienced painter finds a brush that gives him a spot of color of the desired size and shape, and boldly paints a leaf with a single slap of the brush. Perhaps he starts with a good medium green and quickly slaps on spots of color all over the area that is to be the foliage.

Now he must model this foliage area and give it shape. By taking some of the same green paint in a small can and adding black, and perhaps a small amount of blue, he makes a dark green; in the same way by adding white or yellow he makes a light green. The first is for shadows, the second for high lights. This leads to one of the primary principles in painting; *whatever is darker than the ground color will appear sunk, whatever is lighter will appear raised.* His dark and light will have the proper color quality because he has made them out of his base paint. Now with the same brush, he will slap on dark leaves, right over the green ones, wherever he wishes to sink his painting. Wherever he wishes to raise it, say at the ends and tops of branches where light is likely to fall, he will make light-green leaves. He does not try to hide his brush strokes; they are the unit of his painting. Perhaps a light spray of a different green will now pull the entire painting together. Foliage is truly not difficult, if done in this manner, and need not frighten the inexperienced painter.

The same principle of changing color is applicable to painting bricks, or stones, or any series of similar objects. They are unrealistic if they are all one color. The experienced painter, therefore, makes a basic brick color; then by adding varying quantities of white he makes two or three lighter colors. In the same way, by adding purple and black, he makes two or three darker shades. He knows that in nature, no two bricks are ever quite alike. With his five or six varying brick colors, one of which may be almost pink and one almost purple, and with a brush so shaped that one stroke will fill in the area of a brick, he is able rapidly, by varying his colors, to paint the brick surface. After lining in the white mortar, he sprays the surface with purple-black (See Plate VIII B). In the same way, he can make realistic stones, by constantly varying the color of a basic paint.

2. *Lining.* The scene-painter constantly finds it necessary to make lines to indicate molding, paneling, and shading; to show

mortar between bricks or stones; to outline boards; and for an infinite number of purposes. It is necessary that he be able to do this quickly and accurately. So far as possible (that is, unless a free-hand line is called for) he does this with a lining brush and a straight edge. Straight edges may be purchased from supply houses, and are usually about six feet long, two inches wide, and one quarter inch thick. A home-made straight edge can easily be manufactured out of a yardstick, or any long straight piece. It is easier to use if the edge is slightly beveled. The line is drawn against the beveled edge with the bevel down. The width of the line will depend on the pressure put on the brush. It pays to take the time to get the paint of the right consistency, so that it is easy to line with. A little practice will enable the painter to make a smooth even line of unvarying width.

If no lining brush is at hand, it is worth while to make one out of an ordinary small paint brush. A one inch brush is a good size for this purpose, unless the line is to be very wide, when a larger brush will be better. Cut a narrow piece of soft tin (if necessary from a tin can) with a pair of tin shears, about three-eighths of an inch wide, long enough to go one and a half times around the brush. Now wind the tin tightly around the brush about one quarter of an inch from the tips of the bristles. With a hammer, flatten the tin band thus made, so that it holds tightly to the brush. The nearer the band to the tips of the bristles, the finer the line, and the farther away, the broader. Thus, it is possible to prepare a brush to make a line of any thickness.

The most common fault in lining is to hold the brush too parallel to the surface. Again, it is the tip of the brush that should do the painting, and the brush should be only slightly less than a right angle to the surface. In this manner, with paint of a proper consistency, it will be possible to draw a line rapidly with a single stroke. The less repainting, the better.

Often it will be necessary to lay in the lines to be painted with chalk or charcoal. The experienced painter does this by using a snap line, which is a piece of string covered with chalk. If a long line is necessary, the snap line can be held at each end at the indicated points by two persons and tightly stretched while a third one in the middle pulls it up and snaps it. This makes a chalk line on the surface. Usually, several lines can be snapped without rechalking. If a short line is to be snapped,

LIGHT SOURCES

FIG. 55. FLAT DOORS WITH PAINTED PANELS

a bow can be used (see Fig. 58) so that the entire operation can be done by one person.

One of the commoner uses of lines is to indicate paneling, say in a door. The first step is to snap the outline of the panels. If it is simply a plain sunk panel, there will be but one outline; if the panel is surrounded with molding, there may be several lines. On the simplest panel there will be two light lines (high lights) and two dark lines (shadows). Here again the best way to make the paint is to use the base color and make the high light by adding white, and the shadows by adding black (see p. 252), for high lights and shadows are always basically the color of the object. Now it only remains to determine the direction from which the light is coming. If it is coming from above and from the right, the top and the right side of each panel will be shadowed (see Fig. 55). If the panels contain moldings, whatever is a shadow on the top of the panel will be a high light on the bottom, and vice versa. And whatever is a shadow on the right side of the panel, will be a high light on the left. Painting paneling is not difficult and is very useful in scene-painting. The inexperienced painter cannot do better than to observe the lines on real plastic molding. His task is merely to reproduce these permanently with painted lines. Notice the painted paneled wall in Plate IV A.

3. *Dry Brushing.* Dry brushing means painting with a brush from which most of the paint has been shaken or wiped, so that it does not leave a solid stroke, but merely a series of irregular lines. A good brush for this purpose is a three-inch laying-in brush. A stiff-bristled scrubbing brush may also be used. Dry brushing is the common method of suggesting graining in wood. In painting a board fence, we may use a wood-colored priming coat, break the fence into boards with black lines made with a lining brush, and then grain each board by dry brushing it with dark brown, or light yellow, or both. The shadows in Plate XI E are an example of dry brushing. Again, we may pull the painting together and give the fence solidity with a final spray of dark brown or brown-black, or age it with a spray of green-gray.

Dry brushing is also useful in painting panels. In painting the door previously described, we may find that, in spite of the lining, the panels do not appear sufficiently deep. The method of sinking them will be to dry brush a one-inch line of blue-black over the *shadow* line on every panel. This makes what is called the secondary shadow.

4. *Whipping.* In whipping, the painter's tool is a whip, made by attaching four or five ends of rope, each about three feet long, to the end of a stick. This is the common process for sug-

gesting marble. If the marble is to be white, the first step will be a white priming coat. While this priming coat is still wet, the whip should be dipped in black, shaken out, and the surface beaten not too roughly. The ropes spread out and twist in the process, making irregular black marks that suggest marble graining. Often the graining in white marble is both black and green, so the process may be repeated with green. Black marble will begin with a black coat, green marble with a green coat, and so on. Sometimes, when the painter does not wish the graining to be as distinct as that made by a rope whip, he may make a whip of thin strips of cloth and use it in a similar manner. This is often called a flogger.

5. *Stenciling.* Stenciling is a useful and common method of repeating an identical pattern and is usually used by the scene painter in making wall paper. Stencil paper, which is a tough oiled paper, may be bought in most stationers' stores. The pattern is laid out on the stencil paper and then cut out with a sharp knife or razor blade. Sufficient paper must be left to hold the parts of the stencil together, and usually the paper must be mounted on a wooden frame (see Fig. 56). Now the painter holds this prepared stencil against the surface, which may be either vertical or horizontal, and paints the pattern through it. He probably does this by patting the surface with the tip of his brush, and not by stroking as in ordinary painting. A special stencil brush, which is a round brush of short stiff bristles, makes the process easier. Sometimes the pattern can be sponged through the stencil, or the stenciling can be done with a crumpled-up piece of cloth. Once in a while, the pattern may not be painted directly, but the outline can be drawn, or the stencil pattern pounced. A bag of thin cloth, sometimes two or three thicknesses of cheese cloth, is made and filled with powdered chalk or with pigment. This is a pounce bag. It is patted on the surface, through the stencil, and leaves the outline of the pattern. This pattern may now be painted, if desired,

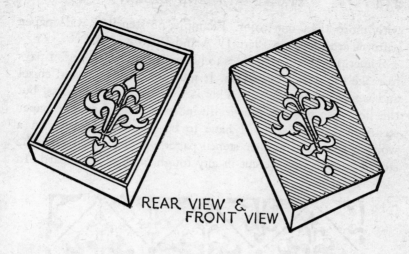

REAR VIEW &
FRONT VIEW

PAT WITH
BRUSH OR SPONGE   POUNCING

FIG. 56. STENCILING A WALL-PAPER PATTERN

with more than one color. Example of stenciled wall paper patterns are shown in Plate IV A and Plate XII B.

Sometimes, if the pattern is to be many times repeated, it pays to make the stencil out of tin. It must be cut with a cold chisel and smoothed with a file. This is a much longer process, but the stencil so made is practically indestructible. Like the paper stencil, the tin sheet will have to be mounted for use on a wooden frame. If neither stencil paper nor tin is available, the stencil pattern may be cut in any tough piece of cardboard. In

Fig. 57. A WALL-PAPER PATTERN, COMBINING THE STENCIL (IN FIG. 56) AND STRAIGHT LINES

that case, the cardboard should be waxed before being used for painting. This can be done by melting old candle ends in a tin can and rubbing the hot wax thoroughly into both sides of the cardboard. It pays to design the wall-paper pattern carefully and if possible, make standard dimensions in the pattern, so that the stencil will lock and space itself. That is, if painting is started on the upper corner of the surface, perhaps the upper corner of the stencil can be placed on the painted pattern at some definite point so as to indicate where the next pattern is to come. If this is not possible, it is necessary to mark out the spaces, probably with a snap line, which takes time.

Often the stencil may give only part of the complete pattern, which may be completed by lines (see Fig. 57), or by a certain amount of free-hand painting.

TRIANGULATION

Often the scene-painter is confronted with the problem of painting some large scene, say a back wall or a landscape, on a drop. This is not difficult if he has a small picture of the drop that is accurately to scale. His method of enlargement will then be triangulation. He must draw measured lines on the drawing breaking it up into accurate squares of a definite size, according to the scale (see page 291). Now he must break up the drop into similar squares, proportionately larger. They may

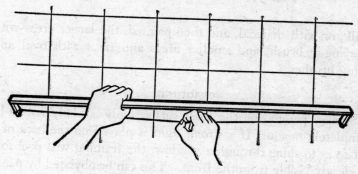

Fig. 58. a snap line

be one foot square, or one and one-half feet, or even two feet square. Now he is able to estimate accurately where the pattern should be drawn on the drop by noticing where the pattern in the small drawing crosses the lines. This is the method commonly used in sign-painting. Every point in the pattern may be estimated accurately by establishing the two points where the pattern crosses two right-angle lines of the square; that is, every point is established in relation to two other fixed points—hence, triangulation. The pattern may be drawn on the drop with

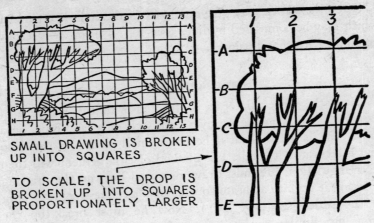

SMALL DRAWING IS BROKEN
UP INTO SQUARES

TO SCALE, THE DROP IS
BROKEN UP INTO SQUARES
PROPORTIONATELY LARGER

FIG. 59. METHOD OF TRIANGULATION

chalk, or with charcoal, and then painted, the larger areas with a laying-in brush, and smaller areas and lines with oval and lining brushes.

OPAQUING

Scenery painted on the front surface only is likely not to be completely opaque. If a strong light is played on the back of a flat so as to shine through a window, the framing will probably be clearly visible from the front. This can be obviated by painting the back of the cloth also, and this process is known as opaquing. The color of the paint is unimportant; black opaques are no better than white. Therefore, a flat may be opaqued with any left-over color. In professional studios, all flats are painted on the back, as well as the front, because the laws require this to be done for the purpose of decreasing the fire hazard. Painting a surface with glue-paint helps to make it fire-resistant. Professionally-made flats are usually opaqued with gray, for a most obvious reason—all excess paint from any operation is thrown in a barrel and saved for opaquing, and almost any combination of several colors turns out to be gray!

PAINTING WITH DYE

In schools and Little Theaters, where scenery is rebuilt and repainted for a succession of plays, it is better, when possible, to avoid using dye colors since it is too difficult to paint them out, or to overpaint them. Sometimes, however, it may be necessary to use them. Any commercial dye may be used, but regular scenic aniline dye will probably give a better result. They can be bought by the ounce, and not the pound, since a small amount will usually color several quarts of water. They may be prepared with either hot or cold water; and sometimes a little glue, or dextrine, is added to prevent spreading. If they do not dissolve completely, they can be boiled in water. They are especially useful in painting transparencies (see p. 276), such as stained-glass windows. Sometimes in drops, sky and water is painted with dye and lighted from behind, and this process gives an effect that can be secured in no other way. Sometimes an entire exterior may be painted on a drop made out of thin muslin, and lighted from behind. Such a curtain is usually called a translucency. Except for special occasions of this sort, the non-professional scene-painter had better avoid dye colors.

FLAMEPROOFING

To render scenic materials completely fireproof is an expensive operation and in most communities is not required. It is commonly required, however, that they be rendered slow-burning, or flameproof. Chemical flameproofing which may be dissolved in water and painted on wood and sprayed on cloth is sold by theatrical-supply houses, and is the most satisfactory material to use for this purpose. A preparation of one pound each of borax and salammoniac, dissolved in three quarts of water, is reasonably effective. The frames should be flameproofed *before* the cloth is stretched, and they must be allowed several hours for drying. Most regular theatrical canvas or duck (see p. 225) comes already flameproofed. If other material is used, the flameproofing may be painted or sprayed on the back of the cloth *after* it is stretched. Painting the back as well as the front surface with scene paint also aids in flameproofing.

SCENE-PAINTING IN SCHOOLS

Although the methods described above are those of professional scene-painters, there is no reason why even the youngest students, in their practice of theater, should not apply many of them. If they are not able to build flats, perhaps heavy screens can be covered with paper and painted appropriately for the play. Several layers of paper can be thumb-tacked on a single screen, and the scenes changed by taking off the top layer. If scene paint is not available, poster paint, which comes in many colors and in large jars, and which is used in much school art work, is suitable. Like the paint of the professional scene-painter, it consists of pigment, size (ground glue), and water. For many children scene-painting can be the most exciting approach to an understanding of color and line; it can be their introduction to the graphic arts.

NEED FOR BOLDNESS AND EXAGGERATION IN SCENE-PAINTING

In scene-painting, as in all other departments of dramatic work, the nerve to try anything is a great asset. The non-professional painter must boldly go ahead and follow directions and learn from his own successes and failures. He must remember that he is painting scenery, and not pictures. Everything about scenery may be intensified and exaggerated. Fine outlines and minor details are lost in the theater. The roughness, even the apparent crudities, of the painting do not show so much under lighting; in fact they often cause the results to be more satisfactory since they make the surfaces more interesting. If the painter makes mistakes, he must just paint them out and try again. The opportunity for experimentation is ever present. The only general rule for scene-painting, therefore, is to proceed boldly, observe results, and learn from experience.

CHAPTER XIX

Types of Scenery

The purpose of scenery may be briefly stated: *to surround the playing space with the most appropriate picture.* The first part of the problem is purely mechanical; we must be sure that spectators cannot look through the scenery and see backstage to the walls of the theater. The settings must *mask.* The second part of the problem, to make the picture appropriate, is an artistic one and is usually considered the function of the scene-designer. It will be discussed in the following chapter. The problem of masking is possible of easy solution to the degree that we understand available types of scenery and scene construction.

Scenery may be classified in many ways. The first possible classification might be according to the construction of the units (see p. 215) into, (1) flats, (2) drops, and (3) plastic pieces. It is also usually classified according to the *structure of the set* into, (1) drop and wing sets, and (2) box sets. A third possible method of classification depends on the *location represented,* so we may divide scenery into (1) interior sets, and (2) exterior sets. There is still a fourth possibility; we may classify scenery according to the *nature of the design.* One obvious division would be (1) naturalistic, and (2) conventionalized; but in this connection we should also find the words *symbolic, realistic, impressionistic,* and many more.[1]

DROP AND WING SET

So far, in the history of the theater, only two fundamental structural types of sets have been discovered, and of these the drop and wing set is the older by two centuries. In a drop and

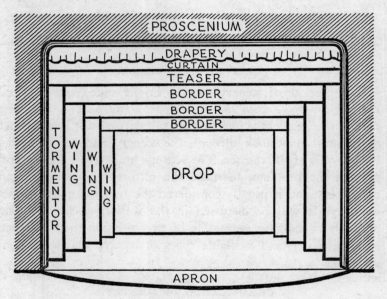

FIG. 60. A DROP AND WING SET

wing set, a full drop masks the back of the playing space, and the sides are masked by wings,[2] which are flats one behind the other and parallel to the proscenium wall (see Fig. 60). The

[1] Gorelik, Mordecai, *New Theaters For Old* (New York, Samuel French, 1940).

[2] The offstage space at each side of the playing-space is called the wings, and the same name is applied to any scenery used in this space. Since until recently, only flats of the sort described here were used, these pieces came to be called wings. It is easy to conceive that the two side areas

wings may be single flats, in which case it is sometimes necessary to slant them so that they will cut the sight lines and really mask. Sometimes it is necessary or desirable to have a jog hinged onto the offstage edge of the wings; this makes it easier to mask with them and also helps them to stand. There must be room, a minimum of three or four feet, between the wings for actors to make entrances. Although these units mask the back and sides, it would still be possible (at least from the front of the auditorium) to see *over* the drop and the wings. Overhead must be masked, then, with a series of short drops, or borders, hanging one behind the other. Usually there are the same number of borders as there are sets of wings, one placed immediately in front of each set. Thus, the complete name of such a setting should be a drop, wing and border set.

Scenery of this sort, often most skilfully painted in perspective, started in Italy in the sixteenth century, spread northward through Europe, and dominated the theater for two hundred years. (See Plate II.)

On these pieces, which *completely masked the playing space,* the old designer painted his picture no matter what he wished to represent. If it was an *interior,* he would paint a back wall on the drop, a series of pillars and side wall areas on the wings, and a ceiling on the borders. If skilfully done, from a sufficient distance the wings and borders might so blend as to give the appearance of a continuous surface. Note, however, that there are no real doors, hence the actors had to enter through the side walls, in the spaces between the wings. This accounts for the stage directions in old scripts such as "Enter RME," or "Enter DLE," meaning right-middle entrance, or down-left entrance. If the setting was an exterior, a landscape might be painted on

in any space might be called its wings, like the wings of a building; but it is interesting to note that in nautical language the wings of a vessel are the part of a hold, or of the lowest deck on which ropes are coiled, nearest the sides. So perhaps this is another example of theatrical language being invented by sailors.

the drop, the wings would become trees, and the borders, painted like foliage and perhaps cut, would become foliage borders. The wings representing trees would often have cut edges, too, made of plywood, to outline the trees; and they would be called wood wings.

BOX SETS

Just when some unknown genius had the idea of turning the wings edge to edge, and thus completely enclosing the playing-space with a box set, is not known. The earliest appearance of such a set in England is supposed to have been in 1832.[3] It was not common in America until late in the nineteenth century. In order that actors may enter a box set, doors have to be inserted, and windows naturally follow. Now the designer must use drops or flats *offstage* to cover the sight lines through the openings; these are called masks. He still has the problem of masking overhead. This may be done by a series of borders, or better yet, he may place a large flat on top of the set, and thus create a realistic ceiling.

All sets, however complicated they appear, are essentially one or the other of these two. If the sides are open, so that actors may enter between the wings at any point, we have a drop and wing set. If the sides are closed by walls, so that the actors must enter through special openings, called doors, we have a box set. This is true even though the set is a cyclorama. If the draperies consist of three continuous pieces, one at the back and one at each side, it makes a box set; but if the sides consist of a series of narrow draperies, hung one behind the other and parallel to the proscenium wall, it is a drop and wing set. There may be combinations of these two kinds of sets, but basically a set will probably be one or the other.

[3] Garrett H. Leverton, *The Production of Later Nineteenth Century American Drama*, Bureau of Publications, Teachers College, New York City, 1936, p. 17.

INTERIORS

It should be obvious that the sets designed by a stage artist are likely to be useful to the degree that he understands the problems of building and painting. In addition to the general methods, described in the two preceding chapters, there is probably much additional information that should be at his immediate command. He constantly finds himself engaged in solving a series of problems, and he often has to suggest, or even teach, a process to some other worker.

1. *Fastening Flats Together.* One of the constant problems in interiors is the fastening of the flats together. The traditional method is to lash them together with hardware and rope. This process will be described in detail in Chapter XXI. However, there are many occasions when this method is not necessary. It is sometimes possible to make an entire wall a single unit, by dropping the flats face down on the floor and fastening them together with long boards (1″ x 3″) nailed or screwed on to the rails. This is called battening the flats together. It is best to use three battens, one at each rail. This is especially useful if the door contains a large opening, say a large doorway, nine feet high and seven feet wide. By battening a small flat (called a header) at the top of the opening, between two other flats, much complicated building may be avoided (see Fig. 61). Such a method, however, results in a wide and heavy piece which is not suitable for traveling, but it is often useful in a school situation, especially when there is a single permanent set. It has, however, another disadvantage, and that is the leaving of cracks where the flats come together on the face of the wall. No matter how carefully flats are built, it is impossible to join them invisibly edge to edge. Therefore, the good designer must know how to avoid cracks in his scenery.

2. *Avoiding Cracks.* The common method is to glue (using white glue) a narrow strip of cloth over the crack. A long strip of cloth used in this way is called a Dutchman. This method

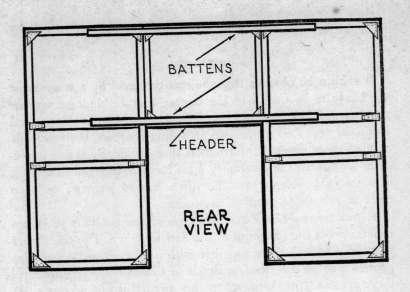

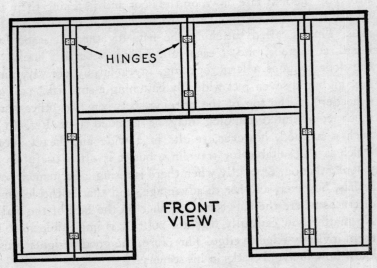

FIG. 61. TWO METHODS OF FRAMING A LARGE DOORWAY

will easily eliminate cracks on a wall of several flats that are battened together. A wall so built, however, cannot be folded. If it is to travel, the Dutchmen must be ripped off, and the wall taken apart by removing the battens. Possibly it can be moved, reassembled, and the Dutchmen pasted on again. If this process is to be used, paperhanger's paste had better be used instead of

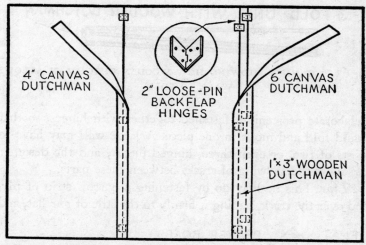

4" CANVAS DUTCHMAN

2" LOOSE-PIN BACKFLAP HINGES

6" CANVAS DUTCHMAN

1"×3" WOODEN DUTCHMAN

FIG. 62. CLOTH DUTCHMEN TO COVER CRACKS IN A WALL OF THREE FLATS

glue. However, it is usually possible by proper designing to avoid any such messy procedure.

a. Hinging Flats Together. The first and easiest method is to make the wall by hinging the flats together, instead of battening them. The hinges (the best for this purpose are one and one-half inch or two-inch loose-pin back-flap hinges) must be placed on the face of the flats. The job is neater if they are sunk to the level of the face of the stile. This process of hinging flats together presents no difficulty if only two flats, or if two flats and a jog, are to be joined. When three or more flats are to be joined, however, it is necessary (see Fig. 62) to insert a wooden piece (1″ x 3″ by the height of the stile) between the two end flats, hinging it to both of them. Such a piece, inserted to make a wall fold, is called a wooden Dutchman. However, if the wall is large, this method results in very heavy pieces, and there may be limits as to the number of flats it is practicable to join with hinges. However, Plates X and XI show

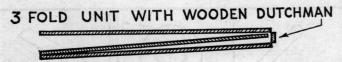

3 FOLD UNIT WITH WOODEN DUTCHMAN

FIG. 63. TOP VIEW SHOWING HOW WOODEN DUTCHMAN ALLOWS WALL TO FOLD

an elaborate proscenium fastened together with hinges, so that it could fold and move in one piece. A large wall may have to consists of two, or even three, hinged pieces; and the designer must avoid the showing of cracks between these parts.

b. Lips. This he may do by fastening a narrow strip of plywood over the crack, nailing it firmly to the stile of *one* flat, and

FLAT   BEAVER BOARD

TOP VIEW OF
CORNER JOINED
BY 2 FLATS WITH
PLYWOOD LIPS

LIP

FIG. 64. METHOD OF USING PLYWOOD LIPS TO COVER CRACKS

one flat *only*. This forms a lip, and the crack is lashed behind the lip. The plywood should be beveled, or rounded, at the front corners, and placed under the cloth covering of the flat. A joint made in this way is usually completely invisible after painting. The flats must be handled with reasonable care, so that the lips are not broken off. A strip of rounded iron is sometimes used in this way if the scenery is designed for hard usage. When a curved surface (see Fig. 64) must be joined to a flat, this is the only practical way to make the joint.

c. Corners. There is still another method. This is to design the wall so that the elements of it always join at a right angle. There is no crack problem in a corner joint. So instead of making a long straight back wall, the designer may move elements

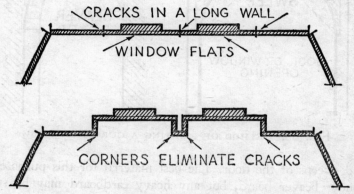

CRACKS IN A LONG WALL

WINDOW FLATS

CORNERS ELIMINATE CRACKS

Fig. 65. METHOD OF USING CORNERS TO ELIMINATE CRACKS

of it either upstage or downstage, sometimes only a few inches, using nailed-on wooden strips to represent the projection in the wall (see Fig. 65). In one of these ways, or by a combination, it is always possible to avoid unsightly cracks in scene walls, and the designer would do well to understand and use them—unless he likes the cracks.

3. *Making Curved Openings.* It is to be hoped that the designer will not always want to use straight edges in all openings. He often may want an arched door or window, so he must understand how to make an arch. The easiest method is to insert wide boards in which the proper curve may be cut at the top of the opening, in the manner shown in Fig. 66. Each piece of wood used in this way is called a sweep. Sweeps can be used at the top of openings, at the bottom of headers, or anywhere a

curved edge is wanted. Oftentimes in an arched doorway where thickness is required, it can be made by nailing a long piece of flexible material of the required width directly on to the stiles

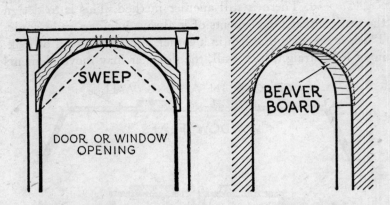

FIG. 66. METHOD OF FRAMING A CURVED OPENING

and sweeps of the door. The best material for this purpose is bender beaver board, but any heavy cardboard may be substituted.

4. *Masking Openings.* Masking openings such as doors and windows presents no special problem in designing interiors. The method is merely to use a drop, or a flat, and to paint on it whatever effect is desired. The common way of masking a door is to use two flats, or a flat and a jog, hinged together so they will stand upstage in a position to block all sight lines when the door is open. Sometimes in a small stage this is not possible. By nailing a piece of plywood or beaver board, the width of a door, on the *back* of the door, so that it projects a few feet above the top, it is sometimes possible to make the door carry its own mask. This piece should be painted a different color from the door, perhaps sometimes even black.

5. *Masking Overhead.* Masking overhead is a more difficult problem, but the designer must master it. Using borders to mask interiors is rarely satisfactory, and when possible it is

better to use a ceiling. The ceiling is simply a large flat, which can be suspended overhead and lowered on to the top of the set. It may be made just like any other piece of scenery. It usually needs to be so large, however, that it is difficult to handle when not in use, especially if there is not a large loft and plenty of rigging. It usually pays, therefore, to make a more practical ceiling.

a. Rolled Ceiling. The most common professional variety is a rolled ceiling, illustrated in Fig. 67. It consists of two long

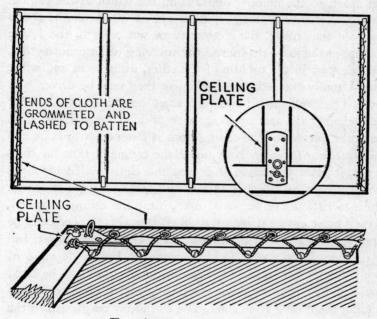

FIG. 67. A ROLLED CEILING

pieces (still called stiles), and a number of short pieces, called stretchers, which keep the stiles the proper distance apart. The problem is how to fasten the ends of the stretchers tightly, but not permanently, to the stiles. The common solution is a ceiling plate, which is a special piece of stage hardware (see Fig. 67) procurable only from a theatrical-supply house. The ceiling plate is fastened permanently to the ends of the stretchers. If the ceiling is of much size, it is wise to use at least two small stove bolts on each plate, in place of two of the screws. The nuts should be pounded back into the wood on the face of the stretcher, and the excess length of the bolt cut off with a hack saw and file, so that the face will be smooth. A round flat headed bolt of a large size, and a winged nut, hold the other end of the plate to the stile. Stretchers should be five or six feet apart, so the number depends on the width of the ceiling. The usual wood for this purpose is 1¼" x 4". After the frame has been thus made, the cloth may be put on with the frame face up, in the same manner as the covering of an ordinary flat. That is, start in the middle of the stiles, using tacks and white glue. Usually the tacks are left in, so they may be driven way down. The cloth should be longer than the ceiling, at least four inches being allowed to hang over at each end. These ends should be hemmed. The ceiling cloth is fastened with tacks and glue *to the stiles only*. Now, after the ceiling is thus far completed, it must be turned over and the cloth pulled over the end stretchers, and lightly tacked on the *back* of the stretcher. These tacks must be removed every time the ceiling is rolled, so they must *not* be driven way in. Better yet, the ends can be supplied with a row of grommets, about eight inches apart, and a lash line. Now a row of blue screws on the inside edge of each end stretcher will allow the ends of the ceiling to be laced (see Fig. 67). The rings on the ceiling plates are used in suspending the ceiling from lines. The cloth may be painted in the usual way and repainted as necessary for different sets. To dispose of the ceiling, a sufficient space must be cleared on the floor, so that the ceiling can be dropped face down—it is to be hoped the floor is clean. By unlacing the ends, or pulling the tacks, removing the wing nuts and lifting out the stretchers, the ceiling cloth may be rolled on the stiles just like a drop. If the rolled ceiling, along with the stretchers, can be tied on to a set of lines, it can be stored in little space above the stage. When next wanted, it can be quickly reassembled, by reversing all the processes.

b. Book Ceiling. A book ceiling is even easier to make since it consists merely of two flats so hinged together that they open and form one piece when placed in position (see Fig. 68).

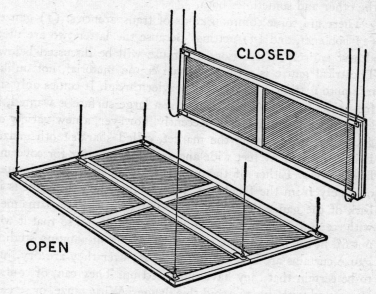

CLOSED

OPEN

FIG. 68. A BOOK CEILING

Any ceiling will need more than two sets of lines. In the above illustration, only the end sets are shown.

Notice that the hinges must be on the bottom side, under the cloth, or else the book will not close. A book ceiling in which the parts are more than six or seven feet wide becomes rather unwieldy, but in many small theaters the sets are rarely more than twelve or fourteen feet deep, so this is a useful device.

6. *Transparencies.* Sometimes the designer wishes to make a dissolving wall. Such was the front wall of the house shown in the scene-sketch for *The Barber of Seville*. Much of the action

in this play was *inside* the house, in a bedroom or a music room (see Fig. 77). The front was, therefore, a transparency. When lighted from the front, it looked opaque; when lighted from behind, the wall became transparent and seemed to disappear. Action was often simultaneously in one room and on the street, so sometimes one room was lighted and sometimes the other and sometimes both.

There are three common kinds of transparencies: (1) gauze, (2) bobbinet, and (3) netting. Because the latter two are used almost entirely in exteriors, their use will be discussed below. Theatrical gauze is a square-woven cotton material, not unlike mosquito netting, but having a heavier thread. It comes only six feet wide, unfortunately, so that if a large surface is wanted, it is necessary to make seams. Recently, however, a new variety of gauze has been put on the market, called shark's-tooth gauze. It is loomed thirty feet wide and so is much better for covering larger areas. Either of these varieties is opaque when lighted obliquely from the front, and transparent when the light is in back of the gauze. They may be painted, in the usual manner, with scene paint which should be slightly thinned so that it will not fill in the holes in the gauze. Sometimes in painting studios, gauze curtains are beaten, like a carpet, after they are dry, just to be certain that they have not filled up. They can, of course, be painted with dye to avoid this danger. Wire gauze, or screening, is the usual theatrical substitute for window glass. It should be galvanized screening, mesh # 16. "Glass" will not always be necessary in all windows, but there are occasions when it is. One of these will be when a window has to contain a cracked or broken pane: the crack or hole is painted with ordinary black scene paint on the screening. A knowledge of how to use gauze, both cloth and wire, puts many theatrical effects within the reach of the designer.

EXTERIORS

In addition to the usual problem encountered in designing interiors, exteriors usually present an additional masking problem. There is, however, no reason why they should be avoided by the non-professional designer. No universal solution can be suggested, although some theorists have recommended that a huge cloth sky-cyclorama would solve every problem. This would be a painted sky-cloth, stretched tightly in a great curve, and completely enclosing the playing-space, so that from every seat in the auditorium only sky would be visible. Besides the great expense of such a structure and the difficulty involved in rigging and handling it, which makes it impractical for a non-professional theater, it has not been completely successful in yet other respects. One of the difficulties is the lack of variety it affords for the entrance of actors. Of course, there can not be doors in the sky; hence the actors must enter always from the front, just in back of the tormentors, or through the floor. Most professional designers therefore, turn, when possible, to some other solution.

1. *Masking Exteriors.* Three other reasonable solutions are possible:

a. *Drop and Wing Set.* The most common, and in many ways the most generally useful, is the drop and wing set (see Fig. 60), first used over three hundred years ago. Plate VIII A shows masking wood wings at stage right.

b. *Plastic Side Pieces.* Sometimes it is possible to use a drop for the background and to invent plastic pieces which will mask the sides. Such plastic pieces might be the outside of a house or other buildings, tall hedges, massive rocks (see Plate III B), and so on. In Plate VIII B, stage right is masked by the house, and stage left by a trellis, vines and offstage wood wings.

c. *Black Side Curtains.* Still another method is to frankly mask the sides with black curtains, like the legs of a black velour cyclorama. These should be as far offstage as possible. In this manner, the designer composes, as it were, in two dimensions, on his back wall. If light is kept off the side curtains, they are very inconspicuous, and excellent exteriors can be made in this manner (see Plate XI E).

Often the designer will use a combination of these methods. In a recent Broadway production of *The Three Sisters* (see Plate VIII A), the exterior set was a combination of every one of these elements. A distant horizon was painted on a drop, which masked the back of the playing-space. A house completely filled in the left side, and since the house was supposed to face a dense pine forest, the right side was masked by a series of many wood wings, representing pine trees. However, not enough wings could be used to mask the right completely; so offstage, a large green-brown curtain, the basic color of the trees, masked such spaces as could be seen through the wings.

Overhead masking can be solved by no such simple solution as a ceiling, and often it is necessary to use a series of borders. These may be foliage borders, especially where there are trees to make them reasonable; but sometimes they probably must be plain blue sky borders or even black borders to match the cyclorama legs. In that case, the higher and less conspicuous they are, the better.

2. *Exterior Drops.* In the non-professional theater, the problem of exteriors is greatly decreased if there is always a good, large, sky drop available. It is still better if the back wall of the stage can be a sky wall (see p. 180). This can be made by making the back wall without openings, plastering it roughly, and painting the plaster a broken-color blue. A plaster wall simulates infinite depth better than a cloth surface because its granular surface catches the light and breaks it up into a more vibrant and diffused medium. In addition, plaster is not sensitive to climatic changes, so it remains free from wrinkles. Also, it does not shake and sway as actors cross behind it. A plaster wall is better if the top and ends are rounded since that tends to hold in the light and to give it even greater diffusion. A

group fortunate enough to have a good plaster wall should probably have a work cloth, or old drop, to hang over it when it is not being used, to keep it clean and unscarred, for scratches on it will completely destroy the illusion of sky. If no plaster sky wall is possible, a good drop, as large as possible, is highly desirable. The important thing to note is that nothing should ever be painted on the wall or drop *except sky*. Landscapes are made by painting them on ground rows and standing them in front of the sky.

3. *Ground Rows*. The modern method of suggesting a landscape is to break it up into its elements and represent each dis-

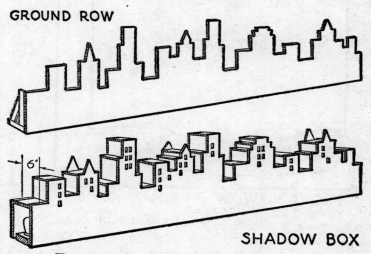

GROUND ROW

6"

SHADOW BOX

FIG. 69. A GROUND ROW AND SHADOW BOX

tance by a low piece of scenery standing in front of a sky. Each of these low pieces is a ground row. Nothing, therefore, ever needs to be painted on the drop itself, so it can be used for an infinite number of exteriors. If the designer wishes to show a distant city, he makes a plywood ground row of the city and stands it on the floor a few inches or so in front of the drop. If he has to show the city lighted up at night, he may make a ground row with two profiles, fasten one six inches in back of the other, cover the edges so light cannot escape, rig some bulbs inside, and cut holes in the face of the ground row to represent the lighted windows. This will be a shadow box. If he wants to make a more elaborate landscape, he might divide it into three ground rows: one for the most distant hills, one for the church and road in the middle distance, and a still lower one for the

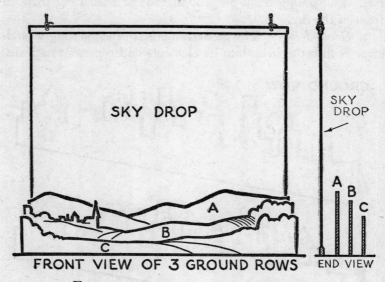

FIG. 70. A SKY DROP AND GROUND ROWS

immediate foreground. These will stand one before the other, a few inches apart, at the foot of the drop. They will be made by cutting the profile out of plywood or beaver board, framing the profile, or fastening it on the edges of jogs to be used on their sides. The ground rows may vary from a few inches to several feet in height. This method makes what might be called a plastic landscape and makes it unnecessary ever to spoil the drop. Plate VIII B shows a ground row in front of a plaster sky-wall. By using lights between the ground rows, it is often possible to secure a much greater variety of lighting and a more convincing distance.

4. *Tree Trunks.* Often the designer will need to use individual trees in an exterior, trees that cannot be painted on a back drop or a wing. Three varieties are possible:

a. Flat Trees. These will be merely framed pieces of the proper outline, perhaps having their roundness painted on them with high lights and shadows. Such trees have already been described on page 223.

b. Plastic Trees. Plastic trees have three dimensions, and the method of making them has been described on page 237.

c. Telescoping Trees. There is still another kind of plastic tree that he may find useful, and this is a telescoping tree. This

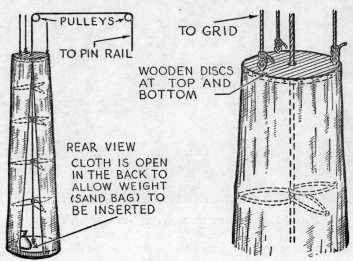

FIG. 71. TELESCOPING TREE

is illustrated in Fig. 71. There are times when the telescoping tree seems the only answer to a problem. I recently did a play which started with a dense forest on the stage. This consisted of sixty telescoping trees. Half of them had to be removed at the opening of the second scene. This was a matter of but a few seconds, for all the crew had to do was to remove the weights from the bottoms, and with the lines on which they were rigged pull them up into the loft and out of sight. Wherever a stump was needed, they carried out and set down in the marked spot a plastic stump. In the third scene, half of the remaining trees had to be cut down, and in the final scene only one remained. Telescoping trees seemed the only reasonable solution, for there was not room offstage to store fifty-nine plastic trees, to say nothing of the task of moving them off.

5. *Bobbinet Drops.* There is one other method that might have been used to represent this dense forest, and that is to use

FIG. 72. BOBBINET DROP WITH APPLIQUED TREES

bobbinet drops and appliqued trees. Bobbinet is one of the transparencies mentioned on page 275. It is a cotton fabric, with a small hexagonal mesh; and like shark's-tooth gauze, it comes thirty feet wide. It is made in four colors: white, black, light blue, and dark blue. Dark blue is generally the most useful. The trees to be a appliqued to a bobbinet drop should be drawn, painted, and cut out. They are then placed face-down on the floor, and the bobbinet spread carefully on top of them so they are in the correct position. A special glue is now necessary, called rosine. This comes in a can, and must be heated by placing the can in hot water. Apply with an old brush, to the edges of the backs of the trees, *through the bobbinet*. The application does not need to be continuous, but can be in gobs, like lumps of sealing wax, which rosine resembles. Rosine remains flexible, therefore the bobbinet can be battened, rolled, and treated exactly like any other drop. A series of two or three bobbinet curtains of appliqued trees makes a splendid dense forest. It has the disadvantage that actors cannot walk down through the forest; and as this was essential in the problem discussed above, it could not be used in that case. However, actors can walk between the drops, and so be seen approaching. Several drops of this sort were used by Cleon Throckmorton to make the several places in a forest in the first production of *The Emperor Jones*. By using the drops in various combinations, quick and effective changes were made, the entire scene shift often consisting of hauling up one drop and lowering in another.

6. *Netting*. The final variety of transparency is netting. This is a square-meshed cotton net, much like fish-net. It too comes in thirty-foot widths and in the same four colors as bobbinet. Again, the dark blue is preferable. Its common use is to support a cut drop or border (see Fig. 73). Netting also keeps the cut edges from twisting. It is used in the same way that bobbinet is used: that is, the border is drawn, painted, and cut out; the netting placed over the back and attached with rosine. One of the most common uses of netting is in making short borders for tree foliage. Most theater trees are made of two parts: (1) a flat or plastic trunk, and (2) a painted mass of foliage—that is, a tab—suspended so that it hangs a few inches in front of the trunk (see Fig. 73). Plate VIII A shows an elaborate cut foliage border on netting. Real foliage and real trees are rarely successful in the theater—they look false under artificial lights, even though they don't have time to wither.

7. *Conventionalized Trees*. Sometimes, the non-professional designer may find that some conventionalized forest pattern is a possible solution for an exterior. Color may be made the main element. A successful setting for *The Tempest* was merely a huge cyclorama of flats enclosing the stage. They had been painted with six-inch stripes of purple and orange. Over these stripes, several different greens were roughly sponged: gray-green, brown-green, yellow-green, and small spots of bright green. The

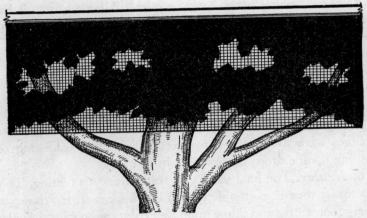

FIG. 73. NETTED FOLIAGE BORDER AND TOP OF PLASTIC TREE
(SEE FIG. 50.)

set, properly lighted, gave the general tone of a thick forest of varying greens, while the vertical stripes of purple and orange, hardly visible through the green, suggested the up and down shadows or tree trunks disappearing in the distance. Another method of making a good forest background is to puddle the surface with the several greens.

It is sometimes wise to conventionalize trees as in the settings for the prologue of *Androcles and the Lion*, in Plate III. The stage design then becomes a mere pattern, which the audience accepts. It sees that no attempt is being made to make real-looking trees and is not bothered by the fact. The one thing to be always avoided is the mixing of reality and fancy. A painted background of a forest, with two or three real trees that have been dragged in from a forest, is always a failure. As artists say, the designer must stay in his medium.

UNIT SETS

Some very interesting suggestions for adaptable scenery have been made. Scenery so designed that the elements may be used in different combinations to indicate different scenes are called unit sets. Gordon Craig has suggested, and used, sets of screens. These screens are of the same heights, but of varying widths— say one foot to six feet. With them a stage of almost any shape may be set, and they are capable of suggesting both interiors and exteriors. Hume, at the Detroit Arts and Crafts Theater, worked out a scheme of combination pieces, consisting of pylons, platforms, flats, stairs, screens, curtains, and other units. With these he set as many as seventeen different performances in one season, in such a way as to win universal approval and praise from all who saw the sets. The experiment is well described in Cheney's *The Art Theater*, in pages that should be studied by all non-professional stage artists. Three scenes of a skilful unit set, designed by Woodman Thompson, are shown in Plate XV; and a much simpler unit set of two scenes is shown in Plate XIV. Unit sets are always a possibility to be borne in mind by a resourceful designer who is forced to work on a small stage or with a limited budget. The sets in Plate XIV were painted a broken-color gray, which is probably the most successful way of painting combination units.

The best broken-color gray can be made by spotting the surface with the three primary colors, red, blue, and yellow. These may be sponged or spattered equally and evenly, although there need be no attempt to touch every spot on the canvas. Each coat must be allowed to dry before the next one is applied. The final coat should be a gray made of about one part of black to four parts of whiting. It may be sponged on, or painted on thinly and evenly with a brush. A surface so made is greatly changed by colored lights. When a blue light is thrown on it, the blue light reënforces the almost-invisible blue spots (picks them out, the electricians say) and makes the surface appear almost blue. The same is true of the red and yellow spots; they are picked out by the lights of their own color, and interesting and puzzling light effects may be secured.

CHAPTER XX

Designing Scenery

THE PROBLEM OF THE DESIGNER

The designer's problem grows out of his understanding of the purpose of scenery; and if he feels that scenery should "mask the playing space with the most appropriate picture," he will feel that his problem falls into two parts. The first is a purely practical and mechanical one: how can he make sets that will *mask*. To solve this part of his problem he needs to know as much as possible about the physical theater, the possibilities of scene building and painting, rigging, sight lines, and so on. If he has more than one set, he needs to understand how the scenery can be handled, and how it can be shifted. In short, he needs to be a clever mechanic. The second part of his problem is the artistic one: how can he make the pictures, the visual element of the play, *appropriate*. To solve this he needs to understand the nature of the theater, how to use color and line in order to create mood, and how to build up the right impression on the audience. In short, he needs to be a competent artist.

NECESSITY FOR APPROPRIATENESS

His key word will be *appropriateness*. He must create a setting that will aid and reënforce the action that is to occur there. The scenery must have a tone, must give the feeling proper for the play. All its elements must be designed to aid in reënforcing the *central idea* that has been agreed upon in the analysis of the script, and on the basis of which the actors have been chosen and the play directed. Now the *color* and *line* of the play can be embodied in the visual elements. A light and amusing Columbine play may demand cool, pale colors and fantastic lines; a somber tragedy would be inconceivable in such a setting. The tragedy may require a dark background, and long, straight serious lines. Even the tragedy, though, will have the possibility of infinite variation. A noble tragedy like Sophocles' *Oedipus Rex* and an earthy tragedy like Euripides' *Electra*, demand different treatment, even though both settings are in front of a palace. As shown in Fig. 5, the artist may emphasize either the long, noble, vertical lines of the columns and doors, or the long, horizontal lines of the steps and the tops of the palace. The passion of Wilde's *Salome*, the robust vigor of France's *The Man Who Married a Dumb Wife*, the delicate irony of Millay's *Aria da Capo*—each of these demands an individualized setting. Notice the variation secured in the sets for *The Beggar's Opera* and *The Way of the World* (Frontispiece) by the use of color and line, even though the mechanical solution is almost identical. Stevenson has written: "Certain dank gardens cry aloud for murder; certain old houses demand to be haunted; certain coasts are set apart for shipwreck." The successful setting is not the one that is most beautiful, or most accurate in period, or most startling; it is the one that best gives the audience the feeling of the play, and that thus aids in creating that unity of effect which is essential to any work of art.

STYLIZATION

This attempt to catch the spirit of the play and to express it in the setting—and also in costumes, and lighting, and manner of acting—is what is sometimes called, perhaps unfortunately, stylizing the play. A stylized play, then, is one in which the responsible artists—director and designer and actors—have attempted to agree upon the *central idea of the script* and to embody it in all the elements of the play. For example, in producing Beaumont and Fletcher's *Knight of the Burning Pestle*, the artist should perceive that the authors have written a burlesque, and he should emphasize and be guided by this spirit to make all the elements in his design slightly grotesque. If he is to use a modified Elizabethan staging, as was done in one performance (see Frontispiece, bottom sketch), even the Elizabethan stage that he designs must yield to this spirit. Instead of the browns and creams that would probably predominate in an exact reproduction of the Elizabethan theater, he may use as basic colors a fantastic purple and green, making the general color of his flats a varied purple, and the woodwork of his doors and windows a pale green. The grotesque shapes of the shingles on the roof, the slant given to all the doors, the irregularity of the window-panes, all these lines are in the same burlesque spirit. The costumes, too, should be exaggerated. The ruffs, the characteristic part of the Elizabethan costume, may be unusually large. They may be made in unusual shapes, and so may the hats and shoes. The colors of the costumes should be even brighter and gayer than they were in the period. And, the acting, too, must partake of this joyous exaggeration.

Stylization is too often thought of as suitable only for weird and unusual plays. Such, of course, is not the case. Even *realism*, to be effective in the theater, demands this sort of stylization. It is more successful to *suggest* nature than it is to *copy* nature. Reality on the stage is just as impossible as it is in all the other fields of art. The basis of all art is the intelligent selection of details.

The modern non-professional designer, then, may well seek for simplification. He need not attempt to reproduce a Moorish palace by an ornate painted interior with elaborate carvings, molding, and cornices; he may suggest it better by a single arched door. He may suggest a rich medieval room in a palace by a single painted tapestry and a few pieces of furniture rather than by an elaborate interior of exact and carefully-painted detail (compare Plate I with Plate II). He will probably be wise to avoid painted shadows and elaborate perspective. He will try to find the one or two objects—the doorway, the window, the fireplace—that may by characteristic treatment give the desired effect. This is the essence of stylization.

STEPS IN THE DESIGNING PROCESS

It is not enough that the designer be able to figure out in his head the construction of the units he wishes made, or that he merely see in his mind's eye the color effects he wishes to secure. Even though he intends to build and paint the sets all by himself, as will rarely be the case, he may forget details. And if he is making plans for other workers to follow, he must have some way of recording his ideas. His best tool for this purpose will probably be that method of representing ideas graphically which is called drawing and painting. He need not create artistic pictures. His skill as a designer depends not on the beauty with which he represents his ideas, but on the soundness and effectiveness with which these ideas can be worked out in the theater. Often a beautiful picture makes a bad stage set, and a not-very-well-executed picture may make a good one. There is a fundamental difference between making a picture on a flat piece of paper and working out a picture in the three dimensions of the stage. The scenic artist's problem also differs in another way from that of the easel artist; his picture is going to be seen from many different angles. Every member of his audience will see it from a different point of view. In a painted picture the point of view does not change and is always that of the artist. So painting a picture and designing a set, even though they have a surface similarity, are two different arts. Nevertheless, a designer should learn all he can about drawing and painting, for he is constantly confronted with the problem of how to represent his scenic ideas.

The first step in the process is the analysis of the script to arrive at the basis of an interpretation. He may call this the fundamental mood, or tone, or atmosphere, or what he wills; the important thing is to decide on a point of view. Especially for a young designer, a good starting place is the *central idea, color,* and *line,* previously discussed in Chapter III. It is to be assumed that the director and the designer, if they are not the same person, will try by discussion to come to mutual agreement. If they cannot do so, one or the other had better resign—perhaps both. They are not likely to be able to make an effective production, a unified work of art, unless they can agree on a basis for it.

The professional designer then usually proceeds to make floor plans, sketches of various kinds, and a model. Designers differ as to the order of procedure, and may often take the steps in varying combinations. The only essential is that visualization become constantly clearer and more detailed in the process. Perhaps the non-professional designer will not need to take all of these steps in every instance, but many times he may wish to do so.

1. *Floor-Plans.* One of the fundamental ways to represent the visualized setting is to draw a floor-plan. This will represent the position of all the scenic units as they would appear in a bird's-eye view. It will show the doors and windows, plastic units like fireplaces, the arrangement of the furniture, etc. The process of doing this will be easier if the designer has a floor-plan of the stage in which the set is to be used (see Fig. 74). In any case, he must know the width of the proscenium opening, the depth of the stage, and what off stage space he has on each side. And above all, he must learn to think and to draw *in scale.* That is, the relation between his drawing and the actual set must be in constant proportion. If his scale is one quarter inch to one foot, then each one quarter inch dimension on the paper will equal one foot on the stage. If the plan of the stage is cross sectioned (Fig. 74), each square will represent one square foot. Cross-section paper makes this process easier. He cannot make a tiny circle in one corner of a square and call it a chair. A normal chair is at least eighteen inches each way, so on the floor-plan it must be represented by an area of at least one and one-half squares each way. A door that is only one square wide

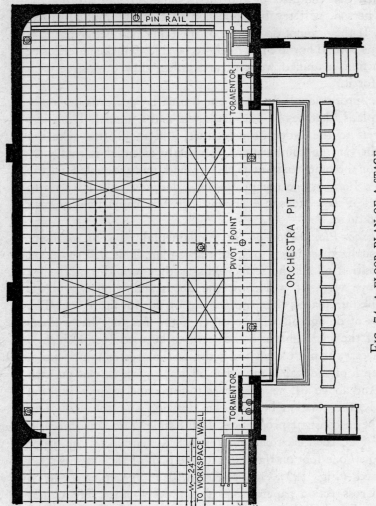

Fig. 74. A FLOOR PLAN OF A STAGE

Floor plans of this sort can be sketched, and printed from a cut, or mimeographed, for the specific stage the designer is to use. Rectangles containing crosses are the symbols for trap doors. The circular symbols show the locations of electrical outlets.

will not be very useful, for in the set it will be but one foot wide, and even children will have to go through it sideways! A normal door is three feet wide and seven feet high. In short, the floor-plan is useless unless it is accurately to scale. A scenic designer must know the sizes of common objects, like doors, sofas, tables, beds, and so on.

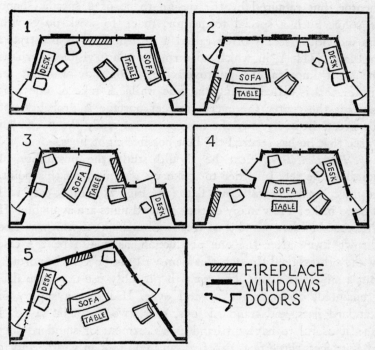

FIG. 75. POSSIBLE FLOOR PLANS FOR A SMALL LIVING ROOM, CONTAINING IDENTICAL FLATS

Probably the designer will make several floor-plans, and he may make many small rough perspective sketches in conjunction with them. Ultimately, he must decide which of his floor-plans is best, probably on the basis of the following elements:

a. Masking. Whether or not the set really masks, should be easily determined from the floor-plan. Sight lines from the poorest seats (see p. 171) through the openings should strike scenery, and not the walls of the theater. The downstage edge of flats must not show; this means that the side walls must terminate at tormentors, and not be merely suspended in the air in back of the curtain. Sometimes, the downstage edge of the walls may terminate in a special flat, similar in use to a tormentor, but required by the design to be of a specific shape or color. Such a special tormentor, made to work only with the individual set, is often called a return. This is illustrated in Plate XIII A, in which no tormentors are visible. Perhaps the sight lines can be improved by setting side walls at an angle; this is called raking the side walls. A rake of one foot towards the center for every six feet upstage is probably not too great. In every way the designer must study the floor-plan to see that he has secured the best possible sight lines.

b. Practicability. Next he should study the possibility of building the set. In order to make up his mind on this point, he must break his walls into flats (see Fig. 75). How easy will it be to make? How many of the required units are available? If the scene-builders are to start fresh and make a set which will be thrown away after the one production, as would be the case in the professional theater, this item will not be very important. But a school or Little Theater will probably use the same flats (repainted, of course) over and over. If it has a supply of standard flats, and standard jogs, much work can be saved. I find it useful to have on hand an assortment of standard jogs of four feet, three feet, two feet, and one foot in width, and to make standard openings in door and window flats. Door openings are three feet by seven feet, and window openings three feet by five feet. My designer must stick to these sizes unless there is some very good reason not to do so. He must move one corner of the set down stage a few inches, or make his back wall a few inches wider. The important point it that *nobody can see the variation of a few inches* in the theater. It is, therefore, wasteful and time-consuming to build a door thirty-five inches wide and seven feet two inches high, if a supply of standard doors, thirty-six inches wide and seven feet high, is at hand. The difference is simply invisible. If the designer wishes to make a door nine or ten feet high, that is another matter. But *slight* variations have little value in design. The good designer will, therefore, study his floor plan to see how he can make the set with the greatest economy of material and labor in view of the scenery possessed by the group.

c. Suitability. He must now test his design for its suitability for the play. Will the play work in the set? No matter how beautiful and economical the floor plan seems, the action demanded in the play must be possible. If some actor is always leaving just as another is entering, a set with a single door will not be very suitable. If persons must hide, there must be a place for them to hide in. If a closet is necessary, the designer must have supplied a closet. If a body is to be discovered in a window seat, the seat must be of a size to take a body. The furniture must be grouped to make reasonable playing areas. Can actors who must sit together comfortably and talk, do so? Is the table big enough for the eight people to sit around it? Is there a good place to hide the revolver? Can three people get through the door at the same time, or will they be hopelessly blocked by the position of the sofa? The designer should study the play and his floor-plan and ask himself many questions of this sort in determining how suitable his design is for the action. Of course, he must also consult the director on these, and similar points.

d. Artistic Quality. His final consideration may be the artistic quality of the set. The least interesting room will probably be one that is perfectly square and symmetrical. So unless he is designing a prison, or a hospital ward, or a poorhouse, the designer may well try to make the floor-plan interesting by breaking up the box. He may do this by adding an alcove, or by making a corner project into the room, or by raking the walls in some way. Some professional designers make one side wall a little shorter than the other, so as to rake the back wall slightly. They think that this allows the audience to see it at a more interesting angle. Part of the problem of making the floor-plan artistic is to see that it makes as much architectural sense as possible. The front door and the door to the kitchen are not reasonable in the same wall, for instance, unless the play makes the point that the kitchen is at the front of the house. The windows must be in what is obviously the outside wall. Two doors leading to different rooms had better not be too close together; stairs should obviously lead somewhere, etc. To the degree that the floor-plan is reasonable and varied it is likely to have artistic quality. Having considered his floor-plan from every angle and having decided on the best one, the designer proceeds to the process of making a series of sketches.

2. *Sketches*. These sketches may be of many kinds. The non-professional designer will often not need to make all of them. In fact, if he makes a model, it may be possible to avoid making any sketches whatsoever. Now, however, he must make many decisions and represent them graphically. The floor-plan shows nothing but the outline of the set on the floor; the width and position of the openings; the placing of the plastic pieces, the furniture, etc. It cannot show *height*. It cannot tell us the shape of the door, nor the kind of chair, nor the outline of the rock or trees. Nor from the floor-plan do we gain any idea of the color. In the process of making sketches, the designer must decide all such details.

a. Perspective Scene-sketch. One of the commonest ways of showing these elements is by a perspective sketch, which is often called the scene-sketch. Scene-sketches in the professional theater are usually in color and represent the scene as it appears from the middle of the auditorium (technically it usually is a horizontal linear perspective). As the eye sees objects in three dimensions, the problem of the artist is to portray all of these three dimensions on a two-dimensional surface—a piece of paper.

Scene-sketch for "The Barber of Seville"

By Lester Polakov

The basic principle of perspective sketching is simple: the further objects are from our eyes the smaller they appear. This means that lines moving away from us appear to grow closer and closer together until they merge at some distant point—called the vanishing point. Thus, in sketching a side wall, the top and bottom lines of the wall will approach each other as they move upstage. If these lines were extended with a ruler they would cross, or meet. The same thing is true of all other parallel lines on this wall, like the top of doors, windows, and fireplaces, etc. The upstage edge of the wall will, of course, be shorter than the downstage edge, because it is further away. Objects equal in size at an equal distance appear the same size. So if there are two similar doors, or two similar windows in a back wall, they should appear the same size in the sketch—if the wall is parallel to the front edge of the stage.

If this sounds confusing, the artist need not in the beginning bother with it. A little bold experimentation will teach him how to represent his ideas with sufficient accuracy. There are many good scene-sketches in which the perspective is not completely accurate. He had better start by boldly taking a piece of paper and drawing on it, in proper proportion, (that is, to scale), the outline of his proscenium opening (technically this is his sight plane). In the center of the opening, perhaps a little below center, he should make a light mark, which will represent his eye level (marked V in Fig. 76). This is his vanishing point. Now all lines that go up and downstage will vanish at this point.[1] At first he may need to use a ruler to get these lines in correctly, but a little practice will enable him to do it by eye. He had better keep in mind three other principles. (1) *All vertical lines* in the set must be represented by lines parallel with the *side* lines of his opening. Such lines will be perpendicular corners in the set, perpendicular door and window stiles, etc. (2) All *horizontal* lines parallel to the front of the

[1] This is true, of course, only in one-point perspective, but the designer had better start with this.

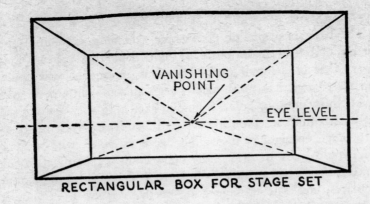

VANISHING
POINT

EYE LEVEL

RECTANGULAR BOX FOR STAGE SET

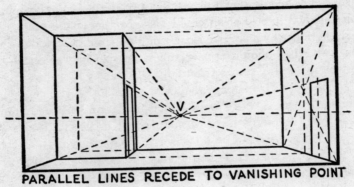

V

PARALLEL LINES RECEDE TO VANISHING POINT

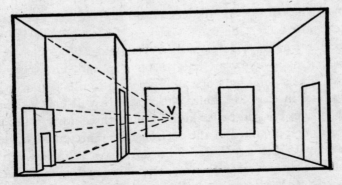

V

FIG. 76. METHOD OF MAKING PERSPECTIVE SKETCH—FLOOR
PLAN #4 IN FIG. 75

stage will be parallel in the sketch with the *bottom* line of the opening. (3) All objects must be kept in proportion. For example, if he is going to draw a fireplace downright (this will be at the left of his sketch, for all stage directions are reversed —see p. 96), which is to be five feet high against a flat that is twelve feet high, the fireplace to be in proportion must be five-twelfths the height of the flat. In the same way, if he wishes to draw a window seat against the back wall, and the seat is twenty inches high, it must be to the total represented height of the back wall as twenty inches is to twelve feet.

These principles are probably most important in helping to correct what appears to be *wrong* in a picture. The inaccurate representation of the scene usually grows out of one of the following violations of principle:

1. The vanishing lines, those going up- and downstage, do not vanish at the same point. This can be easily tested and corrected with a straight edge, such as a rule.
2. The vertical lines are not vertical—because they are not parallel with the sides of the paper.
3. The horizontal lines are not horizontal—because they are not horizontal with the bottom line of the opening. Of course, if these lines are intended to be slanted, or raked, they should *not* be parallel with the bottom line.
4. Objects are not in proper proportion. In a twelve foot flat, a seven foot door must be above the center of the flat, and not below it, etc.

After the sketch, done with pencil or pen, is as accurate as possible, the designer should fill in the colors—poster paint is a good variety to use for this purpose, but any good water color will do. Now he has made a graphic representation of how he wishes the set to look—a perspective sketch. Such are the color sketches in the Frontispiece, and those for *The Barber of Seville* and *The Jealous Husband*. A thoughtful study of them will probably make the method clear.

b. Isometric Sketch. Some artists prefer to make an isometric sketch. This will also be in perspective, but in an isometric

FIG. 77. PERSPECTIVE SKETCH (WITH FRONT WALLS REMOVED) FOR "THE BARBER OF SEVILLE"—SHOWN IN SCENE-SKETCH FACING PAGE 296.

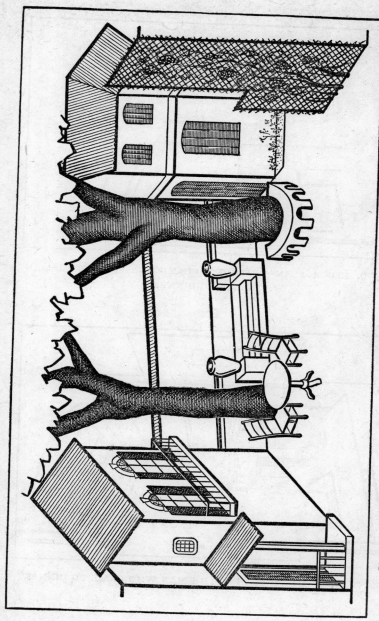

FIG. 78. ISOMETRIC SKETCH FOR "THE JEALOUS HUSBAND"—SHOWN IN SCENE-SKETCH FACING PAGE 304.

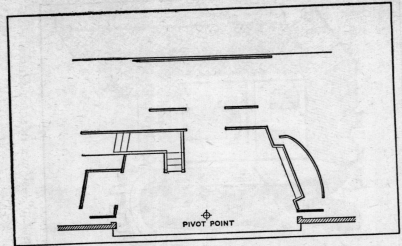

FIG. 79. FLOOR PLAN—WITHOUT FURNITURE—FOR "THE MAN WHO CAME TO DINNER"

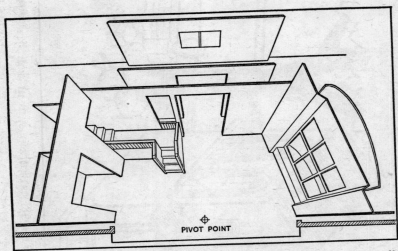

FIG. 80. PERSPECTIVE PLAN—"THE MAN WHO CAME TO DINNER"

sketch all lines have the actual dimension of the object. This has one advantage, at least, in representing scenery: it gives the dimensions accurately. It has the disadvantage that it does not represent the set as it appears to the eye. A study of the sketch shown in Fig. 78 will explain isometric sketching.

c. *Perspective Plan.* A third kind of sketching is sometimes used, and this has the advantage of being purely mechanical. Often this method is called bird's-eye perspective. It consists of making a projection of the actual floor-plan, which must, of course, be accurately to scale. The artist, from a point exactly midway between the tormentors, projects with a straight edge *every vertical* line—that is, every line that is perpendicular to the floor. He then draws in, at the proper distance, the top of the set and all the other lines, and thus represents the set as it would appear from above. Such a projection is shown in Fig. 80, which is a projection of the floor plan in Fig. 79.

d. *Elevations.* No matter which kind of sketches are used, the designer usually finds it necessary to make elevations. These are sketches of the elements of the set, accurately to scale. Technically an elevation is an orthographic projection. The most important elevation in indicating scenery is probably the front elevation; although, if the set is complicated, a side elevation, or even a top elevation, may be necessary. These will represent the scenic unit as it appears from the front, the side, or the top. The illustrations in Fig. 81 and 82 show the method.[2] It is customary to draw the elevations of each unit of a set. If structural details are added, to show methods of building, the elevations will become working drawings. In the non-professional theater, the elevations may be sufficient, and it will not be necessary—assuming that the workers understand scene-building —to make true working drawings.

None of these methods of sketching are too difficult for the

[2] If these front elevations are filled in with color, they will indicate how the set should be painted. Such sketches are called painting elevations and are usually made by professional designers.

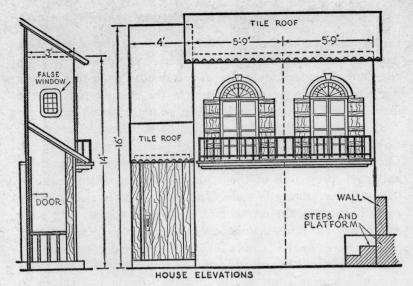

HOUSE ELEVATIONS

FIG. 81. ELEVATIONS FOR HOUSE—"THE JEALOUS HUSBAND"

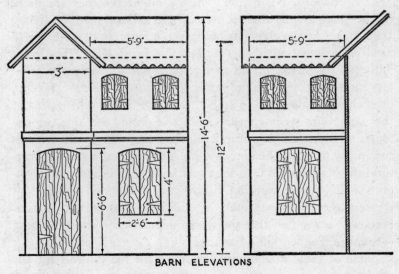

BARN ELEVATIONS

FIG. 82. ELEVATIONS FOR BARN—"THE JEALOUS HUSBAND"

By William Steinel

Scene-sketch for "The Jealous Husband"

non-professional scene-designer who is willing to give the processes thought and practice. They enable him to represent his ideas sufficiently clearly so that other workers can execute them—and that is a primary purpose in designing scenery. They do not have to be beautiful pictures—although many good designs are. The important thing is that they be clear and accurate.

3. *Models.* A model is a miniature stage set, representing each detail as the designer visualizes it. If the model is made and painted in color with sufficient accuracy, it is, perhaps, not necessary to have any sketches. The model will show the size of every piece, the location and shape of every opening, and all the other details necessary for building and painting the set. It has the additional advantage that, being three dimensional, it forces the designer to think in three dimensions—like a stage-designer and not merely like an easel artist. In the process of making a model the designer must solve all the problems of relationship in space that must be solved on the stage. He sees his mistakes as he works over his model, and it is cheaper to throw away a few cents worth of paper than many dollars worth of scenery. It is a profitable and worth-while project for an ambitious designer to study and practice model-making.

Professional model-makers use every sort of material—paper, wood, cloth, soap, sponges, and so on. The non-professional will probably find it wise to begin by using a combination of cardboard and paper. A useful combination is a piece each of medium weight binder's board, black mounting board, and two-ply Bristol board.

a. Base Board. The first step is to lay out the floor of the stage on the binder's board, which is to become the base of the model. This means accurately transferring the floor plan. Cut the base board to stage size.

b. Proscenium Arch. Now, in the same way, lay out on the black mounting board and cut the proscenium opening that is to be used for the particular set. If this piece is large in area, it is an excellent idea to leave flaps around the edges since these can be folded back to give additional strength (see Fig. 83).

   c. Scenic Unit. On the Bristol board, lay out all the scenic units. The main part of a box set may usually be laid out in one piece, with the flats adjacent to one another (see Fig. 83). In fact, this is one of the important principles of model-making: lay out all adjacent surfaces so that they are adjacent on the paper. There is no value in cutting out individual flats and

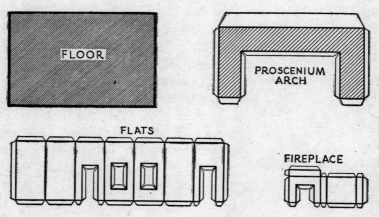

FIG. 83. BASIC PIECES FOR A MODEL—FOR FLOOR PLAN #4, FIG. 75

then sticking them back together again. A clever model-maker reduces his cutting and gluing to a minimum. On the edges of all the elements, flaps at least one-quarter of an inch in width should be left. These are to be folded back in order to keep the paper from warping and to give the model solidity. The flaps at the bottom will also allow the scenery to be pasted to the floor. In the same way, and leaving flaps on the inside edges, draw in the openings, such as doors. After this laying-out process is complete, with scissors and a sharp knife or razor blade, cut out the pieces of the scenery.

d. Scoring. All the lines in all parts of the model where the paper is to be folded should now be scored; that is, lines should be drawn with some blunt instrument like the back of knife blade and a ruler. These lines should be so drawn that the folding will be *in the direction of the scoring.* That is, as the flaps are all probably to be folded back, the scoring should be on their back.

e. Plastic Pieces. Pieces like fireplaces, stairs, columns, etc., may be made in a similar way (see Fig. 83). Trees, rocks, or irregular objects which in the set will be built of papier mâché (see p. 237), may be made accurately to scale by cutting the outline out of paper, and building thickness on front with tissue paper and glue. If it seems preferable, platforms and stairs may be cut out of wood.

f. Painting. Painting should be done before the model is folded. Poster paints, or any good water colors, may be used. Opaque water colors are easier to use than translucent ones. Painting should be as accurate as possible, if the model is to have much value. Any variety of painting may be done in miniature. By using a small-grained sponge, or a thin cloth, it is possible to represent sponging or cloth-rolling, for instance. Spraying can be done with a fixative blower, or with a toothbrush and a knife in the manner described on page 248 for spattering. For lining, paneling, etc., use a fine brush and a straight edge. In fact, the only limit is the ingenuity of the model-maker; he can give himself all the experience of actually painting the set. The paper can be opaqued in the same way that cloth is, by painting the back. Many model-makers opaque sets by painting the back with India ink.

g. Thicknesses. In a good set, hence in a good model, the wall will be given the appearance of thickness by the insertions of door jambs and window frames. Thin strips of paper, cut to scale, may be pasted around the edges of the openings against the folded-back flaps. This will perhaps lead to the necessity of some final touching up with paint.

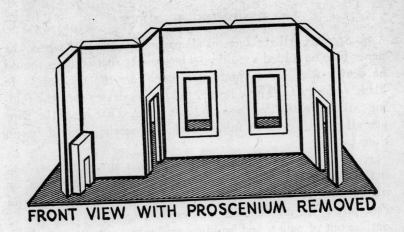

FRONT VIEW WITH PROSCENIUM REMOVED

REAR VIEW WITH PROSCENIUM

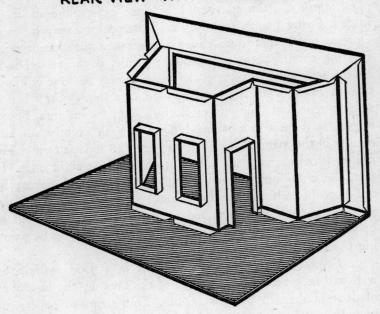

FIG. 84. THE MODEL ASSEMBLED

h. Assembling. Now all the elements should be folded into their proper shapes, and pasted together on the base board with a good strong glue.

If properly made, the model should give an accurate idea of what the scene will look like. It should be strong enough to stand even rough handling in the studio and shop, and it should be accurate enough in size and color so that carpenters and painters can work from it. By experimenting with lights, it is even possible to learn much about the proper lighting of the particular set.

If several artists have varying ideas of how the play might be mounted and each one is required to produce a model, the several models can be compared and the best set selected with more certainty than by any other method.

Complicated models may be made according to the same general principles. Posts, platforms, stairs, or even furniture, may be made of paper and glue and paint. Unless furniture is to be made accurately and to scale, it is better to omit it entirely, however, and to represent it by pasting pieces of paper showing the outlines of the pieces flat on the floor board. If the model is very large, wood or heavy cardboard may be necessary to give it solidity. There is no rule as to method and no limit as to material. The need for ingenuity and cleverness, and the opportunity for true artistic work, makes model-making a most fascinating part of theater practice.

IMAGINATION

One essential element of good stage-design, that has not hitherto been mentioned, is imagination. This is a most necessary ingredient. Designs are likely to be better if the designer does not allow himself to be completely bound by the descriptions and stage directions given by the playwright—at least, in the early phases of his work. In studying a play the designer should not begin by reading the scene descriptions of the author; he should read merely the lines that the actors are to say. If from these lines he learns that the characters are in a kitchen, or living-room, or on a boat, or in a desert, then that setting is essential. If he doesn't gather this, the setting is not essential—the action may be anywhere. Perhaps the playwright has put his action in an inappropriate place, and the designer may suggest a more effective one. The classic authors rarely give us more than a place-indication, and often not that; so in designing classic plays for the modern theater, it is necessary to invent locations. In any case, the designer—in coöperation with the director, of course—can often with imagination make the production more effective.

The setting for *The Barber of Seville* (Fig. 77) is an interesting example of an invented single setting. In the original libretto, there were three locations: in front of the house (a serenade is in progress), a bedroom, and a parlor or music room. The designer, by using a house with a gauze front, has included all these places in a single gay, distorted set, appropriate to the action. He has all the essential elements demanded by the action and dialogue: the balcony, the door, the hiding-place in the basement, etc. Moreover, he has done more, for in the play characters are always secretly entering the house and knocking on the door of an inside room. With this setting we can see them enter; often they come down the street, climb the post up to the balcony and from the balcony onto the roof, and enter the house by a trap-door in the roof. The action can be rapid and continuous. Beaumarchais, the famous author of the play on which the libretto was based, could not have conceived of such a setting, for it uses scenic elements and tricks not invented in his time, but I am sure he would have approved.

So, sometimes, by this sort of device, all the necessary locations can be drawn together in some charming set. An excellent example of this possibility is shown by the Theater Guild setting for Molière's *The School for Husbands* (Plate IX A) where a street, the exteriors of two houses, and the interiors of the same houses (by virtue of the sliding panels which move up to disclose the interiors), were all combined in a gay and charming design. At other times, the designer may do just the reverse and break up the single setting demanded by a play into a more interesting succession of smaller scenes. Sometimes he may transfer the action to a more exciting and more characteristic place.

It is to be hoped that the designer will not wish to make only realistic settings. Of course, many plays, perhaps the majority of those usually produced in the non-professional theater, may demand realistic treatment. But just as there should be variety in the choice of scripts, so there should be as much variety as possible in their treatment by the designer—always providing that the treatment grows honestly out of the script. The designer whose efforts are confined, either by the choice of scripts or by his own limitations, to plays with "one simple exterior" is losing much of the possible pleasure of his art. The true designer wants more interesting and more difficult problems.

If the play has many scenes, perhaps his solution may be a unit set of some sort. This possibility has already been discussed in Chapter XIX. A unit set need not always consist of complete rooms, like those shown in Plate XIV and Plate XV. Often, a few carefully designed flats against a black cyclorama may give an appropriate and effective atmosphere—see "Lincoln's office in the White House" in Plate XII A, and the "Russian parlor" in Plate XII B. Partial sets like these—often called spot sets—are inexpensive to build and easy to shift. Partial sets may, of course, be more elaborate than these simple ones: note the effective modern interior from the Cleveland Playhouse (Plate XIII A) and the ornate 18th century room from the Metropolitan Opera House (Plate XIII B). The designer of *Peer Gynt* (Plate XVI) is using the unit set idea in that he shifts his plastic rocks into varying combinations—the illustrations show only three of the required seven scenes.

The skilful designer will also wish to vary his style, as well as his mechanical approach. If exteriors are required, he may sometimes wish to do realistic ones (Plate VIII), and sometimes conventionalized ones (Plate III A). Occasionally he may be called upon to set a play for which a constructivistic set (Plate V) or expressionistic scenery (Plate VI B) will be appropriate. Sometimes elements built in false perspective (Plate IX B) will give an interesting quality.

Space staging is another method of doing plays with many scenes in an interesting way. In Norman Bel-Geddes' production of *Hamlet* (Plate VII), all the scenes were suggested by rapidly-changing properties and lights on different levels, and this treatment made possible a fast and exciting development of the action—probably in feeling what Shakespeare might have imagined if he had known the modern theater. In a play called *Catherine de Medici* (Plate VI A), all the required scenic elements were built into a single setting, so no shifting whatever was necessary. The script called for a large Gothic exterior door, a small door leading to a bedroom, a large window looking out onto a jousting field, a trap door into a dungeon, some small high windows overlooking an outer gate, etc. All these elements were designed into the set without any regard for logical architectural arrangement, but simply on the basis of where they would be most useful to the director. The program stated simply that the action took place in the Palace of the Louvre, and constantly-changing lighted areas directed the attention of the audience to the action and to the necessary scenic element. In other words, the audience never saw the entire set at any one time, but only those parts which the designer wished them to see.

These are a few of the many possible ways in which the designer's imagination may work to create new and interesting effects. He will probably benefit from seeing the work of other designers, from visits to exhibitions of theatrical drawings and models, from studying books on architecture, and from looking at paintings and drawings of all kinds. Ultimately, however, the virtue of his work and the effectiveness of his designs will probably depend on his skill in combining his mechanical ingenuity and his own visual imagination.

CHAPTER XXI

Handling Scenery

HANDLING A FLAT

As flats are probably the most common scene units in the modern theater, it is essential that stage hands know how to handle them properly. Unless a flat is of excessive height, it can easily be moved by one person. To do so, he must place both of his hands on *one* stile, one hand high and one low, as

Fig. 85. RUNNING A FLAT

far apart as is comfortably possible so as to keep the flat balanced, and slide it along the floor on the bottom rail—which is sometimes called the runner. To drop a flat face-down on the floor, the experienced stage hand slides it into a position leaving plenty of room in the front, and simply lets it fall forward—that is called *floating* a flat. Unless there are large openings in the flat it will fall gently and without noise, cushioned by the air. To pick a flat up again alone is not such an easy matter, but it is perfectly possible. Now, the stage hand must go to the side of the flat, and lift one edge so that the flat stands on a stile. He then moves to the foot (bottom rail), and with both hands on the upper corner and one foot on the lower corner, so the flat will not slide along the floor, he simply pulls it upright keeping it balanced all the while. If the flat is tall (over fourteen foot) he may need an assistant. The assistant starts at the other corner and walks down under the stile, pushing up on the stile. This is called *walking up* a flat.

Several persons may be necessary to lift up a wall of several flats that have been battened together. One person, or more,

FIG. 86. LIFTING A FLAT

must stand at the bottom end of the wall and with his foot keep the bottom rails on the floor—this process is called *footing* the flat. The others lift the top rails and walk up the wall, using their hands on the face of the stiles. A wall is *walked down* by reversing this process—some one foots it at the back, and the others lower it by walking up the stiles with their hands.

If, in the process of handling flats in a performance, a tear should appear in one of them, it can be mended by glueing— with white glue, if possible—a patch of canvas or cardboard on the back. A small can of cold furniture glue is sometimes useful in the shifts. If the tear is serious, it can be more carefully patched after the performance, and retouched by the scene painter.

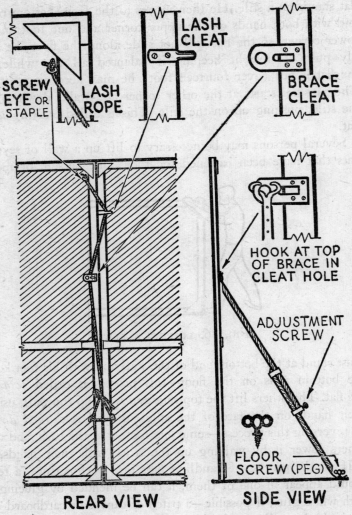

SCREW EYE OR STAPLE

LASH ROPE

LASH CLEAT

BRACE CLEAT

HOOK AT TOP OF BRACE IN CLEAT HOLE

ADJUSTMENT SCREW

FLOOR SCREW (PEG)

REAR VIEW

SIDE VIEW

FIG. 87. LASHING FLATS TOGETHER AND BRACING

LASHING FLATS

The traditional method of joining flats is to lash them together (as indicated in Fig. 87). A lash line (#8 cotton sash cord) is fastened to the top of every right-hand stile. It must be firmly attached with a screw-eye, or a special lash-line eye; or sometimes a hole may be bored in the corner block and the line passed through the hole and knotted. The line should be cut off one inch from the floor. On the left-hand stile, eighteen inches from the top, a lash cleat is fastened; and on the right stile again, about eight feet from the floor, a brace cleat. Lash hooks must be fastened to both stiles, about

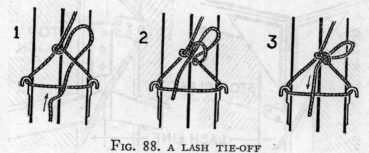

FIG. 88. A LASH TIE-OFF

thirty inches from the floor. The lash line is thrown, with a sharp snap, over the top lash cleat on the adjacent flat, brought back over the brace cleat, to the lash hook on the adjacent flat, and back to the lash hook on its own. The line must be stretched as tight as possible, and tied off by being brought up around the running line, and back on to itself with a single bow knot (see Fig. 88). With experience, this process can be done very quickly. A pull on the loose end of the line unties the knot and allows the line to be snapped off the cleats.

The difference between lash cleats and brace cleats is that the former are merely fingers of metal that may be screwed onto the stile to take lash line, whereas brace cleats contain a hole to take the horn of a brace (see Fig. 87). They may be used interchangeably, so far as lashing is concerned. Wherever a brace is to be used, however, there must be a brace cleat. Instead of lash hooks, lash cleats or three-inch round-headed screws are often used at the tie-off place. In an emergency, large nails may be driven into the stiles, parallel to the covering, to serve as everything but brace cleats.

Cleats need not be placed at the distances indicated above. The important thing is to have some definite system of putting on cleats in any theater, so that they will be the same on the back of every flat. The lash line must always be on the right side of the back, and the tie-off cleats at the same height from

FIG. 89. CORNER LASHING

the floor. Then *any* two flats may be lashed together. Cracks will be left on the face of flats so fastened. This problem has been discussed previously (see pp. 267-271).

The lashing of corners sometimes presents difficulties, but in reality a corner lash is easier to make than a flat joint. Corners should always be arranged so that the crack is right and left, and never downstage—that is, a back wall should be *above* the side walls, and never inside of them. The latter would leave cracks between the back and side walls, which might be visible to the audience. Done the other way, the cracks, if any, will be visible only to the actors. Corners are easier to lash if special devices are used, such as stop cleats or stop blocks (see Fig. 89). Instead of the special stop cleat made for this purpose, any flat cleat may be substituted. A stop block is merely a small block of wood, say 1" by 2" by 8", nailed or screwed on the back of the stile at such a distance from the edge that it holds the flat to be lashed in the proper position so as to make a true corner. Ordinarily, three cleats or three blocks will be sufficient for a flat of any height. One will be placed near the top, one near the middle, and one near the bottom of the stile. The *shape* of the corner is the factor determining which device to use.

BRACING FLATS

The traditional way to brace a wall so that it will be perpendicular and firm is with a stage brace, which is a prop to hold the scenery rigid. It consists (see Fig. 87) of two pieces of wood so arranged that they may be extended or contracted and then solidly clamped together with a thumb screw. They may be purchased in several sizes, and an assortment is useful. At the top end is a pair of hooks, called horns, which is hooked into the hole in the brace cleat. At the bottom is a piece of curved metal (called the rocker), containing several holes through one of which, by the use of a stage screw, or peg, the brace may be fastened to the floor.

Sometimes a wall may be so tall that the braces alone cannot keep it in position: the bottom of the flat must be fastened to the floor also. A special piece of theatrical hardware (see Fig. 90), called a foot iron, is made for this purpose. The foot iron is screwed to the bottom of the flat and fastened to the floor with a peg. Foot irons are useful in pinning a plastic piece in place, or holding a platform on a spot, and for many other purposes. It is partially for the convenience in fastening scenery to the floor, especially for the use of stage screws, that the floor of a stage should always be made of soft wood. If this is not the case, sometimes a beam of soft wood can be fastened permanently to the floor along the back of the stage, by one or two lag screws. It is usually the long back wall that needs bracing, and braces can then all be carried back to this beam. If the stage floor is beautiful hard wood, which must not be marred with a nail, it is sometimes possible to fasten the rockers to short lengths of heavy planks, which may be placed wherever necessary, and held to the floor by weights—a sandbag, or some bricks or stone for instance.

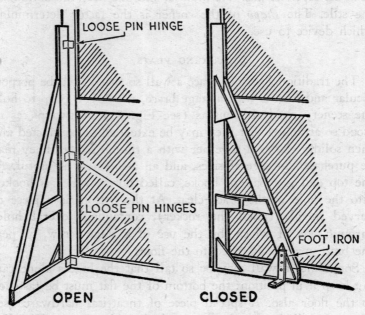

FIG. 90. A JACK

There is another common and useful method of bracing scenery, and that is by using a jack. A jack is a triangular frame, of any size, usually made of 1″ x 3″, and constructed and reënforced in the same manner as a flat. This may be hinged in several places on the back of a stile, so that it will fold back against the flat, and ride with it. In use, it is pulled out perpendicular to the flat and fastened to the floor by using a peg through a foot iron (see Fig. 90). Its advantage is that it holds the wall in several places and thus combines the functions of a brace and a foot iron. Even a small non-professional theater will find use for a collection of jacks of several sizes.

Sometimes, if a wall is very heavy, its moving may be aided by a lift-jack. This is a device made (see Fig. 91) with two stout pieces of wood, two strong hinges, and one or two casters. A lift-jack may be placed at each end of a heavy wall. This sort

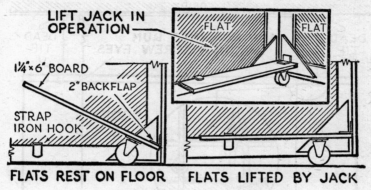

FIG. 91. A LIFT JACK

of jack does nothing to help keep the wall steady, for it works only in the shift when the wall rides on the jacks.

FLYING SCENERY

Drops, borders, even flats, are often flied in the modern theater. The common method for doing this has already been described, on page 177, and it is to be hoped that every non-professional theater will develop some sort of system of rigging to make this possible. If there is not sufficient overhead room so that drops may be hauled up out of sight, it may be necessary to lower them, roll and tie them, before hauling them up for storage. However, if there is room to store the drop folded once, this can be done by tripping it. To trip a drop, it must first be tied off in position with ropes, not through pulleys, of exactly the right length (see Fig. 92). These are called dead ties. Large screw eyes must be placed in the top batten, at the positions of the moving lines. Now the moving lines are brought through these screw eyes and tied off to the *bottom* of the drop. When the lifting lines are pulled, the bottom goes up first, so that the drop is folded. The bottom batten picks up the top one as it reaches it, and the folded drop may be hauled into the

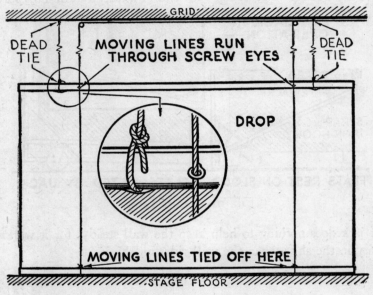

FIG. 92. METHOD OF TRIPPING A DROP

flies against the grid. When the process is reversed, the drop comes down and unfolds, and is held in proper position by the dead ties. The number of lines necessary for this operation will depend, of course, on the width of the drop.

There are several methods of fastening lines to the batten at the top of a drop. One is to bore holes in the batten, so that the lines can be run through the holes (see Fig. 94). Another is to run the lines around the batten by making a slash in the cloth (see Fig. 92). In either of these cases, the best knot to use is a clove hitch with two half-hitches over it (see Fig. 93). A third method, which requires holes in neither the batten nor

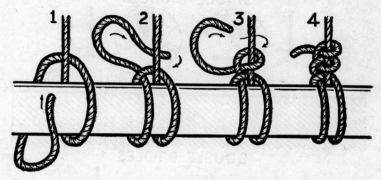

FIG. 93. BATTEN TIE-OFF: A CLOVE HITCH AND TWO HALF-HITCHES

the cloth, is to use a drop holder, which is a special piece of theatrical hardware (see Fig. 94) designed for this purpose.

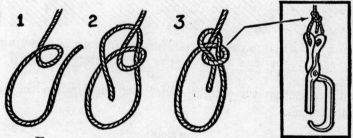

FIG. 94. METHOD OF TYING OFF A DROP HOLDER

The knot shown is a bowline, essential for tying off a drop holder, and preferred by some stagehands for trying a batten to the lines. The latter use of the bowline is illustrated in Fig. 92.

When the gridiron is small, so that only two lines make a set, it is possible to make these two lines support a drop or border of almost any length by the device of using bridles to distribute the weight. When a set of lines is vacant, it is wise to tie the ends together and fasten them to a weight, such as a

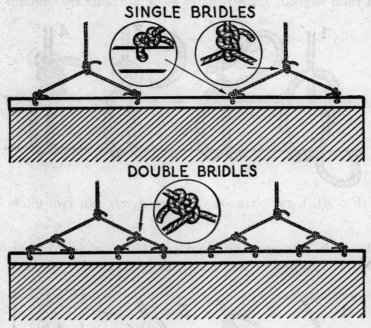

FIG. 95. METHOD OF DISTRIBUTING WEIGHT OF DROP WHEN THERE ARE NOT SUFFICIENT LINES

sandbag, so that the weight will lower them when they are wanted again.

CASTERS

Another common shifting device, used for many purposes in the modern theater, is the caster. A caster is a small wheel, such as is often used on the legs of beds and other heavy furniture. The kind most useful in the theater are three inch, rubber-tired, ball-bearing swivel casters. These are capable of bearing great weight. They may be used on lift-jacks (see Fig. 91), or to roll platforms of all kinds. Sometimes, instead of using lift-jacks, a narrow platform may be used to carry a wall. The wall may be braced to the top of the platform with jacks and braces; and some device for holding the platform in place, like a foot iron and peg, may be necessary. Such a platform, for carrying a wall, is usually called a wagon. Wagon scenery, then, is simply scenery designed to be carried by narrow platforms which move on casters.

Sometimes larger platforms are used in this way—even platforms large enough to cover the playing space, carrying the

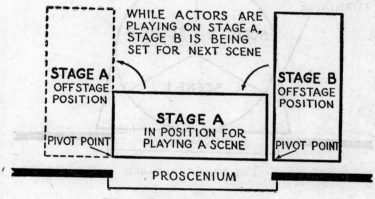

FIG. 96. A JACK-KNIFE STAGE

entire set and furniture. If the stage space is large enough, such platforms are often pivoted at one of the down-stage corners. Two platforms of this size, pivoted at opposite corners so that as one is rolled off, the other is brought on (see Fig. 96), make possible very rapid scene shifts. A new set can be placed on the offstage platform while actors are playing on the onstage one. These platforms work like two blades in a jack-knife, and are often called jack-knife platforms. The entire porch set, shown in Plate VIII B, was carried on a wagon, eight feet wide and twenty-four feet long. The other elements of the set—the tree, the ground row, and the wings—were carried on and set individually.

Still another use of casters, in the attempt to make quick and easy shifts, is to support a round platform, or plate, pinned in the center of the stage, so that it will revolve. The correct name for this is a turn table. It is often called a revolving stage, but a true revolving stage is cut into the floor of the stage and is at the level of the floor. However, both devices are similar in use. A turn table may allow the sets for an entire act, or for an entire

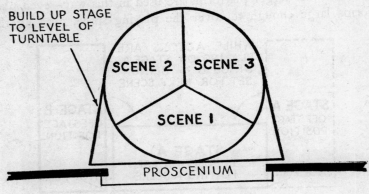

BUILD UP STAGE
TO LEVEL OF
TURNTABLE

SCENE 2   SCENE 3

SCENE 1

PROSCENIUM

FIG. 97. A TURNTABLE

play, to be set up. Then the scene shift consists merely of turning the table to the proper position.

All of these devices are simple in operation, and any non-professional theater which possesses a few clever carpenters and can secure a sufficient amount of lumber and enough casters should have no difficulty in building them.

MISCELLANEOUS HARDWARE

There are certain pieces of hardware, some of them standard and procurable in any large hardware store, and some of them specially made for stage use and obtainable only from theater supply houses, but all of which will make life easier for the stage crew. An assortment of bolts and nuts, hinges, angle irons, and flat angle irons (plus some assorted nails and screws, and a few hammers and screw drivers) are useful in making quick repairs during shifts. Sometimes it becomes necessary to drill a hole, say through a door frame and a stile, and to use a bolt and nut to hold the refractory frame in place. A wing nut of the proper size, which can be tightened with the fingers, makes the operation easier.

The same hinges ($1\frac{1}{2}''$ and $2''$ back flaps) which have been used in scene building for many purposes, now serve as a quick method of fastening two edges together. For example, if two stiles refuse to be lashed edge to edge, a hinge may be fastened, half on each stile, to pin the edges together properly. When the flats must separate, the hinge pin may be quickly drawn. In fact, hinges are widely used for the purpose of pinning the edge of a batten to a stile to add strength, or a window frame into its hole, or a jack against a flat, etc. A special hinge-pin, slightly thinner than the ordinary pin and about six inches long, is made for this purpose, and is much easier to use both in pinning and unpinning. In an emergency a large finishing nail may be used, but a handful of pin-wires is useful and cheap.

It may, too, suddenly become necessary to strengthen the leg of a chair or table, or to reënforce the weak corner of a picture frame. The former may be quickly done by screwing an angle iron in a strategic place, and the latter by a flat angle on the back of the frame.

The most useful piece of special hardware will probably be the stage picture hanger. This consists of two pieces of strap iron, the first containing a bulge (called the socket) with screw holes in each end so it can be fastened against a surface, and the second terminating in a hook which fits into the socket. This is the common method of hanging pictures on sets. A special toggle rail must be placed at the correct height, and the sockets screwed on the face of the flat through the canvas to the rail. The hooks are placed on the back of the frame, and the picture hung by dropping the hooks into the sockets. Picture hangers are used for many other purposes. The curtain battens in Plate

XIV, and the heavy mouldings at the top of the columns in Plate XV, were hung in this manner. As sockets are practically flat, they become almost invisible when painted to match the wall.

Mending irons are flat metal straps which may be quickly screwed on to the back of a broken batten. "S" or keeper hooks are useful in increasing the rigidity of a long wall. Each end of the hook, which is in the shape of a square S, is made to fit a 1" x 3". Thus, by slipping hooks over the top of the flats, or over the toggle rails, it is possible to fasten a long batten temporarily against the back of the wall to act as a stiffener.

Catalogues of theatrical hardware are filled with interesting and useful devices, and will repay study. The alert stage crew will be ready to meet any emergency with speed and skill— *and as quietly as possible.*

SCENE SHIFTS

The handling of the scenery and the changing of the set is another one of the many jobs of the stage-manager. The stage crew needs rehearsals with the scenery just as much as the actors do with their parts of the play. Often the stage manager, or the chief carpenter under his direction, works out in advance the duties of each member of the crew, both for the "set" (which is the process of getting the scene ready) and for the "strike" (which is taking it down again). Sometimes each grip is presented with a previously prepared card which gives him, numbered and in order, the two or three moves he makes in each set and each strike. Like the actors, each member of the crew should have his own duties, which cannot be done by any one else, and he should memorize them accurately.

There are certain definite methods of procedure which should be borne in mind. Rugs, furniture, and properties should, as a rule, be placed on the stage first, and then the set built around them. In the same way, the set should be taken off, then the furniture and properties. It is awkward and time-taking to try to carry heavy pieces through the doorways into sets that are already in place. Flats should be stacked in the order in which they are to be used in making the set. Such a stack is called a pack, and stagehands often call the process of pulling the flats off the stack and into place "running the pack."

Measurements for the placing of a set should be made from a spot under the exact center of the proscenium arch. This is called the pivot point, and in some stages it is marked by a brass plate. Walls are set so many feet back and so many feet to one side or the other of the pivot point (see Fig. 74).

It is of the utmost importance that furniture, as well as sets, be always on the exact spot. When several sets are used, or when a set is to be rearranged, it is helpful to have certain important corners or points marked on the floor cloth or on the floor itself. Chalk or paint will sometimes do, or better still, small pieces of tin may be tacked on the floor to indicate the location of corners. A different shape may be used for each set.

The making and handling of scenery furnishes a never-ending series of interesting problems, involving at times nearly all the arts and nearly all the crafts.

CHAPTER XXII

Properties

DEFINITION

Properties are defined by dictionaries as "all the adjuncts of a play except the painted scenery and the costumes of the actors." Formerly, in periods that took their play production a little less scientifically than ours does, costumes, too, were included among the properties. And custom still includes some articles that might also be classified as costumes—such articles as canes, umbrellas, revolvers, swords, fans, letters, and so forth that are used in the action of the play. Aside from these, properties usually include furniture, pictures and ornaments, noise machines, effects such as snow or rain storms, and many other things that seem to fall to the property man merely because they are not the particular function of any other member of the producing force. The property man is, therefore, a busy and important person. It would seem fitting, perhaps, to give him a more imposing title, such as master (or mistress) of properties. In some organizations he is called the property-manager. Whatever his title, it can never adequately describe all the assorted duties that usually fall upon him and his assistants. A well-organized and competent property department is a necessary adjunct to play production.

IMPORTANCE OF PROPERTIES IN REHEARSAL

It is exceedingly important that properties be introduced into rehearsals as early as possible. Some person, either the property man or the director, or both, should read the play through and

330

list all the properties that are to be needed. Reprints of old prompt-books usually contain lists of necessary articles. If the actual properties cannot be secured much before the performance, other articles may be used in rehearsal. A stick may thus serve for a cane, or an umbrella, or a fishing rod, or a gun, or any other such property. A piece of paper may be used for money, or a dish, or jewelry, or a hat. The important thing is that some physical property be used wherever one is called for. Properties which are introduced at the last moment for the first time are sources of danger. In *The Bishop's Candlesticks*, the Bishop comes into his home, greets his family, and takes a seat at the table for supper. In one performance, the Bishop did all these things nonchalantly with his hat still on his head. Fortunately, the day was saved by his sister who had the presence of mind to go up to the Bishop, sitting quietly at supper in his home, remove his hat, and hang it on the hook that had been provided for it. The audience, it is to be hoped, charged the ungentlemanly action to mere absent-mindedness on the part of the noble Bishop. Such occurrences are entirely unnecessary. The Bishop should have worn some sort of hat at every rehearsal, even if it had been only a paper hat.

FURNITURE ·

Furniture, in a play that is properly planned according to modern ideas, will be chosen by the artist who designs the scenery. When furniture, rugs, pictures, and ornaments are selected from available material, it should be his duty to make the selection. The property man is thus relieved of this responsibility. In a professional theater, the property man is often merely a shopper for the designer. He finds out what furniture and property is available, and the designer makes the selection. Then it is the duty of the property man to arrange for purchase or rental of properties, see to their transport, supervise their return, and look after payment of bills. Whenever the property man does find that he has to do the selecting, he should do it with a complete conception of the play in mind. He should know and follow the modern idea of the play as an artistic unity. The more he knows about the theory of stage design and scenery, the better his selections are likely to be.

Furniture can often be manufactured by an ingenious property department. It may often be made in a manner similar to scenery and with the use of scenic materials. If the back of a chair or sofa is not to show, it should not be finished. Designs and decorations may be applied with scene paint and with papier mâché (see p. 237). To secure a glossy furniture finish, all that is necessary is to shellac the surface. The one thing to be avoided, probably, is the mixing of manufactured and real furniture.[1] The reupholstering of furniture, the making of slip covers and pillows, the sewing up of curtains—all these and many more operations fall to the property department.

MAKING PROPERTIES

The property man will find that manual skill will stand him in good stead. He may have to devise torches by fastening electric torchlights at the ends of sticks and covering the bulbs with colored gelatins. Lanterns may be made of sheet tin, cut to proper shapes, and folded to inclose an electric torch or bulb. Stage food is often required. Bread, covered with hot water just before it is carried on to the stage, is a common device. The bread may be broken or cut to almost any desired shape from potatoes to meat, colored with vegetable dye, and made to steam with hot water. For stage soups, or drinks, a fine grain, like bird-seed, may be used. It, too, can be made to appear just off the stove by the use of boiling water. Real food and drink are usually unnecessary for a play. The actor had much better pretend to eat and drink than really to do so, unless he has to empty a glass. Wine is usually water colored with grape juice

[1] A book exceedingly useful, both to the property man and to the designer is Joseph Aronson's *Encyclopedia of Furniture* (New York, Crown Publishers, 1938).

or vegetable dye; whiskey is weak tea. The property food should be used in as many rehearsals as possible.

STAGE TRICKS

Sometimes the property man may be called upon to devise a stage trick of some sort. In a medieval ballad-play, called *King Herod and the Cock,* the climax of the play comes when the King says that it is just as likely that Christ is to be born as it is that the roasted cock lying before him in a dish will stand up and crow. The cock does so! The trick was performed in this way: During the play a table is carried in by servants and set before the King. It appears to be an ordinary table, but in reality it is a magician's table; a small boy is concealed in a boxlike arrangement close under the table top. The cock is carried in separately by another servant, on a golden platter—made by gilding a tin plate—and placed on the table. The cock is made of cloth, shaped like an ordinary bird, but so arranged that a coat of feathers, and head and a tail, which have been folded under him, appear when he is turned over. Three tiny hooks lie on the table, and a string fastened to each one runs through a hole in the table to the boy beneath. The servant who carves the fowl secretly fastens these hooks to it. At the proper moment the boy crows and pulls the strings, one of which moves the cock's head back and forth. In this manner the cock appears to come to life, to the great amazement of King Herod and the audience.

A similar trick is called for in *The Tempest.* A banquet is set before the King and his followers, who have been wandering, hungry and thirsty, over the mysterious island. At a certain time the food must be made to disappear, while Ariel appears and lectures the courtiers on their evil ways. Again, a trick table was used. This table had a top made of heavy wrapping paper on which was spread a "delicious banquet" of glass fruit. A boxlike arrangement held Ariel just under this paper top; the back was opened so Ariel could crawl in just before the table was carried on by "strange shapes." The King and his friends, after some conversation about the possible source of the banquet, approach it doubtfully. At that moment there is a terrific crash of thunder, a flash of lightning, and then an instant of darkness. Ariel bursts through the top of the table, and the delicious banquet vanishes by dropping into the box. The dismayed courtiers fall back before the accusations of Ariel; at the end of his speech there is more thunder and lightning, and he himself disappears by falling into the boxlike table, which is instantly carried off by the strange shapes. Stage tricks of this sort may call for great ingenuity from the property man and his crew.

COMMON VISUAL EFFECTS

Aside from actual properties, such as articles that are to be used by the actors, furniture, curtains, etc., and stage tricks, which have previously been discussed, the property man is often called on to create effects. The scene-designer usually manages to avoid such problems by standing on an old theater saying: "Manual and mechanical effects belong to the property man, electrical effects to the electricians!" It is, therefore, necessary for the property man to know these common effects. Often they are both manual and electrical, so it is probably more sensible to divide them into visual effects and sound effects.

1. *Fire.* To obtain an illusion of fire, a pile of logs with their centers cut away, may be built up—on andirons, if it is to be used in a fireplace, or on a baseboard if it is to be an open fire. A deep amber-colored electric light and a small fan may be placed at the bottom of the hollow center of the pile. Over the fan should be placed a piece of wire netting to which narrow strips of white, red, and orange crêpe de Chine or georgette should be attached. These strips will catch the breeze and the light, and they will flutter above the tops of the log to create an excellent illusion. It is by a device of this sort that an actor is burned to death in the theater. Smoke may be added if an electric plate is sprinkled with ammonium chloride. Of course,

the mere light will suffice where the effect of flames is not desired. A moving flame may also be created by a painted glass
disc, revolved by motor or clockwork, in front of a spot with a

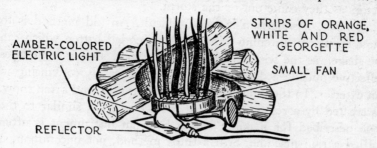

FIG. 98. A STAGE FIRE—FROM THE REAR

focusing lens. This effect may be purchased or rented from a
stage-lighting concern.

2. *Curtains Fluttering.* Electric fans are useful in many other
ways. By their use curtains may wave in the breeze sent through
a window, or a flag may be made to flutter.

3. *Snow.* White confetti, thrown into an electric fan, may be
driven into a window, or across an open window or door, to

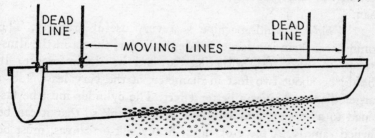

FIG. 99. A SNOW CRADLE

give the effect of snowfall. If the snow is not to come into the
room, the window or door must be covered with cloth or wire
screening. If snow is desired over a large area, a snow cradle
(see Fig. 99) is easy to construct. Torn up newspaper, or corn-

flakes, or some other appropriate substitute, may be used instead of confetti. For snow that is supposed to be on the clothes, wet salt is probably better than confetti. It may be shaken off by the actors as they come out of the storm.

4. *Rain.* Visible rain is more difficult. An old method is to tie a series of glistening wires to a suspended batten which can be shaken as the wires are lighted by a spot. This is sometimes effective outside a door or window, but is rarely convincing in an exterior. In the modern theater, falling rain, and often snow, is created by a revolving disc in front of a spot, similar to the one described for making flames. Such an instrument is often called a rain machine. Still a third method, not uncommon, is to use actual water. A perforated pipe is suspended over the stage, usually near the front, and a hose connection carries real water to the pipe. This method demands some device for collecting the water on the floor, such as a trough, or a slot in the stage with a trough underneath.

SOUND EFFECTS

Other visual effects are sometimes demanded, but sound effect will probably be a greater source of labor for the property man.

1. *Wind.* A wind machine is a very useful property. The commonest form is a large wooden cylinder, shown in the illustration in Fig. 100, with slats around its circumference. It should·be about two feet in diameter, at the very least, and a larger diameter gives a better effect. The cylinder must be fastened to a support and supplied with a crank so that it can be turned rapidly. A piece of cloth, heavy silk or canvas, must be arranged so that it is stretched over the cylinder while it is revolved. The greater the pressure on the cloth, and the more rapidly the cylinder is turned, the louder is the wind. Another form of wind machine, which requires less storage space, but is as a rule less satisfactory, is one made of two smaller, smooth cylinders, fastened about four or five feet apart on a board. One

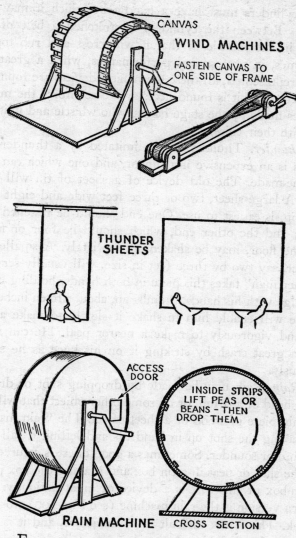

CANVAS

WIND MACHINES

FASTEN CANVAS TO
ONE SIDE OF FRAME

**THUNDER
SHEETS**

ACCESS
DOOR

INSIDE STRIPS
LIFT PEAS OR
BEANS — THEN
DROP THEM

RAIN MACHINE   CROSS SECTION

FIG. 100. SOME COMMON NOISE DEVICES

of the cylinders must have a handle by which it may be revolved. Between the cylinders is stretched a belt of cloth, twisted in the middle so that it will cross and rub together. Oftentimes, in professional performances, when a great storm is to be represented, all these mechanical devices are found to be insufficient; and it is found necessary to reënforce the machines by noises made by the stage hands, who whistle and imitate the wind with their voices.

2. *Thunder*. Thunder is best imitated by a thunder drum, but this is an expensive instrument, and one which can hardly be home-made. The old device of a sheet of tin will usually suffice. A large sheet, two or three feet wide and eight or nine feet long, is easiest to use. One end should be fastened against a wall; and the other end, which should be four or five feet from the floor, may be shaken appropriately. A smaller piece, however, say two by three feet in size, will usually serve. The "thunder man" takes this piece in both hands, holding it by the long edge with his hands, thumbs up, about fifteen inches apart. Practice will enable him to shake it slowly to make a distant peal, and vigorously to make a nearer peal. He can learn to make a great crash by striking it on his knee as he shakes it vigorously.

3. *Rain*. Rain may be made by dropping shot or dried peas on the head of a drum, or on some other object that will sound, as a thin piece of wood or a sheet of tin. The "rain man" must keep taking the shot up in handfuls and letting it fall back on his drum or sounder. Sometimes a good effect is secured by putting the shot or peas in a tin box and shaking the box properly. A rain-box of this sort is a device of great antiquity. A more modern version is the rain machine (see Fig. 100) worked with a crank. This is not difficult to manufacture, and it is also useful for surf or breaking waves.

4. *Hoof beats*. Horses' hoof beats may be imitated by using drum sticks on a sounding box of some sort. However, the traditional method, also of considerable antiquity, is to use two

halves of an empty coconut shell. The performer holds one in each hand and beats with the ends on a hard or soft surface, depending on the effect desired. The long association of this device with cheap melodrama of the "ten, twenty, thirty" style has made it a noise that is to be used with great discretion. It is usually better to allow the audience to imagine the hero riding up to the door—except when a comedy effect is desired.

5. *Crashes.* Crashes off the stage, such as a burglar falling through a window, are usually made by a crash bag; that is, a heavy canvas bag containing broken glass and tin. Such objects may also be placed in a wooden box, which may be allowed to drop. It is dangerous to have broken glass around loose; all crashes should be carefully provided for.

6. *Shots.* When shots are fired and real blanks are not to be used, either on or off the stage, a satisfactory effect may be se-

FIG. 101. A SHOT STICK

cured by striking the floor of the stage with a flat piece of wood. The stick should be about three or four feet long and two or three inches wide. One end should be placed under the heel, and the other end held in the hand two feet or so from the floor. By pressing down with the foot and releasing suddenly the end that is held in the hand, a sharp, shot-like sound can be made. A common method of imitating the sound of distant musketry is to beat a leather cushion or an automobile seat with thin sticks, such as dowels. When a real revolver is to be used, the experienced property man "covers" it with another revolver or a shot stick—in case the first one fails.

7. *Recordings.* There are now on the market an infinite number of recordings by the use of which it is possible to make almost any sound effect. Bands and orchestras, automobiles and trains, airplanes, and many other effects are most difficult—and sometimes impossible—to make manually. Mob noises, such as cheers, boos, applause, may be made offstage by strategically-placed trained groups; but usually it is safer and easier to depend on a good recording. Animal noises of all kinds may be produced by an imitator, but again these all exist on records. Often too, a special text, such as a radio announcement is required by the script; and this can be cut on a recording machine —in a local radio studio, if no machine is available in the school. Therefore, one of the most universally useful devices for sound effects will be a good system of turntables and loud speakers— even a superior phonograph.

NEED FOR ORIGINALITY

The property man must be ready at any and all times to devise methods of creating sounds never before made on any stage! When *The Hairy Ape* was performed first on Broadway, the property man was at a loss for a long time as to how to imitate the sound of the shoveling of coal into the furnaces of a ship, which is demanded throughout an entire scene. After experimenting, he finally hit upon a certain method of shaking iron chains which gave the exact effect. No coal was ever used in the scene. But the stokers, stripped to the waist, with empty shovels went through the motions of feeding coal to the flaming furnaces, the doors of which were constantly opening and closing, making the scene alternately bright and dim. And the "coal man" continued to rattle his chains off stage. From the audience the illusion was excellent. There are no set ways of securing noise effects. Anything that gives the proper sound is legitimate.

HANDLING PROPERTIES

More almost than any other member of the producing force, the property man needs a sense of order and arrangement. He must know where everything is at every moment during the performance, and where everything should be. It is customary to have a property table, or a property box, at a certain definite place near the stage, to which actors can go to get necessary properties just as they are about to make their entrances. Sometimes the property man will have to send an assistant to an entrance to hand an actor a property. He must not neglect to see that the property is taken away from the actor again when it has been used, and restored to the property table. He must, of course, have a complete list of everything that is necessary. Sometimes he may have to work out a system of marking properties to indicate the act in which they are to be used. Colored chalks or colored tapes may prove useful. Above everything else, the property man must be certain that articles are in their proper places. In a serious little play called *The Cottage on the Moor*, an ancient pistol is one of the important properties. A grandfather says to his little grandson, "Get the pistol *down* from the shelf." In one performance, the obedient boy went to the closet, but to his dismay the pistol was not high up on the top shelf, as it had been previously. After a search, he bent over and picked it off the bottom shelf, near the floor. The effect was comical, and the audience laughed. The actors were confused, and the performance went from bad to worse. The slight slip on the part of the property man who had placed the articles in the closet really ruined the performance.

The property man must be ingenious, and he must remember that there may be a difference between dramatic properties and real articles. In a pseudo-Chinese play, *The Turtle Dove*, one of the properties called for is a Chinese newspaper or book. One property man once spent several days, and traveled a long distance, before he finally secured a copy of a real Chinese newspaper. Another property man, collecting his material for another performance of the same play, took a long piece of paper, two sticks, a paint brush and a bottle of black ink, and made in half an hour an excellent Chinese scrollbook, which in the play was much more effective and comical than the real newspaper. Perhaps the perseverance of the first property man and his insistence on the real article is as much to be admired as the cleverness of the second; but there is a moral to the story, nevertheless.

The opportunity that the property man has in using his ingenuity in securing and handling the properties for each new play makes his work ever new and fascinating.

CHAPTER XXIII

Costuming

Costumes are "the scenery worn by the actors." Everything that has been said in previous chapters about the theory of scenery is equally applicable to costuming. Costuming is not good primarily to the degree that it is accurate, or beautiful, or becoming to the wearer; it is good to the degree that it helps act the play by making the story clearer and more effective. It is another one of the visual elements in play production.

The making of theatrical costumes is a very different problem from that of making clothes for ordinary everyday wear. Again, color and line are the all important elements. Fabric, except in so far as it affects color and line, is quite a secondary affair. So is the finish of the costume—the minuteness of the stitches, the fineness of the seam, and the accurate turning of the hem. It is primarily only the sum total of the effect that counts.

AIM IN COSTUMING

Every costume should do two things: (1) it should aid the audience to characterize the wearer; and (2) it should help show his relationship to the other characters.

1. *To Characterize the Wearer*. A costume will succeed in the first aim to the degree that the artist understands and grasps the idea of the character whose costume he is designing. The problem is similar to that of designing a set for a scene. The main aim is appropriateness. The costume, to be

343

successful, must suggest just the kind of person that the action of the play is going to unfold. Hamlet's "inky suit" should show at a glance the despair of the man, whereas the bright costumes of the gay court by which he is surrounded help to characterize the other persons in the play. In the *Show-Off*, Audrey Piper is as instantly disclosed by the checked suit in extreme fashion, the bright tie, the flash-imitation stick-pin, and the yellow shoes, as he is by the empty laugh and the too facile tongue.

2. *To Show Relationships.* It is not enough that the costume be merely suitable to the character; it must indicate his relationships to the other characters. In *Hamlet,* for instance, Horatio, as the friend of Hamlet, may have a costume which is in some ways similar to that worn by Hamlet himself. This will set him off from the courtiers, like Guildenstern and Rosencrantz, who are the friends of the King. But Horatio's costume must also be sufficiently unlike Hamlet's so that the most casual glance will distinguish the two men from each other. In *The Romancers* there are two old men, Bergamin and Pasquinot, who are constantly on the stage together. They must be kept distinct from one another. The coat of one may be longer and fuller than that of the other. One may wear huge cuffs and a striking feather in his hat. One may always carry a stick of some sort. The designer has the same problem that the director has of keeping the characters distinct from one another and yet properly related.

COLOR AND LINE IN COSTUME DESIGN

The two elements upon which the artist must mainly depend in his attempts to attain both of these objects are color and line, which have already been discussed in Chapter III. Remember that, in general, red, orange, and yellow are considered warm colors; they are, therefore, more appropriate for the vigorous, passionate characters in a play. The cool colors, blue, green, and violet, usually suggest calmness and quietness. Old characters should usually be costumed in colors grayed to suggest subdued emotions. Remember, also, that analogous colors suggest harmony and friendship, whereas complementary colors indicate conflict and struggle. The color wheel will prove constantly helpful to the thoughtful costume designer.

Line is the second important element. Remember that long straight lines give the effect of dignity and seriousness, sharp curves and circles suggest lightness and comedy, and jagged lines and angles suggest grotesqueness and excitement. In a costume, up and down lines usually give the effect of tallness and slimness; while cross lines add breadth to a figure. Careful designers consider the silhouette of the costumes and say that each character should have a distinct silhouette as well as a distinct color.

THE COSTUME PLATE AS A REPRESENTATION OF AN IDEA

Just as sketches and models are the best method of representing a setting, so a set of costume plates is the best method of designing costumes. It is not at all necessary to be an accomplished artist to make a set of plates. Any one who has sufficient ability to select costumes for a play has enough ability to make plates, which are only a graphic representation of ideas. They need not be, and in fact should not be, a set of pictures. They need not be finished drawings. They should be merely a representation of the desired line and color. A beautiful set of drawings may be a very bad costume plate. The actual execution of the design on paper is less important than the idea represented.

The idea need not be always represented in great detail and in large scale. In fact, one of the best methods is to sketch all the costumes for the play on a single piece of paper, with the individual costumes not more than two inches in height. This makes it possible to judge the sum total of the entire *set* of costumes, and encourages the designer to work for large and simple effects. Such a plate of costumes is a key to the design-er's scheme, and it might be called a costume-key.

EXAMPLE OF A COSTUME-KEY

This idea will be clearer as we consider it in connection with some specific play, say *Twelfth Night*. Our first step, as always, must be to analyze the script in order to find a basis for a production that will be an interpretation.

1. *Analyzing the Script*. There are many possible plays called *Twelfth Night* (see p. 31). The one we may propose to make is the joyous comedy telling the romantic story of a noble duke and two lovely ladies. It is not going to be a farce-comedy of which the hero is an old reprobate named Sir Toby Belch; nor a tragedy-drama concerning the breaking heart of a faithful, but rather silly, steward called Malvolio. The *theme* is simple and commonplace: "Love sometimes finds a way." Such an obvious—and, if you will, false—theme can have value only as we make the play gay and charming, a pastoral fairy-tale. The *color* of our *Twelfth Night* will be cool, suggesting out-of-doors—blue, green, and purple. The *line* will be curved, exaggerated, and gay.

2. *Arranging the Characters*. Our next step will be to examine the characters, whom we hope to *identify* and *relate* by costuming. We have already decided, in analyzing the script that our major characters are to be the lovers: Orsino, Olivia, and Viola. There might be a play, based on this same script, in which the principal characters would be Sir Toby and Sir Andrew and Viola. There often is one in which the most important characters are Viola and Malvolio! But as we wish to make a romantic play, our leading players are to be the three members of the triangle.

Now we must decide what manner of people these three characters are. This is going to be a matter of casting, too. But we can, by clever costuming, aid the casting—assuming, of course, that the director and the costumer agree and are trying to make the same play! Obviously Orsino must be a virile, heroic, exciting gentleman. It is true that he doesn't have a long part, nor many lines. But he must be prominent. We are going to ask the audience to believe that our heroine, Viola, no sooner sees him than she loves him. He must, therefore, be the kind of man who will instantly win the affection of all the ladies in the audience. It is true that when we first see him, he is melancholy, because his love for Olivia is unrequited. But this is a romantic melancholy, not the despair of Hamlet. Orsino enjoys his melancholy; he imagines himself to be the last of the troubadours! Our second major character, Olivia, is a countess. But at the beginning of the play, she has made a vow to retire from the world for a year because her brother has just died. This act is sensible only if she is a young, naïve, and inexperienced girl. Later on, we are asked to believe that she falls instantly in love with a young man—who turns out to be Viola disguised as a youth. More than this, she avows her love, sends him gifts, and does other indiscreet and unladylike deeds! All these are charming only if she is exceedingly young and innocent. Even a countess can be young. Therefore, our Olivia is going to be, with the help of the director, the youngest, most beautiful, most innocent ingenue even seen in any theater. And Viola! Much of the play she is disguised as a youth. No other character in the play questions this; they all accept her as a young man. Therefore, she must be tall, vital, boyish, frank, vigorous. Many Violas in the theater look more womanish disguised as a man than otherwise! This makes all the other characters stupid.

In order to identify the other characters, we should now relate them to our principal ones. Since we have three major characters, we should have three groups. Orsino has a court, consisting of some gentlemen (Curio, Valentine, and other gentlemen), some pages, musicians, and officers. Olivia has a household, consisting of some ladies-in-waiting (Maria, and others), a steward (Malvolio) and an old servant (Fabian),

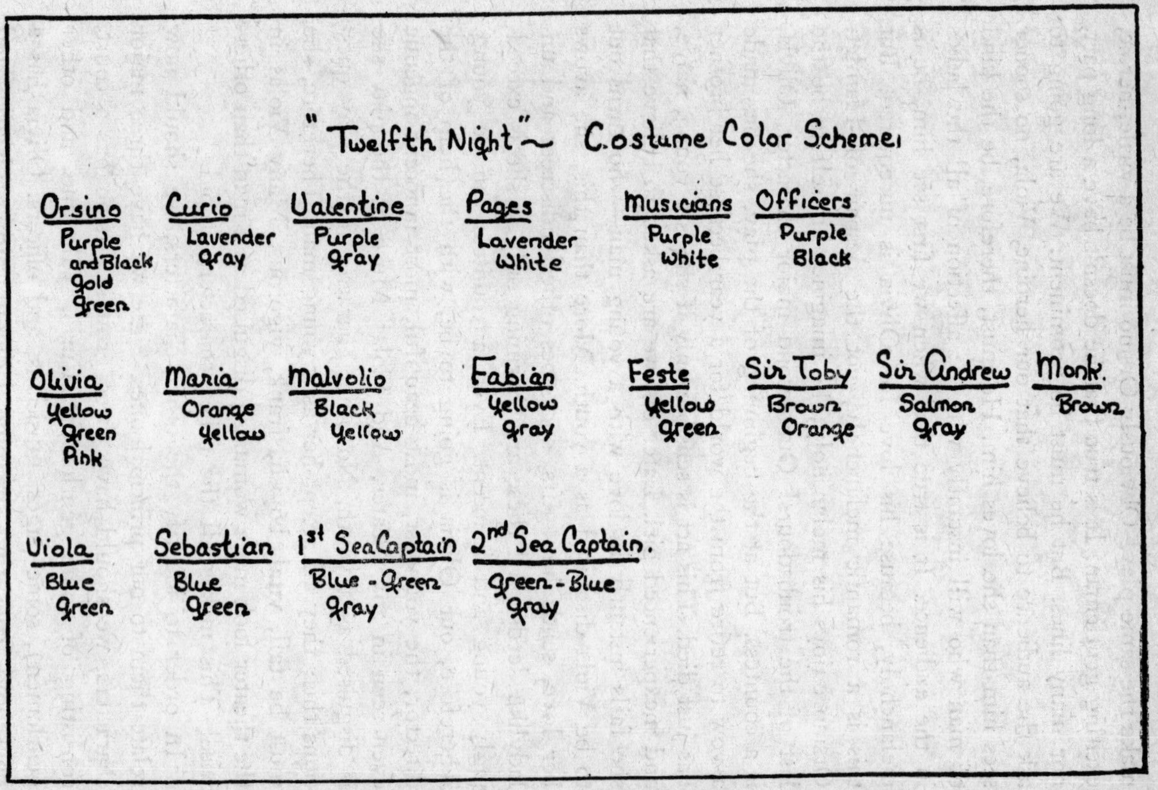

"Twelfth Night" ~ Costume Color Schemes

Orsino	Purple and Black, Gold, Green
Curio	Lavender, Gray
Valentine	Purple, Gray
Pages	Lavender, White
Musicians	Purple, White
Officers	Purple, Black
Monk	Brown
Sir Andrew	Salmon, Gray
Sir Toby	Brown, Orange
Feste	Yellow, Green
Fabian	Yellow, Gray
2nd Sea Captain	Green-Blue, Gray
1st Sea Captain	Blue-Green, Gray
Malvolio	Black, Yellow
Maria	Orange, Yellow
Olivia	Yellow, Green, Ash
Sebastian	Blue, Green
Viola	Blue, Green

FIG. 102. LAY-OUT OF COSTUMES FOR "TWELFTH NIGHT"

Costume-key for "Twelfth Night"

a clown (Feste), an uncle (Sir Toby), and a house guest who has been invited by the uncle to be a suitor for her hand (Sir Andrew Aguecheek). There is also a monk, who lives on her estate, so we must include him. Viola has a twin brother (Sebastian), and a friend, the sea captain who brought her to these shores (Antonio). Finally, there is a second sea captain (unnamed), a friend to Sebastian, so we must include him in this group. We can show these relationships clearly by writing out the groups, as in Fig. 102.

We can also write out the color. As we want a wonderful and princely Orsino, we might think of him as purple. Our Olivia is to be young and naïve; she might use a pale yellow-green. The only basic color left (our play is blue, green, and purple) is blue, which as a strong, clean color is very appropriate for Viola. Because these characters are essentially similar, all gay and charming, and since the nature of the conflict in the play is going to be playful rather than serious, we might well decide to tie these basic colors together with secondary costume colors. As Olivia's color is a yellow-green, we could do this by making green and gold the secondary colors for both Orsino and Viola. Of course, we may use black and white in any or all costumes, for these are not colors— black is the absence of all color, and white the presence of all color. Because we wish to indicate that Olivia is a warm-blooded young lady, in spite of her nobility we might warm up her cool yellow-green with a pale lavender-pink. In taking these steps, we have made many decisions; and whether or not we go further and actually sketch the costumes, we have already arrived at a costume scheme—and one that, because it is in writing, we can show to a director and to the skeptical actors.

3. *Sketching the Figures.* The third step, if we are to carry our costume-key beyond a written scheme, is to sketch the figures on which the costumes are to be drawn. The arrangement of the figures should be identical with the arrangement of the characters in the written scheme; that is, the major characters

(the important ones whose story is told in the incidents of the play) should be at the left of the page, one below the other; the minor characters (preferably in order of importance) in appropriate groups which show their relationship with the major characters.

Sketching the actual figures on which the costumes are to be drawn is not a difficult matter. A few lines suffice, and a little practice will enable the designer to sketch the figure in any

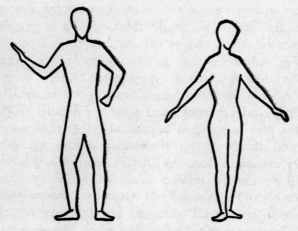

FIG. 103. FIGURES FOR COSTUME KEY

desired posture. A few elementary rules for figure construction are sometimes helpful. The head should be about one-seventh of the total height of the body. The distance from the shoulder to the crotch and the crotch to the knees is about equal. The hand normally reaches to a point half way down the thigh. Each extremity may be estimated to be three-quarters of the part next above it; that is, the hand is three-quarters of the forearm, and the forearm three-quarters of the upper arm; the foot is three-quarters of the lower leg, and the lower leg three-quarters of the upper. However, it is not even necessary to be able to draw the figures, for they can be traced easily from other sketches or illustrations and transferred onto drawing paper. A few figures will serve for many costume plates. Figures two inches high are sufficiently large.

4. *Outlining the Costume.* The next step is to outline the silhouette of the costume. It is important to be certain at this stage that the silhouettes are sufficiently different. For example, in designing a play of Shakespeare's, say *As You Like It* or *The Merchant of Venice,* in which there are several young men all of whom must be dressed similarly, variation

ELIZABETHAN   MEDIEVAL   ROYALIST   CHINESE   MODERN
NOBLEMAN   OLD MAN   TROOPER   MANDARIN   DANDY

FIG. 104. DIFFERENT SILHOUETTES OUTLINED ON IDENTICAL
FIGURE

must be secured by such details as sleeves, cloaks, shoes, and so forth. The basic garments must be tights and doublets or jackets of some sort. One may have large puffed sleeves and trunks. Another will wear a longer doublet, and no trunks. Another may have a long flowing sleeve. Still another may wear ornate shoes that come half way up to his knees. In these ways the necessary variety may be secured. With historic costumes and women's costumes, there is little difficulty in securing individual silhouettes; but the beginner is sometimes puzzled as to what to do about modern men's costumes. The problem is more difficult but can often be solved by the proper choice of collar and tie, by one character wearing his coat always buttoned and another leaving his always opened, by the wearing of topcoats and hats when possible, by spectacles, canes, etc. Where there is possibility for little variety of silhouette, color must be depended upon all the more. Of course, it is not always necessary to have this variety; sometimes the play may demand similarity. But where there is similarity it should always be designed, and not merely accidental.

It is at this point that the designer needs to make his study of the historic period. Any large library will contain books of historic costume plates, and many excellent books are now on the market.[1] The designer should study carefully the historic plates and designs, but he will be unwise slavishly to follow any of them. What he must do is to pick out the typical characteristic of the period he is investigating. For example, he must observe that for many centuries in medieval Europe the basic garments for the men were just two in number, tights covering the legs and thighs, and a jacket of some sort for the upper body. On these two basic garments he may employ his ingenuity to produce an infinite variety of effects. He will do well not to overdress his characters. He should ornament, but not hide the body. One or two interesting details, properly selected and cleverly applied, will make his designs characteristic of the period. A theatrical costume should not be a display of archaeological junk. Its success depends entirely upon its effectiveness.

5. *Indicating the Color*. The final step in making the costume-key is to indicate the color. This may be done with water color, which will be easier to use if it is of the opaque, non-bleeding variety—such as poster paint. The result should be a graphic representation of the artist's idea.

[1] Useful Books:
> Lucy Barton, *Historic Costume for the Stage* (Boston, Walter H. Baker Co., 1935).
> Carl Kohler and Emma Von Sichart, *History of Costume* (London, Watt, 1928).

MAKING COSTUME PLATES

Now, if the artist likes, he may blow up his key into individual costume plates on which he can show greater detail. He should still remember, however, the value of simplification. Invisible details are useless, and too many details make the costumes fuzzy. Just as in designing scenery, the costume artist should work for large, bold effects.

Before making the larger plates, he will find it valuable to study his costume-key. This should show him many important things. In the first place, he should be sure that the costumes have the tone, the color and line quality, that is required. Are they really a *set* of costumes? Do they really express the play? Next, he must be sure that his major characters really have the major costumes. Has some minor costume crept in that is accidentally too effective so that the actor wearing it will wipe out the major characters? For example, in *Twelfth Night* we must be certain that when Orsino enters with members of his court, Orsino will always be the dominant figure. We must not be too inspired in making pages, musicians, and officers. If we have been, we had better weaken the minor costumes—or else improve the major one. Finally, we must be sure that we have both proper similarity and proper unlikeness. In *Twelfth Night* for instance, we have two sea captains. Their common trade would indicate that these two costumes should have many points of likeness. But the value of these characters in the play grows out of a series of errors: the sea captain who is Viola's friend mistakes Sebastian for her and goes to his rescue. In the same way Sebastian's friend is surprised and horrified on seeing that Sebastian (who is really Viola) has become so cowardly and unmanly. We must, therefore, be able to differentiate the two sea captains instantly, or the humor of the scenes is lost. This is partly a matter of casting. One captain may be tall, the other short; or one may be thin and one fat. But costuming must help too. Perhaps one wears an identifying hat, or one wears boots, or one carries a rolled-up blanket over his shoulder. The clever costume designer considers carefully all these items and many more, and so his costumes help act the play.

Costume plates, however simply made, will prove invaluable, whether (1) costumes are to be collected and selected, as will usually be the case with modern costumes, or whether (2) they are to be rented from a professional costumer, or whether (3) they are to be made in the shop of the Little Theater or the school group.

COSTUME CHANGES

The important principle of using color and line to indicate characterization and relationship must not be lost sight of when there are costume changes. It will not do to have a character appear first in blue, then in brown, then in yellow, for no apparent reason. This variety will be merely confusing to the audience. The *variety* in costume sequence must have meaning, too. For instance, in the case of *Twelfth Night*, we shall find that Viola makes a brief appearance as a woman shipwrecked on the coast of Illyria. If, as a youth, her colors are blue-green, her woman's costume must also be blue-green;[2] otherwise, the audience will have difficulty in recognizing her in disguise. In the same play, Olivia, being a wealthy countess and appearing in a sequence of scenes, might very well have more than one costume. These will have effectiveness to the degree that the color sequence has meaning. Thus, her first costume might be a very pale yellow-green to indicate her grief. With the appearance of Viola as a messenger to her, she gains a new interest in life; therefore, she might have a second costume of stronger yellowed-green, with some touches of pink; her third and most triumphant costume should be perhaps a much stronger pink, now decorated with yellow-green. In this

[2] The designer must remember, of course, that blue-green is not *one* color, but only a variety of color sensation (see p. 43).

way, the changing color would help indicate her changing mood. An excellent professional example of this scheme was the costume sequence of Miss Katharine Cornell in *The Barretts of Wimpole Street*. The play opens with Miss Cornell in the rôle of Elizabeth Barrett, a hypochondriac, and a prisoner in her home. The plot of the play is her growing interest in life because of the influence of Robert Browning, who rescues and elopes with her. Her first costume was a slightly purpled gray, her second a grayed reddish-purple, and the final one—in which she makes her escape—a grayed red. Thus, her changes helped act the play by symbolizing her growing courage and vigor. Had the costumes been reversed in order, she would have had to play against them. A sequence of red, to purple, to gray, might be suitable for a character who starts with hope and ends in despair. But the change from a pale and weak color to a more vibrant one, indicates growing strength and hope. Costume changes should have meaning.

SELECTING MODERN COSTUMES

The selecting of modern costumes should not be the haphazard thing it so often is, both on the professional and non-professional stage. Here, even more than in a period play, a costume scheme is essential. The designer can show each actor what he should be, and the actor is usually sufficiently impressed by a drawing to attempt to approach it as closely as possible. When the actor is to provide the costume, it should be brought to the theater and inspected and checked up by some observing person, even though there is no costume plate to check with. Amateurs must be warned about last-minute changes in costume. After the evening dress that the heroine is to wear in the last act has been chosen and approved, it is very annoying to have her appear in Aunt Jennie's Paris dress which she thought would be so much nicer! People are often very anxious to lend coats and sweaters and hats for amateur performances, but last minute inspirations of this sort are to be discouraged as they tend to destroy the entire costuming scheme.

In modern, as in historic costume, the aim must be for appropriateness. It is a human failing for actors and actresses to want to look their best before their friends, but this desire should give way before the artistic demands of the play. When the heroine and her sister are discovered in the first act so poverty-stricken that they are renting the old family home, illusion is dealt a severe blow if the ladies insist on appearing in newly-purchased suits, hats, and furs of the latest style.

Of course, common sense and tact must guide. Selection must be made from what is available. But the point is that selection is necessary, and its purpose and its value should be made clear to everybody concerned.

RENTING COSTUMES

When renting costumes, the costume plate explains what is wanted and saves time and labor. The plate may be sent to the costumer if costumes must be hired from a distance, or a representative of the group may be armed with it when he is interviewing the costumer. As a rule, the plainest costumes, of solid colors, are much the best and should be insisted upon. Especially to be avoided are the gaudy military uniforms of bright colors and synthetic leather that obviously are made for the stage and not for the battle-field.

Even when the costumer does not have what is called for, the costume plate will help in the making of a more satisfactory choice. By selecting items from various eras and nations, it is often possible to create costumes similar to those conceived by the designer.

MAKING COSTUMES

The value of a costume plate when costumes are to be home-made is obvious. It should be the model for the workers who are making the costumes, just as the sketches and stage model guide those making the scenery. When the figures are made small, as is suggested above, it is impossible to represent details about the costume, and this is a virtue and not a failing. Details count very little. The costume-makers should be allowed to get the effects indicated in whatever way seems best to them.

The most difficult costume to make is one calling for a coat such as is worn by modern men. However, even these are not impossible if one skilful person is available to guide the other workers. Costume patterns now exist in great variety for many historical periods. The making of costumes is an interesting and not difficult operation, and there is no reason why Little Theaters and school groups should not have active costume-making squads, just as they have groups working on scenery.

1. *Materials.* The material to be used depends on so many things that general advice can be of little value. Some of the cheaper materials commonly used, however, are serge, melton, duvetyne, burlap, alpaca, velveteen, felt, and baize. Canton flannel is an excellent substitution for felt, and sateen is often used to represent silk. In general, dull-surfaced goods, like serge, are much better than goods with shiny filled surfaces, like sateen. Cambric lining is a very poor material for costumes, and should be avoided. Heavy unbleached muslin is a very useful material, and entire sets of costumes may be made from it. For Greek and Roman classical costumes, calico, challis, cotton crêpe, and cheesecloth are useful. Buckram and tarlatan are also very useful materials for the non-professional costume-maker. They may be used for reënforcing costumes, for collars, cuffs, ruffs, and so forth; and they may be made up into various shapes, such as hats or armor, and covered or painted in the way that is to be presently described.

The one important point about the choice of material is that the same grade of material should be used throughout. An entire set of classical costumes may be made of cheesecloth and muslin properly cut and dyed, but the introduction of one real silk costume will kill all the others. The dramatic art is the art of illusion, and illusion is quickly spoiled by the introduction of one wrong article. The material to be used for costumes, unless they are to be worn many times, is really quite unimportant, so long as this rule of consistency is carefully observed.

2. *Cutting and Sewing.* Skill in the cutting and sewing of costumes may be developed by practice, and there should be members of every producing group who are interested in these arts. The ability to cut from a costume plate is not as difficult as may be supposed. There are many good commercial brands of paper patterns on the market, and these are often very useful. Even without them, however, it is possible to succeed in costume-making. There are a few principles and a few basic cuts that simplify the process immensely.

In cutting, it is usually necessary to make two similar pieces, a right and a left. The common method of doing this is to cut the material doubled, so that two pieces of identical size are made at the one cutting. When the material used has a right and a wrong side (which, however, is not the case with many of the materials recommended above) be sure that two right sides, or two wrong sides, come together so that a right and a left will be made.

Trousers, whether they are to be tight Elizabethan trunks to be worn over long hose, or whether they are to be long loose sailor trousers, should be made in four pieces, as illustrated below. Two pieces make the back, and two the front. The outside seams should be made first, thus putting one front and one back together. Then, starting at the crotch, the inside seam should be made on each leg. Then, starting again at the crotch, and putting the two pieces together, the front and the back may be sewed up to make the top. With this general idea in mind, the clever designer can make any sort of a garment desired for the legs. The material can be cut long or short,

tight or full. It may be gathered at the bottom of the legs
and at the waist, or it may be left straight. It may be left open
part way down the sides, or up the legs. But the main point

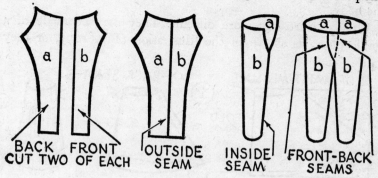

BACK FRONT
CUT TWO OF EACH   OUTSIDE
SEAM   INSIDE
SEAM   FRONT-BACK
SEAMS

FIG. 105. BASIC PATTERN FOR TROUSERS

is to use four pieces, and to put them together in the order
given above.

Skirts may be of two varieties: straight, or circular. A straight

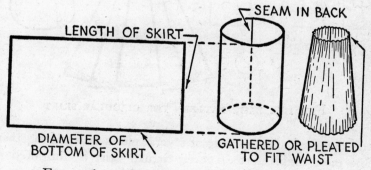

LENGTH OF SKIRT   SEAM IN BACK

DIAMETER OF
BOTTOM OF SKIRT   GATHERED OR PLEATED
TO FIT WAIST

FIG. 106. BASIC PATTERN FOR STRAIGHT SKIRT

skirt consists of a rectangular piece of material, long enough
to give the distance around the bottom. The edges of the
rectangle are sewed together to make a cylinder, which is
gathered or pleated at the top for the waist. There need usu-

ally be but one up-and-down seam; for if the material is wide enough for the length of the skirt, a single cut crosswise of the material will make a piece that is long enough to go around the body.

Circular skirts are more difficult. They may be made of a single piece, as shown in the illustration (Fig. 107), or they

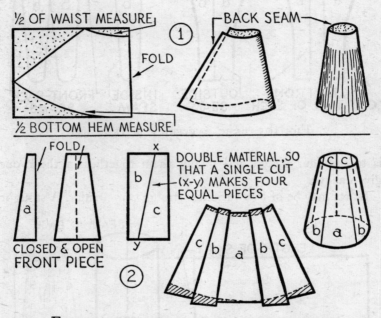

FIG. 107. BASIC PATTERN FOR CIRCULAR SKIRT

may be gored, that is, made of several pieces fastened together. The most simple sort of gored circular skirt is illustrated in Fig. 107. It consists of five pieces; a front piece which must be cut separately (a), and four other pieces (b, b, c, c), all of which may be cut at once from a double piece of material. Material having a pattern that must be kept right side up cannot be cut in this manner since the design in two of the pieces (b, b), would come out upside down. Three measurements are essential for any skirt: the waist measurement, the length, and the distance around the bottom hem.

The basic pattern for a sleeve is also shown Fig. 108. To insure a good easy fit, it is better to have the sleeve a little larger than the armhole into which it is to fit.

The upper parts of a woman's dress, or a man's tunic, may be made just as dolls' dresses usually are, that is, of a doubled piece of material, with the neck hole cut in the center of the fold. One half of the material then hangs down behind, and one half in front. Often, a kimono sleeve can be left, and the

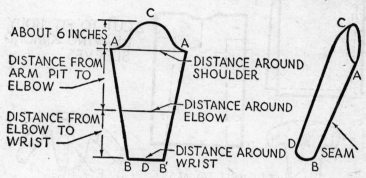

ABOUT 6 INCHES

DISTANCE FROM ARM PIT TO ELBOW

DISTANCE FROM ELBOW TO WRIST

DISTANCE AROUND SHOULDER

DISTANCE AROUND ELBOW

DISTANCE AROUND WRIST

SEAM

FIG. 108. BASIC PATTERN FOR SLEEVE

remainder of the sleeve need be but a cylinder sewed on to the kimono sleeve. An upper garment, made this way (see illustration), may be opened in the back or front, sewed up the sides either shaped or unshaped, left long or short, or treated in any way that the design demands.

Costume-makers will soon build up the necessary ability to make whatever is required. They must decide what few measurements are necessary, and learn to work from them. One-half inch is usually plenty to allow for seams. The excess material on all curved seams must be notched, so that the material will turn back and lie smooth and even. A sewing machine might well be in the workshop of every dramatic organization.

Much time is sometimes wasted in turning hidden hems and making fine seams that affect the value of the costume not at all. This does not mean that work need be careless. But a theatrical costume need not fit like a street suit, and it need not be finished like a costume for general wear. A person need not be an accomplished tailor in order to be able to make excellent and satisfactory costumes. Boldness and

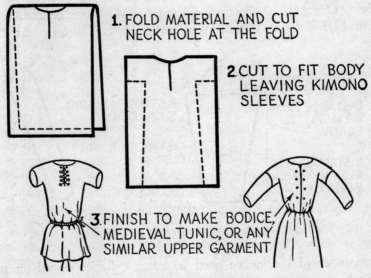

1. FOLD MATERIAL AND CUT NECK HOLE AT THE FOLD

2. CUT TO FIT BODY LEAVING KIMONO SLEEVES

3. FINISH TO MAKE BODICE, MEDIEVAL TUNIC, OR ANY SIMILAR UPPER GARMENT

FIG. 109. METHOD OF MAKING UPPER GARMENT

cleverness in getting effects is the best qualification for a costume-maker.

3. *Dyeing.* What is true of the cutting and sewing of costumes is also true of the dyeing; smooth, even, professional work is entirely unnecessary for the stage. In fact, materials that are dyed so that they are rough and uneven often give better effects under stage lights since they have the roughness of fine fabrics. The lights give them life. Aniline dyes, such as are used in scene painting (see p. 261) are also use-

ful for costume materials and have the advantage of allowing one to work with cold water, but some of the more common commercial dyes are possible. They give good colors, as a rule, and each package gives specific directions. It is wise to follow these directions explicitly. For example, the garment or the material to be dyed should always be soaked with water before being placed in the dye. Some setting agent, salt, or vinegar, or whatever is directed, should always be used. Sometimes, even if colored material is used to make the costumes for a scene, it is wise to dip them all in a weak solution of the same dye to give them artistic unity. A set of calico dresses and shirts for southern mountaineers, for example, might well all be dipped in weak solution of a red-brown color, to give them all the earthy, worn appearance demanded by the play. This weak solution should not change any of the original colors, but should give a universal tint to all of the costumes. The results of theatrical dyeing must always be judged from the distance. It is not how the costume looks to the other characters that counts, but how it appears to the audience.

4. *Painting.* The painting of costumes is an interesting field for experimentation, also. All sorts of decorations and designs may be made with paint. The paint used is similar to that used for making scenery; that is, it is made with hot water, glue or mucilage, and dry pigment. Aluminum or gilt radiator paint may be used for silver or gold color. The material to be painted should be placed on a flat surface, such as an old table covered with paper, and the design painted on with a stiff brush. The paint should be rubbed into the cloth as much as possible. Collars and cuffs and borders may be painted on Elizabethan garments, for example, or the entire surface of a tunic may be covered with a pattern which will give the effect of a fine brocaded surface. Effects, to be of any value, must be large. Finicky and exact work is invisible and useless.

5. *Miscellaneous Articles.* Certain necessary articles are

unusually difficult to make and task to the limit the inventiveness of the non-professional costumer.

a. Tights. Tights are an important part of men's costumes for many centuries, and they are exceedingly difficult to manufacture. They may be made by putting feet in underwear, or by getting large sizes and taking in the leg along the leg seam, but the results are rarely satisfactory. It is much better to purchase the real article. Undyed tights can be purchased at reasonable prices from theatrical costumers, and a number of pairs might well be in the costume closet of every group. The white ones may be dyed light colors; the light colors may be dyed a darker color for the next use, and so on. A satisfactory collection may be soon built up. Medieval characters such as shepherds, farmers, etc., may often have bare legs, or they may have dark trousers or natural-colored coarse underwear cross-gartered or bound to the knee.

b. Shoes. Shoes sometimes are a problem, too. Heavy stockings, cut, or laced, or rolled to suit the occasion, with an inner sole of cardboard, may sometimes be used for medieval cloth shoes. Sandals may be made with inner soles and lacing; or old shoes, with the heels removed, may be cut into the desired shape. Felt, or other heavy material, may be cut and sewed to represent any sort of shoe. The shoes of ladies and upper-class women do not represent so much of a problem, for they seem to have changed very little in the past three hundred years.

c. Armor. Armor is one of the most difficult problems of the non-professional costumer. Many times he can dodge the problem by dressing the characters in surcoats, or in tabards, or in some other long overall garment. Breastplates, or other pieces, may be made of buckram, however, and silvered or gilded with paint. Pieces of tin or other metal, or metal pan cleaners, may be sewed on tunics and painted. Knitted material, like a sweater, may be silvered to make excellent chain mail. Helmets may be made out of buckram, or out of old felt hats, shaped and painted. Armor can always be contrived, if the costumer has the ingenuity to make the proper shape. Long cloaks of some sort are very useful for giving a finish to armor or to other costumes that do not seem to be entirely satisfactory. An assortment of cloaks and capes is a useful addition to any wardrobe.

THE WARDROBE CLOSET

Just as scenery should be saved to be rebuilt and reused, costumes should be saved. A growing costume wardrobe is a useful thing for the non-professional group to build up. Costumes may be remade and redyed to fit the new designs. The problem of designing and making costumes that will be a harmonious part of the whole artistic and dramatic scheme of the play is an interesting one. The most satisfactory results will be attained by broad, simple effects.

CHAPTER XXIV

Make-up

PURPOSE OF MAKE-UP

Make-up may be considered as an extension of costuming. Its purposes are (1) to overcome the effects of the strong lights that are used on the modern stage, and (2) to make the face and head assume the desired characteristics in the same way that costuming does the body.

VARIETIES OF MAKE-UP

It is useful, though perhaps not strictly true, to consider that there are two varieties of make-up: (1) straight, and (2) character. In a straight make-up, a person retains, more or less, his own characteristics. That is, a young man plays the part of a young man, or a young woman plays a young woman. The chief purpose of a straight make-up, therefore, is to overcome the glare of the lights, and to increase beauty. Character make-up requires an actor to change the appearance of his face and head; a young man plays the part of an old man, or a girl assumes a Chinese rôle. Character make-ups require much more skill and experience. In general, however, the processes are similar.

Like all the other processes in theater practice, successful make-up grows out of experience only. There are hundreds of details, and many useful tricks and devices, which can be learned from observation of experienced actors, or from books which deal in detail with make-up only.[1] Usually there are one

[1] See bibliography at end of book.

366

or two persons in every group especially interested in the art, who might well be appointed supervising experts. Each actor, however, should learn enough of the process to be able to make himself up for his own roles. The general principles and the fundamental operations are not difficult to grasp.

VISUALIZING THE MAKE-UP

The first thing to be done is to visualize the desired result: the actor must decide how he wishes to appear. Often he must be governed by the costume plate, which will call for a character of a certain sort. Perhaps the general director, or the art director, will suggest the character's appearance in the play. Perhaps some real person will be the model. With a historical character, portraits may be secured and carefully studied. In any case, in some way, the actor must arrive at a decision. His problem, then, is to make up to match the conception.

MATERIALS

The materials commonly used are as follows:

1. *Cold Cream*. Ordinary theatrical cold cream is cheaper and better for make-up purposes than the common toilet article. Some actors use vaseline or olive oil in place of cold cream.

2. *Grease Paint*. Many varieties of excellent grease paint are now on the market. Grease paints come in all possible hues of flesh colors and are used to give the face the proper color tone. Two types of grease paint are widely used: the first is in the form of a firm stick, usually in a cardboard holder, and the second, a paste in a tube. Choice is merely a matter of individual preference. If an actor is to play a part many times, he should attempt to secure a stick or tube that is just the color he wishes. For example, a young lady playing a straight part might use the color known as *juvenile,* while a young man playing an aged character would use *sallow old man.* Unfortunately, makers of grease paint have no consistent system of marking or of lettering their colors, so that experimentation is sometimes

necessary. With a little experience, it is perfectly possible to mix paints to secure the right colors. For instance, juvenile may be mixed with carmine to give a healthy out-of-doors sunburned appearance; or sallow old man may be mixed with carmine and white to give a good color for middle age. Thus, of all the forty or so flesh colors available, only three or four are absolutely necessary for practically any make-up. A good selection for a make-up box is juvenile, middle age, and sallow old age, or three equivalent colors.

3. *Powders*. Theatrical powders come in many shades, corresponding in color to grease-paint colors. The product of any one manufacturer usually follows in name or number the scheme used to label his grease paints.

4. *Liners*. Liners are smaller sticks of grease paints, in colors that are not normally used to give color tone to the face, such as black, white, gray, blue, and brown. They are used to make lines on the face, such as wrinkles, eyebrows, etc. A complete assortment of liners is useful. Ordinary eyebrow pencils are merely black or brown liners.

5. *Lip Sticks*. Lip sticks are small sticks of grease paint for coloring the lips.

6. *Rouge*. Rouge is of two varieties: moist and dry. The moist comes in small jars; the dry is merely red powder. Instead of moist rouge, many actors prefer a red liner. Dry rouge is often very useful, however, and should be available.

7. *Crêpe Hair and Spirit Gum*. These are the materials out of which stage mustaches and whiskers are made. Crêpe hair is a preparation of wool, woven into a rope. It is sold by the foot. It comes in a great variety of colors, ranging from snow white through grays, black, browns, and blondes, to the most brilliant red. Spirit gum is a combination of gum arabic and ether, with which the crêpe hair is fastened to the face. It comes in small bottles, and is best when it is fresh.

Many other articles such as nose putty, tooth enamel, mascara, and so forth will be found on the list of any manufac-

turer of grease paints, and their uses described in books which
deal only with make-up. But the materials listed are enough
for most purposes. When extended areas of the body need to be
made up, body wash, which can be purchased in various colors,
is better than grease paint. It comes in liquid form, and can be
applied to the skin quickly with a sponge. It washes off easily
with water.

If the actor is to make himself up, he needs a well-lighted
mirror. It may be fixed solidly to the wall, although it is useful
to have it movable, so that it can be set at varying angles. A
small hand mirror is also of great aid. If the lights in the
make-up room are capable of being changed just as the lights
on the stage are to be changed, the actor can see just how
he will look under the stage lights. This is an exceedingly
difficult thing to judge, for lights affect grease paints just as
they do other colors. Most grease paints seem much redder
under ordinary white light than they do under the colored
lights of the stage. Cloths to be used in the process and to
remove the make-up are also necessary. Cheesecloth is highly
satisfactory, and a large supply of cleansing tissue is useful.

Whatever the make-up is to be, whether it is to be straight
or character, male or female, simple or complicated, there is
a certain common process; and this definite process should usually be followed. The development of skill depends on the
operation being done over and over again, until this common
process becomes familiar. The following are the usual steps:

1. *Preparing the Face.* Rub the skin lightly with cold cream,
wipe the cream off the surface, powder the surface, and wipe
the powder off. The cream fills the pores of the skin and also
makes it easier to get off the grease paint afterwards. The powder aids in drying the skin. Too much cold cream must not
be used; many a make-up is spoiled by too much cold cream
at the start. The face should be left perfectly smooth and dry.

This step is merely to prepare the surface for the real painting; it corresponds to the priming coat in scene painting.

2. *Laying on the Ground Tone.* With a grease stick of the desired color, make marks on the face across the forehead, over the eyelids, down the nose, and on the cheeks. Rub this grease paint with the tips of the fingers until it is evenly distributed over all the surface of the face that is to be exposed. If a beard is to be put on, the surface of the face that it is to cover should be left untouched by grease paint or by cold cream and powder. The importance of spreading the grease paint evenly cannot be overestimated, and some practice is needed before this can be done quickly. A good make-up depends upon this step. If the surface is messy, it is impossible to produce a good make-up; the only remedy is to wipe the surface clean and start over again. Be sure that the entire surface that is to be exposed is painted. For instance, paint should extend well up into the roots of the hair and over the ears. The under surface of the chin must not be neglected. The neck is another crucial place; it is very disturbing to see a white girlish neck when a bearded old gentleman turns around to sit down!

At this point in the process, it is possible to change the shape of the face by shading. The basic principle of painting is applicable: whatever is lighter than the ground tone will appear higher, whatever is darker will sink. Thus it is possible to make the forehead squarer by lightening the corners, the nose more prominent by a white line down the front, the chin and cheek bones less prominent by darkening them, and so on. The colors used for this highlighting and shading need not be white and black. Often another base color, which is lighter or darker, is more successful. It is most important too that shadows be well blended, say in the case of hollowed cheeks. The edges of the hollow must fade imperceptibly into the base color, or the effect will only be a dirty face.

3. *Using Rouge.* Cheeks should next be colored with wet rouge or with carmine grease paint. A spot should be made

with the rouge or the stick, and the color should then be worked out over the proper surface with the fingers. Along the edges it should blend into the grease paint of the ground tone. The amount of color, and the exact placing of it, depends largely upon the character of the make-up. An old man of a certain sort may have practically no color in his cheeks, while for a rosy-faced old gentleman a large amount may be used. Observation of people with a good natural color will teach the actor just where the color should appear.

The face may be made to appear narrower or wider by placing the spots nearer together or farther apart. Do not make the spot of rouge too large, and do not overdo with the color. In general, cheek color is placed higher on women than it is on men; that is, for women the color will usually start high up, almost at the eye, and will rarely extend below the level of the nostril. For men, the color may be lower. It may start at a spot half way between the eye and the nostril and extend almost down to the jawbone, and indeed sometimes even a little along the jaw. Women making up as men, or men as women, should remember this observation.

4. *Lining.* The most difficult thing to learn about make-up is how to put on the lines that change the character of the face and give it age and expression. Here again, practice is essential, and observation of the faces of people is the necessary preliminary to practice. The lines are made with the grease paints of dark colors, called liners. The lines cannot be put on directly with the lining stick, however. Some actors melt a small amount of the stick in a pan and make the lines with the warm liquid and a fine camel's-hair brush. Others use a special pencil-like roll of paper, called a stump, or a pointed splinter of wood, such as an ordinary wooden toothpick. One end of the toothpick should be stuck into the liner so that some of the grease paint adheres to it, and with this paint the line is drawn. It is desirable to be able to make the sort of line desired, be it heavy or light, curved or straight; and the beginner may spend

some time practicing on the back of his hand or on his arm. When he feels that he has control over the toothpick, he is ready to proceed with the lining of his face. The color of the liner must then be determined. Heavy lines will probably be black or brown. Many actors prefer dark crimson. A fine network of wrinkles may demand gray. For eye shadow, it is a general custom to use blue or purple for blondes, and brown for brunettes.

a. Eyes. For straight young make-ups, only the eyes will need to be lined. The actor will first draw eyebrows on top of his own, unless his own are naturally so heavy that they do not need to be reënforced. If he wishes to move his eyebrows, as will be the case where he is to make up as a Chinaman, he can hide his own brows by rubbing the hair with wet soap, allowing it to dry, and then covering the surface with grease paint the color of his facial ground tone. Japanese actors have an interesting trick of tying a narrow tape, about half an inch wide, over their own eyebrows. The wig hides the knot at the back of the head, and the tape can be painted to match the rest of the face. After the eyebrows have been satisfactorily adjusted, it is necessary to outline the eye. Otherwise, the eye appears small and expressionless from a distance. Usually men merely outline their eyes. With a toothpick covered with grease paint, a line may be drawn under the eye, as close to it as possible, from the inner corner to a point just beyond the outer corner. During this process the eye had better be kept open, looking upwards. Then, with the eye closed, a similar line should be drawn along the edge of the eyelid; this line is to emphasize the eyelashes. It should meet the line drawn under the eye just beyond the outer corner.

Most women begin with the eye-shadow. They run a line on the top of the lid, just above the eyelashes, and with a finger blend it into the base color. The color of this line often corresponds to the color of the pupil of the eye. The blended line should not be too wide; for most make-ups it is perhaps a quarter of an inch in width. The eye may then be outlined in the manner described above with a color distinctly darker than the eye-shadow. Some actresses paint a series of little vertical dark lines over the eye-shadow; this has the effect of extending the lashes up on the lid. Others use false eyelashes, which come on a court-plaster strip, and which may be fastened with spirit-gum. Still others use mascara to darken their own eyelashes, or bead their lashes with cosmetic. None of these processes must be overdone—unless the character is required to be obviously made-up.

b. Wrinkles. For middle age, or old age, it may be necessary to draw wrinkles. The best method is to screw up the face, so that it falls into wrinkles, and then to draw the wrinkles so formed. They will thus be made in the natural places, in the places where they will really be when that particular face grows old! The actor may well attempt to assume an expression suitable to the character he is playing. If he is to be a cheerful old man, he should feel happy, smile, and wrinkle up his face; if he is to be sour, he should attempt an unhappy appearance. Then, with his paint, he should try to make this appearance permanent. This is the scientific background for the rather hazy advice that one must inwardly assume the character before he can successfully make up for it.

Observation will show the actor that there are certain basic wrinkles that are practically universal. The first of these are the wrinkles across the forehead. They are usually three in number, and they dip down slightly in the center of the head over the nose. Usually there is a short line over the bridge of the nose, and one or two small vertical wrinkles over the top of the nose, where it runs into the forehead. The next common set of wrinkles is at the outer corner of the eyes, where there is a fine set of lines radiating from the corner. These are popularly known as crows'-feet. A third line is usually found at the inner corner of the eye, from which it runs down into the cheek for one or one and one-half inches. This line is formed by the falling of the skin under the eye into a pouch. A fourth line, or set of lines, runs from the lower corners of the nose down towards the mouth; it is caused by the sagging of the cheek muscle. Finally, there will be lines from the corners of the mouth, and crosswise between the lower lip and the chin, caused by the weakening of the muscles of the lips.

Wrinkles may be made to appear deeper by the use of white lines alongside the black ones. Thus, if the actor wishes to show a deeply furrowed forehead, he may sketch in the wrinkles

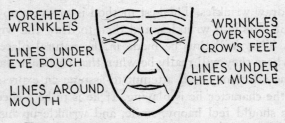

FOREHEAD WRINKLES

LINES UNDER EYE POUCH

LINES AROUND MOUTH

WRINKLES OVER NOSE CROW'S FEET

LINES UNDER CHEEK MUSCLE

FIG. 110. BASIC WRINKLES FOR OLD AGE

with black, and then just above each wrinkle draw a corresponding line with white grease paint.

Two principles, if kept in mind, will greatly simplify the matter of suggesting age with make-up. The first is that parts painted darker than the prevailing ground tone will appear depressed, and parts painted lighter will appear elevated. Thus, an actor wishing to make sunken cheeks, or sunken temples, will work a little black or gray into the desired place after putting on the ground tone. If, on the other hand, he wishes to make his cheek bones, or his nose, more prominent, he will work in a little white. The second principle is that in middle age the muscles of the face sag, so that middle age and young old-age may be indicated by underlining the muscles; but in old-age, the muscles tend to disappear, so that it is best portrayed by indicating the outline of the skull. As temples and cheeks are made to appear sunken by being darkened, so the corners of the forehead, the cheek bones, and the jawbones should be made to stand out skull-like by being made lighter.

The neck and the hands must not be neglected; they should be colored and wrinkled as well as the face.

5. *Penciling the Lips.* The next step is to color the lips. For a youthful make-up an ordinary lip stick, or a carmine liner, will give the proper tone. Color should, as a rule, be placed at the center of the lips and worked outwards in each direction. It should not be carried clear to the corners of the mouth, especially in women, or the mouth is likely to appear unnaturally wide. In old age, the lips lose their color, so for an old make-up it is necessary to tone down the lips with blue or gray. This should not be neglected, for red lips on an old man are very noticeable, especially if they are seen through venerable whiskers.

6. *Putting on the Hair.* Hair for the face may be purchased already made up into mustaches or whiskers on wire or gauze frames, and such a device is useful if the same make-up is to be used night after night, or if very quick changes of make-up are necessary. It is not very difficult to make a false mustache by attaching crêpe hair to a piece of gauze. As a rule, however, the non-professional actor will find that the most satisfactory sort of false hair will be that fastened directly to the face. Usually it appears much more natural, if it is properly made; and it doesn't pay to go to the expense or the labor of a ready-made beard for a few performances.

Hair on the face, whenever it doesn't match the color of that on the head, is usually lighter; therefore, whenever it is impossible to match the wig or the hair, crêpe hair of a lighter shade should be chosen. Two or three shades lighter is better than one shade darker. The big, black, obviously false mustache that marks the villain is usually caused by using hair that is too dark. The rope of crêpe hair should be pulled out at one end and worked out to a proper thinness with the fingers or a comb. The kinks can usually be combed out without difficulty; but if absolute straightness is desired, the crêpe hair can be soaked in water, after it is pulled out, and then be allowed to dry for several hours.

For a mustache, the hair should be cut or pulled off the rope, properly shaped, and then cut in the center and fastened to the lip in two separate pieces. The mustache should always be made of two pieces, no matter how small it is. This allows a little triangle of flesh to be left on the upper lip, between the two parts, which is always observable in nature. Besides, it makes speaking in a mustache easier, as the lip is not constricted as it would be by the single band of hair. A very small amount of hair is needed. Most non-professional actors tend to use too much, which looks very unnatural. The upper lip, on which the hair is to be placed, should be covered with the spirit gum, which should be allowed a moment to grow tacky, before the hair is placed on it. Then the hair should be pressed against the lip for a moment with the hand or with a piece of cloth. If too much hair is used, the surplus can be pulled off after the gum is dried. The mustache can then be pulled out into any desired shape, or trimmed to fit the fancy just as real hair might be.

Hair on the other part of the face should be put on in the same manner. A full beard is best made with six pieces: the two parts of the mustache already described, two side pieces, a throat piece, and a chin piece. The two side pieces are placed on the cheeks and should be long enough to come down and mingle with the hair from the chin; say, five or six inches long. They may be placed high to join the side hair of the wig, or of the head, or they may be started lower, leaving a shaved place above. These side pieces come just in front of the ears, but a little line of flesh should always be left between them and the ears. Hair never grows clear back to the ears. The throat piece is gummed under the chin, with the hair coming forward. This is an important piece which must never be omitted. The unnatural appearance of some false beards is often due to the fact that they appear to be pasted on to the front of the face; in a natural full beard there is always hair growing *under* the chin, unless that part is shaved. The chin piece is fastened to the front of the chin, stretching downward from the lower lip. Its length and heaviness will usually determine the fullness of the beard. All these pieces, after they are thoroughly fastened on, may be worked together and pulled into the desired shape. For a rough shaggy beard, appropriate for a peasant or a mountaineer, the hair may be left rough and ragged,

FIG. III. PARTS OF A BEARD

as torn from the rope. For a more cultivated person, the same sort of manufactured beard may be trimmed with scissors, just as a real one would be by a barber. No matter how small the full beard is, it should be made with all these six pieces. And even a goatee, unless it is a very tiny one that sprouts only from the lower lip, should always be made of two pieces: a throat piece and a chin piece.

Crêpe hair is also useful to make eyebrows, especially for old men, or old women, who need gray shaggy brows. A small piece of hair should be pulled to the proper shape and fastened on with gum. The spot on to which it is to be fastened must be left clean of grease or paint, or else the gum will not stick to the face.

In general, the most important thing to remember is not to

use too much hair. Usually the outline of the chin can be seen through any beard, no matter how full it is. If the false hair appears too thick and heavy to be natural, the actor should pull off tufts of hair until the mustache or beard does seem natural. The rule is to stick the hair on to the surfaces where it would naturally grow, and then to pull and cut the hair, to thin and trim it, until it seems right.

7. *Powder.* The final step is to put a coat of powder over the entire make-up. At this point before powdering, many actresses put a small spot of wet rouge, or carmine liner, inside the corner of each nostril to overcome the natural shadow there, and on the inner corner of each eye to increase its brilliancy. This is a good practice, if done discreetly. The powder should match in color the ground tone. It should be applied generously with a powder puff, and the surplus should be brushed off gently, so that the lines of the make-up will not be blurred. A useful tool for this purpose is a baby's brush with very soft bristles. If the cheeks do not seem to be red enough after this coat of powder, they can be colored with dry rouge. This completes the normal make-up.

If a wig is to be used, it may be slipped on before the final powdering. A partially bald wig must be put on before the second step, however, so that the ground tone of grease paint may be carried up on to the wig, to cover the place where it meets the forehead. The hair may be successfully whitened with powder; orris root, obtainable at any drug-store, is probably better than face powder, but many actors use zinc oxide in water. The wet zinc oxide may be applied with a tooth brush, and the excess, after drying, combed out of the hair.

To remove the make-up, rub cold cream over the face, and wipe with a clean cloth. The false hair should be pulled off first, and the gum that remains may be dissolved with alcohol.

If the non-professional actor becomes thoroughly familiar with this make-up process, he will find that it is a relatively simple matter, with sufficient practice, to make up for any sort of character.

DRY MAKE-UP

It is not always necessary, however, to use grease paint. For a straight character, a dry make-up is often sufficient. This is a make-up consisting merely of powder, rouge, and penciling of the eyes and lips. That is, it is a make-up without grease paint. The process is that described above, with the omission of the second step, the laying of the ground tone of grease paint.

SOME SUGGESTIONS

There are certain general suggestions that the inexperienced actor may well keep in mind.

Observation is the basis of all good make-up. If a young man wishes to make up as an old one, he can do no better than to study the faces of old men. He can notice how the beard grows, and where the lines come. He must also study himself, and see how the idea can be best expressed on his own face. He will probably see real people whom he would never dare to imitate, because a successful imitation would look too unreal. As in all the other departments of dramatic art, the selection of proper details is the basis of success.

Queer make-ups, involving black eyes, knocked-out teeth, and other such irregularities, should be used sparingly. They are very rarely necessary, and still more rarely truly comical.

If a number of actors are to be made up—say, a group of a hundred children for a pageant—a make-up team is a useful device. One person can be appointed to make eyebrows, another to rouge cheeks, and still a third to redden lips. The children can go from one to another, and a rapid and effective system can be worked out. In general, however, in a case of this sort, make-up should be used sparingly, unless it is made necessary by glaring lights which would cause faces to appear white and ghastly. It is only under the glare of real stage lighting, or on the assumption of a true character, that make-up need be complete and elaborate.

Finally, if strange make-ups are to be used, they should be used until every one becomes familiar with them. A boy who is wearing a beard and an old man's make-up cannot be expected to act well if he is wearing it for the first time on the night of the performance. A good comedy make-up with which the other actors are not familiar may cause them to laugh in the wrong places. Boys wearing long wigs, as cavaliers, or boys playing women's parts, must have an opportunity to become at home in their make-up. In make-up, as in all other branches of dramatics, foresight and practice are necessary to success.

CHAPTER XXV

Stage Lighting

THE IMPORTANCE OF STAGE LIGHTING

It is entirely proper that lighting should be the technical element of play production that has been left for final consideration. Not only was it the last element to be developed historically, but we are only just beginning to realize that it is perhaps most important of all since it is more capable of fusing the play into an artistic and unified design than is any other single element. Its important bearing on the success and effectiveness of the scenery, costuming, make-up, and even upon the action of the play, can hardly be over-estimated. As Irving Pichel says, in light "we have the only single agency in the theater that can work with all the other agencies binding them together—that can reveal with the dramatist, paint with the designer, and act with actors." [1] It is rare that light is used by non-professional producing groups as effectively as it could be.

THE PURPOSES OF STAGE LIGHTING

Stage lighting has certain definite purposes, of which the four most generally accepted are the following:

1. To illuminate the stage and the actors.
2. To suggest the light effects in nature, and thus to state the hour, season, and weather.

[1] Irving Pichel, *Modern Theaters* (New York, Harcourt, Brace and Co., 1925), p. 69.

3. To help paint the scenery by heightening the color values and by adding light and shade.

4. To help act the play by symbolizing its meaning and reënforcing its psychology.

These purposes are stated more or less in the order in which they came to be recognized. In most parts of Europe, plays were given out-of-doors in the light of the sun until three hundred years ago, and light effects were impossible. Then, hesitatingly, drama crept indoors. This change began in England during the time of Shakespeare; in his young manhood all the public theaters were outdoor theaters, but by the time he retired there were two or three regular indoor theaters in London, notably the famous Blackfriars, in which he had an interest. In these indoor theaters, artificial lighting became a necessity; the stage was flooded with the light of as many candles as possible so that the audience could see the actors. For many generations this was the main purpose of the lighting. Gradually some attempt was made to regulate the amount of light according to the time of day in which the action was supposed to be taking place, by increasing or decreasing the number of candles. With the introduction of oil, then gas, and finally electricity, this could be done better and better. The last two purposes have been but recently recognized. We are only beginning to see what can be done on the stage with light.

In general, of course, the same lighting accomplishes all four purposes. This may all be illustrated by almost any example of good stage lighting. In the final scene of *Cyrano de Bergerac*, the light may illuminate the stage and old Cyrano, who sits dying in his chair in the garden; the yellow light of the late afternoon gradually fades to the blue of twilight, while a leaf drifts down occasionally from a tree to indicate that the year as well as the day is drawing to a close; the dying light, streaming in from one side of the stage, may help paint the scene and cast increasing shadows of the tree, of the wall that crosses the back of the stage, and of gaunt old Cyrano himself; and finally, the rapidly fading light may symbolize the action by showing the darkness—the shadow of death—that creeps closer to Cyrano throughout the scene and engulfs him at its close.

A knowledge of these purposes should be held constantly in mind by the artist who arranges the lighting for any scene, All good lighting continually achieves all four purposes.

THE PROBLEM OF STAGE LIGHTING

Like all other theater artists, the lighting expert has a double problem. The first part is purely physical and mechanical: What sort of lighting units can he use? Where should he place them? How can he make his installations safe? How can he best control the lighting? The other half of his problem is artistic, a problem in aesthetics: How can he use light most effectively to act the play?

After all, most of our machinery of the theater is of the simplest type—ropes and pulleys, and simple bracing. In a double sense, the electrical equipment is approached with more awe. While most people know a little about the simpler laws of mechanics, electricity, guarded by an element of danger, is a matter too recondite to be brought into the fold of everyday information out of mere curiosity, or to be reasoned out as the childish working of a pulley can be figured out by common sense; it has to be studied and learned. And besides being outside of common matter-of-fact, light is mystery itself, unplumbed nature, a fraction of the inscrutable life of the world led by strings to the stage. If the little playhouse is without any mechanical convenience, if its stage is cramped and mean, it can still achieve visual beauty through light. This force brings into the playhouse the most vibrant, subtle and affecting gift of the physical world, barring only the human presence.[2]

Stage lighting deserves, and requires, the most careful study. To build up an adequate equipment and to learn to use it skilfully, should be the determination of every earnest group.

[2] *Ibid.*, p. 64.

1. (A)

(B)

2.

REFLECTOR   LENS

BARREL   LAMP

3.

1. STRIP LIGHTS
   (A) OPEN FACED STRIP
   (B) COMPARTMENT STRIP

2. SPOTLIGHT AND
   CROSS SECTION

3. FLOOD LIGHT

FIG. 112. THE THREE BASIC LIGHTING UNITS

LIGHTING UNITS

Although the modern theater uses an infinite number of lighting devices, some simple and some complicated, there are in all only three fundamentally different kinds of units—except for incidental light fixtures, like chandeliers, brackets, etc. The three units are easy to recognize.

1. *Strip Lights.* The first of these is the strip light: a series of bulbs (called "lamps" in the language of the trade and the catalogues) arranged alongside of one another in a long, narrow row, or strip, so that they work as a unit. Strip lights may be either (*a*) open-trough strips, or (*b*) compartment strips. The former is the older variety and consists merely of a series of bulbs, one beside the other, usually six or eight inches apart, and wired in two, three, or even more circuits. Usually such a unit is backed by a metal reflector, often painted white, and if the reflector is bent in a sharp curve so as to cover both the back and top of the bulbs, the unit is sometimes called a semi-open trough (see Fig. 112). Such units, six feet or more in length, were in the early days of electricity commonly used as footlights and border lights. An even cruder form of this variety of unit, consisting of a real trough of tin, containing several bulbs and usually in one circuit, is still often used to light an offstage alcove made by the masking behind a door or archway, hence sometimes called a cove light. Modern strip lights are usually of the compartment variety, in which each bulb is in an individual compartment (see Fig. 112). Such lights vary greatly in size; the smaller units, built for small bulbs, are used commonly as footlights; and larger units are suspended overhead as border lights. Hence, large compartment strips, consisting usually of six or nine compartments, each one taking a 200 or 300-watt bulb, are often called border lights (see below).

2. *Spot Lights.* The second common variety of lighting unit is the spot light, which has two essential features: a concave mirror

behind the bulb to collect and reflect the light rays, and a condenser lens in front of the bulb to concentrate them. (See Fig. 112.) A spot light thus throws a spot of strong, concentrated light over a small area. These elements are contained in a shaped metal housing often in the form of a cylinder, sometimes called the hood, sometimes the barrel. Spot lights vary in size from very small ones, containing bulbs of 100-watt capacity, to large ones with 3000-watt bulbs. Many have special trade names,[3] such as kleiglites, baby Hercules spot lights, lekolites, fresnelites, and so on. The most common sizes of bulbs used in spots are probably 500 and 1000 watts. Spot lights smaller than 500 watts, usually 250 to 400, are often called baby spots. Whatever the name or whatever the size of bulb, each spot light functions as a spot light by virtue of a mirror and a lens, which give it the capacity to throw a large amount of light through a comparatively long distance over a controlled area. Most spots are capable of being focused by a device which allows the bulb to be moved from immediately behind the lens, where the spot illuminates its largest area, to the back end of the hood or barrel, where it covers its smallest area. As this operation does not decrease the total *amount* of light, lights are brightest when most "spotted,"—that is, when the bulb is farthest from the lens.

3. *Flood Lights*. The third and final variety of unit is the flood light, which, as the name implies, floods a wide area, All floods are individual bulbs in a housing with an open front. The housing may be square or round, large or small. It may hang from a pipe overhead, or be supported by a standard from the floor. The characteristic that makes it a flood is that it has an open front and is without any mechanism for refracting and concentrating light. It floods. Some spot lights, arranged so that the lens is easily removable, are sold as spot-flood lights. When a lens is used, the unit is a spot light; and

[3] See catalogues of stage lighting companies, which will usually be sent on request and which repay study.

when the lens is removed, it is a flood light. A compartment strip light is really a series of adjacent flood lights, so perhaps it would be a little more philosophical to say that there are really only *two* kinds of stage lighting units: (*a*) those that condense light and (*b*) those that do not, or in other words, (*a*) spot lights, and (*b*) all other or non-spot lights. However, the usual division into the three varieties is practical and functional.

PLACING OF UNITS

After choosing the most appropriate unit, the next problem of the electrician is to decide how to install it so it will be most useful. Lights are usually identified in two ways: from (1) the place in which they work, and (2) the kind of unit. Again, although lights may be placed anywhere on the stage, they normally fall into six classifications:

1. *Footlights.* The most universally known stage light is probably the footlight, which is placed along the front edge of the stage and throws light up and back over the playing-space. In pre-electricity days, when light from candles or lamps could not be concentrated, footlights were the main source of stage lighting. The danger of an actor tipping over a candle with his cloak or skirt, and thus setting himself and the theater on fire, often led to such lights being placed on little boats and floated in a long trough of water along the front edge of the stage. Hence, footlights were often called floats. With the development of electric lighting and modern units which could throw over long distances, footlights became less and less important, and a controversy developed as to whether they had much, or any, value. The argument against footlights was that they formed a wall of light between the audience and the play, and that they lighted the bottoms of chairs and tables and the bottom of the actors' chins and noses, and other areas not usually high-lighted by nature. The argument, however, seems to be directed only against a dominance of

light from below, and it has almost died out. Most modern authorities feel that footlights, if they can be controlled so as to give a variable amount of light, still have great usefulness. Footlights are usually strip lights, made in sections for greater ease in handling. Sometimes, however, small spots are used as footlights, often in combination with strips. In order to identify such units it is customary to number them from

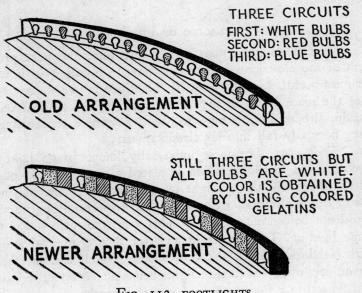

THREE CIRCUITS
FIRST: WHITE BULBS
SECOND: RED BULBS
THIRD: BLUE BULBS

OLD ARRANGEMENT

STILL THREE CIRCUITS BUT
ALL BULBS ARE WHITE.
COLOR IS OBTAINED
BY USING COLORED
GELATINS

NEWER ARRANGEMENT

FIG. 113. FOOTLIGHTS

left to right (facing the audience, of course), so the electrician can mention footlight strip #2, or footlight spot #4. Each unit is thus named in two ways, and unmistakably, from (1) the place where it is being used and (2) the nature of the unit.

2. *Border Lights*. Border lights hang above the stage and throw their light down over the playing-space. In the modern theater, they are usually compartment strips, but in old theaters, and in too many school theaters, they may be open-

faced strips, as shown in the illustration. There may be several borders, one behind the other, commonly spaced about seven or eight feet apart. The number will depend on the depth of the stage, the traditional number being three; however, a large stage may have four or five. They are numbered from front to back, so the border nearest the proscenium wall is the first border. Only the first border is usable in a set with

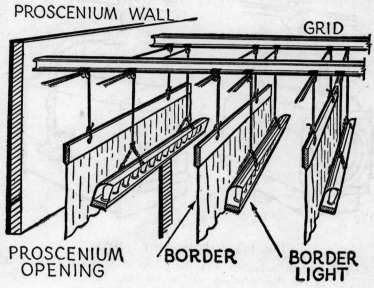

FIG. 114. BORDER LIGHTS

a ceiling, so it is the most important one. The usual way of rigging borders is to hang them from long battens extending often a foot or two beyond the proscenium opening on each side. In most theaters these battens are of one and one-half inch or two-inch pipe, hung for safety from wire cable. Although borders are usually strip lights, they are often reenforced with spots. Indeed, the common rigging for the first border is one or two sections of strips in the center and as many spots as possible beyond the strips at each side of the batten (see Fig. 122). Because in old theaters the first border and footlights were often the only lights used for concerts, for which the set was shallow, the first border is often called the concert border. Sometimes it is still called the X-ray border since one of the earliest forms of good compartment strip lights was a variety having corrugated glass reflectors and named

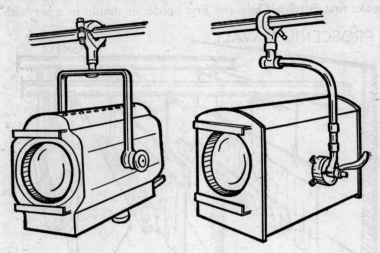

FIG. 115. HANGING SPOT LIGHTS

Left shows spot suspended with clamp and yoke, and right shows C clamp and curved pipe, or off-set yoke, to side stud. Straight pipe hangers are also common.

an X-ray border by the manufacturer. In most theaters these have long since been replaced by lights having spun-aluminum reflectors. Footlights alone illumined the front of the actor, but made him cast a hard high shadow on the backdrop. Light from overhead, from the borders, equalized the lighting and killed the shadow. So for many years, foots and borders were the traditional method of lighting almost every scene. With the development of modern lighting units, especially spots, the combination became less necessary; and in modern lighting, foots and borders are used largely for blending or general lights, to smooth out the areas more brightly lighted by spots. In large modern theaters, the first border may be a bridge, suspended over the stage above the proscenium opening, on which electricans can stand to direct spots during the performance. As in all other naming of stage lighting, border lights are indicated by numbers, from downstage to upstage, and from left to right. Thus, border spot #17 would mean the *seventh* spot in the *first* border; while border strip #22 would mean the *second* strip in the *second* border.

3. *Tormentor Lights.* Another common place from which light is thrown is from the tormentors, usually from spots arranged between the proscenium wall and the tormentors (see Fig. 122). These lights throw into the sets from the wings. They are sometimes individual lights on standards, or they may be a row of spots on a pipe or a ladder, and sometimes they are whole banks of lights on a tower. As usual, they are numbered, tormentor spot #1 being nearest the floor. Usually the name must indicate which tormentor is referred to, as right tormentor spot #5. Strips are also sometimes used as tormentor lights. The tormentor lights, together with those on the first border, are often referred to as *proscenium arch lights.*

4. *Auditorium Lights.* Often lights are placed in the auditorium itself. They may be on the front of a balcony, or behind trap-doors in the ceiling, or hidden in false beams against the ceiling, or in booths in the back wall. If so, they may be referred to as balcony, or ceiling, or beam, or booth spots. Wherever they are placed, they have the common characteristic that they throw into the acting area through the proscenium opening, and they should all be thought of as auditorium lights.

5. *Floor Lights.* Often it is necessary to throw light through actual openings, like windows in the set. Such units may be a single flood on a standard, or a whole battery of spot lights on a tower. Often a series of strip-light sections is used at the

bottom of a drop, whereas the top part is illuminated by a border. All lights that work on the floor, whether floods, or spots, or strips, are floor lights.

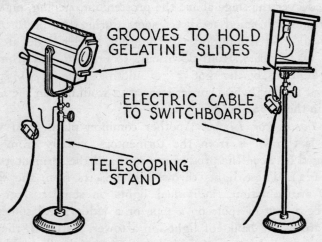

GROOVES TO HOLD GELATINE SLIDES

ELECTRIC CABLE TO SWITCHBOARD

TELESCOPING STAND

FIG. 116. FLOOR LIGHTS

6. *Incidental Lights.* The final classification consists of the practical units in a set that actually give off light, such as the glow in a fireplace or lighted bulbs in chandeliers and brackets or torches, lanterns, candles, etc. These units often can be helpful in actually furnishing light for the set. Usually, however, they need to be reënforced by a border spot or a light from some stage source, but the actual amount of illumination they give must be considered. All practical lights in a set—that is, fixtures that actually are lighted—are incidental lights. It is important that the actual light source, such as the bulbs in chandeliers or lamps, are not so bright as to be annoying to the audience; small bulbs should probably be used, and often they must be shielded by masks or shades.

Wherever lights are used, they must fall into one or another of these classifications; and by naming and numbering them properly, it is possible to indicate accurately each unit and thus eradicate misunderstandings and save time.

THE PHYSICS OF LIGHTING

It is not necessary—although it is perhaps desirable—that the non-professional electrician be completely familiar with the subject of electricity. But there are certain elementary concepts and many practical processes with which he should be familiar.

1. *The Nature of Electricity.* Electricity, one of the fundamental quantities in nature, as an electric current is a form of energy. Its practical use is based on the discovery that when a coil of wire is rotated in a magnetic field, an electric current is created which may be made to flow through wires. A dynamo is a machine with a rotating coil, called the armature, and a field, made for the purpose of converting mechanical energy into electrical energy. The mechanical energy, necessary to turn the armature, may be supplied by a waterfall or by a steam engine. In order to use the mechanical energy, we must go to the place where it exists. But by turning it into electrical energy, we are able to transport it, through wires and with slight loss, hundreds of miles. There we can, by the use of another electrical machine, which is usually called a motor, transform it back into mechanical energy and use it to turn the wheels in a factory, or to run a vacuum cleaner, or to spin a fan. However, an electric light uses electricity directly, and is merely a special wire, surrounded by a protective glass bulb, which becomes highly incandescent when an electric current flows through it. That is, the current heats the filament, and causes it to glow.

2. *Conductors and Non-Conductors.* It is very fortunate that there are in nature some materials, like copper and other metals, through which electricity flows readily. There are also some, such as rubber, asbestos, porcelain, glass, wood, etc., through which electricity does not flow readily. Substances of

the first kind are called conductors, and of the latter, non-conductors. In order, therefore, to make a flow of electricity we need only a good conductor of sufficient size and length (a wire), surrounded by a bad conductor, which we call insulation. We must know, however, that electricity will not flow through one wire, but needs always at least two. It may flow from the dynamo out of one of these wire legs, and back the other, in which case it is called direct current—for short, D.C. On the other hand, it may reverse its direction of flow at regular intervals, which makes it alternating current, or A.C. For many instruments, such as light bulbs, some motors, etc., it does not matter which kind of current is used. Some instruments —especially radio sets—may be used only with one special variety of current. Any complete path for electrical energy, say from a dynamo to a bulb and back again, is called a circuit. A circuit, therefore, is a complete path for electricity. We may branch a circuit, by splitting the two wires as many times as we wish. In popular language, each of these branches is also called a circuit. Our problem in the theater is how to divide a large circuit that enters the building into many small circuits, one leading to each light unit or other electrical instrument in which we want to use electricity. We need, too, to control the flow in each of these small circuits. The usual device for this purpose is called a switchboard, which will be discussed below. However, we also constantly need to terminate our circuits in different places (say, move a spot light from the first border to the back of the auditorium), and in order to do this we must be able to extend the length of the circuit. For convenience, we usually have two wires, carefully insulated from each other, in a single unit (see Fig. 117) called a stage cable. Our practical problem, then, is how to join cables end to end with safety and speed so as to make a circuit of the desired length.

3. *Extending a Circuit*. In the theater there are three common ways of extending a circuit, of which the worst is probably

to make a splice. However, there are times when we must do this, and then it must be done correctly.

a. Splice. A splice is made (see Fig. 117) by scraping the insulation off the ends of two wires and twisting them together, so that the current can easily flow from one to the other. In order to make the splices safe to handle, we must now surround each one with insulation. Two forms of insulation come prepared for this purpose: (1) rubber tape, and (2) friction tape. When the voltage is as large as 110, it is customary to bind the splice first with rubber tape and to protect it with friction tape, which is tougher and longer wearing; for small voltages, such as are obtained from dry cells, friction tape alone is usually sufficient. If the splice is to be a permanent one, the wires are often spliced together and then soldered. What we do in making a splice is to join the conductors and surround them with non-conductors. Of course, there must be no current in the cables while they are being spliced, or the current would flow out of the wire and into the splicer—people are excellent conductors.

b. Connectors. Connectors are devices for joining lengths of cables without the necessity of making a splice. They consist of two blocks (see Fig. 117), one of which contains two sleeves (the female) and the other two prongs (the male) which fit tightly into the sleeves. Each sleeve and each prong ends in a flange and screw, around which the scraped wire may be wound and fastened tightly by turning down the screw. Again, this device joins conductor to conductor, and surrounds them with insulation. Its functioning will be familiar to anyone who has ever plugged a lamp into an outlet in a baseboard. Connectors come in pairs and in several sizes, the most common sizes being 5 ampere (see below) and 15 ampere. Their usefulness in stage lighting is obvious. Usually light units have short wires leading out of them (called pigtails) which are insulated with asbestos fabric. In joining the pigtails to the cable, we should have to go through the lengthy process of

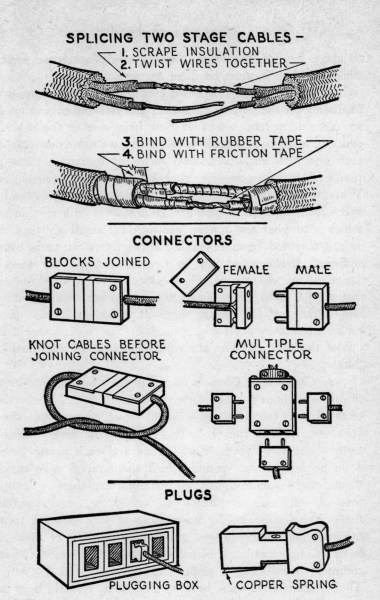

SPLICING TWO STAGE CABLES –
1. SCRAPE INSULATION
2. TWIST WIRES TOGETHER

3. BIND WITH RUBBER TAPE
4. BIND WITH FRICTION TAPE

CONNECTORS

BLOCKS JOINED

FEMALE   MALE

KNOT CABLES BEFORE
JOINING CONNECTOR

MULTIPLE
CONNECTOR

PLUGS

PLUGGING BOX   COPPER SPRING

FIG. 117. METHODS OF CONDUCTING ELECTRICITY

making a splice, except that by putting a connector part on each end, we can complete the circuit simply by joining the parts of the connector—if they are the same size! In the same way, we can connect any light unit with any cable; and if each cable has a connector on each end, any cable to any cable. With sufficient connectors available, we shall rarely have to take the time to make a splice. Multiple connectors are sleeve connectors to which several prong connectors can be joined, and are useful in connecting two or three lighting units to one cable, or feed line. The sleeve connector should always be on the end of the joint nearest the power; prong connections at the power end would be dangerous because every time a piece of metal, such as a knife or a screw-driver blade (or a finger!) were put across the prongs the circuit would be completed, and current would begin to flow. Usually, the cables are knotted (see Fig. 117) before the connector is joined, so that the parts will not accidentally pull apart.

c. Plugs. Plugs are similar to connectors in principle (see Fig. 117) and consist of blocks of insulation with copper springs on the edges which make tight contact with copper plates on the inside of a receptacle, which is usually of porcelain. They are commonly used when the load is over 15 amperes, and in switchboards and in floor pockets. Recently, connectors have been widely used to replace plugs and plugging boxes, and the latter need be used in a small theater only occasionally for heavy loads.

4. *Measures of Electricity.* It has been repeatedly necessary in discussing how to extend a circuit to refer to the electrical load. This is because wires and all electrical units fed by wires, have a capacity to take a certain amount of current. This amount is its load, and over-loading leads to disaster. In order to avoid over-loading, we must understand how electricity is measured.

a. Wattage. A watt is the unit of measurement of the total *capacity*, or load, of a circuit. The greater the number of watts, the greater the power in the circuit. If we make the common analogy between the flow of an electric current and the flow of water, the wattage is comparable to measures of water volume, such as gallons, quarts, and pints. Thus, the brightness of a bulb can be said to depend on its wattage, and we increase the amount of light by replacing a bulb of low wattage with one of higher wattage. For lighting homes, we commonly use bulbs of 25, 40, 60, 75, and even 100 watts. In the theater, even small spots take 250 or 400-watt bulbs, and a 5000-watt spot light is not rare. Compartment border strips usually take 200- or 300-watt bulbs. The wattage rating of bulbs is usually clearly marked on the glass end. Similarly, a definite wattage is indicated on all electrical instruments—fans, vacuum cleaners, toasters, coffee pots, stoves, and so on.

b. Voltage. A volt is a unit of measurement of electromotive force and is roughly comparable to the pressure in a flow of water. Voltage is determined at the source, and the user of electricity normally accepts this as his operating voltage. In the early days of commercial electricity, voltages varied widely, but it has now become almost universally standardized at 110. Most bulbs and instruments, therefore, are made for this voltage, and are so marked.

c. Amperage.[4] The ampere is the unit of *intensity*, but may be compared in the analogy to water to the size of the flow. It is determined—other things, such as the material in the wire, being equal—by the size of the wire. In general, then, the amperage capacity of a wire depends on its diameter. The most common conductor, in stage cable, is annealed stranded copper, and the most common insulation is rubber surrounded by a braided cotton fabric. In standardized small cables, size #1 carries 100 amperes, and higher size numbers indicate

---

[4] The development of the use of electricity has been an international affair. Ampère was a French physicist, Volta was an Italian physicist, and Watt, a Scottish inventor. The unit of electrical resistance, important in theory, but not essential to basic practice of the stage electrician, is named after a German electrician, Ohm.

smaller amperage. Thus, #6 carries 50 A; #8, 35; and #12, 20. The most common variety of stage cable, which will be the only one necessary in most small theaters, is #14, which has a capacity of 15 amperes.

5. *The Essential Formula.* In theater practice, one of the constant problems of the electrician is determining the capacity (or wattage) of any circuit. This is an easy matter if he understands one simple formula: *the wattage in any circuit is the product of its voltage multiplied by its amperage.* This is commonly expressed: W = V x A (the initial letters of these measures—*without a period*—is their common abbreviations.[5] Thus, if he knows that V is 110 and A is 60, the W of a circuit will be 6600 (110V x 60A = 6600W). In a 110 V circuit of ordinary #14 stage cable, which has a capacity of 15 A, the W will be 1650 W. It, therefore, can safely carry one 1500-W spotlight, or three 500-W spotlights, or, in fact any load *less than 1650 W*. If we wish to use *more,* either voltage or amperage must be increased, and it is usually more practical to increase the amperage by using a larger wire. The principle is clear if the analogy to water is remembered. To increase the amount of water coming out of a pipe we have only two possibilities: (1) we can cause it to flow faster by increasing the pressure (which is the voltage), or (2) we can enlarge the size of the flow (which is the amperage) by increasing the size of the pipe. In electricity, we have the same two possibilities. If we wish to use more lights on a stage, it is necessary to increase our total wattage: if the voltage, as is likely to be the case, is fixed, our only method is to increase the amperage, and that means substituting larger feed wires. In order to do this, we must trace the wiring back towards the power source, and find some branch with sufficient amperage so that our larger wires can be spliced into them. This branching-off place (usually called a "panel-box") may be in some part of the building itself,

[5] Electricians with feeble memories can remember the abbreviation for West Virginia—W. Va.

but sometimes it may be necessary to go to the panel box in the street. Sometimes, indeed, it is necessary to go to a main power feed line several blocks away. However, in a school or Little Theater, where the stage panel box supplies insufficient power, it is often possible to increase its capacity by running a few hundred feet of larger cable to a panel box only a short distance away. The question of what is adequate capacity is discussed below. Everyone who works as an electrician on any stage will find the formula $W = V \times A$ constantly useful. Knowing any two elements, he is always able to find the third one. Thus, if he decides, by adding up the capacity of all his lighting units, that he wants 20,000 W, and he knows he has 110 V, it is easy to determine that the necessary amperage is 180 plus—because 20,000 divided by 110 is 180 and a little over!

6. *Fuses*. The safe and practical use of electricity depends on the invention of some unknown electrical genius, and the invention is called a fuse. If a water pipe were subjected to

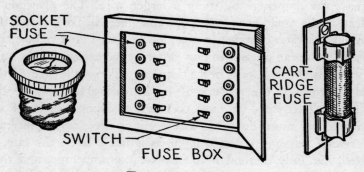

FIG. 118. FUSES

great strain because of variation in the pressure behind the flow of water, it might occasionally burst at its weakest place. The same is true of an electric circuit. It is subjected to an occasional surge of electricity, which causes it to grow so hot that the weakest place in the wiring will burn. To protect the circuit, therefore, we can make an artificial weak place in it. This artificial weak place consists of a metal wire which has sufficient resistance so that it heats up and melts when the capacity for which it has been made is exceeded. In other words, it *fuses*—literally, melts from the heat. If we enclose the special fuse wire in a fireproof box, the melting will take place in the box and do no harm. At this point, our analogy to water breaks down. If a pipe bursts, the water continues to pour through the uninjured pipe up to the break; but if an electrical circuit is broken, the flow of current stops, and the circuit beyond the break becomes dead. Thus, the fuse is a safety device, for when it burns, it automatically cuts off the entire circuit. This is why circuits should never be over-fused. The limited capacity of the fuse protects the wiring in the circuit, and inserting a fuse of a larger capacity merely removes the safety factor, and allows the next weakest element to burn if there is an unexpected surge of current—which should not be, but often is.

A surge may be caused in either of two ways: (1) by an overload, or (2) by a short circuit. An overload is made when the sum total of wattage in the light units greatly exceeds the wattage capacity of the circuit. If we have an ordinary 15 A circuit with a capacity of 1650 W, and attach a 3000-W bulb, we make an overload, and the surge of additional current will probably burn out the circuit. A similar surge may be caused if the two legs of the circuit are joined before reaching the load; this is the case when a metal blade of some kind touches two bared wires and makes a *short* circuit.

7. *Switches*. The principle referred to above—that when a fuse blows, thus making a gap in the circuit, the flow in the circuit stops—is the basic idea behind a switch. A switch is merely a mechanical contrivance for making or breaking the contact, and it may be placed anywhere in the circuit. Whenever a person, even though completely ignorant of electricity, pushes a button on a wall to turn on a chandelier, or turns a button on a lamp to put it off, what he is really doing is making

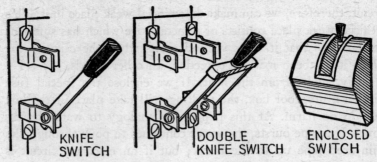

KNIFE SWITCH   DOUBLE KNIFE SWITCH   ENCLOSED SWITCH

FIG. 119. SWITCHES

or breaking a connection in the circuit. Most circuits in the theater are 15A, or bigger, and in such a circuit the common form of switch is a small copper bar with an insulated handle, so that it can be pushed into a copper spring, thus completing the circuit. This is called a knife switch (see Fig. 119). Sometimes, for additional safety a double knife switch is used.

8. *Dimmers.* In home wiring, most circuits are fitted with fuses and switches, for we want the circuit to operate in safety, and we wish to be able to turn the lights off and on. In the theater, however, we often wish to control the amount of current in a circuit for the purpose of decreasing the amount of light given off by a bulb. The instrument for doing this is a dimmer. Recently new forms of dimmers have been developed, but the most common, and still most widely-used form, is the resistance dimmer, technically a rheostat. This is based on the principle that electricity, even in a good conductor, encounters resistance; the current is slightly decreased as if by friction and thrown off in the form of heat. If we had, therefore, a long circuit—say of several miles—so much pressure might be used up that it would not light a bulb at the end of the circuit. By changing the length of this wire—that is, by varying the resistance in the circuit—we should be able to control the amount of current flowing into a light. We do not need to use miles of wire, however, if we replace the good copper conductor by

a conductor having a higher resistance—often German silver, an alloy of copper, zinc, and nickel is used for this purpose. The commonest form of such a dimmer is called a plate dimmer (see Fig. 120), in which the resistance wire is baked in a disc of moulded refractory material, which forms a tough solid plate. A revolving arm, through which the current flows, allows us to cut into the circuit a short section of the wire, hence only a slight resistance, or more wire to increase the resistance, until we have included it all, and thus reached the capacity of the dimmer. Of course, when the arm is in its first position, the current flows through no resistance, so the circuit is

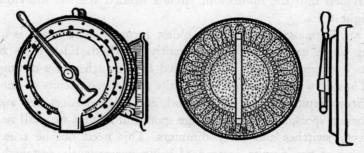

FIG. 120. DIMMER

maintained at its full capacity. Like all electrical instruments, dimmers vary in their capacity, so they are marked for wattage. A dimmer works accurately only when it is of the same capacity as the load. Thus, to control a 1000-W bulb, we should use a 1000-W dimmer—except that the standard dimmer of this size is marked 1100-W. A 2000-W dimmer will have no effect on a 50-W bulb, for enough current will flow even though the complete resistance to light the bulb to capacity. In the opposite way, a 500-W dimmer will abruptly take out a 1000-W bulb, but will probably burn up in the process. Thus, the problem of the stage electrician is to keep a balance between the capacity of his dimmers and the bulbs he wishes to control with them.

THE SWITCHBOARD

This problem of the control of stage lighting is greatly simplified if all the circuits can be brought together in one place and arranged so as to be handled by one individual. This place is commonly called the switchboard. It is a combination of fuses, switches, and dimmers, so arranged as to control all the circuits. There is no such thing as a standard switchboard, each one being made according to special specifications for the theater in which it is to be used. The main power lines, feeding in the current for use on the stage, must come into the board and there be divided into the number of circuits needed for the individual light units.

1. *Permanent Board.* The oldest form of switchboard is one in which each light is permanently installed. Each light has its own circuit, which is controlled by a switch and a dimmer. Thus, if we wish to use forty units (say three circuits of foots, three circuits each of first, second, and third borders, ten auditorium spots, and eighteen stage spots and floods) we shall need forty switches and forty dimmers. This need not be true if some of the circuits, instead of being permanently fastened to units, lead to stage pockets, for by plugging different lights in the pockets we shall have a certain amount of flexibility. But in general, this is an expensive system, for when light units are not being used in a particular play, their circuits are idle. A board to handle even forty circuits will cost several thousand dollars. Probably it will be equipped with some sort of interlocking system, to combine different dimmers so that they can be controlled with one lever or one wheel. The most modern permanent boards have many flexible features, such as electrical master dimming and changeable connections between controls and loads. Thus, it is no longer "permanent," and to distinguish it from the old type it is often called a Flexible Board. Even such a system, however, since the installation is permanent, cannot be taken on the road or transferred from one

theater to another. Moreover, in spite of the fact that it has many advantages, it will take up a large amount of space, and is very expensive.

2. *Portable Board.* To overcome these difficulties, a much cheaper and more flexible variety of board has been developed, called a portable board. Instead of being permanently installed in some definite place in the theater, this board is usually installed in a wooden box, lined throughout with metal and

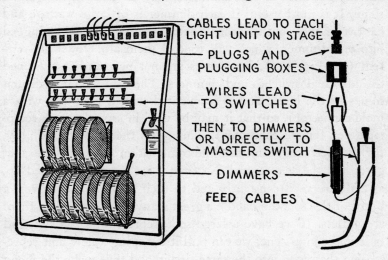

FIG. 121. PORTABLE SWITCHBOARD AND WIRING DIAGRAM

mounted on casters. Even a large portable board need be no larger or heavier than an upright piano, but if great capacity is needed, it can be made in sections. Usually, there is a series of outlets (which may be either plugging receptacles or sleeve connectors) at the top, a line of switches and fuses below them, and a bank of dimmers at the bottom (see Fig. 121). These dimmers may work individually, or they may have some interlocking system. Such a board has great flexibility and will cost at most several hundred dollars instead of several thousand. Professionally, it has the advantage that it can travel with the show, and it can be manufactured to fit requirements of a specific play. In arriving at a new theater, the electrician wires it by bringing lines from the panel box of the stage to his portable board, on which his moves are all memorized; he does not have a new set-up to work out, and a new switchboard to learn, in each new theater. A portable board is highly recommended for the non-professional theater. A board even with only a dozen outlets, and three or four dimmers, may be sufficient for a small stage. It is most useful if each dimmer is of large wattage and has two or three outlets; then several light units may be plugged into one dimmer, which will control them all. Under this system (see Fig. 121), light units are not permanently fastened to individual switches and dimmers. The cable from each unit comes to the board and is terminated with a plug (or with a male connector), so that it may be used in *any* plugging receptacle (or female connector). This gives the utmost flexibility, for the electrician can make the combination for each scene that gives him the best control. No circuits are permanently tied up, and all are used constantly and to their capacity. Moreover, a board of this sort can handle a great many more units than there are outlets. If we have a large spot, representing the sun, and fade it out in a scene, we can pull it out, plug a new unit representing the moon into the same circuit, and thus make the moon rise with the dimmer that faded the sun. Each circuit may be used constantly. Moreover, this system has the advantage that it need not all be purchased at once, but may be improved as finances permit. If the box containing the switchboard is correctly planned and made large enough, with a number of non-dimming circuits, it is a simple matter to add dimmers later. A very small initial outlay may lead in time to a complete switchboard. The size and scheme of the board will depend on the amount of equipment, the number and kinds of lights, etc., and this is discussed below. But even a small theater should try to secure from 60 to 100 amperes, and probably the more the better. A larger board and more equipment can gradually be acquired over the years if sufficient electrical power is available.

MINIMUM EQUIPMENT

The question of a minimum equipment is a delicate one, for it depends on the skill and ingenuity of the electricians, the amount of money available, the program of plays, and many other items. More than these, however, it depends on keeping

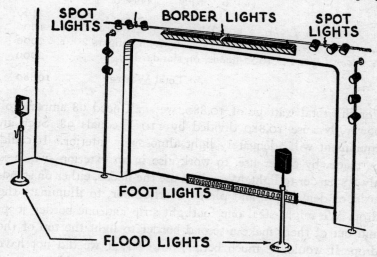

FIG. 122. MINIMUM EQUIPMENT ON STAGE

the equipment flexible. Strip lights may be needed as border lights in one play, but will be more valuable in the next play used on the floor to light a drop, or standing on end behind the sides of the arch as tormentor lights. A spot light may work in the auditorium, and then on a tormentor pipe, and then on a second border batten. So the details of any minimum scheme must be left to the situation in any group. However, it will perhaps be useful to suggest a sort of ideal minimum—which need not be taken as an absolute minimum! In any case, the lights may be divided according to the places in which they will normally work (see p. 387). The following, then, is suggested for a small stage, with an arch opening of about thirty feet, and a stage depth of twenty to twenty-five feet:

Wattage

1. *Footlights.* 3 5′ strips, [6], with bulbs on 6″ centers or 27 40-W bulbs 1080
2. *1st Border Light.* (*a*) 2 6-compartment strips—12 200-W bulbs 2400
   (*b*) 6 "baby" spots—6 400-W bulbs 2400
3. *Tormentor Lights.* 2 500-W spots, on standards 1000
4. *Auditorium Lights.* 4 500-W spots, with hangers 2000
5. *Floor Lights.* 2 1000-floods, on standards 2000

Total Wattage...... 10880

For this total wattage of 10,880, we shall need 98 amperes of power, because 10,880 divided by 110 V equals 98. Such an equipment will adequately light almost any interior.[7] It could be made, by clever use, to work also in an exterior—which is always harder to light. We might use the floods, either on standards, or demounted and placed on the floor, to illuminate the drop. We might steal one footlight strip and one border strip, and out of them make a second border to light the top of the drop. It would be much better, however, if we did not have to resort to such practice. Our ideal equipment requires units to light a backdrop, so we might add:

6. *2nd Border Lights.* 7 hanging individual floods of 500-W each (3500-W); *or*, 4 9-compartment strips of 100-W each 3600
7. *Floor Lights.* 4 9-compartment strips of 100-W each . 3600

Total Wattage...... 7200

[6] It is better if the footlights do not fill the opening, for the bulbs at the end merely illuminate the proscenium wall. If the footlight strips in a theater are too long, it is wise to unscrew and remove some of the end bulbs.

[7] Normally this amount of equipment would cost, if new, about $450. By careful shopping, and by picking up used equipment, this could be greatly lowered.

These units [8] would be adequate to light any skywall or drop, and would be highly desirable. They would require about 65 additional amperes (7200 divided by 110 equals 65 plus), thus making a total of about 160 A for the complete equipment. Probably less would do (150, or even less), for not all light units will be used at once. Our ideal minimum equipment, then, would consist of these seven items, and would demand 150 amperes for lighting. Groups for whom this seems excessive should not be discouraged. They can get along with many fewer lighting units and much less power. They will have to substitute skill and ingenuity for equipment.

HOME-MADE LIGHTING UNITS

It is by no means impossible to create lighting units that will serve the purpose of the standard units.[9] It is desirable, of course, that they be made carefully by persons familiar with electrical practice.

1. *Home-made Strips.* A series of light sockets may be fastened to a piece of wood three or four inches wide and the desired length. A bent piece of tin, eight or ten inches wide and of the same length as the baseboard may be fastened on to act as a reflector. It should be painted white inside, and painted black on the outside. In such a strip, the bulbs should always be arranged as in the illustration, so that they throw the light from the side. They give more light in this position; there is a dead spot at the end of most bulbs. These home-made strips may serve as footlights, or border lights, or proscenium-arch lights.

2. *Home-made Spots.* A tin cone or horn makes a substitute spotlight. It had best be made around a single large bulb mounted on a socket which has been set on a square of wood.

---

[8] These units would cost approximately an additional $100.

[9] See Theodore Fuchs, *Stage Lighting* (Boston, Little, Brown & Co., 1929). Unfortunately, this book is out of print, but copies may be obtained in most large libraries. The entire book will repay careful study.

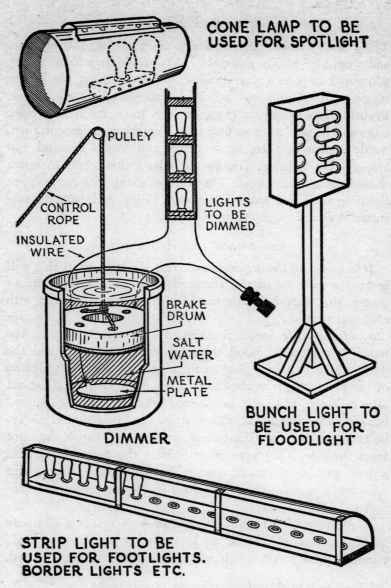

CONE LAMP TO BE USED FOR SPOTLIGHT

PULLEY

CONTROL ROPE

INSULATED WIRE

LIGHTS TO BE DIMMED

BRAKE DRUM

SALT WATER

METAL PLATE

DIMMER

BUNCH LIGHT TO BE USED FOR FLOODLIGHT

STRIP LIGHT TO BE USED FOR FOOTLIGHTS. BORDER LIGHTS ETC.

FIG. 123. HOME-MADE LIGHT UNITS

A tin reflector can be tacked to the back edge of the wooden block. Holes above the bulb will be necessary for ventilation, but it will be necessary to rivet a tin hood over the holes or they will let out light. Of course, this substitute will have no lens, which is the most important single element of the spotlight. But the home-made article will cast a limited spot of light. It will work better if the inner rim of the cone is painted black for a distance of six inches or so. This black rim helps to make the light from the cone less diffuse by preventing it from being reflected by the extreme edge of the cone—it prevents the light from "kicking off," in the technical jargon of the stage electrician.

3. *Home-made Floods.* For a flood light, a bunch light is the best substitute. When electricity was in its infancy, before the powerful bulbs of the present day had been devised, bunch lights were universally used. It consists of nothing more or less than a box arranged to contain a number of small bulbs. It throws a diffuse light over a large area, just as a flood does. If a wooden box is used, it had better be lined with tin. It may be set on a standard, but if it appears at all top-heavy, it should be fastened to the floor whenever it is used. This may best be done with one or two stage screws. The amount of light may be regulated by unscrewing some of the bulbs. The variation possible with a bunch light is, therefore, from a single bulb to the united strength of the total number of bulbs. Color may be introduced by the use of colored bulbs, or by arranging a device at the front of the box to hold gelatine slides.

4. *Home-made Dimmers.* Salt water conducts electricity, and has a reasonably high resistance. Most home-made dimmers depend on this principle. A large porcelain jar, or a wooden tub, may be filled with water and several handfuls of salt. The circuit to be dimmed must be cut (with the switch off!) and each end of the wire fastened to a metal disc, such as an old stove lid or an automobile brake drum. One of these plates should be placed in the bottom of the tub, the other suspended over

the tub, say with a pulley and line, so that it can be lowered into it. Experimentation will show that when the current is turned on and the top plate dropped into the water, the light will begin to glow. As the plates are allowed to approach each other the light will burn brighter, and it will come to full brightness as they touch. By moving them apart, the light will be dimmed. If the water boils, the dimmer is overloaded, and a larger vessel and more water should be quickly substituted. Such devices are practical, however, only in small numbers and for small units, and it is better to secure regular dimmers.

In making home-made electrical devices, care must be taken to make them safe. Unless they are built under the direction of some highly competent person, the units should probably be checked over and approved by some licensed electrician. There is no reason why students should not have the satisfaction of making such units as have been described, but *they must not be thrown together hastily and carelessly.*

COLOR IN STAGE LIGHTING

In addition to wishing to control the amount of light given by a unit, the stage electrician also needs to control the color of the light. There are two common methods for doing this:

DYED BULBS

FIG. 124. DYEING BULBS

1. *Lamp Dye.* The first is to dye the bulb. A special lamp dye is made for this purpose and can be secured from any stage-lighting company. The dye may be secured in several colors, such as amber, straw, red, blue, and green, and comes in a bottle surrounded by a can. In dyeing, the dye is poured into the can,

which is lifted so that the lighted bulb is covered with the dye (see Fig. 124). The bulb to be dyed must be heated because dye will not spread smoothly nor dry evenly on cold glass. The dye left in the can should be poured back into the bottle and saved for future use. Dyeing is practical only with bulbs of small wattage, sixty or under. On larger bulbs it rapidly burns off.

2. *Gelatine Medium.* The second method is, therefore, much to be preferred, for it can be used with bulbs of any size. Gelatine is a transparent medium, which may be purchased from theatrical supply houses in a much larger number of colors than dye. It comes in sheets, approximately twenty inches square. A supply of these in assorted colors that are commonly used, might well be kept on hand. Frames to hold the gelatines come with the lighting units, but additional ones may be easily made of either wood or tin. Gelatine curls with the heat, and it is easily broken, so that many of the large frames have fine wires stretched across the face (as in the flood light frame, Fig. 125) to help protect the gelatine. It should be the work of a few moments only to change the gelatines in the frames, but it is useful to have several slides for each unit, so that it will not be necessary to make changes during the course of a performance.

The colors in gelatines that will be found most useful will be ambers, straws, reds, blues, and greens. With these, almost any effect can be secured. Frosted gelatine, which throws a white light, is also essential, but it must be used discreetly, for it diffuses the light and thus tends to turn a spot light into a flood. It is of great value, however, to soften the edge of a spotlight. By putting it in a slide with another color and tearing a jagged hole in the center of the frost (see illustration), a soft edge is secured. The commonest color for the representation of sunlight is amber, but some modern stage artists are opposed to using this color at all. They point out, quite correctly, that it kills many of the other colors commonly used

WOODEN FRAME TO HOLD GELATINE IN FLOOD LIGHT

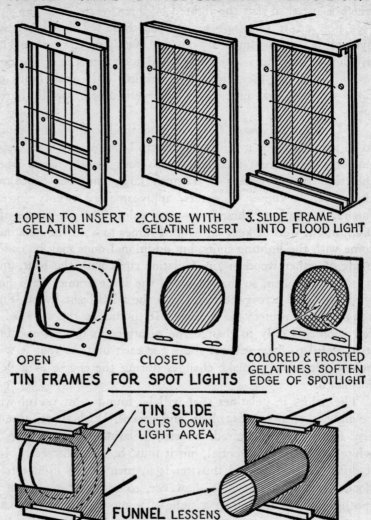

1. OPEN TO INSERT GELATINE
2. CLOSE WITH GELATINE INSERT
3. SLIDE FRAME INTO FLOOD LIGHT

OPEN CLOSED COLORED & FROSTED GELATINES SOFTEN EDGE OF SPOTLIGHT

TIN FRAMES FOR SPOT LIGHTS

TIN SLIDE CUTS DOWN LIGHT AREA

FUNNEL LESSENS LIGHT SPILL

Fig. 125. GELATINES AND SLIDES

in scenery, costume, and make-up. They recommend that the effect of sunlight be secured by a combination of several gelatines, for instance, straw, steel blue, and light pink.

Gelatines may be placed doubled in a frame, so that the light shines through a double medium. If a single sheet allows too much light to shine through, another sheet of the same color may be used. Two different colors may be placed together to create a third color. Many lights have grooves in front to take two slides, so that slides may be placed one before the other, and the two colors mixed by this method. These grooves also serve to hold other useful equipment. Sometimes it is necessary to lessen the light area covered by a spot or flood light. Regular shutters, similar to those in a camera, are sold by supply manufacturers; but pieces of tin and cut-offs, may be used for the same purpose. A funnel (see Fig. 125) is often used on the front of a spot to cut down the light spill; sometimes it is called, for obvious reasons, a hat. They may be purchased from supply houses, but can quite easily be made from stove pipes or tin cans of the proper diameter.

COLOR PRIMARIES

A consideration of color in stage lighting makes it necessary to point out that *light primaries* differ from pigment primaries, discussed in Chapter III. Most authorities state that light primaries are red, green, and blue. It is true that with these three colors a white can be made. It would seem then that the ideal color scheme for stage lighting would be red, green, and blue; for with these lights we should be able to make all other colors. A practical problem presents itself, however. The use of green and blue color media results in light of such low intensity that we should need lighting units of enormous size. Many modern theaters, therefore, use a *four* circuit system, which allows them to use as basic colors, red, yellow, green, and blue. In any case, probably few school theaters will have four circuits in foot and border lights, and it works well enough to have three. For many years, common colors used were red, white, and blue. Perhaps magenta (purple-red), pale straw (yellow), and a not-too-dark blue, or blue-green, is a good combination. If there are only *two* circuits, it is possible to secure good balance by doubling the blue lights since they will cast less light than either of the other colors; thus, one circuit may be alternate red and yellow (or white), and the other entirely blue. Even with only *one* circuit, it is an excellent idea to use varicolored bulbs, for a manufactured white light brings out much more effectively the colors in the sets and costumes. Every color is brightest under a light of the same color; that is, if there is red in the lighting, a red costume is made still more brilliant. In the same way, complementary colors tend to kill each other and to gray a costume. Warm colors in lighting reënforce warm colors in costumes or scenery, whereas they dull cool colors; of course, the reverse is also true. Therefore, lighter colors, such as straw, lemon, steel blue, and so forth, because they contain more of the complements, usually produce less color change than do more brilliant and vivid colors. These lighter colors are, therefore, more generally useful.

LIGHTING A SCENE

Lighting a scene is easier if the artist has a technical background. Often he can speed up the process by deciding in advance what units he wants to use, where he wants them placed, how he wants them ganged up at the switchboard, what colors will be best, and so forth. This he can often write down in some sort of a lighting plot (see Fig. 126). All the placing of the units, the anchoring of the spots, and the color of the gelatines shown in Fig. 126, can be worked out in advance. Then the actual work on the stage can be guided and rapid, and not hit or miss. This sort of preliminary scheme is especially important if the time to be spent in lighting the play is limited. With the scheme in hand, spots can be changed so as to cover the right areas, their focus made larger or smaller, new gelatine slides

F<small>IG</small>. 126. SCHEME FOR NIGHT LIGHTING AN INTERIOR

Diagram No.	Name of Light Unit	Function of Unit	Color
1 & 2	Floor strips #21 & 22 Border strips #21 & 22	Light sky wall " "	Dark blue " "
3	Floor strip #11	Light grow row	Med. blue
4	Floor flood #2	Throw moonlight through window	Steel blue
5	Floor spot #1	Throw firelight	Amber
6 & 7	Border spots #13 & 14	Reënforce upstage lamp on table A	Amber
8 & 9	Border spots #11 & 12	Reënforce downstage lamp on table B	Amber
10	House spot #11	Reënforce acting area around lamp B	Med. straw
11 & 12	House spots #12 & 13	Cover center playing area and blend lamps	Light blue
13	Floor flood #1	Light alcove	Dark straw
14 & 15	Foot and 1st border strips	Blend and tone lighting: use very low	Straw, pink, and blue

prepared and inserted, and, when necessary, units moved to different locations. At length, however, the exciting moment comes when the artist begins to light the scene.

Now he is like an artist painting a picture. Some experts begin by using spot lights to light the playing areas and then add foots and borders to give the desired tone. Others begin with the general lighting and then add spots to make the playing more visible. Perhaps it doesn't matter where the start is made. Ultimately, the lighting must be tested with actors in the scene. Therefore, if actors aren't available at the moment, other persons—probably stage hands—must substitute for them. It is impossible to be certain that an empty scene is being properly lighted, even though it creates the proper effect, for one of the things that requires utmost attention is the way light falls on the faces of the actors. Care must be used to see how the shadows fall and how they change during the movements of the actors. Often as an actor moves across the stage there is a dead spot which must be corrected by changing slightly the angle of a spot or by increasing its lighting area by changing the focus. Sometimes there will be a hot spot caused by too much light in one area. Ultimately, the lighting will be all a matter of balance, and this is where dimmers are desirable.

The uninitiated may think that dimmers are useful only where a transition in lighting is used: in which the sun sets, or the moon rises. Such is not the case. Dimmers are of even more importance to control the intensity of light that must be thrown by various units. The footlights cast a little too much light and account for the shadows on the back wall, or the top of the set is too brightly lighted and the border must be slightly dimmer. Dimmers are used constantly in good lighting to obtain balance. However, if no dimmers are available, ingenuity must take their place. Less light can be obtained from footlights and border strips by turning out a few bulbs, especially if those bulbs light the walls instead of the acting area; more light from these units can be created by changing to larger bulbs. The amount of light given depends, also, on the distance of the light unit from the surface illuminated; therefore, it is often possible to improve the balance by bringing units nearer or by moving them

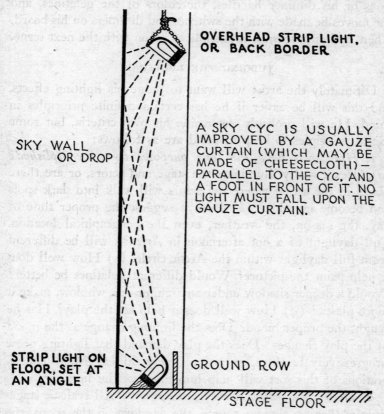

OVERHEAD STRIP LIGHT, OR BACK BORDER

A SKY CYC IS USUALLY IMPROVED BY A GAUZE CURTAIN (WHICH MAY BE MADE OF CHEESECLOTH) — PARALLEL TO THE CYC. AND A FOOT IN FRONT OF IT. NO LIGHT MUST FALL UPON THE GAUZE CURTAIN.

SKY WALL OR DROP

STRIP LIGHT ON FLOOR, SET AT AN ANGLE

GROUND ROW

STAGE FLOOR

FIG. 127. LIGHTING A SKYWALL OR DROP

If realistic sky lighting is desired, the floor unit should be of larger size or should contain more bulbs than the suspended unit, because a sky is nearly always brightest at the horizon. See Plate XI E.

further away. Experimentation can suggest many ways in which the lighting may be improved. Lighting cannot be determined in the abstract, even though the person in charge knows just what effect he desires. It is a matter of time, perhaps of hours.

When at length the effect is reached, the electrician must write it down. He must indicate what units he is using, the positions of his dimmer handles, the colors of the gelatines, and the moves he made with the switches and dimmers on his board. Then, and only then, is it possible to go on with the next scene.

JUDGING THE LIGHTING

Ultimately the artist will want to judge his lighting effects, and this will be easier if he has certain definite principles in mind. He will probably determine his own criteria, but some useful principles to keep in mind are as follows:

1. *How well have the four purposes been accomplished?* (*a*) Does it really illuminate the stage and actors, or are there places in the action where the actors will walk into dark spots and become invisible? (*b*) Does it suggest the proper time of day, the season, the weather, even the geographical location. Full daylight of a hot afternoon in Arizona will be different from full daylight within the Arctic circle. (*c*) How well does it help paint the picture? Would different gelatines be better? Would a deeper shadow under an arch, or in a window, make it more plastic? (*d*) How well does it help act the play? Has he caught the proper mood? Does the lighting change as the mood of the play changes? Does the play demand that lighting grow progressively brighter, or progressively duller? Many considerations of this sort will help him improve the lighting.

2. *Does the lighting come from a source?* All realistic stage-lighting has an obvious source, the windows in the room, the lighted chandelier, the torches, the candles, and so on. If the scene contains windows and the action is in the day, the light in the scene should *appear* to be coming through the windows. Rarely, of course, will it be possible to throw all the light that is necessary through the windows. It may be necessary to use footlights, a front border, and some proscenium-arch or auditorium lights. But enough light should be cast in at the window

Designed by Frederick McConnell

PLATE XIII A (above). *Portrait in Black,* by Ben Roberts and Ivan Goff

A Living Room. This is an interesting setting which the designer states is based on the theory that "realistic sets may be handled spatially, and need not be boxed in with a secondary proscenium." In other words, the audience is allowed to see past the edges of the set and above the top of it, so that it has the effect of existing in space. In such a set, the ceiling may be supported entirely by the walls, with a cantilever construction to support it at the center. (See p. 311.)

PLATE XIII B (below). *The Marriage of Figaro,* by Mozart

An 18th century bedroom. Another spot set, much more elaborate than those in Plate XII, but based on the same scheme, and masked with curtains in the same manner. (See p. 311.)

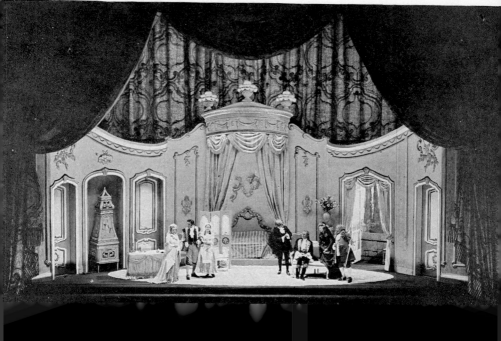

PLATE XIV. *The Butter and Egg Man*, by George Kauf

A unit set, designed by John Baird. Both the theatrical office (A) and the hotel room (D) are made of the same flats. The pylons remain in place. In B, the are being shifted, and C shows a new plastic door being inserted for the bed scene. (See p. 285 and p. 423.)

Columbia University: a laboratory production

Do

PLATE XV. *Malvaloca*, by S. Alvarez-Quintero and J. Alvarez-Quintero

A beautiful unit set, designed by Woodman Thompson, to represent a cloister of a Spanish nunnery, a courtyard, and an interior. The set was the unusual height of thirty feet and ceilingless; some of the elements were flown, and some moved on casters. (See p. 285 and p. 424.)

PLATE XVI. *Peer Gynt,* by Henrik Ibsen

A famous unit set by Lee Simonson. The illustrations show but three of the seven scenes: mountain road, in the hall of the Troll King, and before Aase's hut. (See p. 238 and p. 424.

to throw a faint shadow of the frame on the floor. Persons walking near the window should cast a shadow *away* from the window, just as they would in real life. There should usually be shadows in good lighting, although very faint shadows; for a shadowless room under natural lighting is non-existent. Probably the easiest way to get this effect is to fill the room with just about the amount of light desired and then to bring enough through the window to give the proper natural effect. The same process should be followed in all other circumstances. If there is a lamp, or a lantern, or a fireplace, which would be a source of light naturally, that source should be utilized. A circle of light may be thrown by a spotlight from overhead around a table on which a lamp is standing. A spotlight from over the proscenium arch may reënforce the light from a fireplace. In lighting an outdoor scene, more light should be cast from one side than from the other; only when the sun is directly overhead is outdoor light even, and it is then most uninteresting. Sometimes an excellent effect is secured by throwing green or blue light from one side, the "non-sun" side, and straw light from the other side; this helps to make faint but interesting shadows. Black, heavy shadows are usually to be avoided; but faint shadows, which will be hardly noticed by the unobserving, are essential. Scene-designers should do their part to secure good lighting by providing in their designs apparent sources for light.

3. *Have extremes of darkness and brightness been avoided?* The scene should not be flooded with white garish light, nor be so dark that the audience is obliged to strain in order to see what is happening. Overlighting is a common fault, but underlighting is probably more generally annoying to an audience. Dark scenes should be of short duration since they are tiring to the ear as well as to the eye. Often the effect of darkness can be secured by starting with the scene dimly lighted and then by bringing on more light so slowly that the change is imperceptible to the eyes of the audience. This gives the psycho-

logical effect of the eye growing accustomed to the darkness so that it sees better.

4. *Does the "day" and "night" lighting have the proper quality?* The quality of "day" lighting is diffusion; that of "night" lighting, concentration. Many artists try to secure this difference by doing day scenes with a dominance of strip lights, which cast a diffused, all-over light, and by using a dominance of spots in night lighting. This is also aided by the distance to the lighting unit. The wonderful quality of sunlight is caused by the distance it travels; its rays are almost parallel. Therefore, it is a helpful principle to use lighting units farthest away from the area for day lighting and to use the nearest units for night lighting.

5. *Have all possible imperceptible changes in the lighting been worked out?* If there are light changes, of course he wants his fades to be slow and smooth so that the audience will not be conscious of them. But there are many other possible imperceptible fades which may improve the lighting. Some of the cleverest effects are those of which the audience may be entirely unaware. If a character has to make an important speech from a certain position, it may be that his face would be indistinct and uninteresting under the normal lighting of the scene. A baby spot properly directed and brought up slowly at the correct time may give this character just the proper lighting without any one in the audience being aware that there has been any change in the lights. If a ghost is to appear, as in "Julius Caesar," the normal lights may be dimmed out and green light run in so gradually that the audience does not notice the change; but this lighting trick will intensify the entrance of the ghost and make it many times more effective than it would otherwise be.

6. *Has color been used to the greatest advantage?* Does his lighting kill or reënforce the colors in the sets and costumes? Often he may wish to put the costumes in the set while lighting it. In every way possible, the good artist will try to see that he

has assisted, and not spoiled, the effects that the scene and costume designers have tried to make.

Like all the other artists involved in making the production, the person responsible for the lighting—whether he be the electrician, or the designer, or the director—must constantly keep in mind the basic idea on which the production has been made. If it is a gay and brilliant play, he can kill it with dull and gloomy lighting; if it is a delicate fantasy, or a noble tragedy, he can hurt it with bright and garish lighting. Lighting is good or bad not to the degree that it is ingenius and mechanically skilful, but to the degree that it helps to build up the great sum total of effectiveness that is the play.

THE VALUE OF STUDY

The person who wishes to excel in stage lighting, can do much to improve his skill even when he is not actually working on the lighting of a stage. A thoughtful study of stage photographs, and other pictures, will prove a constant help. Many of the photographs reproduced in this book have been chosen partially because they are interesting from the point of view of lighting, and because they illustrate some of the principles discussed.

For example, the lighting of the skies in Plates IV B and XI E is better than that in Plate VIII B, in which the sky is not brightest at the horizon, and hence shows no gradation. Some of the illustrations (see Plates XII A, XII B, and XIII A) show the effectiveness, especially in partial sets, of a spotted pool of light in the center that fades off to blackness at the edges of the stage. An excellent example of outdoor lighting appears in Plate VIII A, in which the "sun" is obviously stage right: note the high light on the right sides of both the plastic and painted trees, and on the right wall of the house. The difference between day lighting and night lighting is shown in Plate XIV: in A, the source is the windows at the left, therefore the light decreases steadily from the left to the right wall; in B, the source is the chandelier and lamps, so the light is pooled in the center and kept off the side walls. Finally, Plate XV and Plate XVI illustrate clearly a possible difference between realistic and non-realistic lighting, and all six of these photographs are worthy of careful study. Note the wonderful plastic quality of the sets in Plate XV, which is caused partly by the lighting. In each set, there is a clear source of light: in A, it comes through the open arches in the left wall; in B, from the stairway up left; and in C, through the window down left. In Plate XVI, although a few units are shifted and the rocks re-set to make the scene-change, the primary differences are created with light. In set A, the dominant light is from a strong off-stage spot, perhaps to suggest a non-realistic setting sun; in B, which represents an underground cave, the lighting is in pools from overhead spotlights; and in C, there is even flood-lighting to suggest cool northern daylight.

In addition to the study of stage pictures, which are always instructive to the stage artist, the lighting effects created by nature will be a never-ceasing source of instruction, delight, and awe. Perhaps he will come to agree that light is a force which brings to the playhouse ". . . the most vibrant, subtle and affecting gift of the physical world, barring only the human presence."

PART IV
Organization and Management

CHAPTER XXVI

The Permanent Organization

THE VALUE OF A PERMANENT ORGANIZATION

The organization of the producing group is an important factor in the economical and effective process of play production. The process is made tremendously easier if there is a permanent group. The old system of getting together a number of amateurs in a community and giving a play is fortunately becoming very rare; amateur theatricals have given place to non-professional play production of a much more worth while variety. In the school or college the exigencies of the situation often demand that classes, or even less well-organized groups, be allowed, or even encouraged, to produce plays. But in both community and school, the advantages of a permanent dramatic organization are many. The full value of dramatics can never be secured unless there is some method of attracting and discovering ability and giving it a chance to grow. Newer and untried members can be started in smaller rôles and less important positions, and advanced as their progress warrants until they are able to bear heavy artistic and executive burdens. They can learn from their predecessors and teach their successors. In this way a valuable mass of experience should be created.

The form taken by the permanent organization should be one that will allow the ablest members of the group to control the activities—this is, perhaps, the only rule that can be laid down for guidance. Two different types of organization are found. The first is that controlled by a board of directors and is exemplified by the typical Little Theater organization. The second is the more common club type of organization, which is probably more workable in schools and colleges.

OFFICERS OF THE PERMANENT ORGANIZATION

In either case, however the group may be organized, there are certain definite functions to be performed, and there should be officers to perform them, whatever titles are used to indicate their position.

1. *Executive Head.* Every organization will need an executive officer of some sort whose duties are to call meetings, to preside at the meetings, to carry out the decisions made, to appoint committees, and in general to guide the policy of the organization. In a Little Theater, this executive head is often the director. Sometimes he is a salaried official, who gives a great part, or all, of his time to the work. In addition to being the executive head, he should be able to assume artistic control and to direct the actual work of play production. If the club organization is used, the executive head may be a student president. In most situations, he should restrict his function to administration and need not be responsible for the artistic guidance of the club. This should be the function of the faculty director, who must usually assume actual charge of the work, because of his superior skill in play production and his comparative permanency in the club. Perhaps it is wise not to define the duties of these two officers too sharply, but to allow the situation and their tact to govern. In either case, these officers will need assistance, so there might well be some assistant directors in the Little Theater, and some vice-presidents in the club.

2. *Treasurer.* In either kind of an organization, some official must be in charge of the funds. In Little Theaters, this is sometimes the duty of a business-manager, who may be a professional assistant to the director; in club organization, this officer is more likely to be called a treasurer.

3. *Secretary.* For any producing group, the secretarial work is heavy and should often be heavier than it actually is. It may,

therefore, be wise to have several officers to share in this labor. There might be a corresponding secretary to carry on the duties implied by the title—write official communications, keep files of letters, etc. This officer might well be a sort of permanent press representative and do what is possible to keep the organization and its activities before the eyes of the community or the school, especially between productions. Another official, a recording secretary, might be appointed to keep the minutes of the organization and to record its activities. He should keep a file of programs and reports of performances, a collection of newspaper clippings and criticisms, pictures of performances and actors—in short, everything that may be of future interest or that will help to build up tradition. Groups having a theater, or the permanent use of an auditorium, may add interest to their work by making the lobby, the lounge, or some other part of the building a picture gallery. They may display photographs of their own performances, sketches and designs, posters, old programs, etc. In some groups, this officer is called the historian. It is a simple matter, by a skilfully planned campaign, to produce an aura of great and respectable antiquity in a short period of time. The value of this sort of tradition is most helpful.

4. *Caretaker of Club Property.* One duty that should be performed by the officers of a dramatic club is so often neglected in schools and colleges that it may be better to have a special officer for it. That duty is to act as the caretaker of club property. He might be called the caretaker, or the trustee, or any other appropriate title. The office may be competitive, the outgoing officer appointing from among the candidates one who shows the greatest skill. This official should check off the scenery and properties taken from storage for any given performance, give his permission for its being rebuilt, and see that as much of it as has future usefulness is saved after the performance. Only by such a scheme can the proper physical requirements be built up in order to make elaborate productions possible.

A similar duty should, of course, be performed in respect

to costume. In small organizations it may be done by the same official, but in larger ones a separate office may well be created. Master (or mistress) of the wardrobe is an ancient and appropriate title.

EXECUTIVE COMMITTEE

To avoid the obvious difficulty of attempting to settle questions of policy or detail in general business meetings, especially when the organization has a large membership, it is wise, probably, to have a governing board of some sort. Most Little Theaters have a board of directors as a governing committee. For a dramatic club, a small executive committee, consisting of the officers, or some of them, and a few elected members can function much more easily than the large body of members; but it is usually wise to bring the decisions of such an executive committee before general business meetings for approval. Not only does such a procedure lead to a better feeling and more general interest, but valuable suggestions are often thus received from unexpected sources that might otherwise be lost.

MEMBERSHIP

In either case, however the group is organized, one important principle should be kept in mind: the membership should be comparatively large—much larger than it usually is. It should not be an organization of actors only. There should be room for every one who has an interest that can be tied up with play production—every one, that is, who is willing to manifest that interest in some concrete manner. No group consisting only of actors can make a successful organization. For every actor there should be two or three other persons who are interested in scenery and costume designing, in carpentry and painting, stage-managing and stage-lighting, business-managing and advertising, or in any of the other activities that must come together in the full process of successful play production.

Of course, it is probably unwise to admit every one who

merely expresses a wish to become a member of such a group. But every one who wishes should be given an opportunity to prove his ability in acting or in any of the varied activities of stagecraft or management. He should be allowed to become a member of the organization by successfully doing definite work of some sort. Those who wish to act should be encouraged to report to the director when plays are being cast, and they should be allowed to become full-fledged members only after they have played in a performance. Those interested in the crafts ought to be on the list of the stage-manager, who should give them work as opportunity offers. And prospective business-managers should be given the chance to prove ability in that field. Some such competitive system is a great aid in building a flourishing organization.

SPECIAL MEMBERS

It is often helpful in school and college dramatic clubs to have degrees of membership. One common method is to give an award of some sort for dramatic service, comparable to a letter in athletics. A point system is sometimes used. For example, playing a major part in a performance, or being a manager of some sort, might count two points; while a minor part or an assistant-managership might count but one. An accumulation of a certain number of points, five or seven or any predetermined number, might give membership in this higher class. Those having this award, which may be made obvious by their having the right to wear a pin or an emblem of some sort, will constitute a small inner group of the most experienced members. They may have special voting privileges, or the right to attend certain special meetings, or whatever authority is dictated by fancy and situation.

THE SCHOOL THEATER

The school theater is probably both aided and complicated by the growing tendency to make dramatic arts a subject in the curriculum. A generation ago, almost all theater practice in schools and universities was completely extra-curricula. There has, however, been a steady movement towards the introduction of classes for the serious study of phases of theater practice. Often, especially if the classes are not numerous or are in some way restricted so that they cannot by themselves practice elaborate play production, the classes can be made to feed some sort of a permanent organization, which can include students who have neither the time nor inclination to take the courses. Thus, a combination of curricular and extra-curricular activity benefits all the students and allows the school to make bigger and better productions than could be made by the play-production classes alone. In the classes, students may develop special skills, and the productions create real situations in which they may practice these skills. To secure the utmost benefits for students from the practice of the theater, some plan must be devised for a long-time program. The permanent organization makes this possible. Students are developed by being in a series of plays—not only actors, but painters, carpenters, costumers, ushers, managers, and so on. To allow students who are interested in the art of the theater to be involved in only one production in their school career is comparable to allowing athletes to participate in one game. As a good athletic program provides continual activity for students, so should a good dramatic program. This can be provided only by a planned series of dramatic productions, and not by a frantic class play, which the students undertake without previous training. And in properly planned and guided dramatic activity, there is a possibility of the development of talents of many sorts—not merely acting—and an unusual opportunity for socialization and leadership. The permanent organization should not be merely a social group, but a body of earnest-minded and serious artists, bound together by interest in a common activity.

FUNCTIONS OF A PERMANENT ORGANIZATION

A live Little Theater or dramatic club will probably not be content merely with the giving of performances. It has other possible functions in the community or the school especially if there are no dramatic arts classes in the school. Members may meet together for the study of phases of play production. They may bring lecturers, or even professional dramatic troupes, before their public. They may attend dramatic performances of professional or other non-professional groups. They may build up a dramatic library and strive in general to raise the level of dramatic knowledge and appreciation. They may hold meetings for the study of plays.

The fostering of original dramatic composition is another function that may be performed by a dramatic organization. Contests may be held and winning scripts may be presented. Play production tournaments may be another interesting and valuable activity. University theaters sometimes conduct state-wide conferences and contests. There is no lack of possible activities for an ambitious and imaginative group.

Nevertheless, the primary purpose of any organization will probably be to produce a series of plays. Each time a production is undertaken, it will be wise to follow the practice of the professional theater, which is to create a specific organization, or staff, to take charge of the specific production. In the theater, the producer makes the primary decisions that lead to the production. He chooses the script, determines the dates of the performances, furnishes the necessary financial backing, and engages the staff necessary for the operation. In the Little Theater, and in schools and colleges, a permanent organization occupies the position of the producer. The organization should make the general decisions, either directly by vote of the membership or by the action of a Board of Directors or an Executive Committee. These are the administrative decisions necessary to set the project in motion and to guide its progress. But just as the producer leaves to the staff the multitude of decisions necessary in the actual process of producing and managing the play, so the permanent organization will be wise to turn over these functions to a competent group of officers for each specific production. In the professional theater, the staff engaged for the specific play, along with the actors working in it, become a company, named from the play being produced. Thus, there might be the *Taming of the Shrew* Company, or the *Imaginary Invalid* Company, or the *Springtime for Henry* Company. A professional producer may have several companies working at the same time, each engaged for the specific purpose of producing a single script. Indeed, he might, in the case of a successful play, have several different companies, each presenting the same play; one may be playing in New York, one touring in the South, and one playing on the West Coast. Each company is a complete working unit, capable of performing all the necessary operations, such as acting the rôles, transporting and shifting the scenery, caring for the costumes, lighting the stage, publicizing the performances, selling the tickets, keeping the financial records, and so on.

The advantages of a similar scheme in the non-professional theater are obvious. The permanent organization, if it is properly organized for its primary purposes, will not be structurally suitable for the actual task of play production. It will, it is to be hoped, be made up of members trained in the many necessary operations. By creating the staff to do the actual work in the specific situation, the permanent organization performs its proper function as a holding body. At the conclusion of the operation, the staff is automatically discharged, just as the actors are. The staff, or certain members of it, may be officially appointed to function again in the next production, in the same or in different capacities. But there should never be any automatic hold-over, any more than there is in case of the actors. The actress who plays the heroine in one production does not automatically become the heroine in the next one, and neither should the stage-manager, nor the electrician, nor the property man, nor the business-manager automatically continue in the same position. Indeed, the business-manager of one production may become the hero of the following one, and one of the actors may wish to try his hand at house-management. Thus, the function of the permanent organization is to create a series of companies, each of which will be disbanded when its task is done. Active members of the organization may function on the staff of production after production, in the same way that earnest and skilful actors may appear in play after play. But in each case, it should be only by specific reappointment. Thus, the treasurer need not be the business-manager of each production; perhaps he need never function as a business-manager. As treasurer, his task is to keep the financial records of the organization. He should receive the report of each business-manager and make the report part of his accounting. But he will be most unwise if he himself handles the publicity, sells and collects the tickets, and keeps the day by day financial record of every production. To do these things is the duty of the business-manager, not the duty of the permanent treasurer. The same is true of all the other officers of the permanent organization. The secretary is not, as secretary, responsible for the publicity of specific productions; nor is the president in charge of directing. If these officers are to function on the staff of a specific production, it should be by special appointment or election.

This scheme helps to create interest on the part of all the members of the permanent organization. It makes it possible for many more persons to assume responsible positions in the course of a season. It allows the organization to be planning and working on several productions at the same time. It makes possible the selecting and training of large numbers of persons in all of the many interesting operations involved in producing a play.

CHAPTER XXVII

Organizing the Staff

As has been suggested in the preceding chapter, the permanent organization, whether it be a Little Theater or a dramatic club in a school or university, will not be well organized to do the actual work involved in making a production; therefore it is wise to create a special group of officers to take charge of each production. This group is usually called the production staff. When a play is being given by a temporary group of some sort, such as a school or college class, the need for this organization is still more acute. To attempt a performance without a complete organization for it, is to court confusion and disaster.

Just how the staff should be organized must be governed by the elaborateness of the intended production, its purpose, the number of performances, the skill of the available people, and many other elements. However, it must always be governed too by the tasks that are involved in producing a play. These tasks are suggested by the definition, discussed previously, that a play is a "story presented by actors on a stage before an audience." After the story, or the script, has been chosen, in the process of transforming it into a play, we must be concerned with three elements: the actors, the stage, and the audience. It is therefore logical and useful to conceive of the work of the staff as falling into three divisions: (1) actors must be chosen and rehearsed, (2) the stage must be prepared with scenery, lights, properties, etc., and (3) an audience must be attracted. Hence, a scheme that works well and that follows,

436

in general, modern professional theater practice, is to organize the staff into three units, as suggested by the diagram. Each of these units should be headed by a competent officer, and they must work harmoniously together to produce the best possible play. These officers may be called the director, the designer,

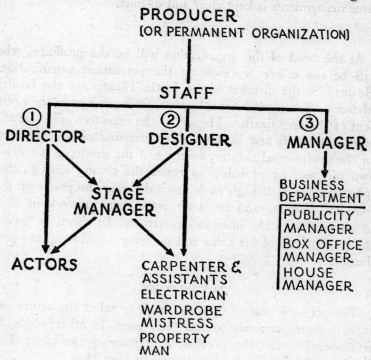

FIG. 128. ORGANIZATION OF A STAFF

and the manager; and they are concerned respectively with the actors, the stage crew, and the business department.

There must be some general official to supervise and coordinate the work of these officers; and as has been previously suggested, in the professional theater this is usually the duty of the producer. However, there is much confusion over terms and much variation in the actual organization of production staffs. Some producers may be their own directors and actually themselves rehearse the actors; others take a more active part in management, and leave the directing to some one else. The same variation will probably exist among non-professional groups. It will be helpful, however, if the division between the three departments is kept clear and distinct.

THE PRODUCER

At the head of the organization will be the producer, who will be the officer representing the permanent organization. He may be the director of the Little Theater, or the faculty adviser or director in a school group, or in some cases the president of the organization. He acts as the executive officer of the production staff, and he guides and coördinates the activities. In the professional theater, even when the producer is not his own director, he probably approves the casting and watches rehearsals; even though he is not a designer, he passes on the technical designs; and he is almost certain to work in close coöperation with the business department. In short, he guides the work of all of his aides and in general builds up the production.

THE DIRECTOR

The primary task of the director is to select the actors and to help them get ready to play their parts. In other words, he is responsible for the process of rehearsing the play. This process has been discussed at length in Part II.

In all non-professional producing groups, the aim might well be to develop directors. In schools and colleges, experienced students may be given the opportunities to direct, perhaps under the watchful eye of the faculty director. Sometimes there may be programs of one-act plays, with a student assistant director in charge of each play.

The stage-manager is the chief and most important of the assistants to the director. His functions in rehearsal are numerous and important, and they have been previously described. He controls the actors under the instructions of the director and is in charge of the production after preparations are complete. Since he is also responsible for the scenery, properties, lighting, and so forth during the performances, he is a bond between the director and the designer. In the performance, he is not only in charge of the actors, but also of the technical crew. He is responsible for the smooth running of the performances, and his duties have been discussed at length in Chapter XIII. Many directors, in the professional theater, start as stage-managers.

Sometimes the director may have special assistants, responsible to him, and connected with the general scheme only by their relationship to him. He may have a special assistant to direct the music or the dancing, if they are demanded by the play and if he is unable to direct them himself. Or he may have an art director to advise him in that field. Sometimes the scenic-designer may act in that capacity. Or the director may have special coaches to help the actors with their lines, or their pantomime or with some other special feature.

THE DESIGNER

The designer is, in general, in charge of the visual elements of the production. It is desirable, of course, that he work in close coöperation with the director and that they aid each other in carrying out the idea agreed upon for the production. His functions have been previously discussed in Part III. Sometimes there may be a "technical director" in a staff. He is usually an expert in stage rigging, carpentry, scene-shifting, and other such technical matters. He should work in close coöperation with the designer, and if we should try to fit him into the diagram (Fig. 128), sometimes he might be placed above the designer, and sometimes below. Probably the work will be carried on more harmoniously if such a decision need not be made, and if the designer and the technical director work pleasantly together. Often, in the non-professional theater, they may be one and the same person. The designer's duties, like those of the director, end with the start of the performances, and he has to depend on the stage-manager to see that his plans are carried out—that scenery is properly handled, that properties are in their correct places, that the lighting remains as arranged, and so on. The stage-manager cannot do all these things in person; therefore he needs a number of competent assistants.

One of his principal assistants is the stage carpenter. When scenery used to be built and painted in the theater, as was once almost universally the case, the stage carpenter was in direct charge of the operation. In non-professional situations, this might well still be the case. All the students that work on the building and painting of scenery will, therefore, technically be assistant carpenters. In the professional theater, the scenery is now usually prepared in a studio and delivered to the theater. The carpenter's job is to receive it, make whatever changes are necessary, and to take direct charge of the scene shifts. His assistants—who are commonly known as stage hands—are often called "grips," and their main job is making the scene changes.

The electrician is in charge of the lighting. His task is to arrange the lights so as to secure the effects demanded by the designer and the director, and then to see that the lights are properly worked throughout the performance. Sometimes, he too needs assistants, especially if floor lights have to be reset, if gelatine slides have to be changed, or if special effects are demanded during the performance.

The wardrobe-manager is in charge of costumes. In olden days, he, or she, under the direction of the producer or the director, often had charge of purchasing or making them. Now, costumes for most professional productions are made in special costume studios under the direction of the designer, who often has a special assistant to supervise this work. The wardrobe-manager's task is usually only to receive the costumes, see that they are properly distributed, and supervise their care and repair. In the non-professional theater, however, the costume department may be a large and flourishing organization, which assumes responsibility for the manufacture and care of costumes under the direction of the designer, for their handling in production, and for their cleaning and storing after use.

The property man has charge of the properties, which are all of the articles used in the performance that are not part of the sets or costumes. His duties have been previously discussed in Chapter XXII. In addition to securing necessary articles, he is responsible during the performance for their handling. He and his assistants shift the furniture; distribute the hand props used by the actors, such articles as sticks, pistols, fans, dishes, candles, and so on; and then collect them again after they are used. In the professional theater, the grips are not allowed to touch furniture or props. The property man usually has a station somewhere back stage, near a property table or closet, from which he can control the situation. He, or an assistant, takes the property to be used to the proper entrance for delivery to the actor as he goes on, and he collects it on the actor's exit and replaces it in his closet so that it can be used again the following performance.

As is suggested by the diagram, Fig. 128, the stage manager has a position of dual responsibility, in that he represents both the director and the designer. In his first capacity, he must see that the play is performed by the actors as it was directed; in his second, he has charge of the technical crew and must check up on the carpenter, the electrician, the wardrobe-manager, and the property man. His responsibility for all these activities and his importance during the performance have been discussed in Chapter XIII. Like all the other members of the staff, his duties may become so numerous that he needs assistants; therefore in any staff there may be several assistant stage-managers. Their duties are to do whatever work is assigned to them, such as prompting the play, calling the actors, making technical checkups, and so on.

THE BUSINESS-MANAGER

The third general division is business-management. The function of the business-manager is to secure an audience by proper advertising and publicity, to control the sale of tickets, and to manage the audience while they are in the theater. He usually needs at least three assistants to aid him in accomplishing these purposes, a publicity-manager or press agent, a box-office manager, and a house-manager. The duties of the business-manager and his assistants are numerous and important, and they are discussed in the following chapters.

COMBINATION OF OFFICES

In non-professional groups, it may often be necessary, or even wise, to make combinations of some of the offices suggested. The teacher-director is usually confronted with the necessity of being the producer-director, and perhaps in many cases he guides in person the building of scenery, or the making of costumes, thus becoming also the designer. If, in addition, he is in financial charge of the production, he also becomes the manager. If he finds it necessary to assume all these responsibilities, he is especially in need of a good staff, and competent student-assistants can be of untold value. Even though the teacher-producer guides all these processes, he need not do them all in person. A good student stage-manager can be of great assistance in the process of rehearsing and performing. A good stage carpenter can assume the responsibility for the handling of scenery, a property-manager can help to secure the properties, and so on.

There is likely to be less confusion if the department division remains distinct. Thus, the business-manager may logically assume the duties of the box-office manager or the house-manager, but he should rarely be the electrician. If it is necessary to use actors in the business department, or as members of the producing staff, their dual position ought to be distinctly recog-

nized. The important point to be kept in mind is the three-fold division of the production staff, which grows out of the nature of the functions that must be performed in producing a play. This threefold division exists no matter how large or small the production. Even when a play is presented in a class room, there may be actors, a stage crew, and a business department. The student who clears the space for the performance and moves whatever articles have to be moved is really a stage-manager. And the student who acts as host, who sees that the audience is comfortably seated, is the house-manager, just as truly as the professional house-manager who controls a staff of ushers and cares for the comfort and safety of an audience of two thousand spectators.

CHAPTER XXVII

The Business Department

THE IMPORTANCE OF BUSINESS-MANAGEMENT

The importance of skillful and efficient business-management in the production of a play is apparent when the object of the venture is to be a commercial success, or to make money. Even when this is not the case, as will be true—it is to be hoped—with most school, college and Little Theater productions, business-management remains an important phase of the activity because no play that plays to uncomfortable and restless audiences can be successful. Therefore, even when the purpose is to produce a play for the purpose of the fun and education involved, the business department has an important function to perform.

This business department is usually headed by an officer called a manager. His assistants are usually (1) a box-office manager (or treasurer), who is responsible for the sale of tickets and the handling of the money, (2) an advertising manager or press representative, who tries to secure as much publicity as possible for the play, and (3) a house-manager, who is responsible for the control of the audience during the performances. Each of these officers may need assistants. The box-office manager cannot sell all the tickets in person; the press representative probably cannot write all the necessary publicity and make all the necessary contacts single-handed; and the house-manager needs door men and ushers to help him admit the audience, get them in the correct seats, distribute programs, and handle the audience in emergencies. The business department, there-

fore, may be in many cases a large organization. This managerial organization is often loosely known in the professional theater as the front of the house, and normally they have little direct relationship with the actors or the stage crew. Their function is to make the contacts with the public, and in the nonprofessional theater, a good business department can aid greatly to give a pleasant and successful quality to the process of play production.

THE BUDGET

One of the first, and most important, tasks of the business-manager and his assistants will probably be to work out a budget. This step will be important even though no financial profit is anticipated. If the purpose is merely to avoid losses and to put the receipts back into other productions, as may often be the case in universities and Little Theatres, it is necessary that expenses be estimated and controlled and compared with probable box-office take. A careful manager will, therefore, estimate a probable income and will figure a sufficient margin so that if his income is not all he expects it to be, he will nevertheless clear expenses. One of the primary duties of the manager is to balance his budget, and in order to do this he must know all the items of expenses and keep careful track of expenditures as they occur. He must, therefore, work out some scheme of daily reports from his assistants.

Normally, a theatrical budget will break down into the following items:

1. *Rental of theater.* Even though the group has the free use of a school assembly hall or a university building, there may be expenses under this item, such as special janitorial services, special cleaning, etc.
2. *Royalty.* This should be one of the first items attended to by the business-management. If royalty is demanded for the use of the play, it should be paid well in advance, and the letter of permission, giving the group the right to use the play, should

be carefully preserved. When the play is royalty free, there may be such items as the purchase of scripts, typing, etc.

3. *Production.* This should include all the expenses of scenery, costumes, properties, lighting, etc. Often it will include trucking, cleaning, purchasing special make-up, rental of special electrical equipment, replacing of gelatin in the lights, and many small items like dye, needles and thread, etc., which must not be neglected if the budget is to have accuracy.

4. *Printing.* Tickets, programs, posters, advertising, and many other such items, often make printing a primary expense.

Many times there may be special items, such as salaries, transportation for actors, and so on. It should be clear that the best business manager is the one who can think most clearly in terms of *income* and *expenses:* his duty is to boost the income as high as possible, and, without being niggardly or injuring the production, to keep expenses as low as possible. He must try to estimate, accurately and in advance, all the necessary costs of the production. Of course, many budget decisions cannot be made by the business department alone, and probably a good budget must be worked out in coöperation with all the other departments.

After the production the business-manager should make a complete financial report, which should include, of course, the actual expenses, the income, and the profit or loss. The job of the business-manager is to oversee the work of all his assistants, and to assume the financial responsibility for the production. This job is not complete until all the bills are paid, until the receipts and records have been put in order, and until a final all-inclusive financial report has been worked out. His task, therefore, does not end with the fall of the final curtain, but may occupy him for several days, or weeks, thereafter. This report should be permanently recorded in some way for the benefit of future managers. In management, as in all other departments of non-professional play production, it is important that the experience gained in one production be passed on for the next.

BOX-OFFICE MANAGEMENT

One of the first jobs of the box-office manager will be to have tickets printed, but this requires some previous decisions which cannot be made by the box-office manager alone, or indeed not even by the business-manager. These decisions should probably be made by the producer, or perhaps by vote of the entire membership of the permanent organization. Such decisions might comprise the price, or prices, of admission; the question of whether or not seats are to be reserved; the problem of whether seats are to be sold only at a box-office or by members of the organization in general; and so on.

1. *Ticket Prices.* The price of admission will probably be determined by local custom, the purpose of the production, and

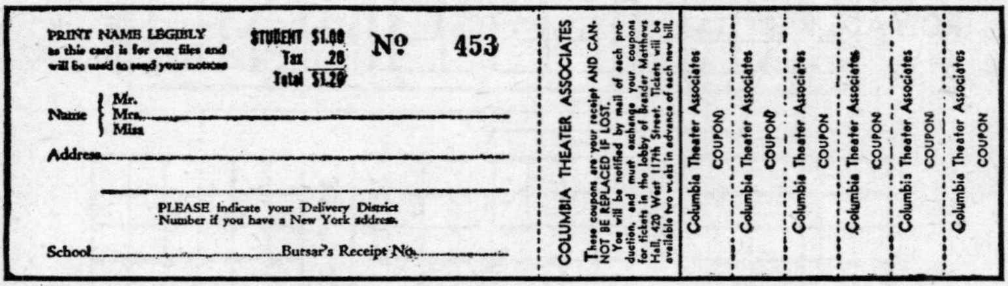
PRINT NAME LEGIBLY
as this card is for our files and
will be used to send your notices
STUDENT $1.00
Tax .20
Total $1.20
No 453
Name Mr.
Mrs.
Miss
Address
PLEASE indicate your Delivery District
Number if you have a New York address.
School Bursar's Receipt No.
COLUMBIA THEATER ASSOCIATES
These coupons are your receipt AND CANNOT BE REPLACED IF LOST.
You will be notified by mail of each production, and must exchange your coupons for tickets in the lobby of Brander Matthews Hall, 420 West 117th Street. Tickets will be available two weeks in advance of each new bill.
Columbia Theater Associates COUPON
Columbia Theater Associates COUPON
Columbia Theater Associates COUPON
Columbia Theater Associates COUPON
Columbia Theater Associates COUPON
Columbia Theater Associates COUPON

FIG. 129. A SUBSCRIPTION STUB AND COUPONS

many other factors inherent in the specific situation. Some groups charge a single price for all tickets; others have a varying price determined by the location of the seat to be occupied by the ticket-holder. The important thing is that the ticket give the necessary information about price and location. If several productions are made during a season, it is often advantageous to introduce some sort of subscription scheme by which subscribers can buy season tickets, perhaps at a reduced rate. In this case, it is not always necessary to have the actual tickets for the individual performances of the entire season since a strip of coupons may be sold (see Fig. 129), and the coupons may be exchanged for seats to the performances shortly in advance of each date. A subscription scheme does, however, imply that the subscribers be promised a certain number of performances and therefore binds the group to make the promised productions.

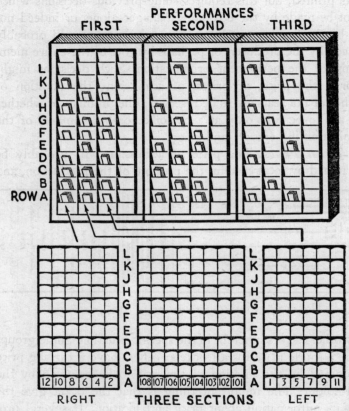

FIG. 130. TICKET RACK AND SEATING ARRANGEMENT OF THREE
SECTIONS

2. *Reserved Seats.* Whether or not seats are to be reserved is also a matter that must be decided before tickets are printed. In general, it is probably more satisfactory to number the seats, so that purchasers may know in advance where they are to sit. In a well-arranged auditorium, the numbering of the seats

(see Fig. 130) shows at a glance which seat is called for by the ticket. Rows are usually designated by letters, starting with the row nearest the stage, which is Row A. The letter "I" is often omitted because it looks like a number, and in the hurry of seating spectators, the ushers may make a mistake. This leaves but twenty-five letters, which is usually enough since rarely are there more than twenty-five rows of seats in a theater. If there are, it is better to repeat the first letters of the alphabet than to start re-lettering at the back of the house. Thus, if necessary, the first three rows may be AA, BB, and CC, after

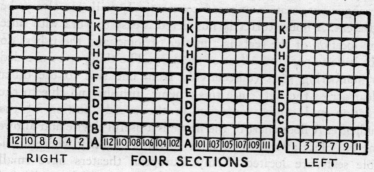

FIG. 131. SEATING ARRANGEMENT OF FOUR SECTIONS

which the rows may be lettered as usual with a single A, B, C, etc. Then the general principle still holds, that the letters at the beginning of the alphabet are in the front of the house.

In a similar way, the individual seats are numbered from the middle of the house towards the outside, with the odd numbers at the left of the house and even ones at the right. Thus, if the seats are correctly numbered, in an arrangement with two sections, C6 will be the third seat to the right from the middle aisle in the third row. If there are three sections, the left one is usually numbered 1, 3, 5, etc., the middle section 101, 102, 103, etc., and the right section 2, 4, 6, etc. A similar scheme may be worked out for four sections. If there are five or more sections, which will rarely be the case, it becomes necessary to name the sections, and have them printed on the ticket along with the row and number of the seat. The five sections are usually indicated as left, left center, center, right center, and right—corresponding, from the audience point of view, to the actor's names for sections of the stage (see Fig. 12). Unless the auditorium is very narrow, or unusually wide, the three section arrangement is probably best. When possible, it is wise to avoid a middle aisle, as this is the most desirable part of the house from the point of view of spectators. The box office manager— and the house manager and ushers—must know that in this arrangement, seats numbered consecutively will not always be adjacent. A house correctly numbered is easy to work with since the location of the seats is a matter of logic, and the ushers do not have to perform a feat of memory. The thing to be avoided is numbering seats consecutively from one side to the other clear across the hall since this scheme furnishes no clue to the location and causes confusion in the speedy seating of the audience. A floor-chart of the house is a useful device and allows the box-office attendant to show spectators exactly where available seats are located. Many European theaters have small models of the auditorium at the box office to aid in explaining the location of seats, and the making of such a model may be an interesting project.

3. *Racking Tickets.* In order to sell reserved-seat tickets accurately, the box-office manager must have some scheme that enables him to see at a glance what tickets are left. For this purpose, some device to hold tickets is necessary, and this is called a rack. A complicated rack may have a slot for each ticket in the house, in which case an empty slot means a sold ticket. More often, racks are made to hold sections of tickets (see Fig. 130), each slot containing the tickets of one section of one row. On Broadway, it is a law that no seat can be more than eight seats from an aisle, so no section can be wider than sixteen seats. Therefore, no slot in the rack needs to hold more than sixteen tickets, and the average is probably nearer twelve.

The manager should see to it that the box office is supplied with racks that will hold the tickets for a production. These can often be purchased in various sizes, or they can be manufactured, like the one in Fig. 130, out of plywood or tin.

When there is no single box office to which purchasers come, or when a committee, or the membership of a group, make a general attempt to sell tickets throughout the community or the school, it sometimes complicates sales to have the seats reserved and the tickets numbered. Customers may not wish to buy numbered tickets unless they are certain that they are going to get the best possible seats, and any salesman can have only a limited assortment. Some groups attempt to overcome this difficulty by having the members sell preliminary tickets which may be exchanged for reserved-seat tickets at the box office at certain definite hours, or even just previous to the performance. In general, however, it is best to have as few persons as possible selling reserved seats; so unless a convenient central box office can be established, perhaps it may be wise to resort to tickets of general admission. Of course, the box office, even though it is only a table in the lobby, should be open for the sale of tickets at a certain definite time, perhaps two hours before curtain time on the evenings of performances and should remain open at least through the first intermission.

4. *Dressing the House.* A good box-office manager who understands his job is courteous and obliging to his customers at all times and must be able to keep his head and his temper. He must work rapidly and accurately. He represents the organization in its contact with the public, which begins to judge the production from the method in which the tickets are handled. In addition to being able to explain quickly the location of the seats still available, to choose the right tickets, and to make change accurately and quickly, the box-office manager is often able to distribute the audience, especially in cases where he is certain that the house is not going to sell out completely, so that they make the impression of a full house.

He does not, unless the customers demand it, sell every seat in the front half of the auditorium, leaving the rear half completely unoccupied; but he tries to distribute the audience by leaving occasional pairs of unsold seats. This practice, which is called dressing the house, makes the theater feel better both to the audience and to the actors.

5. *House Tickets.* One of the common methods in dressing the house is to pull out of the racks, before box-office sales begin, a certain number of tickets, perhaps ten or fifteen pairs, to be used last, or in emergencies. These are called house tickets. They should be distributed throughout the auditorium, and not be a single block in any one section. These house tickets are used by the box-office manager, at his discretion, as complimentary seats for important guests, or to fill last-minute orders, or to make adjustments for errors—if any have been made. A box-office manager always feels safe if he has a few extra pairs of good seats for emergencies in the last few minutes before curtain time. If the play is successful, they can usually be sold at the last moment. If the play is not completely sold out, a few pairs of empty seats, in scattered locations, do no harm.

6. *Complimentary Tickets.* Complimentary tickets are those which are not purchased, but which may be given away to distinguished guests, or to reviewers, or to theatrical agents scouting for talent, or to any persons who cannot be expected to pay for the privilege of seeing the performance. In making an accurate financial accounting of the proceedings of the evening, which is one of the tasks of the box-office manager, he usually needs some method of distinguishing those seats which are complimentary from those that are purchased, and a common method is to punch a hole in each end of the complimentary ticket. These tickets are sometimes called Annie Oakleys, because—tradition has it—a famous lady marksman of that name in Buffalo Bill's Wild West Show used to create complimentary tickets by shooting bullet holes in them. Holes are punched at each end of the ticket, so that one will be in the stub—the

numbered part retained by the customer—to indicate to the house manager that the holder hasn't paid for his seat. He is what is called in theater language a "deadhead." The hole also tells the box-office manager that he shouldn't refund the money that the deadhead hasn't paid! The hole on the other end, which is torn off and retained by the doorman, and turned in for the house count, indicates to the box-office manager that he must not count this ticket for money. If he does, his account will not balance. It is only a scrap of paper.

For this reason, passing out complimentary tickets is often called "papering the house." This is a practice that schools and Little Theater might sometimes try—commercial theaters do! By judicious papering, a small house may sometimes be built up to one of reasonable size. Aside from the advantage of giving the actors sufficient audience so that playing is an agreeable experience, it may be a method of introducing the organization to new and prospective paying customers. Paper should be distributed judiciously, however, only to persons who can not be expected to attend otherwise. Blocks of complimentary tickets may be sent to other schools and colleges for distribution, or to large department stores, factories, and offices. Blocks of tickets of this sort should not be too large, for it is inevitable that some of the tickets so distributed will not be used. The danger in this practice, if it is too widely and openly used, is that all prospective patrons may wait for the paper, and the group may ultimately find itself playing to deadheads only!

7. *The Printed Ticket.* The actual printed form of the ticket is another consideration that requires thought and decision. The traditional theater ticket is on thin cardboard, approximately 1½" wide and 3¾" long. It must contain all necessary information, such as the name of the theater, the name of the play, the date of the performance, the price of the ticket (including the federal tax, if there is any), the time of the curtain, and the location of the seat. Regular theater tickets can be secured from printers equipped to do the special job of numbering the tickets.

Usually a seating plan of the auditorium must accompany the first order, and thereafter the printer can supply accurate sets of tickets properly numbered. It costs slightly more if the color of the tickets are to vary for different parts of the house, as for the orchestra and balconies, or if different colors are to be used for different performances. Where there are to be several performances, therefore, tickets are often distinguished from one another only by the date, which is usually clearly indicated by a large numeral for the day of the month (see Fig. 132). In order to distinguish clearly between seats for evening and matinee performances, the numeral indicating the date is

FIG. 132. A STANDARD TICKET

usually made small on matinee tickets, and the initial letter of the day is printed in large, bold type. Thus, S indicates a ticket for a Saturday matinee, W a Wednesday matinee, etc. By recent regulation of the Federal Bureau of Internal Revenue, it is required to print the seat number at each end of the ticket. This makes it impossible for the door man to make the mistake of giving the customer the unnumbered end, which entitles him to no seat! Non-professional groups not wishing to go to the expense of having tickets supplied by the regular ticket-printing concerns, can often get a satisfactory job from a local printer (see Fig. 133), and, if seats are to be reserved, the tickets can be neatly numbered in black ink by hand. Care must be taken to do this clearly so that the numbers can easily be read in a darkened auditorium, and accurately, so that no two tickets will entitle the bearers to sit in the same seat! A ticket that is well printed and attractive and that looks like a theater ticket is usually worth the slight extra expense.

FIG. 133. AN IMITATION OF A STANDARD TICKET

8. *The Box-Office Report.* The final task of the box-office manager, at the close of each day's work, is to make up a statement of the condition of the box office. He records the number of tickets sold, the prices, the amount of money on hand, and the remaining number of unsold tickets. His position is a responsible one, for he should keep complete financial records; and it is for this reason that he is often called a treasurer.

In addition to his daily statement, the box-office manager should make a final Box-office Report, showing the disposition of tickets for the entire run of the play, similar to the imaginary one shown in Fig. 134. Aside from the obvious necessity of accounting for the tickets, and giving the essential financial statement, such a report gives much interesting and valuable information. It might well be carefully studied by the Board of Directors or the Executive Committee, or whoever else is responsible for the policies of the organization.

For example, a study of the statement shown (Fig. 134) indicates that although two houses (Friday and Saturday eve-

BOX OFFICE REPORT

Production: "The Beaux Stratagem"

Date: April 20th to April 23rd.

House Capacity: 290.

Day	Coupons		Cash	Comp.	Total Issued	Unsold	Attend.	Unused Seats
	Gen.	Stu.						
Wednesday	62	70	120	4	256	34	250	6
Thursday	60	56	68	5	189	101	169	20
Friday	66	102	115	7	290	-	284	6
Sat. Matinee	44	36	77	-	157	133	140	17
Sat. Night	73	83	128	6	290	-	283	7
TOTALS	305	347	508	22	1182	268	1126	56

RECAPITULATION OF TICKET DISTRIBUTION

Exchanged for General Subscription coupons..................305

Exchanged for Student Subscription coupons..................347

Sold for Cash..508

Complimentary.. 22

                       1182

FINANCIAL STATEMENT

305 General coupons @ .50....................................$152.50

347 Student coupons @ .25.................................... 86.75

508 Cash admissions @ 1.00.................................. 508.00

                      $747.25

FIG. 134. A BOX-OFFICE REPORT

nings) were sold out, there was never a capacity attendance. During the course of the run, fifty-six patrons secured tickets which they did not bother to use—an average of ten a performance. Perhaps this might lead to the policy of selling a limited amount of standing room, even though the theater is small: obviously there are always going to be some vacant seats, so a certain number of standees can probably be seated at any performance.

Again, as could be expected, Friday and Saturday evenings are the most popular performances—every theater man believes there should be more Fridays and Saturdays in a week! The Board, however, will probably be disappointed to note that on Wednesday, there were thirty-four unsold seats and six unused ones. Thus, even for the Opening Night, which should be gala, the actual attendance was only two hundred and fifty—five-sixths of capacity. Perhaps some steps can be taken to arouse more enthusiasm for opening nights.

The smallest audiences were on Thursday night and Saturday matinee. Perhaps, for the next production, some parties can be arranged for these performances, or the business manager can be instructed to indulge in a little discreet papering. Perhaps it is even possible that the Saturday matinee performance, at which the attendance was less than fifty percent of capacity, should be dropped from the schedule, unless some way can be found of building it up. The state of the weather may have had something to do with it, however, and a beautiful afternoon may have cut into attendance; or perhaps the performance collided with a football game.

Another interesting speculation, which the statement suggests but cannot show, is the number of possible patrons turned away on Friday and Saturday evenings. If a large number were disappointed, it might be wise to initiate the experiment of performing on Fridays and Saturdays only—performances could be given on two consecutive weekends. Or perhaps the opening is on the wrong evening. If performances began on Friday, the patrons turned away over the week end might buy tickets for the following Monday and Tuesday, thus making better houses than can ever be secured for Wednesday and Thursday.

Many other analyses such as these may be drawn from a study of an accurate box-office statement, and such speculations are an interesting possibility not to be neglected by alert school and Little Theater organizations.

ADVERTISING MANAGEMENT

The advertising manager is the official responsible for giving publicity to the specific production, and his task must grow out of the local situation. Nevertheless, whether the producing organization be in a school or university, or in a more general community as will be the case with a Little Theater, advertising must usually take one of three forms: paid advertising, newspaper publicity, and special publicity stunts.

1. *Paid Advertising.* Probably the theater advertising most familiar to the general public is in the form of billboards, which range in size from the large panels seen in roadside displays to the small panels placed on the sides of buildings in cities and towns. These displays are not made up of single sheets of paper, but of a series of sheets assembled in the proper order. The basic sheet, which is the unit, measures twenty-six inches by twenty-seven inches; and displays are named according to the number of sheets used to make the complete poster, as three-sheet, eight-sheet, sixteen-sheet, and twenty-eight sheet. This sort of advertising is probably rarely used by the non-professional theater. A single poster, printed on cardboard, varying in size from 12″ by 15″ to 18″ by 24″ is probably a more useful form of advertising. Professionally, posters of this sort are known as tack-ups. They can be displayed not only on bulletin boards in the school, but sometimes they can be tacked up on walls and fences throughout the community, or placed in the windows of shops. Even when no such poster is to be printed, a few hand-made ones may be valuable. A contest for a play poster in a school or community usually stimulates interest in a coming performance. The text for such a poster should probably be specified, so that contestants will not omit some vital item. The text should in-

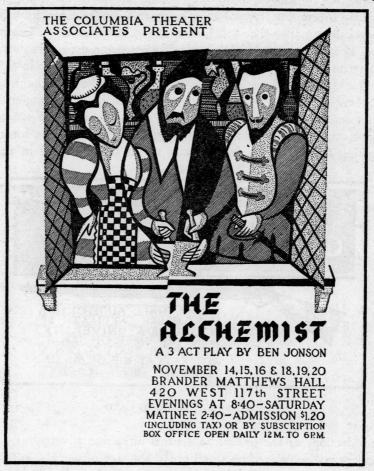

THE COLUMBIA THEATER
ASSOCIATES PRESENT

THE ALCHEMIST

A 3 ACT PLAY BY BEN JONSON

NOVEMBER 14,15,16 & 18,19,20
BRANDER MATTHEWS HALL
420 WEST 117th STREET
EVENINGS AT 8:40 – SATURDAY
MATINEE 2:40 – ADMISSION $1.20
(INCLUDING TAX) OR BY SUBSCRIPTION
BOX OFFICE OPEN DAILY 12 M. TO 6 P.M.

FIG. 135. A POSTER

clude not only the name of the play and the dates of performances, but the price of tickets, the time of the curtains, the
method of procuring tickets, and so on.

Another method of advertising that may be useful in school
and community productions is what the professional theater
calls heralds or throwaways. These are either small printed

single sheets, about the size of a theater program, or folders, containing matter that will interest a reader in the play. Often, on Broadway, heralds for several other current performances may be inserted in a program. Otherwise, they may be left in piles in public places, in hopes that they will be picked up by passers-by, or they may be distributed by mail. In the non-professional theater, advertising of this form may be sent out to special mailing lists, built up by asking spectators to fill in forms giving the names of friends who might be interested in the

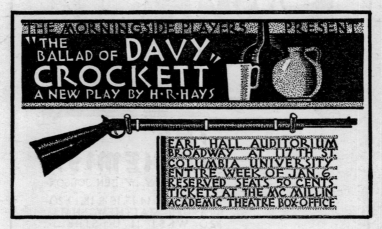

FIG. 136. A MAILING CARD

productions of the group. Sometimes attractive advertising circulars can be printed on small cards, the size of postals, so that they can be mailed. Such cards, ready to be addressed and stamped, may be given to members of the audience, to the players, and to other members of the general organization. A clever advertising manager will try to devise schemes of this sort which will enlist the aid of the entire student body or the entire membership of the group.

A final form of paid advertising, universally used in the professional theater, is small paid newspaper advertisements, of a few lines only, announcing the performances. In any city having several theaters, a block of such advertisements is a feature of the daily papers. Many non-professional groups use this form of advertising in local, or in school or university, papers.

2. *Newspaper stories.* But the real theater advertising manager prides himself on the amount of *free* publicity he can secure for his production in the daily press. This publicity takes the form of stories which he sends out as press releases. Often he distributes them several days in advance of the date he wants them to appear and marks them in an upper corner, "to be released on such-a-date." These stories will begin with the decision to produce a certain play and continue with the appointment of a staff, the choosing of the cast, the appointment of a director or a designer, the beginning of rehearsals, reports on the progress of rehearsals, changes in the cast, incidents happening to persons prominent in the cast, the approach of the opening, and so on. Often he accompanies such stories with pictures of actors or other persons involved in the production. Stories and pictures of this sort may often be useful in the advertising campaign of the non-professional theater. They might be sent not only to the school or university papers, but to local public papers, or even to the papers of nearby communities—especially when actors come from those localities. This activity calls for some person who is capable of writing good stories and who is sufficiently ingenious to find occasions for them. Often he may be a special official called a press representative.

3. *Special Publicity.* In addition to these traditional methods of securing publicity, there is often an opportunity, especially in a school or college, for some inventive person who can create special stunts. If set models, or drawings, are made for the production, sometimes these can be displayed in a corridor of the school, or even in a window in a store in the community, where they will attract attention. When an auditorium is in daily use, it helps advertise the play to leave a scene on the stage, even

though it is not yet completed, so that it will be seen by all who enter the auditorium. Sometimes, too, it is possible to have short special acts, or stunts, as part of some assembly or chapel exercise. Special displays, collections of pictures, photographs of actors, etc., can often be created for use in the lobby, both before and during the performances. In short, the only limit to the possibility of arousing interest in the community will be the dictates of good taste and the inventiveness of the officials in charge of that activity.

PROGRAMS

The programs that are to be used in the performances are another problem that will demand the attention of the business-manager and his assistants. An attractive program, whether it is mimeographed or printed, will do much to help prepare the audience for a pleasant evening. Items that it should contain will be the name of the play and the author; the list of characters and actors; the location and times of the scenes; the production staff; and all special credits, such as scene-designing, lighting-designing and execution, credits for costumes or furniture borrowed, etc. An often-omitted item that should be inserted is the length of intermissions. Sometimes a "Who's Who in the Cast" is valuable, especially if it can list previous appearances of actors appearing in the present production. Another feature, often interesting, is some discussion of the present play, its history and its author, the point of view from which the production was made, and perhaps the future plans of the organization. In short, the program can be made an attractive pamphlet, dealing with the past, present, and future work of the organization. A series of good programs becomes a permanent historical record; therefore it is worth while to make them as interesting as possible.

Some groups more than cover the expense of an elaborate program by inserting paid advertising secured throughout the community. Other groups feel that a program without advertising is more dignified and attractive, and that it is sufficiently important to be a legitimate item in the expense of producing the play. In any case, the program policy is something that needs to be considered, and some attractive form, used in a series of productions, does much to give the work unity and continuity.

HOUSE-MANAGEMENT

The final function of the business department is to receive the audience, seat them in the auditorium, see that they are comfortable, and to be alert for any of the possible emergencies that arise when a large group of persons are assembled. For this purpose, the business-manager should have a special assistant to take charge of this operation who is usually called the house-manager.

1. *The House-Manager.* A good house-manager does little actual work himself during the performance. He has arranged for a door man, a head usher, several other ushers, a cloak-room attendant, and whatever other assistants he needs. He himself stands in the rear of the auditorium and supervises the handling of the audience, alert for their comfort and safety, and ready to solve any difficulties that arise. Before he opens the door to the audience, the house-manager should see that all his assistants are in their proper places, so that seating the audience can proceed rapidly and efficiently. He should, so far as possible, be certain that the auditorium is comfortable in temperature. On a warm evening, he may have previously opened doors and windows and had the heat turned off. Perhaps he tries to get the auditorium sufficiently cool so that it will not heat up too rapidly after the audience is admitted. If there are noisy fans or ventilators, he must know how to turn them off during the performance. In short, he must understand the heating and ventilating of the house, so that he can keep it as comfortable as possible.

2. *The Door Man.* The door man collects the tickets and admits the audience. When the auditorium has several doors,

all but one should be closed during this process. The door man stands just outside the door being used and says, "Tickets, please." Sometimes an aisle is made with stanchions and ropes, so that this process can be made as orderly as possible. When the seats are reserved, it is necessary for the door man to tear the tickets and to give the customer the stub end of the ticket, or the one on which the seat number is marked. Professional tickets are numbered on both ends, so it is difficult to make a mistake. Usually, the door man takes the tickets presented to him and quickly riffles them with his thumb to determine if they are correct in number, for the current performance, and for the right theater. On Broadway, where there are often two or more theaters with adjacent entrances, it is a very common occurrence to have customers present tickets for the theater next door, and a good door man likes to discover this before he tears the tickets. After assuring himself on all these points, therefore, he tears the ticket, giving the stub end to the customer and dropping the other end in a slot in a box in which he collects the tickets for the performance. Later on, it will be the task of the house-manager to count these tickets and to make a report to the box-office manager.

3. *The Head Usher.* The duty of the head usher is to stand just *inside* the door, to glance at the ticket stubs, and to direct the customers to the proper parts of the house. This demands that he know the numbering system accurately. He should be able to direct "The front of the right aisle, please," or "The back of the center aisle," or "The middle of the left aisle." This implies that he knows where the sections divide, so that he may direct people by the shortest route. He must be able to direct them to the aisle to which their seats are nearest, so that they will be obliged to climb over as few spectators as possible in order to reach their seats. In short, he controls traffic, and the orderly distribution of the audience depends on his skill and efficiency. Often, too, the head usher makes a list of persons who may possibly be called out of the auditorium by some

emergency during the performance by listing their names and seat numbers. Such a person may be a doctor, whose office may need to reach him in an emergency.

4. *Ushers.* The ushers are the officials most directly and most continuously in contact with the audience; and if they work efficiently, they can do much to give the performances a professional atmosphere. Most amateur ushers move too much —like most amateur actors! The head usher should assign one or two of his assistants to each aisle. When there are two ushers to an aisle, one should station himself in the front of the house, while the other takes the rear. Each usher stays near his station and allows the spectators to come to him, as directed by the head usher; he does not fight his way constantly against the traffic to the head of his aisle. He does not need to walk up and down the aisle. He helps to reduce traffic by allowing the audience to come to him. Then, while handing out the programs, he notes carefully the numbers on the stubs, indicates the correct seats, returns the stubs, and sees that the spectators take the seats indicated. If, by error, they have come to the wrong aisle, he points out the right one, but does not himself conduct the party to the station of another usher. It is, of course, of great importance to seat people in the correct seats— and on the first try. Spectators being changed during the early part of the performances are a great annoyance, both to the actors and to the other spectators. Efficient and accurate ushering exhausts neither the ushers nor the audience.

When the performance starts, the ushers move quietly to the head of the aisles. If the spectators are admitted while the play is in progress—and this is usually the wisest policy—at least one usher in each aisle will need to be supplied with a flashlight. Flashlights must be used discreetly and not allowed to shine on walls and ceiling, or on the stage, or in the eyes of the audience. Ushers should be careful to keep them pointed to the floor and use them only to see the numbers on tickets and to guide late comers to the correct seats.

Finally, the ushers must do everything possible to avoid noise during the performance. They should not indulge in loud whispered conversations with late comers, and above all they must not talk with one another. No matter how many times they have seen the play, and even though they are now bored by the proceedings, their task is still to create a quiet and pleasant atmosphere in which the play can be enjoyed by the audience. On the other hand, they must not become so absorbed in the play that they neglect their duties. Good ushers are constantly alert to be helpful. They are always ready to remove fainting ladies without disturbing the other members of the audience, to keep the audience calm in case of accident or fire, and to remain cool and self-possessed in any of those other emergencies that sometimes arise at theatrical performances.

BIBLIOGRAPHY

This list mentions only a few of the many books which the student will find interesting and valuable either for reference or for further study. Some of the books are old, and some unfortunately are out of print. I have included them because it seems to me that no newer books have as yet replaced them. Most of them are still widely available in libraries and in theater collections. The *Dramatic Bibliography* of Blanche Baker (New York, H. W. Wilson, 1933) lists almost all the important books on the theater published in English previous to 1932. It is supplemented by the excellent bibliography, compiled by George Freedley, in *The Theater Handbook*. Many of the other books listed below contain bibliographies and references to other volumes. Thus, any student investigating a subject finds himself guided from book to book, until ultimately he is forced to make a selection, as I have been, of those volumes that he finds most helpful and stimulating.

M. S.

PART I

THE THEATER AND THE SCRIPT

CLARK, Barrett H., *European Theories of the Drama* (Revised Edition), New York, Crown, 1947.

An anthology of the writing of critics and theorists, starting with Aristotle. Maxwell Anderson says: "This is the only book you need if you want to study dramatic theory."

CRAIG, Edward Gordon, *On the Art of the Theater,* New York, Dodd, Mead, 1925.

The theory of theater practice, as explained by one of the important leaders in the "new theater" movement of a generation ago.

GORELIK, Mordecai, *New Theaters for Old,* New York, Samuel French, 1940.

A thought provoking history of stage production, describing old and new forms and techniques in the theaters of Europe and America, by a well-known designer.

HAMILTON, Clayton, *The Theory of the Theatre,* New York, Henry Holt & Co., 1939.

A collection of essays on all phases of the theater and theater practice.

JONES, Robert Edmond, *Dramatic Imagination,* New York, Duell, Sloan and Pearce, 1941.

An interesting series of essays on the arts and problems of theater production.

LAWSON, John Howard, *Theory and Technique of Playwriting*, New York, Putnam, 1936.

A thoughtful discussion of the problem of the playwright, which necessarily touches on many other phases of theater practice.

MATTHEWS, Brander, *A Study of the Drama*, Boston, Houghton, Mifflin Co., 1910.

Still one of the best introductions to the general problems of the theater practitioner. A.L.A. Catalogue (1926): "A clear and unpedantic study from an original point of view."

SIMONSON, Lee, *The Stage Is Set*, New York, Harcourt, Brace & Co., 1932.

Although primarily a study of stage design, by a famous designer, the book discusses the relationship of the theater to the society in which it flourished, from ancient Greece to contemporary New York.

SOBEL, Bernard (Editor), *The Theater Handbook*, New York, Crown, 1940.

A cyclopedia of theatrical information, containing a series of interesting articles, a synopsis of nearly one thousand plays, and a valuable bibliography compiled by George Freedley.

YOUNG, Stark, *Theatre Practice*, New York, Scribner's, 1926.

A provocative volume of essays on acting and the theater.

PART II

DIRECTING AND ACTING

Directing

DEAN, Alexander, *Fundamentals of Play Directing*, New York, Farrar and Rinehart, 1941.

Foreword: "An expansion of the first third of Alexander Dean's Syllabus of a course in play directing and includes the material covered in his first-year class in directing at Yale."

BROWN, Gilmor and Alice Garwood, *General Principles of Play Direction*, New York, Samuel French, 1936.

Handbook on phases of directing and acting by the director of the Pasadena Community Playhouse.

HOPKINS, Arthur, *How's Your Second Act?* New York, Samuel French, 1931.

Despite the title, a terse and constructive discussion on the art of direction in the professional theater.

Acting

ALBERTI, Eva, *A Handbook of Acting*, New York, Samuel French, 1932.

A theory (with exercises) of development based on pantomime, used by a successful teacher.

BEHNKE, Kate Emil, *Speech and Movement of the Stage*, London, Oxford, 1930.

A mature and thoughtful book for the thorough grounding of the actor.

BOLESLAVSKY, Richard, *Acting: The First Six Lessons,* New York, Theater Arts, 1933.

An interesting presentation of fundamental ideas, charmingly narrated in dialogue form.

BOSWORTH, Halliam, *Technique in Dramatic Art* (Revised Edition), New York, Macmillan, 1934.

The fruit of a professional's experience, not entirely conventional in theory, but detailed and practical.

CALVERT, Louis, *Problems of the Actor,* New York, Henry Holt & Co., 1918.

An illuminating book by a famous actor "to assist the beginner to find his own technique."

D'ANGELO, Aristides, *The Actor Creates,* New York, Samuel French, 1939.

Class discussions, as carried on at the American Academy of Dramatic Arts, including such considerations as the development of character and the preparation of a role.

FRANKLIN, Miriam, *Rehearsals, The Principles and Practice of Acting for the Stage,* New York, Prentice-Hall, 1942.

A discussion of the principles of acting, and many useful exercises.

KJERBUHL-PETERSEN, Lorenz, *The Psychology of Acting,* Boston, The Expression Company, 1935.

Translated from German. An extended and valuable study of the problem of emotion in acting.

STANISLAVSKI, Constantin, *An Actor Prepares,* New York, Theater Arts, 1936.

Essays on the art of acting by the founder and director of the Moscow Art Theater.

PART III

STAGECRAFT AND DESIGN

Scenery and Properties

ARONSON, Joseph, *The Encyclopaedia of Furniture,* New York, Crown, 1928.

An invaluable reference book of descriptions and illustrations of period furniture.

BURRIS-MEYER, Harold and Edward C. Cole, *Scenery for the Theater,* Boston, Little, Brown & Co., 1941.

"The organization, processes, materials, and techniques used to set the stage." An indispensable book for advanced students.

ISAACS, Edith J. R., *Architecture for the New Theatre,* New York, Theatre Arts, 1935.

Collected articles by prominent stage designers and theater architects.

KRANICH, Frederich, *Buhnentechnik der Gegenwart,* Munich and Berlin, Oldernburg, 1929. 2 vols.

Although the text is German, the wealth of illustrations of stage machinery, equipment, and modern theater construction, makes this a useful and usable book on professional practice.

KROWS, Arthur, *Equipment for Stage Production,* New York, Appleton-Century, 1928.

A discussion of professional practice in stage arrangement, unit construction, mechanical effects, etc.

MEYER, Franz Sales, *A Handbook of Ornament* (Revised Edition), Chicago, Wilcox and Follett & Co., 1946.

An excellent handbook on the elements and application of decoration. Copiously illustrated. Includes architectural features, furniture, armorial weapons, utensils, jewelry, etc., from ancient to modern times.

PICHEL, Irving, *Modern Theaters,* New York, Harcourt, Brace and Co., 1925.

A most readable and valuable book on the planning and construction of a small theater.

SELDEN, Samuel and Hunton D. Sellman, *Stage Scenery and Lighting,* New York, Crofts, 1936.

A book designed for amateurs but based on professional practices, presented in a not too elementary nor overly technical manner.

SPELTZ, Alexander, *Styles of Ornament* (Revised Edition), New York, Grosset & Dunlap, 1936.

A standard work, first published in 1904, representing "the entire range of ornament in all its different styles from prehistoric times till the middle of the 19th century and to illustrate the different uses to which it has been applied."

Costuming and Make-up

BARTON, Lucy, *Historic Costume for the Stage,* Boston, Baker, 1935.

An indispensable book on the history of costume from the Egyptian period to the Twentieth Century, with suggestions on practical reproduction of costumes and accessories, and on costume construction.

CORSON, Richard, *Stage Make-up,* New York, Crofts, 1942 (New Edition, 1947).

An excellent and well-written handbook, with diagrams, color charts, and half-tones.

DOTEN, Hazel R. and Constance Boulard, *Fashion Drawing,* New York, Harpers, 1939.

An excellent book on the problem of costume rendering, though not written primarily from the point of view of the theater. Contains good short section on period costumes.

KOHLER, Carl and Emma Von Sichart, *History of Costume,* London, Watt, 1928 (re-published, Philadelphia, David McKay, 1937).

A splendidly detailed history of costume from 2000 B.C. to 1870 A.D., illustrated with half-tones and patterns.

LISZT, Rudolph G., *The Last Word in Make-up,* New York, Dramatists Play Service, 1942.

Detailed instructions, especially good for advanced student.

PELLEW, Charles, *Dyes and Dyeing,* New York, McBride, 1918. (Republished 1928.)

The standard book on the use of dyes, with instructions in all types of dyeing and decorating with dyes, and description of equipment needed.

STRENKOVSKY, Serge, *The Art of Make-up,* New York, Dutton, 1937.

A thorough and comprehensive study, for the advanced student.

Lighting

FUCHS, Theodore, *Stage Lighting,* Boston, Little, Brown & Co., 1929.

A complete and thoughtful study of stage lighting, its theories, and its modern practices.

McCANDLESS, Stanley R., *A Method of Lighting the Stage* (Revised Edition), New York, Theater Arts, Inc., 1939.

The theory of creating special effects and proper lighting of stage areas.

NELMS, Henning, *Lighting the Amateur Stage,* New York, Putnam, 1932.

A practical guide for equipment and layout.

(See also chapters on lighting in Pichel, and in Selden and Sellman, previously mentioned.)

PART IV

ORGANIZATION AND MANAGEMENT

BERNHEIM, Alfred L., *The Business of the Theater,* New York, Actors Equity Association, 1932.

A skilful report of the development and practice of theater business as it existed in 1932, still valuable.

DEAN, Alexander, *Little Theater Organization and Management,* New York, Appleton, 1926.

The Little Theater's place in the community and a complete guide to its structural organization.

HALSTEAD, William P., *Stage Management for the Amateur Theater,* New York, Crofts, 1937.

A thorough and practical book on organization and management, with an excellent index to works on stagecraft.

KROWS, Arthur Edwin, *Play Production in America,* New York, Henry Holt & Co., 1916.

A survey of standard professional practice, out of date only in its scale of prices and expenses.

STANTON, Sanford E., *Theater Management,* New York, Appleton-Century, 1929.

Discussion of bookings, publicity, billings, duties of the box office manager, etc.

INDEX